INSPIRE / PLAN / DISCOVER / EXPERIENCE

SWITZERLAND

SWITZERLAND

CONTENTS

DISCOVER 6

Welcome to Switzerland....8
Reasons to Love Switzerland....10
Explore Switzerland....14
Getting to Know Switzerland....16
Switzerland Itineraries....22
Switzerland Your Way....30
A Year in Switzerland....54
A Brief History....56

EXPERIENCE 60

Bern....62
Mittelland, Bernese Oberland and Valais....80
Geneva....114
Western Switzerland....130
Zürich....158
Northern Switzerland....174
Central Switzerland and Ticino....200
Eastern Switzerland and Graubünden....238

NEED TO KNOW 268

Before You Go....270
Getting Around....272
Practical Information....276
Index....278
Phrasebook....285
Acknowledgments....287

Left: Decorative elements adorning Basel's Rathaus
Previous page: A hiker overlooking Lake Lugano
Cover image: Picturesque village in Lauterbrunnen

DISCOVER

The crystalline River Limmat bisecting Zürich

Welcome to Switzerland....8

Reasons to Love Switzerland....10

Explore Switzerland....14

Getting to Know Switzerland....16

Switzerland Itineraries....22

Switzerland Your Way....30

A Year in Switzerland....54

A Brief History....56

WELCOME TO SWITZERLAND

Think Switzerland, and yodelling, cheese, cuckoo clocks and chocolates might spring to mind, but this country has so much more to offer. Magnificent natural beauty, charming medieval villages, cosmopolitan cities and a healthy dose of Alpine air - Switzerland's small size belies its beguiling charms. The varied scene is coloured by a fascinating history and the unique mix of four official languages only add to the appeal. Whatever your dream trip to Switzerland includes, this DK Eyewitness travel guide is your perfect companion.

1 A warmly lit train passing the iconic Matterhorn.

2 Charlie Chaplin statue, overlooking Lake Geneva.

3 Evening in buzzy Zürich West.

4 Narcissus blooming across Les Pléiades, Vaud.

Once a group of independent cantons, the Swiss Confederation has come a long way since its foundation in 1291. Today's federal state is an intriguing blend of different customs, languages and dialects, lending the country a rich heritage. The year's myriad traditional festivals, where alphorn players and Swiss wrestlers take centre stage, are woven into the country's cultural tapestry. And there are stunning historic landmarks to explore across the land, from the castles of Bellinzona in the south to St Gallen's abbey quarter in the north. As much as it is rooted in the past, Switzerland looks to the future, with cutting-edge nightlife in Zürich, world-class art galleries in Basel and superb fine dining across the country from Geneva to St Moritz.

Away from its buzzing cities, Switzerland is a land of the great outdoors, and the country's network of hiking, biking and skiing trails is as well organized as its public transport system. In a single day, you can encounter breathtaking glaciers, high-altitude lakes and iconic mountains, and be back in time for fondue and schnapps.

With so many different things to experience, Switzerland can seem overwhelming. We've broken the country down into easily navigable chapters, with detailed itineraries, expert local knowledge and colourful, comprehensive maps to help you plan the perfect visit. Whether you're staying for a weekend, a week or longer, this DK Eyewitness travel guide will ensure that you see the very best Switzerland has to offer. Enjoy the book, and enjoy Switzerland.

REASONS TO LOVE SWITZERLAND

Small in size but big on experiences, Switzerland is awash with fascinating sights, exhilarating activities and intriguing traditions, presented in one remarkably beautiful package. Here, we pick some of our favourites.

1 BERN'S OLD TOWN

A UNESCO World Heritage Site, the Swiss capital's medieval Old Town is a real beauty. Its charming *lauben* (covered walkways) shelter independent boutiques, little cafés and buzzing bars hidden beneath cellar doors *(p62)*.

2 SCENIC RAIL JOURNEYS

Part of the fun of travelling around Switzerland is the journey itself. The country's rail routes are truly extraordinary, both as feats of engineering and for the incredible scenery they pass through.

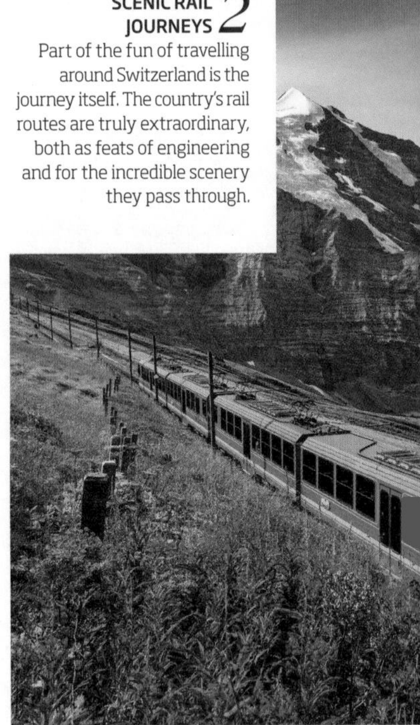

3 RURAL TRADITIONS

From *Schwingen* (wrestling) to *Hornussen* (a combination of golf and baseball), via cowbell ringing and alphorn playing, the past is still very much a part of modern Swiss life *(p48)*.

4 LAKE LIFE

Despite being a landlocked country, Switzerland's myriad lakes mean getting near the water is always easy. Lakeside beaches throng all summer with sunbathers and swimmers, while quiet hiking trails lead to remote Alpine lagoons.

SLEDGING IN THE JUNGFRAU 5

Take an exhilarating toboggan ride in this stunning mountainous region. Top of the list is the longest run in Europe – the epic 15-km (9-mile) descent from the top of the Faulhorn to the village of Grindelwald.

FONDUE 6

Breathe in the irresistible aroma of molten cheese. Fondue *Moitié-Moitié* – half Gruyère, half Vacherin Fribourgeois – is best washed down with a glass of local Chasselas wine.

HISTORIC TREASURES 7

Whether St Gallen Abbey, Bellinzona's castles or the fairy-tale Château de Chillon in Montreux, Switzerland's rugged terrain is littered with history-laden sights that rival its natural wonders for your attention *(p46)*.

ART IN BASEL 8

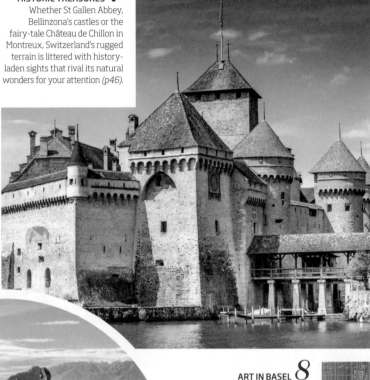

Art enthusiasts flock to Switzerland's cultural capital for its annual artistic showpiece Art Basel, but its world-class galleries and museums are a joy all year round *(p178)*.

9 WORLD-CLASS SKIING

From the epic powder runs of Zermatt *(p90)* – the highest resort in Europe – to family-friendly slopes, Switzerland offers a remarkable choice for skiers, freeriders and snow-boarders on and off-piste.

10 HUT TO HUT HIKING

Join the Swiss in their national pastime - hiking to cosy cabins across the Alps. Whether run by the Swiss Alpine Club or privately owned, each offer the camaraderie of spending the night in the mountains.

ZÜRICH'S NIGHTLIFE 11

The largest city in Switzerland, Zürich is a go-to place for night owls. Head to dynamic Langstrasse *(p168)*, a reformed red-light district, for pubs, clubs and cocktail bars.

WINE TASTING IN LAVAUX 12

Blanketing the hillside above Lake Geneva *(p142)*, the Lavaux Vineyard Terraces are a fine place for a Swiss wine initiation. Take a stroll along the myriad wine trails, where *vignerons* (winegrowers) lure visitors with tastings.

EXPLORE SWITZERLAND

This guide divides Switzerland into eight colour-coded sightseeing areas, as shown on the map below. Find out more about each area on the following pages.

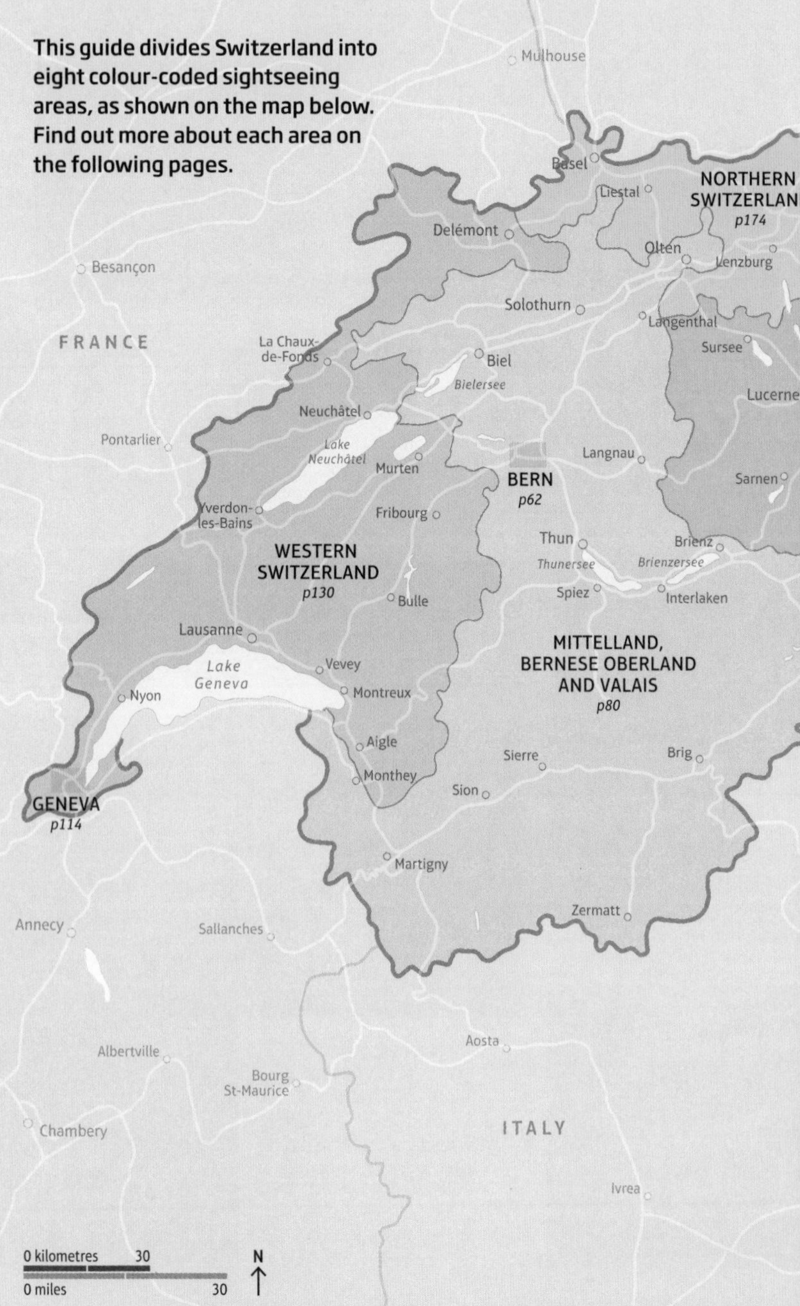

GERMANY
Ehingen
Rottweil
Memmingen
Stockach
Ravensburg
Kempten
Schaffhausen
Kreuzlingen
Eglisau
Frauenfeld
Bodensee
Lindau
Arbon
Bregenz
ZÜRICH
p158
Winterthur
Dübendorf
St Gallen
Watwil
Muri
Zurichsee
Rapperswil
Cham
Pfäffikon
Walensee
Buchs
LIECHTENSTEIN
Bludenz
Landeck
AUSTRIA
Schwyz
Glarus
Stans
Urnersee
Bad Ragaz
Altdorf
Chur
Klosters
Scuol
Davos
Ilanz
Susch
EASTERN SWITZERLAND AND GRAUBÜNDEN
p238
Andermatt
Zillis
Silandro
Airolo
St Moritz
CENTRAL SWITZERLAND AND TICINO
p200
Mesocco
Bregaglia
ITALY
Locarno
Bellinzona
Lake Maggiore
Lugano
Lake Lugano
Varese
Milan
Novara
Vercelli

WESTERN EUROPE
UNITED KINGDOM
NETHERLANDS
POLAND
GERMANY
BELGIUM
CZECH REPUBLIC
AUSTRIA
SWITZERLAND
SLOVENIA
Bay of Biscay
FRANCE
ITALY
CROATIA
SPAIN
Mediterranean Sea

GETTING TO KNOW SWITZERLAND

Cradled by Europe's highest peaks, Switzerland is the capital of Alpine drama, and rich in world-class art, culinary adventures and fascinating folklore. Outside the cities, Switzerland is a land of mesmerizing natural beauty with twisting valleys, dizzying mountains and shimmering lakes.

PAGE 62

BERN

The gateway to the Alps, Switzerland's oft-overlooked capital has a wealth of attractions – from its medieval Old Town (a UNESCO World Heritage Site) to urban swimming in the clean waters of the Aare River. The city is also the seat of Switzerland's government and the Houses of Parliament are often open to the public. Always at the heart of the country's intellectual culture, Bern is a laid-back place for serious thinkers. The former haunt of Albert Einstein has plenty of café-lined squares and pretty gardens to chew over the day's politics, ponder Modern Masters and debate matters of time and space.

Best for
A magnificent Old Town

Home to
Zytglogge, Kunstmuseum

Experience
The boutiques, cafés and restaurants hidden under the lauben, *covered walkways that line the Old Town streets*

PAGE 80

MITTELLAND, BERNESE OBERLAND AND VALAIS

One of the most beautiful areas in the country, this is a region of soaring peaks and deep valleys. Mountain lovers should make a beeline to Interlaken to soak up the sky-high vistas and ride the train to the Jungfraujoch. To the south, in the canton of Valais, looms the country's most famous peak: the Matterhorn. For the ultimate journey, catch the train to see hanging valleys and leviathan-sized glaciers from the comfort of a carriage.

Best for
Breathtaking panoramas from top-of-Europe summits

Home to
Zermatt and the Matterhorn, Aletsch Glacier

Experience
Hiking along the incomparable Aletsch Glacier

PAGE 114

GENEVA

The capital of the French-speaking part of the country is the jewel of the Swiss Lake District. Pocket-sized and impeccably clean, it offers timely distractions for clock-watchers and more casual travellers. The pedestrianized Old Town, a mini-maze of bijou squares and Neo-Classical cathedrals, is a delight to get lost in. Beyond the city limits, you'll find CERN, the world's largest particle physics laboratory, the creased hills of Saint-Cergue, and enough lakeside vineyards and castles to keep you here longer than planned.

Best for
Museums, culture and lakeside excursions

Home to
Musée d'Art et d'Histoire

Experience
Taking a tram to the lovely Italianate district of Carouge, with its independent shops and Saturday market

→

PAGE 130

WESTERN SWITZERLAND

Stretching from the Jura mountains and Vaud Alps to the shores of lakes Geneva and Neuchâtel, this is one of the most densely inhabited parts of the country. City-breakers flock to buzzing university city Lausanne and the hip-shaking jazz bars of Montreux, while foodies relish the iconic cheese of Gruyères, fondue-friendly Fribourg and Lavaux's winegrowing nirvana. In between all this, let time slow down in the historical watchmaking hubs of Le Locle and La Chaux-de-Fonds.

Best for
Jazz, wine and watches

Home to
Lake Geneva, Château de Chillon

Experience
Taking the scenic GoldenPass train line from Montreux to Interlaken

PAGE 158

ZÜRICH

Often ranked as one of the world's most liveable cities, Zürich has more to offer than its reputation of wealth. Switzerland's largest city punches above its weight as a 21st-century design hub without losing its medieval mojo. Just take a stroll through the zigzagging lanes of the Old Town Niederdorf to the Limmat River, and you'll wend a path past weathered churches, candy-box clock towers, avant-garde galleries, traditional chocolatiers and high-end boutiques. Most visitors use it as a jumping-off point, but the city's mix of culture and cuisine demands attention.

Best for
A city buzz

Home to
Schweizerisches Nationalmuseum

Experience
Swimming in a badi, *an outdoor pool on the lake or river*

PAGE 174

NORTHERN SWITZERLAND

Encompassing the river lands of the Rhine, which winds from Basel's Old Town to Bodensee in the east, this region is full of contrasts. Basel is well known for its ambitious skyline – shaped by architects such as Mario Botta and Zaha Hadid – and few cities are so defined by their relationship with art. Elsewhere, hot springs have been attracting visitors to Baden since Roman times. To the east, the rolling vineyards of Regensberg yield some of the prettiest landscapes.

Best for
World-renowned art, thermal springs

Home to
Basel Kunstmuseum, Baden

Experience
The huge annual expo Art Basel

→

PAGE 200

CENTRAL SWITZERLAND AND TICINO

Most journeys through this alluring region begin in Lucerne, where a boat trip on Vierwaldstattersee drifts past jaw-dropping cliffs. To the south is the town of Andermatt, with five-star hotels and golf courses. On the other side of the Gotthard Tunnel spills Italian-speaking Switzerland, home to the lakeside towns of Locarno and Ascona, clifftop monasteries, crystal-clear swimming spots, and belly-hugging pizza and pasta.

Best for
Superlative scenery and tasty Italian food

Home to
Kloster Einsiedeln, Bellinzona

Experience
Riding up – and up – the Burgenstock mountain's spine-tingling outdoor elevator

PAGE 238

EASTERN SWITZERLAND AND GRAUBÜNDEN

The Switzerland of storybooks is alive in the east. Dairy farmers and cheesemakers get to work in postcard-ready mountain huts and picturesque farmsteads, while sawtooth peaks rise above turquoise lakes. The region is known for outdoor adventures and the famous "champagne powder" of the ski resorts of Arosa and Davos. Beyond the mountain resorts lie tranquil Lake Constance and historic St Gallen to the north.

Best for
Outdoor thrills, folk singing and traditional life

Home to
UNESCO-protected St Gallen Abbey, Swiss National Park

Experience
Participating in local celebrations

1 Bern's monumental 15th-century Münster.

2 Kleine-Scheidegg ski area in Bernese Oberland.

3 Boats on Oeschinensee.

4 Interlaken's Old Town.

Switzerland's diverse regions are bursting with historic towns, breathtaking natural scenery and myriad activities. These itineraries will help you make the most of your visit to this beautiful country.

4 DAYS

in Bern and the Bernese Oberland

Day 1

Morning Start the day with a stroll round the arcades and boutiques of Bern's Old City *(p62)*. Swing past the 15th-century Münster to marvel at its intricate tympanum before heading to the Zytglogge clock tower *(p70)*.

Afternoon After lunch in the atmospheric Kornhauskeller *(p73)*, take bus 12 to the wave-like Zentrum Paul Klee *(p77)* and immerse yourself in modern art.

Evening Head to the Altes Tramdepot *(https://altestramdepot.ch)* for views of the Old City and enjoy traditional Bernese cuisine with a stein of house beer, brewed in copper vats in the the restaurant.

Day 2

Morning Take the train to the town of Interlaken *(p84)*, which sits between lakes Thun and Brienz. Explore Jungfraujoch *(p102)*, then head to the pretty village of Lauterbrunnen *(p103)*.

Afternoon Dine on a traditional Swiss lunch of *Flammenkuchen* (flambéed tarts) and fondue. The 141 bus will take you through lush countryside to the breathtaking Trümmelbach Falls, Europe's largest subterranean waterfall, and one of many that surround the village. From here you can hike the "Black Monk" mountain to experience the full majesty of the ten glacier falls beneath.

Evening Take the 141 onwards to the village of Stechelberg, where you can ascend the 2,970-m (9,744-ft) Schilthorn via a four-stage cable car. Its solar-powered revolving restaurant, Piz Gloria *(p103)*, featured as Blofeld's lair in the 1969 James Bond film, *On Her Majesty's Secret Service*. Dine on one of the 007 burgers, then head down to the car-free village of Mürren *(p104)* for a night at the Alpenruh hotel *(p105)*, near the cable terminus.

Day 3

Morning Hike or snowboard along some of Mürren's 51.5 km (32 miles) of trails, then take the train to have coffee at the historic Bellevue des Alpes hotel in Wengen *(p105)*.

Afternoon A short walk from the hotel yields fabulous views to the Männlichen; a train also takes visitors to Eigerglestcher station. The train tunnels up through the mountains to Jungfraujoch *(p102)* for incredible glacial vistas. It's a three-hour hike on the Eiger Ultra Trail (or a quick cable-car ride) back down to Grindelwald *(p102)*.

Evening Ease those tired muscles in the sauna and spa rooms of the luxurious Hotel Belvedere Grindelwald *(p105)*.

Day 4

Morning Ride the cable car to Pfingstegg or walk to Gletscherschlucht, a spectacular canyon of rock and ice with great views over the Bernese Oberland mountains. For a speedy return, head back to Pfingstegg and zoom down the summer toboggan run to Grindelwald.

Afternoon Enjoy a light lunch at C und M Café Bar *(p103)*, then take the train back to Interlaken West for a leisurely steamer ride over Thunersee to the town that gave the lake its name. The pier is a few minutes' walk from the railway station for a train back to Bern.

←

1 People entering the sobering International Red Cross and Red Crescent Museum.

2 The audience mingling at the iconic Montreux Jazz Festival.

3 Rolling hills leading to Lutry.

4 Charlie Chaplin standing on the banks of Lake Geneva.

5 A visitor exploring a display at the Olympic Museum.

5 DAYS

in Western Switzerland

Day 1

Morning Starting at Geneva's Jet d'Eau *(p124)*, stroll north into the Old Town for coffee in the main square. Around the corner is Cathédrale St-Pierre *(p120)*, where far-reaching views reward those who climb the north tower.

Afternoon After a spot of lunch at Café Papon *(www.cafepapon.ch)*, catch the tram to visit the International Red Cross and Red Crescent Museum *(p126)*.

Evening Feast on contemporary Swiss cuisine at Chez Philippe *(www.chez philippe.ch)* and test the mixologist's skills at L'Apothicaire Cocktail-Club *(p125)*.

Day 2

Morning Take the train to Lausanne *(p134)* and explore the market *(Wed & Sat, weekly)*. Climb the medieval market steps to visit the beautiful cathedral *(p140)*. Break for lunch at L'Eveché *(www.leveche.ch)*.

Afternoon Take the M2 metro down to Ouchy *(p139)* and the absorbing displays of the Olympic Museum *(p138)*. From here, it's an easy stroll to seasonal bar Jetée de la Compagnie *(p139)* for an *apéro*.

Evening Book ahead for a table at live jazz club Chorus *(p136)* and enjoy dinner and drinks before the show starts.

Day 3

Morning Travel out to the medieval village of Lutry where the local market offers everything you need for a picnic in the terraced vineyards of Lavaux *(p145)*. If you're feeling energetic, you can hike the 11-km (7-mile) trail through the vines to the pretty town of St-Saphorin.

Afternoon From St-Saphorin, it's a three-minute train ride to Vevey *(p142)* and Chaplin's World, where re-created film sets and curated displays of personal items reveal the man behind the "Little Tramp". A ferry will get you there from Lutry in all of 30 minutes.

Evening Dine overlooking the water at Vevey's KJU *(p155)*, which turns into a club as the night wears on.

Day 4

Morning It's only five minutes by train from Vevey to Montreux *(p144)*, where you can follow the lakefront to Château de Chillon *(p146)*. Spend an hour or two exploring the medieval island and the 13th-century chapel of St-George.

Afternoon Catch a boat back to Montreux in time for lunch, then head to the summit of Rochers-de-Naye via a 55-minute cogwheel railway ride with stunning views over Lake Geneva *(p142)*.

Evening Head to Montreux Jazz Café *(www.montreuxjazzcafe.com)* for dinner.

Day 5

Morning Take the train to the cheese-making town of Gruyères *(p152)*. Sample its famous cheese and learn how it's made at La Maison du Gruyère. Then head up the hill into the medieval centre.

Afternoon Tuck into Le Gruyère fondue for lunch, and round things off with fresh meringues and cream, a local speciality. Explore the surreal world of H R Giger at the museum dedicated to his works.

Evening Journey back to Geneva, and enjoy a light dinner at buzzy open-plan bistro Natürlich *(www.naturlich.ch)*.

8 DAYS
in Central Switzerland

Day 1

Hop on a train in Basel *(p178)* and speed past the countryside to Schwyz *(p228)*, the birthplace of modern Switzerland, stopping in Zug for lunch. Once in Schwyz, check into Wysses Rössli *(www.wysses-roessli-schwyz.ch)*, a traditionally furnished 17th-century hotel overlooking the main square. Then find a café for a fortifying *Kirsch* (cherry schnapps); the "area is famous for it. Later, enjoy seasonal, modern dishes at family-run restaurant Schwyzer-Stubli *(www.schwyzer-stubli.ch)*.

Day 2

Spend a couple of hours at the Museum of the Swiss Charters of Confederation, where the earliest documents of the Swiss Confederation are kept. Round the corner is the Schweizerisches Nationalmuseum, which has interesting multimedia displays on life in Schwyz from 1300 to 1600. Take the Rolenflue-Mythenregion cable car up (and up) for pleasant mountain strolls. Return to town for a dinner of *Älplermagronen* (macaroni and cheese) made with Sbrinz, the quintessential cheese of the region.

Day 3

Catch the train to Lucerne *(p204)*, and get carried away in the Swiss Museum of Transport *(p210)*. Take a picnic aboard a boat from the adjacent pier across to Alpnachstad for the world's steepest rack railway to wander Mount Pilatus *(p214)*. Then descend from Alpnachstad by the cable car to Fräkmüntegg, where there is a hair-raising toboggan run, and arrive in Lucerne's city centre in time for dinner.

Day 4

Start the day with a rendezvous with Modernist Masters at Lucerne's Museum Sammlung Rosengart *(p208)*. Cross the Seebrücke to the Bourbaki Panorama to see the world's largest round mural, a visual history of the 19th century. Have a hearty lunch at family-friendly Hofgarten, round the corner. Then catch a train to Stans *(p227)*, where you can board the funicular to Kälti, and transfer onto the double-decker open-top cable car up to the Stanserhorn summit. On your way back to Lucerne, stop for drinks at Seebistro LUZ *(www.luzseebistro.ch)* – its setting overlooking the Reuss is terrific.

6

1 Pretty houses lining Basel streets.

2 Schwyz's church piercing the sky.

3 A bridge crossing the Reuss.

4 Amazing vistas at Pilatus.

5 Views from the Gotthard train.

6 A funicular climbing Monte Brè.

Day 5

Take a steam-powered paddle boat to Vitznau for a trip up to Mont Rigi *(p226)* on Europe's first rack railway. Pause for lunch at Rigi Kulm-Hotel *(www.rigikulm.ch)*, Switzerland's first mountain inn, and enjoy one of many walks in the area. Descend the mountain via Arth-Goldau for the train back to Lucerne.

Day 6

Take the Gotthard Panorama Express to Flüelen and then a train to Bellinzona *(p224)* to visit Castelgrande, Sasso Corbaro and Montebello. When hunger strikes at Montebello, sample some *salame* – a local speciality. Explore the pleasant historic town before taking the short trip to Locarno to watch the sunset over Lake Maggiore. Stay at the gorgeous Belvedere *(www.belvedere-locarno.com)*.

Day 7

Take the train south to Lugano *(p220)* for a meander through its pretty cobbled streets. At Cassarete, catch the funicular up to Monte Brè for long views of Lake Lugano *(p218)* and the snow-capped mountains in the distance. Find a restaurant with a terrace for lunch, whatever time of year – cosy lap blankets are available when temperatures plummet. Return to the city centre and hail a cab to the small town of Montanola for a dinner of dry-rubbed pork and a bowl of wine at Grotto del Cavicc *(p231)* – a favourite haunt of German-Swiss author Hermann Hesse.

Day 8

Fuel up on Italian pastries and neat shots of espresso at Grand Cafe Al Porto *(www.grand-cafe-lugano.ch)*, then enjoy a morning exploring the best art in the city at LAC Lugano Arte e Cultura. Take one of Switzerland's most scenic railway journeys, the Centovalli. The narrow-gauge line to Domodossola crosses numerous valleys over hair-raising bridges and viaducts, weaving through woods with views over the river below. Change at Domodossola, to return to Zürich or Basel.

1

3

2

4

A WEEK *in Valais*

Day 1

From Geneva, take the train to the Rhône Valley beside Lake Geneva, which affords fabulous views of the French Alps and the Lavaux vineyard terraces. The train skirts the castle at Chillon *(p146)*, the backdrop of Lord Byron's poem, *The Prisoner of Chillon*. Disembark at Martigny *(p106)* to visit the impressive Fondation Pierre Gianadda, which hosts changing world-class art exhibitions. Come evening, watch the sun set over the ruins of the Roman amphitheatre, then dine on traditional wood-fired *raclette*.

Day 2

After breakfast, take the branch railway from Martigny to Le Châble for the cable car to the famous ski resort of Verbier *(p106)*. For even more dramatic views, brave one of Europe's largest cable cars to Mont Fort. In the winter, test your mettle on bunny slopes and monster moguls, breaking for steaming mugs of hot chocolate. When it's warmer, the region is famed for equally good hiking trails and bike paths. Return to Martigny and continue east along the Rhône Valley to Leuk. From here the postbus will take you up the twisty mountain road to one of the spas of Leukerbad *(p113)*, such as Les Sources des Alpes *(www.sourcesdesalpes.ch)*.

Day 3

Spend a lazy morning recuperating in a thermal spa, followed by a wander round the historic village. Fuel up on some fine charcuterie in a brasserie, before testing your fitness on the former trading route to the Gemmipass, which zigzags up the mountain, offering ever-wider views. At the top is the historic Hotel Schwarenbach *(www.schwarenbach.ch)*, which inspired Guy Maupassant's short story *L'Auberge*. Head back to your hotel and go for a quick plunge in the pool back at the spa before dinner.

Day 4

Continue east to Visp and take the handy narrow-gauge railway up to the car-free resort of Zermatt *(p90)* and its iconic mountain, the Matterhorn. The fascinating

5

1 Admiring art displays at Fondation Pierre Gianadda.

2 A panorama pointing out landmarks at the resort town of Verbier.

3 The iconic Matterhorn reflected in a clear mountain lake.

4 Walkers viewing the Aletsch Glacier.

5 Wooden chalet lining Zermatt.

Matterhorn Museum tells the story of the drama surrounding the first ascent in 1865 and describes how the mountain's distinctive silhouette has come to be so well known. One of the best walks from the town of Zermatt is the Matterhorn Trail to Schwarzsee and its tiny chapel, passing through the hamlet of Zmutt where restaurants serve specialities from Valais. Have a drink (or stay) at the Monte Rosa Hotel *(www.monterosazermatt.ch)* where famed mountaineer Edward Whymper stayed before his fateful ascent of the Matterhorn.

Day 5

Rise early to take the Gornergratbahn train to watch dawn break over one of the finest viewpoints of the Matterhorn, and grab a quick breakfast at the Kulmhotel Gornergrat *(www.gornergrat-kulm.ch)*. Take to the 360 Trail for great views of the Monte Rosa massif *(p111)* and a panorama of 29 peaks, or, if you're feeling energetic, try the longer Five Lakes Walk. Later, catch the train from Zermatt to Morel for the cable car up to Riederalp, gateway to the Aletsch Glacier *(p94)*.

Day 6

After breakfast, take the cable car to Moosfluh for the start of the spectacular Aletsch Panoramaweg, a 12-km (7-mile) walk beside the 23-km (14-mile) Aletsch Glacier, the centrepiece of the Aletsch Arena World Heritage Site. Stop for a reviving afternoon tea at Villa Cassel in Riederfurka, just above Riederalp *(summer only)*; Sir Winston Churchill was a regular guest at Sir Ernest Cassel's holiday home here. Back in Riederalp, tuck into tasty locally sourced *chinoise* (hot pot) and *raclette* at Restaurant Derby *(www.derby-riederalp.ch)*, then rock out to live music, performed here throughout the ski season. Stay overnight in one of the Swiss Alpine Club (*www.sac-cas.ch*) huts that can be found dotted around the area.

Day 7

Make your way to Morel for the train back to Geneva. Alternatively spend a leisurely day taking the scenic route to Zürich via Andermatt and the train through the stunning Schöllenen Gorge to Göschenen on the old Gotthard main line.

Monumental Peaks

A fundamental part of Swiss life, the Alps are a playground for hikers, bikers and rock climbers – and the ingenuity of Swiss engineering has made many peaks accessible to the less active visitor, too. Perhaps the most majestic of all is the iconic Matterhorn *(p90)*; this pyramid-shaped behemoth looms over the village of Zermatt *(p90)*. Still a challenge for even the most seasoned mountaineers, it's best admired from afar – take the train to the rocky ridge of Gornergrat for a stunning view of the majestic summit.

Two hikers walking over an icy path, with the Matterhorn in the distance

SWITZERLAND FOR NATURAL WONDERS

Switzerland brims with sublime natural beauty that has inspired painters, writers and photographers for centuries. But little can truly do justice to the immensity of its mountains, the sparkle of its Alpine lakes and the sheer might of its glaciers. Prepare to bow down to Mother Nature.

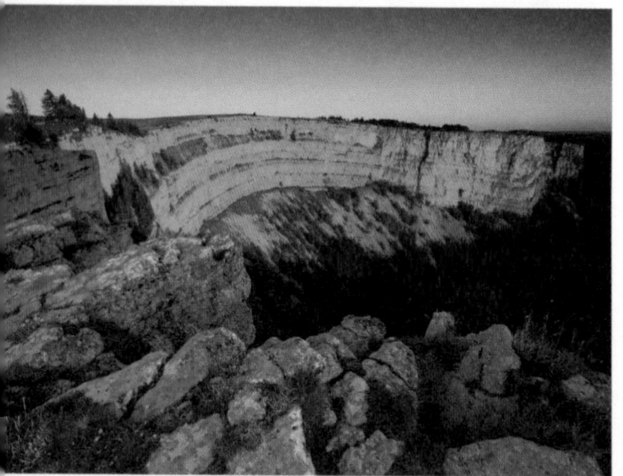

Geological Marvels

Geological features carved out over millennia add their own unique beauty to this fascinating landscape, from Europe's largest waterfall to deep gorges. In western Switzerland, the one to see is the Creux du Van *(p157)*. A range of hiking trails, which include saunters and challenging treks, lead to fabulous views across the amphitheatre of this grand canyon.

Sunlight curving along the towering walls of the Creux du Van

MAJESTIC MOUNTAINS

Pilatus
Paraglide on thermals around the mountain.

Rigi
Ride Europe's first mountain railway to the top.

Rochers-de-Naye
Spot marmots and Alpine flowers on hiking paths.

Monte Generoso
Catch the rack railway to Ticino's most scenic spot.

Mont Fort
At the summit watch the sun rise over the valley.

Aletsch Glacier

Though many are shrinking at an alarming rate, Switzerland's enthralling glaciers remain an unforgettable experience. Among the most impressive is the 23-km (14-mile) Aletsch Glacier *(p94)*. It is particularly stunning when the glistening ice river contrasts with the autumn forests around it.

A visitor getting up close to the thick wall of ice on the underside of the immense Aletsch Glacier

Enchanting Lakes

Landlocked Switzerland may be, but you're never far from water. Head into the mountains to seek out popular Oeschinensee *(p96)*, a swatch of turquoise surrounded by dramatic cliffs, or south to the sunny Mediterranean-esque Lake Lugano *(p218)*, a starting point for wonderful hikes.

→

Cows grazing in front of the placid expanse of Oeschinensee

Retail Therapy

Switzerland's cities are havens for discerning shoppers of all stripes. Lose yourself in the grand department stores and quaint boutiques of Zürich's busy Bahnhofstrasse *(p168)*. For a more historic affair, visit the western district of Bern's old town. The arcades along Münstergasse *(p74)* bustle during the Tuesday and Saturday morning street market, while Bundesplatz *(p72)*, near the city's main shopping hub, hosts a morning flower market. Farmers markets are also held in Bern's central squares.

→

Shops lining the Bahnhofstrasse in Zürich

SWITZERLAND FOR CITY LIFE

Picture Switzerland and mountain summits, glassy lakes and Alpine fields - rather than city streets - might spring to mind. But the vast majority of people live in the country's fashion-forward capitals of cool, each one offering a fascinating glimpse into Switzerland's chic side.

Take to the river

The best way to see Basel is by water. Walk down to the Rhine and take one of the four Fähren passenger ferries. As old as they are timeless, the wooden vessels are assisted by a steel cable; simply wait at one side and ring the bell. From the river, marvel at the spires of Basel Münster *(p184)* or hop off to explore Kleinbasel *(p183)*. When in Zürich, follow the Limmatquai boulevard *(p171)* for views over the Limmat.

→

The spires of Basel Münster glimpsed over the Rhine

City Tipples

Come evening, Switzerland's cities offer the perfect excuse to kick back with a glass of something special. Zürich has truly perfected the art of the cocktail - head to the bright lights of Langstrasse *(p168)* for a selection of chic bars serving up the best new mixes. By some estimates, Switzerland hosts the highest number of micro-breweries per capita in the world, so good beer is never in short supply. For great hops, make for the garden terrace of Bern's Café Einstein au Jardin *(p73)* to sample the Einstein brew.

Alfresco drinking in Bern's old town

TOP 5 CITY EVENTS

Basel Carnival
The county's largest "Fasnacht" runs from February to March.

Lucerne Festival
This arts fiesta (Aug-Sep) packs in 100-plus classical concerts.

Locarno Film Festival
In August, Piazza Grande is recast as an arthouse cinema.

National Day
Fireworks take place in every city and town on 1 August.

Wine in Lavaux
Wineries offer tastings once a year, during the grape harvest.

Revellers participating in the annual Zürich Pride celebrations ↑

LGBTQ+ celebrations

Despite only allowing same-sex marriage in 2022, Switzerland has a vibrant LGBTQ+ community, with plenty of queer music festivals and welcoming cafés. Progressive Zürich is the most switched-on city to visit, with the annual Zürich Pride *(p54)* every June a lynchpin for the country's gay and lesbian communities. Geneva also has a growing LGBTQ+ nightlife scene, with Geneva Pride the community focal point.

40,000

The average number of attendees at the annual Zürich Pride march.

Visitors perusing exhibits at the Schweizer Kindermuseum

SWITZERLAND FOR FAMILIES

With rope parks, toboggan runs, water parks and forests to high-tail it through, Switzerland is the perfect family getaway. In winter, the snow-dusted peaks become a fairy-tale landscape for children, while the summer thaw brings dozens of water-based attractions to life.

Into the Wild

Switzerland's great outdoors is a wonderland for children of all ages. In the winter, hit the bunny slopes in family-friendly resorts towns, such as Wengen *(p104)* and Kandersteg *(p105)*. When the weather warms, heed the call of mountain lakes and myriad hiking and cycling trails through Switzerland's natural wonders.

Walkers on the 5-Seenweg (Five Lakes Walk), near Zermatt

Rainy-Day Activities

Child-friendly museums are the perfect place to be when it's too rainy (or snowy) to be outside. Make for Zürich's Schweizerisches Nationalmuseum *(p164)* and its "A Magic Carpet Ride Through History", an interactive journey that starts in an Arabian palace and ends on a vintage railway carriage. Over in Baden, "children's culture" is celebrated at the Schweizer Kindermuseum *(p193)*, where the whole family can play together.

↓ The Schweizer Kindermuseum's elegant building, dating from 1890

INSIDER TIP
Babies at High Altitude

It's easier than you might think to travel with youngsters in Switzerland. Kids under six travel free on trains, and there is often space for prams. Resort town tourist offices have information on buggy-friendly walking trails, if baby-wearing is out of the question. Nappy-changing facilities are common, and some restaurants provide high chairs.

Theme Parks

With such large-scale landscapes on offer, Switzerland can appear daunting for little ones. They'll have no problem at Swissminiatur, an open-air park on the shores of Lake Lugano *(p218)* with pocket-sized models of monuments and national icons, plus tiny trains choo-chooing between the knee-high sights. In Graubünden, children can step back in time and re-create the adventures of Heidi, Switzerland's littlest explorer, at Heididorf *(www.heididorf.ch)*.

↑ Families enjoying the Swissminiatur park in Lake Lugano

Death by Chocolate

The Swiss won't let you forget that milk chocolate was invented in Switzerland in the 1880s, and it's possible to visit dozens of factories and artisan chocolatiers across the country to find out how they did it. Unearth the sweet history at Maison Cailler's historic Broc chocolate factory near Gruyères *(www.cailler.ch)*, or visit the Chocolarium of Maestrani in Flawil *(www.chocolarium.ch)*; it's one of the few chocolate factories in Switzerland that lets you onto the production floor.

→

Chocolate workshop at Maison Cailler's famous factory

Did You Know?

Chocolate is a primary source of wealth for the Swiss; famous brands include Nestlé, Lindt and Toblerone.

SWITZERLAND FOR FOODIES

Flanked by the powerhouses of France and Italy, Switzerland's culinary scene can get overlooked. Yet, its talented chefs and food fairs are quickly turning its cities into foodie destinations. Across the Alps you'll find age-old traditions and belly-hugging experiences that'll stay with you forever.

Regional Varieties

At the vanguard of the Swiss food revival is traditional go-to comfort food, and each region has its own classic dishes. In Graubünden, that's a tasty version of *Älplermagronen* (macaroni cheese elevated with speck), while in Zürich you'll find *Zürcher geschnetzeltes mit rösti*.

←

Hearty *Zürcher*, a dish with veal, onions, mushroom and a hash brown in a creamy sauce

←

Birchermuesli, the wholesome and classic Swiss breakfast dish

A Hosanna to Healthy Living

Created by the famous Swiss physician Dr Bircher-Benner, Birchermuesli has rapidly changed the way the world eats breakfast. The simple meal is made from grated apple, cinnamon, rolled oats, seeds, nuts and dollops of yogurt – with the intention of combatting the ill effects of tuberculosis through better diet – and can be found at every hotel buffet. Strangely, it was actually never intended for breakfast, but as a starter to every meal.

TOP 4 FOOD FESTIVALS

St Moritz Gourmet Festival, January
Nine days of culinary highs in the mountains.

Risotto Gran Prix, Locarno, August
Chefs go head-to-head in an open-air cook-off on the spectacular Piazza Grande.

Food Zürich, September
Ten days with more than 150 dining events, from sizzling street food to five-star banquets.

Zibelemärit, Bern, November
This centuries-old festival celebrates the humble onion.

A World of Cheese

From Appenzeller to Sbinz, the Swiss love cheese and there is plenty of it to enjoy. Build an appetite on the Emmen Valley Cheese Trail, starting in Burgdorf, then tuck into some of the country's world-famous dishes, such as fondue (bubbling melted cheese for bread dipping) and *raclette* (grilled cheese for coating potatoes) – the subjects of lifelong obsessions for cheese lovers everywhere. Cheesy festivals and artisanal markets can be relished across the country all year.

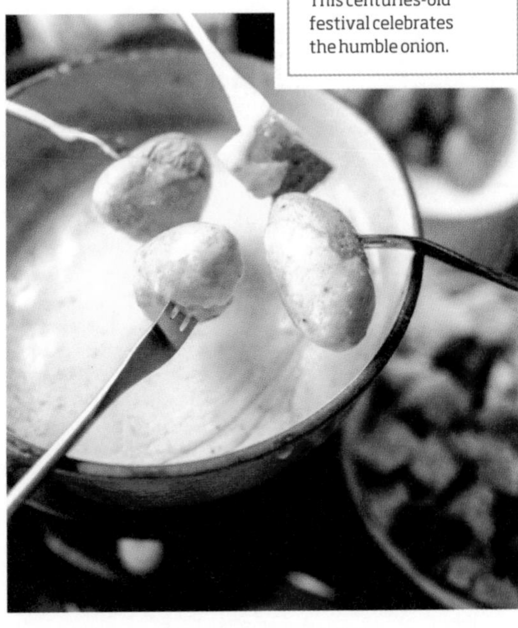

→

Dipping potatoes and bread into a bubbling cheese fondue

All Eyes on Basel

Basel is first and foremost a city of art and culture. There are more museums here than anywhere in Switzerland; it's the home of Art Basel (one of Europe's premier art shows) and the term Art Brut (Raw Art) was coined here. Start at the Kunstmuseum *(p186)*, the world's oldest public fine art gallery, then pay homage to local kinetic sculptor Jean Tinguely at Museum Tinguely *(p183)* on the banks of the Rhine. For 21st-century art, finish up at the Kunsthalle *(p181)*.

→

Admiring works by Fernand Léger in the Kunstmuseum

SWITZERLAND FOR ART LOVERS

Switzerland's artistic heritage is second to none, with a succession of world-class galleries, museums and renowned art fairs. National treasures include Alberto Giacometti, Ferdinand Hodler, Jean Tinguely and Paul Klee, but there are countless collections of artists from around the world too.

Hats Off to Paul Klee

Call it Expressionism, Cubism or Surrealism, but one thing's clear: Paul Klee is one of Switzerland's greatest artists. He called Bern home and it is there that you'll find the Zentrum Paul Klee *(p77)*, a wave-shaped museum designed by architect Renzo Piano, dedicated to Klee's life's work. The vast collection showcases the versatility of his art, balancing masterpieces alongside lesser-known artworks.

←

Combining history and high spirits in *Uebermut* (1939) by Paul Klee

TOP 4 BEST ART MUSEUMS

Kunstmuseum Bern
Opened in 1879, this is one of Switzerland's oldest art museums.

Kunsthaus Zürich
A modern art home to international stars and prominent home-grown figures such as Giacometti and Hodler.

Löwenbräu-Areal Complex, Zürich
Once a brewery, now an unmissable cultural centre.

Musée d'Art et d'Histoire, Geneva
An impressive gallery in the west of the country.

←
Admiring art displays in the Bilderlust exhibit, Kunstmuseum (Basel)

Birthplace of Dadaism

Zürich's most famous art moment came during World War I when a counter-culture movement emerged focusing on anti-war politics and an anti-bourgeois ethic. It was called Dadaism and its ground zero today is Cabaret Voltaire *(p171)*, one of Switzerland's most vibrant avant-garde art spaces and jazz bars.

→
Performance art at Zürich's artistic nightclub, Cabaret Voltaire

INSIDER TIP
Comic Collection

Basel's Caricature & Cartoon Museum *(www.cartoonmuseum.ch)* celebrates narrative drawing, with one of Europe's most kaleidoscopic collections of caricature, comics and graphic novels. The museum was extended and restyled by Swiss architects Herzog & de Meuron.

Hotels with Character

They don't build straightforward places to stay here. Many have the otherworldliness of a James Bond villain's lair, including Bürgenstock Resort *(www.burgenstockresort.com)*, which is perched on a mountain plateau above Lake Lucerne *(p204)* with a cantilevered infinity pool, Europe's highest outdoor elevator and a fabulous funicular. Another is Grand Resort Bad Ragaz *(www.resortragaz.ch)*, a wellness wonderland with oversized baths to set the heart racing.

→ Bürgenstock Resort offering majestic views over Lake Lucerne

SWITZERLAND FOR ARCHITECTURE

Switzerland's angular mountains have long captured the imagination, but the country is also a ground zero for sharply styled buildings created by fanciful architects who are always eager to impress.

Capital of Curves

Basel offers a notable display of architecture, and "starchitects" Renzo Piano, Mario Botta and Zaha Hadid are all here. Fondation Beyeler *(p196)* has Renzo Piano's fingerprints all over it. Museum Tinguely, designed by Swiss architect Mario Botta *(p183)*, is also a tour de force, while Basel's Kunstmuseum *(p186)* is a fine example of Modernist architecture.

→ Renzo Piano's Fondation Beyeler, near Basel

Time Travel

Not all Switzerland's eye candy architecture is from the here-and-now. Lake Geneva's Château de Chillon *(p146)*, the country's most visited castle, has Savoy-era great halls and courtyards, while the capital Bern is crammed with marvels from the Middle Ages; in particular, seek out the Zytglogge clock tower *(p70)*, the late-Gothic Cathedral and Renaissance-era fountains. Taking you further back in time, the Avenches *(p155)* was once the capital of Roman Helvetia and has Roman baths, old city walls and a stunning amphitheatre.

Château de Chillon on the banks of Lake Geneva

ALPINE ARCHITECTS

Herzog & de Meuron
The work of this renowned Swiss duo can be seen all over their home city of Basel, but they also designed the summit restaurant and cable car station at Chäserrugg.

Mario Botta
The Ticino-born architect has tackled Switzerland's challenging landscape several times, including designing the three-storey building at the top of Glacier 3000.

Bearth & Deplazes (1915-59)
In an extraordinarily isolated location, the Monte Rosa hut was designed by this firm from Chur as a contemporary version of a medieval *donjon*.

Picturesque Centres

Few spots in Switzerland encapsulate the country's traditional village architecture quite like Gstaad *(p106)*. From the main promenade lined with shops and galleries, to the rising spire at the heart of the village, Gstaad embodies Swiss romanticism. In St Gallen *(p244)*, eastern Switzerland's largest town, you can see traditional oriel windows, an iconic feature of rural Swiss design.

↑ The beautiful promenade in the heart of Gstaad

On the Water

In a country with around 7,000 lakes, much of local life takes place around - and across - the water. Paddle steamers cruise Lake Geneva *(p142)* and Lake Lucerne daily, in season. On Lake Maggiore *(p234)* speedboats ping-pong between Locarno and Ascona. Away from the lakes, river boats cruise the scenic Rhine between Schaffhausen *(p242)* and Stein am Rhein *(p257)*.

A paddle steamer on the turquoise waters of Lake Geneva

SWITZERLAND FOR SCENIC JOURNEYS

One of the best ways to appreciate the beauty of Switzerland's diverse landscape is to travel through it. Whether you're driving, walking or taking the train, you'll soon discover that there is truth in the saying "it's the journey not the destination".

Tour by Train

The views outside train windows are just as impressive as the Swiss railways' obstacle-defying engineering. Each time the Bernina Express *(p274)* emerges from one of the 55 tunnels between Chur and Tirano, the scene changes, from lake to forest and back again. To really soak up the panoramas, ride the world's slowest "express" train, the Glacier Express *(p274)*, which takes about seven hours to travel the mountainous 290 km (180 miles) between Zermatt and St Moritz.

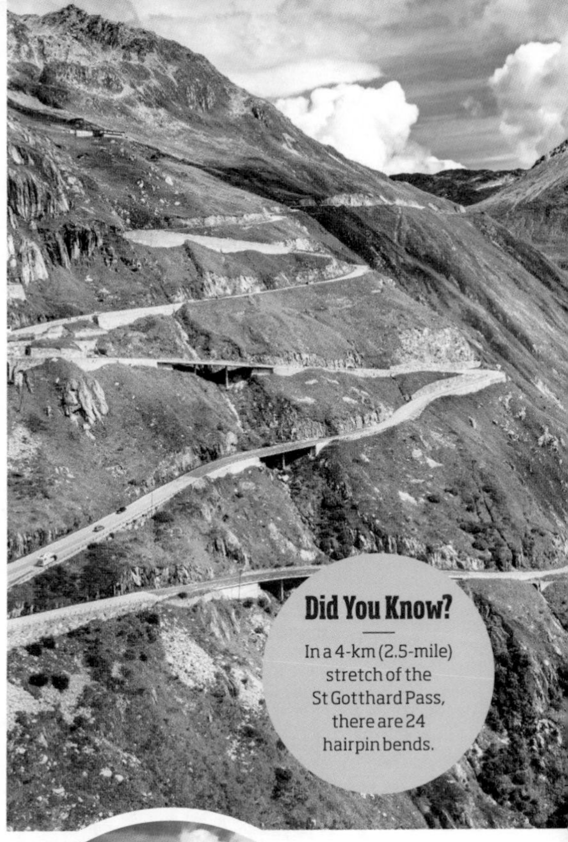

→

A series of hairpin bends on the St Gotthard Pass

Hit the Road

Driving isn't always about speed and convenience; sometimes it pays to take the scenic route. The traffic-free St Gotthard Pass *(p233)*, a route through the Swiss Alps, offers sweeping curves, hairpin bends and mountain views. The vistas from the Umbrail Pass - Switzerland's highest paved road - are similarly rewarding.

HIDDEN GEM

Flower Power

Zermatt's railway station marks the start of the Botanical Trail. This fairly easy 4-km (2.5-mile) hiking route offers sightings of ubiquitous edelweiss, rare orchids and wild ibex on its way to Trift.

Did You Know?

In a 4-km (2.5-mile) stretch of the St Gotthard Pass, there are 24 hairpin bends.

←

Hiking along the rugged, ice-laden Aletsch Glacier Trail

Lace up your Boots

The Swiss swear that the best way to see their country is on foot and on summer weekends they love nothing more than donning hiking boots and heading up the nearest mountain. Join them on the Lauterbrunnental Glacial Valley route, which takes in 12 waterfalls, the 6-km (3.5-mile) Eiger Trail, the Aletsch Glacier Trail across Europe's largest ice flow, or the Five Lakes Walk around the Matterhorn.

The iconic red Bernina Express trundling over a viaduct

Flying High

It might be better known for its winter sports, but Verbier *(p106)* contains some of the most renowned paragliding schools in Europe *(www.verbier-summits.com)*. Appenzell's Ebenalp cable car *(p258)*, meanwhile, affords access to consistent thermals for experienced paragliders. For those without a head for heights, airborne freedom can be found on Grindelwald's First Flyer, a zipline offering startling views over the Eiger and Jungfraujoch summits.

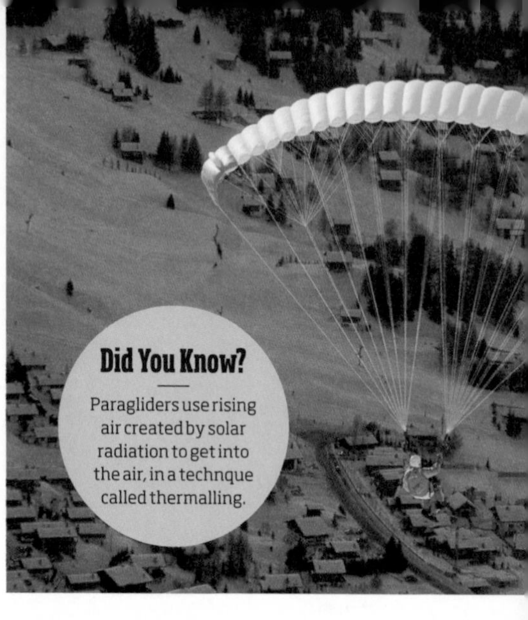

→

Winter paragliding above the Alpine village of Verbier

Did You Know?

Paragliders use rising air created by solar radiation to get into the air, in a technque called thermalling.

SWITZERLAND FOR OUTDOOR ADVENTURES

With their enviable backdrop of sawtooth peaks, sheer canyon drops and hairline ridges, it's no surprise the Swiss have a love affair with white-knuckle adventures. Weekends see the cities empty out as locals embrace the elements, and there's ample opportunity to join them, too.

Epic Canyoning

Combining the best elements of hiking, climbing, swimming and abseiling, canyoning is a heart-racing activity. Sometimes, it's also the only way to access a hidden corner of the country. Switzerland's top spots include the Valle Verzasca *(p230)* and Valle Maggia *(p231)* for the Val Grande canyoning route. Swiss River Adventures *(www.swissriveradventures.ch)* shows beginners the ropes.

A group of visitors preparing for a swim in the serene waters of Valle Maggia

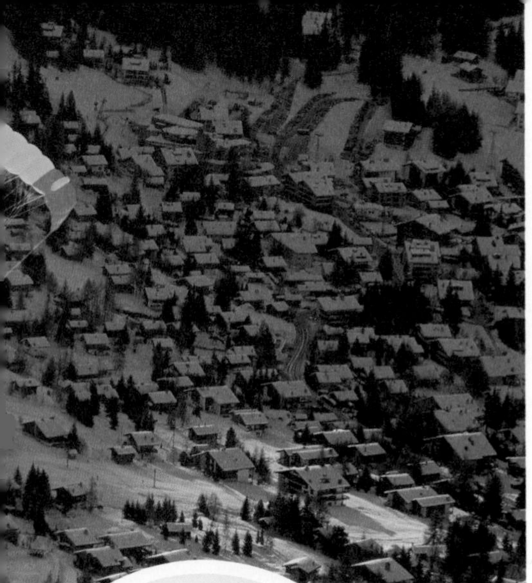

MORE GREAT ADVENTURES

Olympia Bob Run, St Moritz
The oldest bobsleigh track in the world.

Via Ferrata, Aletsch
Climb above the largest glacier in the Alps.

Whitewater Rafting, Lower Engadine
Thrills on the river En.

Titlis Cliff Walk, Engelberg
Cross Europe's highest suspension bridge.

Take to the Trails

Given how many hiking trails there are in the country, the Swiss might as well have been born with rucksacks on their backs. The oldest trail is the Tell Trail, which loops around Lake Lucerne *(p204)* in the footsteps of William Tell, the country's famed hero *(p229)*. Other pathways worth seeking are those in Appenzellerland's Alpstein, the Haute Route across Valais and the wine-tasting routes through the Lavaux Vineyards near Lausanne *(p145)*.

←

Hiking the trails in the lush hills around Lake Lucerne

Soaring Cycles

Pedal power is all the rage in Switzerland, but with so many mountains and lakes to roam on two wheels you need to be choosy. Highlights to consider are the huge and deservedly popular mountain biking park in Lenzerheide *(www.bikekingdom.ch)* and the white knuckle downhill trails of Graubünden *(p261)*. Though cycling in the country is often hilly, the cycle highways around Zürich offer gentler routes for all abilities.

→

A stunning descent down Val di Poschiavo in Graubünden

Museums and More

The Schweizerisches Nationalmuseum *(p164)* in Zürich is the *grande dame* of Switzerland's cultural trove. Explore the galleries and you'll find some of the museum's best kept secrets, including sledges. The Swiss Open-Air Museum *(p89)* at Ballenberg has 100 old buildings and numerous crafters to bring it to life.

A traditional building on display at the Swiss Open-Air Museum

SWITZERLAND FOR HISTORY BUFFS

With so many breathtaking natural attractions, it can be easy to overlook Switzerland's history. But the chance to observe Roman ruins, castles of various viscounts and timeless UNESCO Heritage Sites shouldn't be passed up. Be sure to fit these unmissable national treasures into your schedule.

TOP 4 HISTORICAL SITES

Avenches Roman Amphitheatre
This amphitheatre hosts an opera festival and regular concerts.

Augusta Raurica, Basel
A Roman archaeological site on the south bank of the Rhine *(p196)*.

Rutli Meadow, Lucerne
The spot on the shores of Lake Lucerne where modern Switzerland was founded.

Sasso San Gottardo, St Gotthard Pass
A former secret military bunker built in WWII, now a museum *(p233)*.

The Most Visited Castle

Discover a perfect marriage of history and locale at Château de Chillon *(p146)*, an island castle located south of Veytaux on Lake Geneva. The intriguing stories of the Counts of Savoy who controlled the fort, and its role as arsenal and prison, are rivalled only by the extraordinary natural drama that surrounds it.

→

The imposing Château de Chillon overlooking the tranquil Lake Geneva

UNESCO World Heritage Sites

In a country rich in UNESCO sights, it's hard to pick a favourite. Bellinzona's magnificent castles *(p224)* and Bern's Zytglogge clock tower *(p70)* are among the best. The abbey at St Gallen *(p246)* is a perfect example of living history: its library has one of the world's most stunning book collections.

Celestial beings adorn the domed ceiling of St Gallen's abbey ↓

↑ The ornate façade and soaring twin towers of the abbey at St Gallen

→

Contestants in a bout of *Schwingen*, a Swiss form of wrestling

SWITZERLAND FOR SPORTS FANS

Switzerland offers a wealth of variety for sports fans, from armchair pundits to anyone ready to play. The country is renowned for its world-class winter sports, down the slopes and on the ice, and as the summer heats up, so too do the tennis courts and biking trails.

Anyone for Tennis?

Switzerland may have its medal-winning skiers and figure skaters, but tennis has become the de facto national sport thanks to a string of star players, such as Roger Federer and Belinda Bencic. The good news is there are plenty of places to practise, as well as a number of ATP World Tour championships at which to spectate. Consider the Geneva Open (May), Gstaad Open (Jul) or, the big one in Federer's home city, the Swiss Indoors tournament in Basel (Oct-Nov).

Olympic gold medallist Belinda Bencic in action at the women's Fed Cup in Geneva

Keep up the Tradition

The Swiss have loved watching and playing sports for centuries. *Schwingen*, also known as Swiss wrestling, dates back to at least the 13th century. Bouts were originally fought between farmers and cattle herders and bulls are often still awarded as prizes. Other historic sports include *Hornussen*, where players attempt to hit a heavy puck as far as possible, and *steinstossen*, where stones weighing up to 50 kg (110 lb) are thrown like a shot put.

TOP 4 SPECTATOR SPORTS

Ice Hockey, Davos
Catch the world's oldest ice hockey tournament.

Sailing, Geneva
Watch the Bol d'Or Mirabaud, the world's largest inland regatta.

Tour de Suisse Cycling, Various
Cheer on cyclists on this proving ground for the Tour de France.

Football, Various
Join fans at a local game between August and May.

→ Sculpture of cyclists in the Olympic Museum's expansive grounds

Active History

A meditative walk around the Olympic Museum in Ouchy, Lausanne *(p138)* is the perfect introduction to Switzerland's sport obsession. The International Olympic Committee is based in the city, but it's the museum where you can enjoy a comprehensive look into the history of the movement, including halls dedicated to Olympic torches, sports memorabilia and medals. Zürich, meanwhile, is home to the FIFA World Football Museum *(p173)*, which charts the highs and lows of the world's most popular sport. Understandably, the most famous biggest draw is the chance to take a the original World Cup trophy.

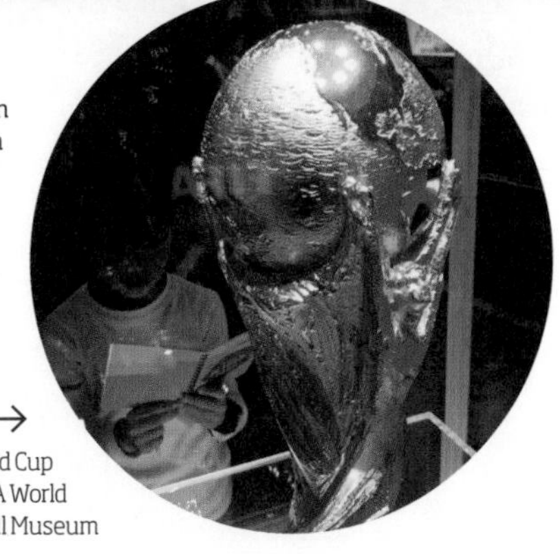

→ The World Cup trophy, FIFA World Football Museum

Heidi and Graubünden

Johanna Spyri's novel *Heidi* tells the story of an orphan girl who is taken to live with her grandfather high up in the Swiss Alps near Chur. The most popular work of Swiss fiction has been translated into 50 languages, and captured the imagination of children the world over. Kids can re-create her adventures at Heididorf *(p35)*, a village above Maienfeld *(p261)*.

Children reenacting characters Heidi and Clara walking across a meadow

SWITZERLAND IN BOOKS AND FILM

Switzerland's jaw-dropping landscapes have inspired some of the most-read classics in literature, and can often be seen as the backdrop in Hollywood blockbusters. There are museums, festivals and reenactments held across the country to honour Switzerland's effect on the imagination.

J R R Tolkien and Lauterbrunnen

For most *Lord of the Rings* fans, Middle-Earth means New Zealand, yet it was the sheer cliffs, fairy-tale grottoes and deep, dark forests of the rugged Bernese Oberland *(p80)* that inspired J R R Tolkien's elvish valleys, troll-filled woods and craggy fortresses.

→

The view of the Bernese mountains that surround turquoise Oeschinensee

INSIDER TIP
Licence to Chill

Sip martinis shaken to Bond's specifications at nearly 3,000 m (9,850 ft) at the awe-inspiring revolving restaurant Piz Gloria *(p103)*, designed by Konrad Wolf.

The Alps and 007

James Bond's high-altitude antics have brought viewers into the Alps three times. The first was the high-speed chase up to the Furka Pass in *Goldfinger* (1964). Next was *On Her Majesty's Secret Service* (1969), where its villain has a mountain lair on Schilthorn (now the Piz Gloria restaurant), and Bond embarks on a black run in an Alpine blizzard. Then came the astonishing jump over the Contra Dam in *GoldenEye* (1995).

Did You Know?

The Bond production team financed the completion of Piz Gloria in exchange for filming rights.

→

The terrace at Piz Gloria, with glorious mountain views across the Alps

←

The grisly iron statue of Frankenstein's monster in Geneva

Mary Shelley and Geneva

The haunted (and hunted) scientist Victor Frankenstein was born when Gothic writer Mary Shelley was challenged to write a ghost story during a dark and stormy night while staying on Lake Geneva in 1816. The result was the instant horror classic *Frankenstein*, which has been commemorated all across the western tip of Switzerland. Visit the Plainpalais area of Geneva to see the statue of Frankenstein's monster; the grounds of private Villa Diodati, where Shelley was first struck with the idea; and the Fondation Martin Bodmer *(www.fondationbodmer.ch)*, which has an archive of material related to the book's creation.

Boarding Call

Skiing is the top choice of sport in Switzerland. However, there are also some resorts that favour snowboarders. With four snow parks, a freestyle slope and Europe's largest half-pipe, Flims Laax Falera is made for boarders. Take a lesson with LAAX School *(www.laaxschool.com)* before showing off your moves. Grindelwald *(p102)*, in the Jungfrau region, is one of the best options for novice riders.

→ Snowboarding fun at Flims Laax Falera

SWITZERLAND FOR SNOW SPORTS

Switzerland's mountains draw visitors all year round but for snow-sports fans there's only one time to visit: winter, when the high altitude guarantees great powder. Whether you're after an adrenaline-fuelled ski session or a family-friendly toboggan ride, Switzerland will not disappoint.

Cool Runnings

Adrenaline junkie? Visit St Moritz's Cresta Run, where the first competitive luge and bobsleigh races were held, and try your hand at skeleton bobsleighing *(www.cresta-run.com)*. If you're after something a bit more gentle, hire a toboggan or *velogemel*. Invented in 1911 by a local businessman and woodcarver who faced mobility problems, the *velogemel* is a wooden snow-bike unique to the mountain village of Grindelwald *(p102)*. It's easy to use: push off with your feet and steer with the two handlebars.

Snow sent flying through the air by the blades of a traditional toboggan

Take a Tube

The most family-friendly snow sport? Snow tubing, where parents and kids zoom down specially designed slopes in inflatable tubes. And, with more snow-tubing tracks than anywhere else in Europe, Switzerland offers plenty of opportunities to try it. Leysin *(p150)* has 11 tracks alone, including several for under-fives, and at Zermatt *(p90)* you can even snow tube on the glacier.

←
Icy tracks in Valais make for a fun snow-tube ride

TOP 3 FAMOUS SWISS SKIERS

Madeleine Berthod (b 1931)
Won gold in the women's downhill at the 1956 Olympic Games.

Vreni Schneider (b 1964)
Voted "Swiss Sportswoman of the Century".

Simon Ammann (b 1981)
Ski jumper, recipient of four Winter Olympic gold medals.

Hit the Slopes

With scores of ski resorts and thousands of kilometres of pistes, it's little wonder the Swiss Alps are a popular training ground for the best winter sports athletes. If you're after classic Alpine skiing, choose a mega resort, such as Verbier *(p106)* or Davos *(p261)*. For glitz and glamour, it's hard to beat Zermatt *(p90)* and Gstaad *(p106)*. St Moritz *(p264)*, meanwhile, is a top choice for cross-country skiers.

HIDDEN GEM
Empty Slopes

Swiss ski slopes are world famous, but there are still some under-the-radar pistes if you know where to look. Car-free Bettmeralp, for instance, rewards intrepid skiers with empty runs.

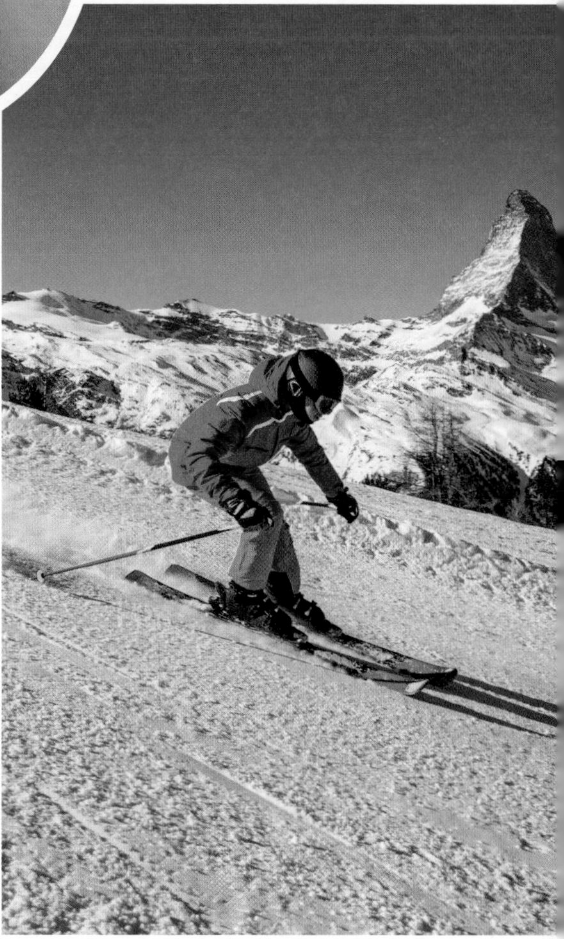

→
A skier zooming across the powdery slopes of the Zermatt ski resort

A YEAR IN SWITZERLAND

JANUARY

Inferno Downhill *(late Jan).* In Mürren, the world's oldest and longest downhill ski race is open to all.

World Economic Forum *(late Jan).* Davos plays host to heads of state and public events.

△ **International Hot Air Balloon Festival** *(late Jan–early Feb).* Competition and passenger flights high above Château d'Oex in the Alps.

FEBRUARY

△ **White Turf** *(first three Suns).* Champagne flows as thoroughbred horses make snow fly on St Moritz's frozen lake.

Carnival *(late Feb–early Mar).* It's party time in every village during *Carnaval* (in French), or *Fastnacht* (in German), with world-famous parades in Basel and Lucerne.

MAY

Combats de Reines, Aproz *(early May).* In Aproz, the unique Herens breed of feisty cow lock (blunted) horns in bovine battle to determine next year's "Queen of queens".

△ **International Cheese Festival** *(first Sun).* Visitors – and judges – snaffle samples made by cheesemakers from around the world, vying to be crowned Supreme Champion in Gruyères.

JUNE

△ **Art Basel** *(mid-Jun).* World-renowned art fair, with sister events in Miami and Hong Kong.

Zürich Pride *(mid-Jun).* The streets in the city centre come alive with one of the largest celebrations of LGBTQ+ culture in the world.

Montreux Jazz Festival *(end Jun).* Music fans flock to venues across the city for this legendary festival.

SEPTEMBER

△ **Désalpage** *(mid-Sep–early Oct).* Bringing the cows down from high Alpine pastures is celebrated in every rural Swiss village, with children leading highly decorated cows through the streets.

OCTOBER

△ **Chestnut Festival** *(mid-Oct).* During a celebration of chestnuts across Ticino, more than 2,000 kg (4,400 lb) are consumed in a day in Ascona.

MARCH

Festichoc *(early Mar)*. Visitors tour artisan workshops, ride on the chocolate train and sample all the chocolate they can stomach in Versoix for free.

△ **Engadine Marathon** *(second Sun)*. Well over a thousand cross-country skiers trudge across frozen lakes and woods to rustic S-chanf; open to all.

APRIL

Verbier Xtreme *(end Mar–early Apr)*. Skiers and snowboarders compete with pros on Verbier's challenging terrain.

△ **Landsgemeinde** *(late Apr)*. Switzerland's unique open-air assembly takes place in Appenzell, where some 3,000 citizens stand and vote on all public matters.

JULY

Paléo *(late Jul)*. An eclectic range of rock, blues and funk is performed in circus tents around Nyon.

△ **Swiss Open** *(end Jul)*. The world's best tennis players battle it out on impeccable clay courts for the title of champion, in Gstaad's ultra-chic surroundings.

AUGUST

△ **Swiss National Day** *(1 Aug)*. During the day, a parade snakes through Zürich, while bonfires and fireworks illuminate every mountaintop across the country by night to celebrate the founding of the Swiss Confederation.

International Film Festival *(mid-Aug)*. Thousands of spectators grab a seat in Locarno for outdoor viewings on a huge screen, of premieres as well as old favourites.

Lucerne Festival *(mid-Aug–mid-Sep)*. Internationally renowned summer programme of galas and concerts showcase the best of classical music.

NOVEMBER

△ **Onion Fair** *(late Nov)*. At this uniquely Swiss event, people flock to Bern from across the country to ring in the onion harvest. A wild confetti-throwing battle signals the official end of the festival.

DECEMBER

L'Escalade *(12 Dec)*. Celebrating the successful defence of Geneva from an attack by the Duke of Savoy in 1602, thousands march through the city in period costumes.

△ **Christmas Markets** *(throughout)*. Open-air markets appear across the country. While those in Basel, Bern, Zürich and Montreux are among the biggest, Stein am Rhein and Fribourg's are particularly charming.

A BRIEF HISTORY

Thanks to its strategic location in the heart of Europe, Switzerland has been highly sought after for centuries. In 1291, the Swiss Confederation was created to stave off foreign rule. The alliance expanded until modern Switzerland was born in 1848. Although its international neutrality has kept it out of many major events, this small country remains one of the continent's powerhouses.

The Crossroads of Europe

As early as 500 BCE, the lands that now comprise Switzerland were settled by two tribes, the Celtic Helvetii and the Etruscan Rhaetians. By 58 BCE, the region was incorporated into the Roman Empire and peace and prosperity reigned: agriculture flourished, towns grew and new roads encouraged trade. From the 5th to the 13th centuries, different factions fought over the territory until it was swallowed into the Holy Roman Empire in the 800s; it continued to be a battleground for powerful feudal families, notably the Habsburgs, Savoys and Zähringens.

1 A 17th-century map showing Basel. ↑

2 The 1315 Battle of Morgarten against the Habsburgs.

3 A statue depicting folk hero William Tell.

4 Destruction of icons during the Reformation in 1524, Zürich.

Timeline of events

500s BCE
The Helvetii and Rhaetian tribes begin to settle in the Alps.

390 BCE
Gallic armies heading for Rome cross the Grand St Bernard Pass.

217 BCE
Hannibal comes over the Alps with his elephants.

200 BCE onwards
The Roman rulers introduce their religion, language and underfloor heating.

742
A feudal system develops as Charlemagne draws the region into the Holy Roman Empire.

Birth of the Swiss Nation

In 1291, men from Unterwalden, Schwyz and Uri, the "Three Forest Cantons", gathered to form an alliance against foreign power. The Swiss Confederation was born, eventually giving rise to the legend of William Tell, the fearless countryman who defied Habsburg rule. Over the next 200 years, other cantons joined the fight for independence, which they finally gained in 1499. Renowned for their valour, Swiss troops became sought after as mercenaries. However, a shock defeat at the 1515 Battle of Marignano led the nation to declare an eternal peace with France; this led to laws preventing the Swiss from fighting in foreign wars, and gradually brought about complete neutrality.

The Reformation

The Protestant Reformation of the early 16th century created bitter conflict between Catholic cantons and those embracing the new creed of reformers such as Huldrych Zwingli (1484–1531) and Jean Calvin (1509–64). Despite this religious rift, all the cantons remained loyal to the Confederation throughout the wars of religion that swept Europe in the 17th century.

MÈRE ROYAUME'S FOOD FIGHT

On 11 December 1602, the Duke of Savoy's troops attempted to scale Geneva's walls in a surprise attack. Catherine Cheynel ("Mère Royaume"), a mother of 14 children, grabbed a cauldron of hot vegetable soup and poured it over the attackers, killing one of them. This caused such a commotion it roused the townspeople to defend their city.

1291

The Swiss Confederation stands against the Habsburgs.

1315

The Swiss defeat the Habsburgs at the Battle of Morgarten, consolidating the Confederation; the 1499 Swabian War brings independence.

1506

The Swiss Guard is engaged to protect the Vatican.

1516

Huguenot refugees introduce the craft of clock-making.

1680s–90s

Swiss mathematicians Jacob and Johann Bernoulli work on probability and calculus.

1

2

3

The Foundation of Modern Switzerland

Napoleon invaded Switzerland in 1798 and replaced the cantons of the Confederation with the short-lived, unpopular Helvetic Republic. The Swiss Confederation was restored in 1803, but French jurisdiction lasted until Napoleon's defeat by a British-led coalition of European armies at Waterloo in 1815. In the wake of civil war, a new constitution, drawn up in 1848 and revised in 1874, established today's system of direct democracy, with the cantons collectively ruled by a federal assembly in Bern. With political stability, the country flourished. New commercial banks were established, and the construction of the railway network and new roads opened up Alpine areas to burgeoning tourism; industries from watchmaking to chocolate manufacture thrived.

Neutrality through Two World Wars

During both the world wars, Switzerland maintained a state of armed neutrality. As a result, it was sought after by both the Allied and Axis countries as a location for commerce (thus boosting the growth of the Swiss banking industry), espionage

WOMEN'S SUFFRAGE

Swiss women were only granted the right to vote in federal elections in 1971; in 1991 Appenzell Innerrhoden became the last canton to give women a vote on local issues. Since then, women have made great strides in the political arena. In 2010, the country was one of just five worldwide to have more women than men in the cabinet that year.

Timeline of events

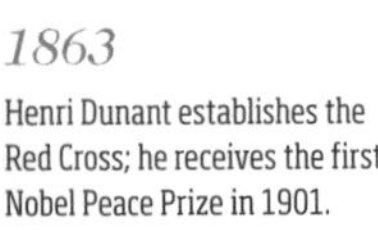

1863

Henri Dunant establishes the Red Cross; he receives the first Nobel Peace Prize in 1901.

1874

A revision of the Swiss constitution allows direct democracy by referendum.

1912

Carl Jung publishes his ground-breaking book, *Psychology of the Unconscious.*

1914–18

Switzerland organizes Red Cross units but remains neutral during World War I; the 1919 Treaty of Versailles reaffirms Swiss neutrality.

4

and secret diplomacy. It also became a safe haven for refugees fleeing violence from all across Europe, even as it provided anonymity for Nazi officials seeking to exchange pillaged gold and other looted assets for hard currency. The postwar years coincided with a period of unprecedented financial and industrial growth as the country, unscathed by the ravages of war, basked in its insular neutrality and political isolationism.

Switzerland Today

Although this small, wealthy Alpine nation still enjoys its political neutrality and its role as a tax haven, it has now finally become more involved in European matters. The country joined the United Nations in 2002 and the Schengen Agreement in 2005 as a result of public voting, and signed the Paris climate agreement in 2016, although it remains outside the EU to date. As it looks to redefine itself in a changing world, Switzerland's asylum and immigration laws have become highly contentious. Nonetheless, as host to the headquarters of several important international organizations, it continues to play a key role in world affairs.

1 Artwork depicting Napoleon at Zürich.

2 Swiss World War II General Guisan, 1939.

3 Women campaigning for the vote in 1971.

4 Headquarters of the Red Cross, Geneva.

Did You Know?

The date of Henri Dunant's birthday - 8 May - is celebrated as World Red Cross Day.

1928

The inaugural Winter Olympics are held in St Moritz.

1996

The "Nazi Gold" scandal reveals Swiss banks had bolstered the German economy.

2008

The nation scraps routine passport controls at all its borders.

2018

The government initiates "national empowerment", sponsoring tourism in Tunisia to try to curb illegal immigration.

EXPERIENCE

Cross-country skiers on the Zermatt ski pass

Bern......62

Mittelland, Bernese Oberland and Valais......80

Geneva......114

Western Switzerland......130

Zürich......158

Northern Switzerland......174

Central Switzerland and Ticino......200

Eastern Switzerland and Graubünden......238

The ornate portal at the main entrance to the Bern Münster

BERN

Lying on a narrow, elevated spit of land set in a sharp, steep-banked bend of the River Aare, the city of Bern was founded by Berthold V, Duke of Zähringen, in 1191. According to legend, the duke decided to name the new settlement after the first animal that he killed on his next hunt: this was a bear *(Bär)*, and the duke duly named the town Bärn. After the demise of the Zähringen dynasty, Bern became a free town. Growing in power and prosperity, it joined the Swiss Confederation in 1353.

In 1528, the Bernese declared themselves in favour of the Reformation, and supported the Protestant cause. By the 16th century, Bern, led by a prosperous nobility, was a powerful city-state that in the 17th and 18th centuries further expanded its territory through the annexation of surrounding lands. It lost some of its territories following an invasion of Napoleonic forces in 1798, but it remained important enough to be chosen as the Swiss capital in 1848. In the early 20th century Albert Einstein published his theory of relativity in Bern, and the city became a refuge for prominent anarchists, thus securing Bern's reputation as a place of progress.

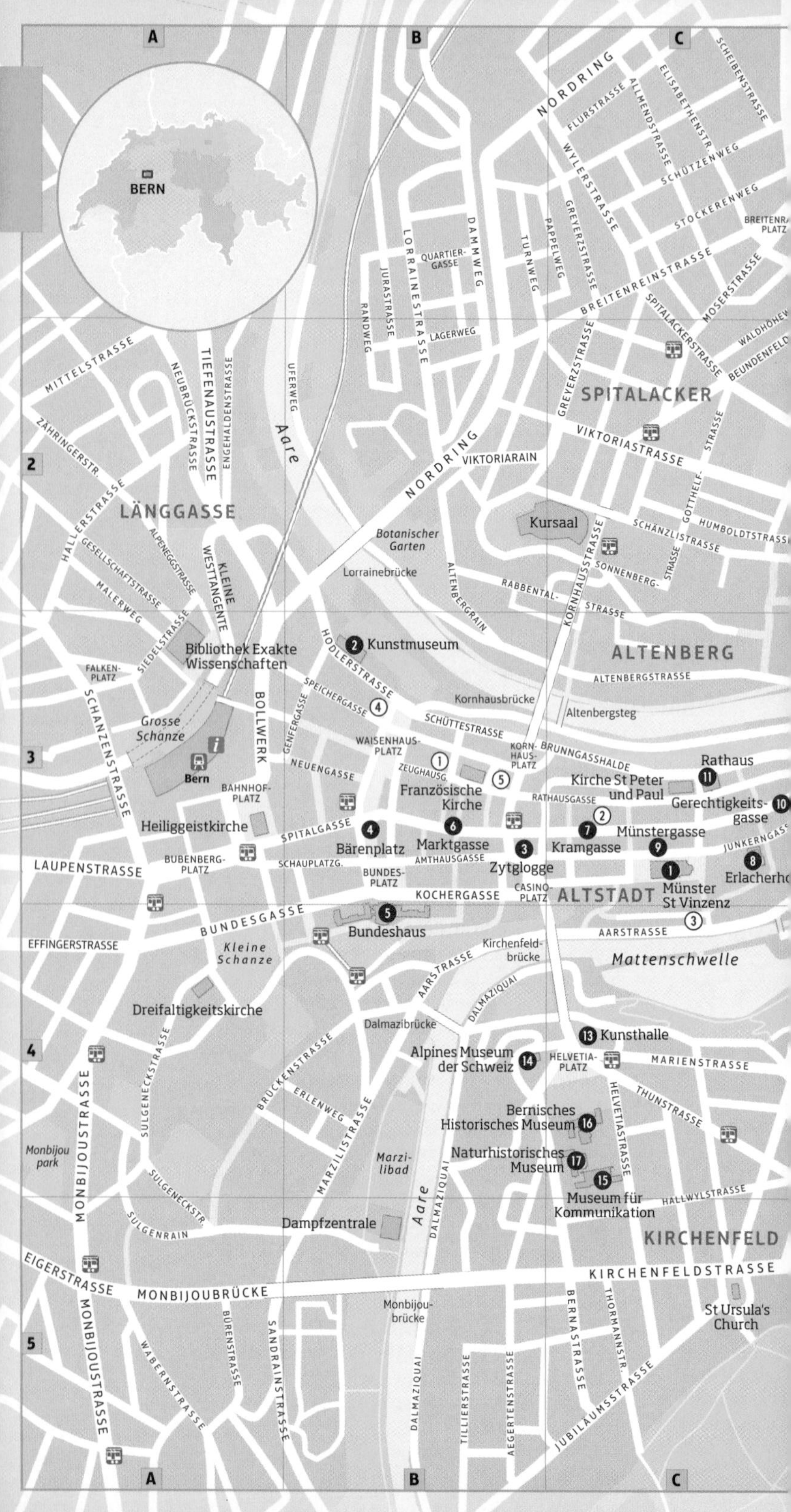

A
B
C
BERN
NORDRING
LÄNGGASSE
SPITALACKER
ALTENBERG
ALTSTADT
KIRCHENFELD
Aare
Botanischer Garten
Lorrainebrücke
Kursaal
2 Kunstmuseum
Bibliothek Exakte Wissenschaften
Grosse Schanze
Bern
BAHNHOF-PLATZ
Heiliggeistkirche
Kornhausbrücke
Altenbergsteg
Französische Kirche
Rathaus
Kirche St Peter und Paul
Gerechtigkeits-gasse
Münstergasse
Bärenplatz
Marktgasse
Zytglogge
Kramgasse
Münster St Vinzenz
Erlacherh
Bundeshaus
Kleine Schanze
Dreifaltigkeitskirche
Mattenschwelle
Kirchenfeld-brücke
Dalmazibrücke
Kunsthalle
Alpines Museum der Schweiz
HELVETIA-PLATZ
Bernisches Historisches Museum
Naturhistorisches Museum
Museum für Kommunikation
Monbijou park
Marzili-bad
Dampfzentrale
Monbijou-brücke
St Ursula's Church
MITTELSTRASSE
ZÄHRINGERSTR.
HALLERSTRASSE
GESELLSCHAFTSTRASSE
MALERWEG
ALPENEGGSTRASSE
SIEDELSTRASSE
FALKEN-PLATZ
SCHANZENSTRASSE
NEUBRÜCKSTRASSE
TIEFENAUSTRASSE
ENGEHALDENSTRASSE
KLEINE WESTTANGENTE
BOLLWERK
UFERWEG
RANDWEG
JURASTRASSE
LORRAINESTRASSE
QUARTIER-GASSE
DAMMWEG
LAGERWEG
TURNWEG
PAPPELWEG
GREYERZSTRASSE
WYLERSTRASSE
FLURSTRASSE
ALLMENDSTRASSE
ELISABETHENSTR.
SCHEIBENSTRASSE
SCHÜTZENWEG
STOCKERENWEG
BREITENRAINPLATZ
BREITENREINSTRASSE
MOSERSTRASSE
SPITALACKERSTRASSE
WALDHÖHEW
BEUNDENFELD
VIKTORIARAIN
VIKTORIASTRASSE
GOTTHELF-STRASSE
HUMBOLDTSTRASSE
SCHÄNZLISTRASSE
SONNENBERG-STRASSE
RABBENTAL-STRASSE
ALTENBERGRAIN
KORNHAUSSTRASSE
ALTENBERGSTRASSE
HODLERSTRASSE
SPEICHERGASSE
GENFERGASSE
SCHÜTTESTRASSE
WAISENHAUS-PLATZ
NEUENGASSE
ZEUGHAUSG.
KORN-HAUS-PLATZ
BRUNNGASSHALDE
RATHAUSGASSE
JUNKERNGASSE
SPITALGASSE
BUBENBERG-PLATZ
SCHAUPLATZG.
AMTHAUSGASSE
BUNDES-PLATZ
CASINO-PLATZ
KOCHERGASSE
LAUPENSTRASSE
BUNDESGASSE
EFFINGERSTRASSE
AARSTRASSE
DALMAZIQUAI
MARIENSTRASSE
THUNSTRASSE
HELVETIASTRASSE
HALLWYLSTRASSE
SULGENECKSTRASSE
BRÜCKENSTRASSE
ERLENWEG
MARZILISTRASSE
SULGENECKSTR.
SULGENRAIN
MONBIJOUSTRASSE
EIGERSTRASSE
MONBIJOUBRÜCKE
KIRCHENFELDSTRASSE
BÜRENSTRASSE
WABERNSTRASSE
SANDRAINSTRASSE
TILLIERSTRASSE
AEGERTENSTRASSE
BERNASTRASSE
THORMANNSTR.
JUBILÄUMSSTRASSE
2
3
4
5

BERN
Must Sees
1 Münster St Vinzenz
2 Kunstmuseum
3 Zytglogge
Experience More
4 Bärenplatz
5 Bundeshaus
6 Marktgasse
7 Kramgasse
8 Erlacherhof
9 Münstergasse
10 Gerechtigkeitsgasse
11 Rathaus
12 Bear Park
13 Kunsthalle
14 Alpines Museum der Schweiz
15 Museum für Kommunikation
16 Bernisches Historisches Museum
17 Naturhistorisches Museum
18 Zentrum Paul Klee
Eat
① Lötschberg
② Wein und Sein
Drink
③ Einstein au Jardin
④ Turnhalle
⑤ Kornhauskeller
D
E
F
1
2
3
4
5
Rosengarten
Schosshaldenfriedhof
Zentrum Paul Klee
Untertorbrücke
Nydeggkirche
Nydeggbrücke
Bear Park
SCHOSSHALDE
Egelsee
Petruskirche
Dählhölzliwald
OSTERMUNDIGENSTRASSE
LAUBEGGSTRASSE
ARGAUERSTALDEN
ALTER AARGAUERSTALDEN
MURISTALDEN
KLEINER MURISTALDEN
MURISTRASSE
OSTRING
BUCHSERSTRASSE
THUNSTRASSE
THUNPLATZ
BRUNNADERNSTRASSE
WELTPOSTSTRASSE
SCHOSSHALDENSTRASSE
KASERNENSTRASSE
SCHÖNBURGSTR.
SCHÄNZLISTR.
LERBERSTRASSE
BRECHBÜHLERSTR.
SALVISBERGSTRASSE
BITZIUSSTRASSE
WEISSWEG
BEVELERWEG
HASPELWEG
SPITTELERSTRASSE
FRIEDLISTRASSE
BRÜGGLERWEG
BANTIGERSTR.
WATTENWYLWEG
STEIGERWEG
TAVELWEG
HÖHEWEG
EGELBERGSTRASSE
FAMILIENSPAZIERGANG
BÜRGLENSTRASSE
GANTRISCHSTRASSE
GIACOMETTISTRASSE
BUCHSERSTRASSE
EGELGASSE
BURGERNZIELWEG
JOLIMONTSTRASSE
KASTHOFERSTRASSE
GRUBERSTRASSE
MURIFELDWEG
ALLEEWEG
WITTIGKOFENWEG
MÜLINENSTRASSE
STAUFERSTRASSE
WERNERSTRASSE
KALCHEGGWEG
LOMBACHWEG
WILLADINGWEG
ELFENAUWEG
ELFENSTRASSE
SEMINARSTRASSE
ENSINGERSTRASSE
STEINERSTRASSE
GRYPHENHÜBELIWEG
ALPENSTRASSE
A6
0 metres 400
0 yards 400
N

1

MÜNSTER ST VINZENZ

C3 Münsterplatz 12, 30 Winter: noon-4pm Mon-Fri, 10am-5pm Sat, 11:30am-4pm Sun; summer: 10am-5pm Mon-Sat (Sun: from 11:30am) bernermuenster.ch

A splendid example of the German-influenced late-Gothic style, Bern's Münster is the most recent of Switzerland's great Gothic cathedrals. Work on the cathedral began in 1421, however it was not until 1893, when the spire was added, that the building was finally completed.

The Münster is the country's tallest cathedral and largest ecclesiastical building, at just over 100 m (328 ft) high. It was originally located outside the city walls, near what is now Kreuzgasse; today the cathedral dominates Münsterplatz in the city's Old Town. The architect Matthäus Ensinger of Ulm designed it as a three-aisle basilica with fan vaulting, side chapels and a tower. The main construction took place during the city's conversion from Catholicism to Protestantism. As a result, the the cathedral features two styles: the choir's religious symbols are Catholic, while the arms on the ceiling's keystones are Protestant.

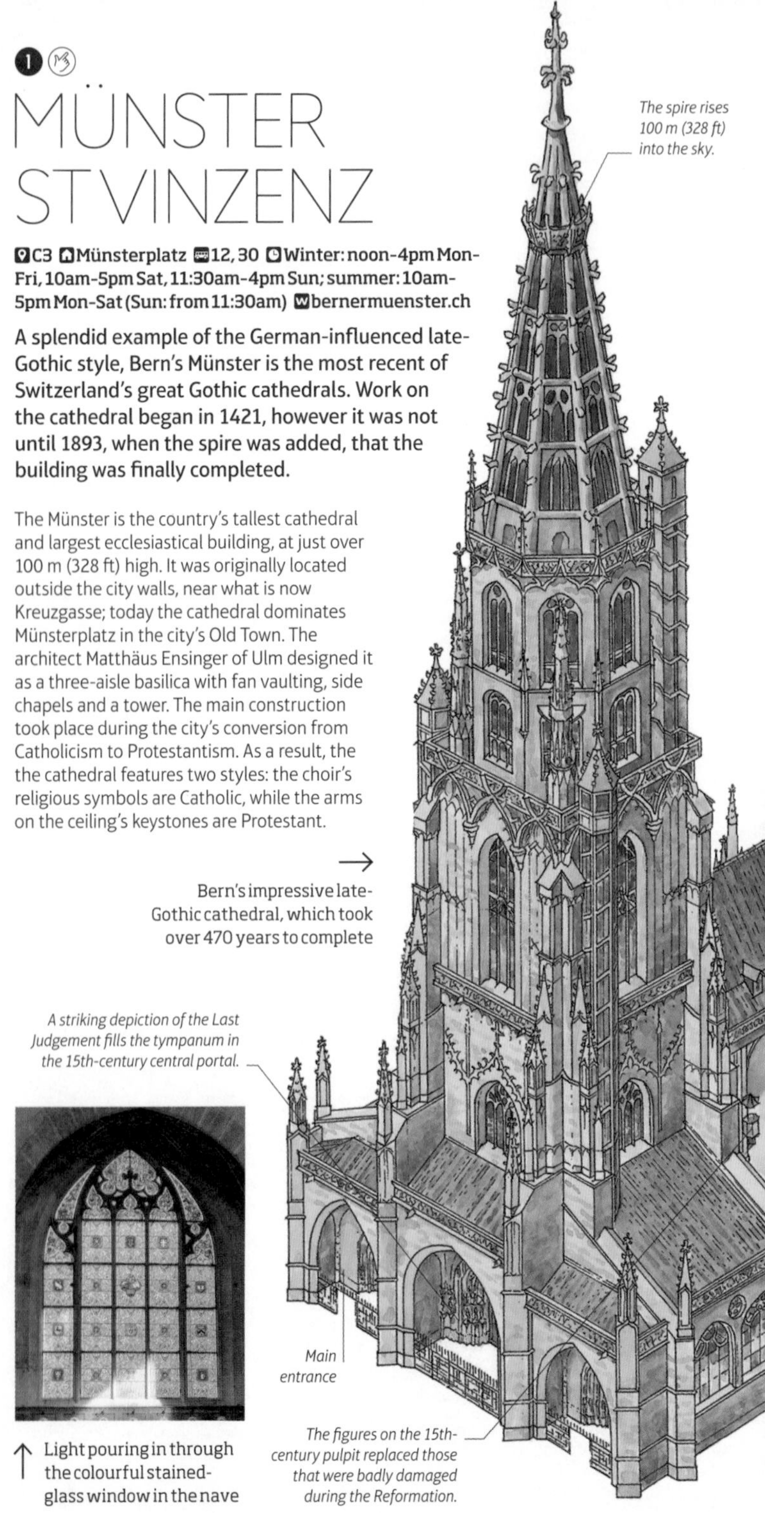
The spire rises 100 m (328 ft) into the sky.
A striking depiction of the Last Judgement fills the tympanum in the 15th-century central portal.
Main entrance
The figures on the 15th-century pulpit replaced those that were badly damaged during the Reformation.

→ Bern's impressive late-Gothic cathedral, which took over 470 years to complete

↑ Light pouring in through the colourful stained-glass window in the nave

↑ The Münster's tower and spire, stretching skywards above Bern's quaint Old Town

The central stained-glass panel in the choir depicts Christ's Passion and Crucifixion.

The nave culminates in the stained-glass windows of the choir.

Flying buttressess transmit the weight of the roof outwards and downwards to the outer walls.

The rib vaulting, by Daniel Heintz, dates from the 1570s.

GREAT VIEW
The Tower

Fortune favours the brave. For a small fee, you can climb up the 344 steps that scale the cathedral's tower to the lookout point, which perches high above the entrance. The reward is fantastic views, spilling over the rooftops of the city across to the snow-covered mountains of the distant Bernese Oberland.

↑ The figures of the Foolish Virgins standing on the left side of the main doors

2

KUNSTMUSEUM

B3 Hodlerstrasse 8-12 11, 18, 20, 21 10am-9pm Tue, 10am-5pm Wed-Sun kunstmuseumbern.ch

Housing more than 4,000 paintings, and 50,000 other items including drawings, prints and photographs, Bern's Museum of Fine Arts is Switzerland's oldest art museum with a permanent collection and the perfect place to explore centuries of world-class art.

Spanning the 14th to the 20th centuries, the Kunstmuseum's constantly evolving collection includes Early Renaissance paintings, 16th- and 17th-century Old Master paintings, and 19th- and 20th-century French paintings, including works by Delacroix, Manet, Monet, Cézanne, Braque, Gris, Picasso, Klee and Kandinsky. Look out, in particular, for Picasso's *Drunken Doze*, a work from his early Blue Period, and Klee's *Ad Parnassum*, a piece produced at a time when he was fascinated with Pointillism. Swiss artists, among them Ferdinand Hodler and Albert Anker, are well represented.

The museum runs public tours on Tuesdays and Sundays – though only occasionally in English – and a children's workshop on Saturdays and Sundays (once a month in English).

GALLERY GUIDE

The layout of the Kunstmuseum is quite simple: its collection of Old Master paintings is displayed in the basement, while the 19th-century paintings are exhibited on the ground floor, alongside temporary exhibitions. The 20th-century collection, comprising work by Picasso and Klee, occupies the first floor.

1 This winter landscape of broken ice carried downstream by a wide river *(Ice on the River)* was painted in 1882 by the Impressionist Claude Monet.

2 Visitors survey some of the well-curated works on display at the Kunstmuseum.

3 Busts line the walls of the Kunstmuseum's grand 19th-century staircase.

↑ Working alongside paintings by Ferdinand Hodler, inside the Neo-Renaissance Kunstmuseum *(inset)*

3

ZYTGLOGGE

B3 Bim Zytglogge 1 6,7,8,9 10, 12, 19, 30 Apr-Oct: 2:30-3:20pm daily; Nov-Mar: 2:30-3:20pm Sat

The eclectic Zytglogge, also widely known as the Zeitglockenturm, is Bern's most striking central landmark. Located at the heart of the medieval Old Town – a UNESCO World Heritage Site – this clock tower is one of the most visited sights in the city.

The clock tower was the town's west gate from 1191 to 1250, when it was superseded by the Käfigturm. Rebuilt after the fire of 1405, the Zytglogge was then used as a prison. Its astronomical clock was made by Caspar Brunner in 1527–30 and contains mechanical figures, including bears and a crowing cock that begin their procession on the clock's east face four minutes before it strikes the hour. A guided tour allows visitors to observe the clock's original mechanism, as well as see the rooms in the tower and admire the view. English-language tours take place daily in the summer season.

Internal mechanics of the astronomical clock on display in the tower

GREAT VIEW

Nighttime Sight

Although the views from the tower are impressive, you don't need to buy a ticket to appreciate the Zytglogge. From Easter to October and in the run-up to Christmas, the clock tower is illuminated after dusk each day, making it a magical sight.

Detail of the astronomical clock, with its brightly coloured face and dials

The tall spire and clockface of the Zytglogge rising above the red-roofed buildings of the Old Town

THE TOWER'S BELL

With a diameter of 127 cm (50 in) and a weight of 1,400 kg (3,100 lb) the tower's hour bell has remained unchanged since the tower's construction. An inscription carved on the bell reads, in Latin: "In the October month of the year 1405 I was cast by Master John called Reber of Aarau. I am vessel and wax, and to all I tell the hours of the day." Below it hangs the smaller quarter hour bell, cast in 1887 to replace the cracked 1486 original.

The softly lit arcade under Bern's iconic Zytglogge, at twilight

EXPERIENCE MORE

Bärenplatz

B3 6, 7, 8 12, 30

This elongated esplanade looks more like a wide street than a square. Seamlessly continued by another square, Waisenhausplatz, on its north side, only a fountain marks the division between the two.

Bärenplatz (Bear Square) is named after the bear pits that were once located here; since 2009, the bears have been housed in a Bear Park on the other side of the River Aare *(p75)*. The Waisenhausplatz (Orphanage Square), now a police headquarters, owes its name to the former orphanage that was once housed in this fine Baroque building.

On the east side of both squares stand the Dutch Tower and the **Käfigturm** (Prison Tower). The Käfigturm has a slender lantern tower topped by a spire. It was incorporated into a wall that was built to the west as Bern expanded, and was the town gate from 1250 until 1350. From 1643 to 1897 the tower was used as a prison, and since 1999 it has been a venue for political seminars, forums and exhibitions.

On its southern side the square adjoins Bundesplatz, which is lined with cafés; a fruit and flower market is held here on Tuesday and Saturday.

Käfigturm

Marktgasse 67 031 322 75 00 2-6pm Mon, 10am-6pm Tue-Fri, 10am-4pm Sat Mid-Jul-mid-Aug

Did You Know?

Bern hosted the 1954 World Cup Final, in which West Germany defeated Hungary.

Bundeshaus

B4 Bundesplatz 3 10, 19 parlament.ch

The imposing seat of the Federal Assembly, the Bundeshaus (parliament building) stands on a cliff overlooking the Aare Valley. Although it faces north onto Bundesplatz, its most attractive aspect is from the south – from Monbijoubrücke, a bridge on the Aare.

The building was designed by W H Auer in a bold Neo-Renaissance style, and completed in 1902. Its central part contains a spacious domed hall, with paintings illustrating important events in Swiss history. Access is by guided tour only. Free English-language tours take place on Saturdays at 2pm (book online in advance).

The Bundesterrasse, a wide promenade behind the Bundeshaus, offers a panoramic view of the Alps. A funicular near the western side of the Bundeshaus takes visitors down to the bottom of the Aare Valley.

INSIDER TIP
Lights on Bern

Every autumn, the Bundeshaus exterior stars in the highly inventive Rendez-vous Bundesplatz, a brightly coloured sound and light show. Performances are free of charge and take place several times a day.

The medieval Käfigturm, the old town gate, on picturesque Marktgasse ↑

Marktgasse

B3 6, 7, 8, 9 10, 12, 19, 30

Laid out in the 13th century, Marktgasse runs east to west from the Zytglogge, the original town gate, to the Käfigturm, the later gate. Now the centre of Bern's shopping district, Marktgasse has two Renaissance fountains: the Anna-Seiler-Brunnen, which commemorates the woman who founded Bern's first hospital in 1354, and the Schützenbrunnen (Musketeer Fountain). On the adjoining Kornhausplatz is the macabre Kindlifresserbrunnen (Ogre Fountain).

Off the northwestern side of Kornhausgasse stands the Französische Kirche (French Church). Built in the 12th century, it is the oldest church in Bern. It was taken over by French Protestants, most of them Huguenot refugees, in the 17th century.

The Neo-Renaissance façade of the stately Bundeshaus

7

Kramgasse

C3 6, 7, 8 10, 12, 19, 30

With Gerechtigkeitsgasse, its eastern extension, Kramgasse marks the main axis of Bern's early medieval town plan. It is lined with handsome historic buildings fronted by long arcades and has three fountains: the Zähringerbrunnen (1542), with a bear in armour holding the standard of Berthold von Zähringer, Bern's founder; the Simsonbrunnen (1545), with a figure of Samson subduing a lion; and the unadorned Kreuzgassbrunnen (1778). Located at Kramgasse 49 is the **Einsteinhaus**, where the great German physicist and mathematician Albert Einstein lived from 1903 to 1905 and where he began to develop the theory of relativity while working at the patent office. Einstein's apartment is now a museum, displaying his writing desk and other objects from his time in Bern.

Einsteinhaus

Kramgasse 49
10am-5pm daily Jan
einstein-bern.ch

DRINK

Einstein au Jardin

Perch on the garden terrace, with a famous Einstein brew in hand, and admire the view.

C4
Münsterplattform
einstein-jardin.ch

Turnhalle

This cool concert hall bar is located in a former school. Chill out with a local brew in the busy courtyard.

B3
Speichergasse 4
turnhalle.ch

Kornhauskeller

Enjoy brews under vaulted ceilings at Bern's most sumptuous beer cellar.

B3
Kornhausplatz 18
kornhaus-bern.ch

8

Erlacherhof

C3 Junkerngasse 47
12, 30 To visitors

Junkerngasse was once home to Bern's wealthiest citizens. At No 47 is the Erlacherhof, a Baroque mansion built by Hieronymus von Erlach, mayor of Bern, and completed in 1752. Designed in the French style, its wings are set at a right angle to the main building, enclosing a grand courtyard. To the rear is a formal French garden.

The Erlacherhof is now the official residence of the mayor of Bern and the seat of the city's government.

Münstergasse

C3

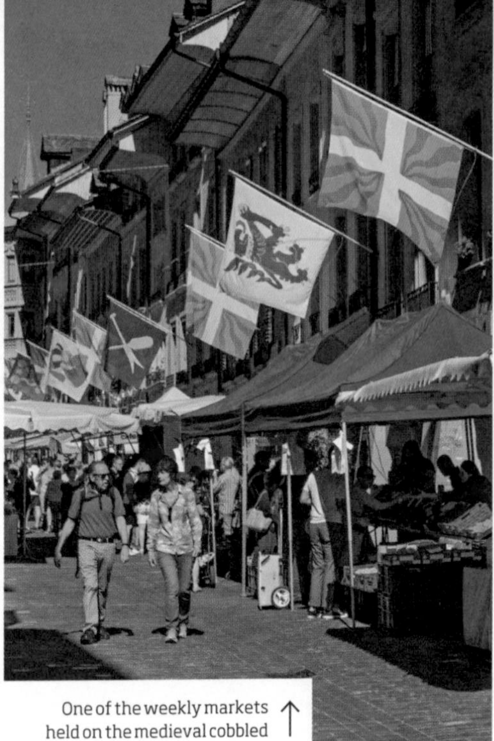

One of the weekly markets held on the medieval cobbled street of Münstergasse ↑

Running parallel to nearby Kramgasse, Münstergasse links Theaterplatz with Münsterplatz, which is lined with arcaded buildings. On Tuesday and Saturday mornings (and Thursday from April to October), this square is filled with a busy meat and cheese market. During Advent, it is replaced by a large Christmas market.

Where Münstergasse and Theaterplatz meet stands the **Stadt- und Universitätsbibliothek**, the City and University Library. This 18th-century building stages exhibitions on the history of Bern and on literary subjects.

A fountain with the figure of Moses holding the Ten Commandments stands at the corner of Münstergasse and Münsterplatz, opposite the Münster. He points to the second of them, which forbids idolatry, one of the main tenets of the Reformation.

On the Münster's south side is the Münsterplattform, a terrace with trees and Baroque pavilions from which there are views over the River Aare.

Stadt- und Universitätsbibliothek
Münstergasse 61 031 631 92 11 8am-9pm daily

EAT

Lötschberg
This place has large communal tables, no reservations and a cheese-focused menu.
B3
Zeughausgasse 16
lotschbergbern.com

Wein und Sein
Set in a cosy town cellar, this one-Michelin-star wonder offers à la carte Swiss cuisine and a top-notch wine list. Dine on the terrace in summer.
C3
Münstergasse 50
weinundsein.ch

10

Gerechtigkeitsgasse

C3

Some of the oldest and most beautiful arcaded buildings in Bern line this street. Many of them were built as guild houses, and their façades are heavily decorated with motifs reflecting the relevant trade. Gerechtigkeitsgasse, or Street of Justice, also has a fountain, the Gerechtigkeitsbrunnen, which features a figure personifying Justice.

Where Gerechtigkeitsgasse leads to Nydegggasse a castle once stood, probably about 100 years before Berthold V chose the location as a secure spot on which to establish a new town. In the late 15th century the castle was replaced by a small church, the Nydeggkirche, and in the 19th century a stone bridge, the Nydeggbrücke, was built over the deep gorge of the Aare, connecting the Old Town with Bern's eastern end.

11 

Rathaus

C3 Rathausplatz 2 12, 30 sta.be.ch/en

The seat of the canton and the city of Bern's legislative assembly since it was built in 1406–16, the Rathaus is an attractive building with an elegant Gothic façade and double staircase.

Since the 15th century, the Rathaus has undergone several major restorations, and the ground floor was completely rebuilt in 1939–42. However, it still retains its Gothic character. The Visitors' Gallery is open to the public when the assembly is in session, and free guided tours are held once a month (book ahead online).

Near the Rathaus stands the Neo-Gothic Catholic church, Kirche St Peter und Paul, completed in 1858.

12 

Bear Park

D3 Grosser Muristalden 6 12 24 hrs by appointment tierpark-bern.ch

Located near the town's old bear pits, this forested 6,000-sq-m (64,590-sq-ft) modern park is home to three brown bears. Sloping down to the river, the park has numerous caves and pools that provide the bears with a truly natural environment. There is no feeding time, rather food is hidden for the bears to forage.

Next to the old bear pits, in a former tram depot, is one of the town's two helpful tourist offices, as well as a restaurant serving local cuisine and beer brewed on the premises.

A steep path from the old bear pits leads up to the Rosengarten, containing over 200 varieties of roses.

13   

Kunsthalle

C4 Helvetiaplatz 1 6, 7, 8 19 11am-6pm Tue-Fri, 10am-6pm Sat & Sun kunsthalle-bern.ch

The Kunsthalle, a building in the Modernist style, was founded in 1918 and has retained its prominence as a showcase for modern art. It has no permanent collection, but stages a continuous programme of exhibitions by prominent artists.

BERN'S BEARS

Brown bears have been indelibly associated with Bern since the town was founded in 1191. They were kept in pits *(Bärengraben)* on the far side of the Nydeggbrücke, just across the river from the Old Town's eastern extremity, from the early 16th century. The old pits are still there, linked by a tunnel to the Bear Park.

↑ The Gothic façade of the Rathaus, a typical example of Bernese architecture

14   

Alpines Museum der Schweiz

B4 Helvetiaplatz 4 6, 7, 8 19 10am-5pm Tue-Sun alpinesmuseum.ch

Through various media, including videos, dioramas and paintings inspired by the Alps landscapes, this museum describes the geology, topography, climate and natural history of the Swiss Alps, and documents all aspects of human activity in the mountains.

The displays include a graphic explanation of how glaciers are formed and how they are melting, and a model of the Bernese Oberland. Separate sections are devoted to various aspects of Alpine life, including transport, industry, tourism and winter sports. The daily life and culture of Alpine people are also described, as are current concerns for the environment. One exhibit in the section devoted to the history of mountaineering is *The Climb and the Fall*, part of two dioramas by Ferdinand Hodler, illustrating the history of the conquest of the Matterhorn.

INSIDER TIP

Swim in the River Aare

On a particularly hot day nothing beats being carried along in the bracing current of Bern's River Aare. Jump in the river for a swim or bathe in the refreshing Marzili swimming pool.

15  

Museum für Kommunikation

C4 Helvetiastrasse 16 6, 7, 8 19 10am-5pm Tue-Sun mfk.ch

The history of the human endeavour to make contact across long distances is compellingly laid out at the Museum of Communication. The displays span the gamut from bonfires to satellites. Multimedia presentations dive into radio, described as "the window to the world", and explain how cyborgs are the progeny of simple punch cards. The permanent collection gets visitors singing along at karaoke and trying their hand at hacking.

Also of interest are the "communicators", a group of expert hosts who move through the museum to get conversations flowing. The ever-changing temporary exhibitions might cover digital detoxing or political cartoons.

→ The wave-like Zentrum Paul Klee, designed by Renzo Piano

An exhibit in the interactive Museum für Kommunikation

16  

Bernisches Historisches Museum

C4 Helvetiaplatz 5 6, 7, 8 19 10am–5pm Tue–Sun bhm.ch

Laid out over seven floors of a Neo-Gothic building reminiscent of a medieval fortified castle, Bern's Museum of History holds some 500,000 artifacts and is also home to the Einstein Museum.

Among the most interesting exhibits here is a spine-chilling depiction of the Dance of Death, a copy of a 16th-century monastic wall painting, but the pride of the museum is its collection of 12 Burgundian tapestries, the oldest of which date from the 15th century. Among the most notable is the Millefleurs-tapisserie (Thousand Flowers Tapestry).

Other sections are devoted to archaeology, with displays of Stone Age, Ancient Egyptian, Celtic, Roman and Islamic artifacts. The Einstein Museum provides an engaging account of Albert Einstein's ground-breaking discoveries, as well as the life and loves behind the genius.

17  

Naturhistorisches Museum

C4 Bernastrasse 15 6, 7, 8 19 2–5pm Mon, 9am–5pm Tue, Thu & Fri, 9am–6pm Wed, 10am–5pm Sat & Sun nmbe.ch

With roots dating to the early 19th century, Bern's Museum of Natural History is one of the oldest museums in Switzerland. It is best known for its numerous dioramas of stuffed animals shown in re-creations of their natural habitats. There are sections devoted to Africa, Asia and the Arctic, but the most impressive displays focus on the wildlife of the Alps. On view is the stuffed body of Barry, a St Bernard dog famous for his feats of mountain rescue in the 19th century. The museum also has a large collection of Alpine minerals and fossils.

Did You Know?

A skilled musician, Paul Klee chose the visual arts because modern music was "creatively unattractive".

18   

Zentrum Paul Klee

F3 Monument im Fruchtland 3 12 10am–5pm Tue–Sun zpk.org

This arts centre houses the world's largest collection of works by Swiss artist Paul Klee (1879–1940). Of the 4,000 paintings and drawings in its collection, about 200 are on display at any one time. There are temporary exhibitions, guided tours and events such as concerts, theatre, readings and workshops, as well as a separate children's museum, Creaviva. The undulating building by Italian architect Renzo Piano, and the surrounding sculpture park, are designed to blend in with the landscape.

A SHORT WALK
OLD TOWN

Distance 2 km (1 mile) **Nearest tram** 6, 7, 8
Time 30 minutes

With long cobbled streets lined with red-roofed houses and picturesque arcades, Bern's Old Town (Altstadt) is the best-preserved historic town centre in Switzerland. The layout of its streets, which are punctuated by colourfully painted fountains, has remained largely unchanged since the early 15th century. This was also the period when the Münster and the Rathaus, two of its great landmarks, were built. While the western district of the Old Town is filled with shops and busy street markets, its older eastern district has a more serene atmosphere.

↑ Zytglogge's ornate golden clock face

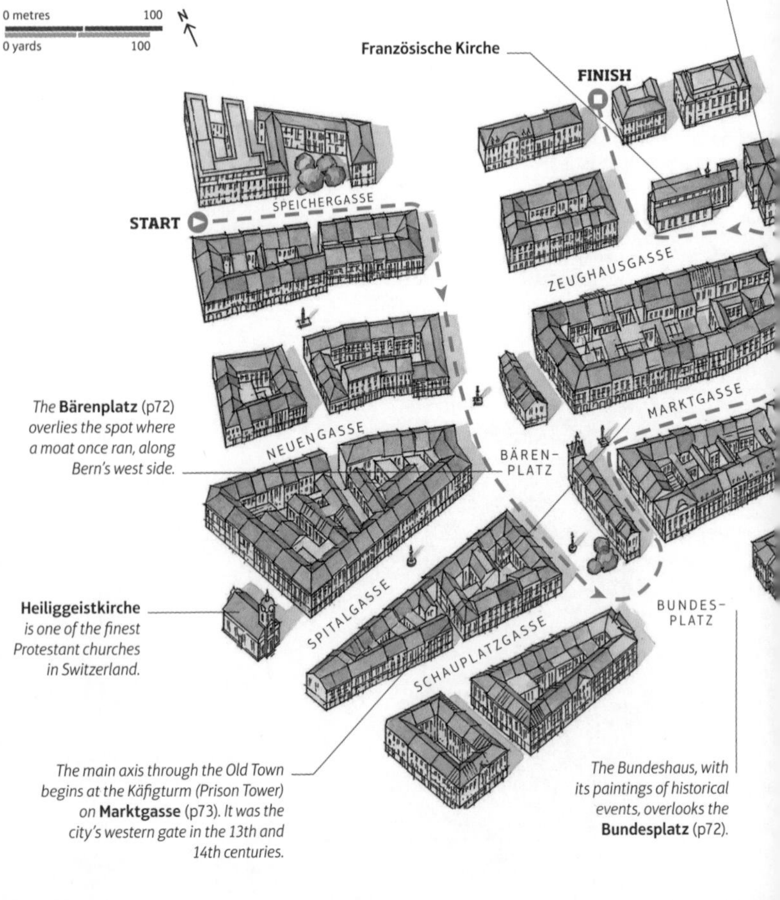

Now a cultural centre, the 18th-century **Kornhaus** *granary was built over vaulted wine cellars that currently house a restaurant.*

0 metres 100
0 yards 100

Französische Kirche

FINISH

START

SPEICHERGASSE

ZEUGHAUSGASSE

MARKTGASSE

NEUENGASSE

BÄREN-PLATZ

SPITALGASSE

SCHAUPLATZGASSE

BUNDES-PLATZ

The **Bärenplatz** *(p72) overlies the spot where a moat once ran, along Bern's west side.*

Heiliggeistkirche *is one of the finest Protestant churches in Switzerland.*

The main axis through the Old Town begins at the Käfigturm (Prison Tower) on **Marktgasse** *(p73). It was the city's western gate in the 13th and 14th centuries.*

The Bundeshaus, with its paintings of historical events, overlooks the **Bundesplatz** *(p72).*

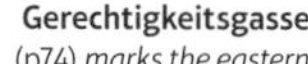

Did You Know?

The Französische Kirche is the oldest church in Bern.

Gerechtigkeitsgasse (p74) *marks the eastern section of the main axis through the Old Town. The house at No 68 is the Weavers' Guild, the façade featuring a gilt griffin. Another striking landmark is a fountain with a statue of Justice.*

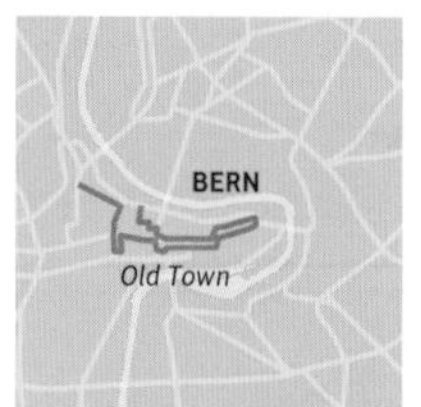

Locator Map
For more detail see p64

From 1191 to 1250 the **Zytglogge** (p70) *clock tower was the city's western gate, and it was later used as a prison. Its chimes begin at four minutes before the hour.*

Rathaus (p75), *the town hall, is fronted by a double staircase and a Gothic loggia that leads to the main entrance.*

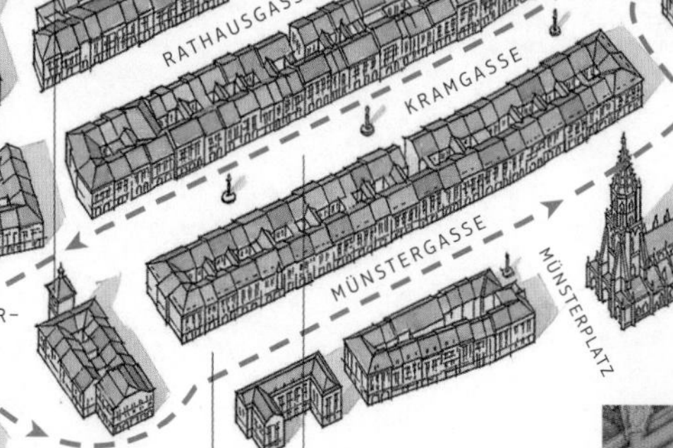

The most striking feature of Bern's Gothic cathedral **Münster St Vinzenz** (p66) *is the magnificent central portal, surrounded by painted figures.*

On Tuesday and Saturday mornings the arcades along **Münstergasse** (p74) *host a bustling street market.*

The main axis through the Old Town is continued by **Kramgasse** (p73). *This street begins at the Zytglogge, the clock tower marking the western limit of the oldest part of the Old Town.*

→ Relief on the main portal of Bern's Münster St Vinzenz

Flower-filled meadowland beneath the iconic Matterhorn

MITTELLAND, BERNESE OBERLAND AND VALAIS

Peppered with the cultural centres of Basel and Bern, these three regions in the western central section of Switzerland are beloved for their combination of magnificent, diverse landscapes and artistic heritage. The rolling farmland and numerous lakes attracted Celtic tribes to the Mittelland in around 500 BCE. Following the Roman invasion in 15 BCE, the region became crisscrossed with roads that linked the towns that sprung up across the plateau. By the Middle Ages, these roads brought skilled crafters and trade to cities across the Mittelland and Bernese Oberland, such as Bern and Solothurn. At the same time, the people of Valais, in the south, had developed engineering methods to build a new trade route across the St Gotthard Pass. This new route allowed formidable alliances to be forged between centres of power in the north and south, so strengthening the ever-expanding Swiss Confederation.

While much of the region remained agricultural, by the 19th century the more mountainous areas began to develop a thriving tourist industry. Artists and writers, from Felix Mendelssohn to Mark Twain, flocked to hike in the fresh mountain air. Today the large international resorts of Verbier, Crans-Montana, Zermatt and Saas-Fee draw tourists year-round.

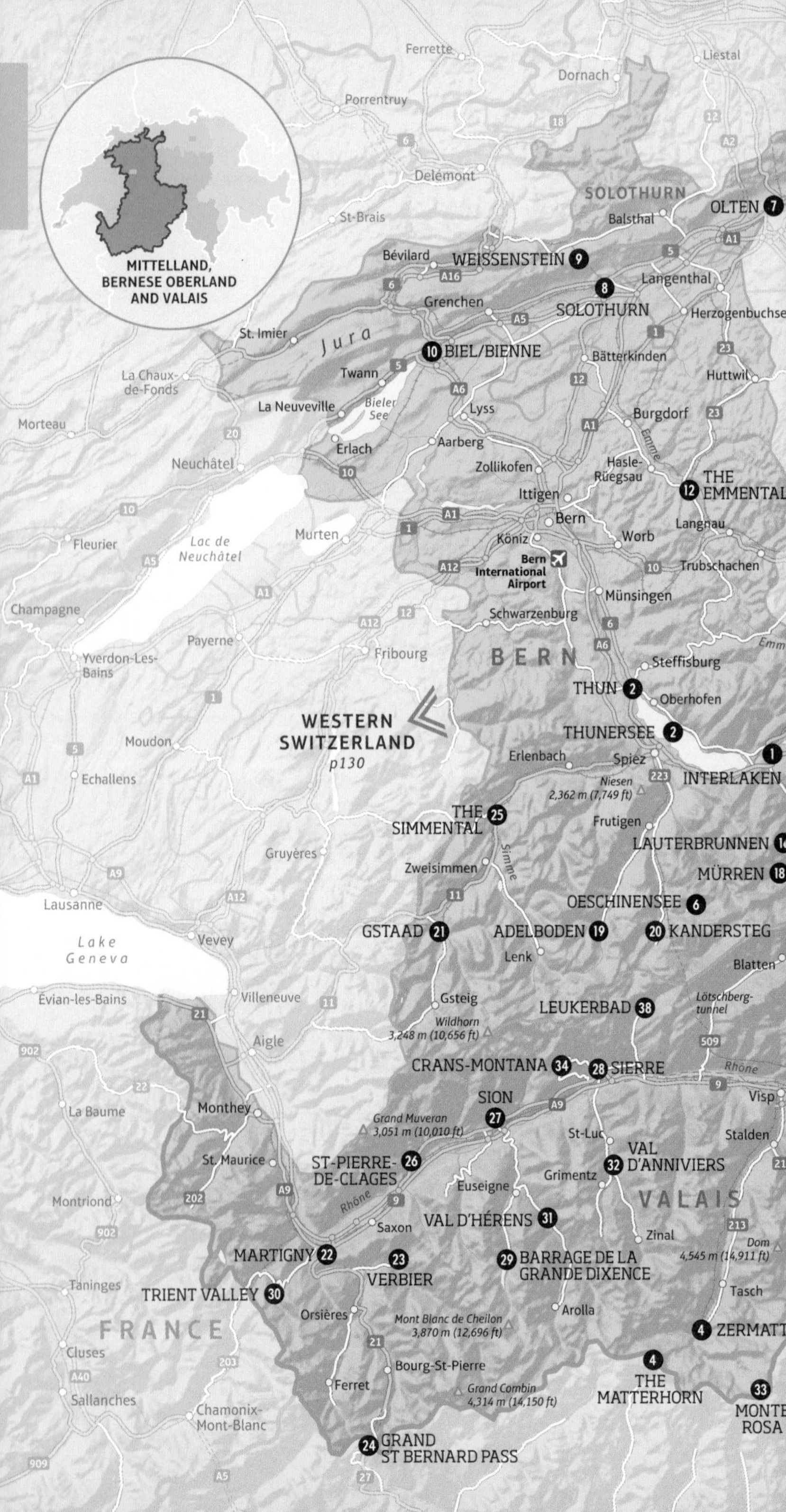
MITTELLAND, BERNESE OBERLAND AND VALAIS
OLTEN 7
WEISSENSTEIN 9
SOLOTHURN 8
BIEL/BIENNE 10
THE EMMENTAL 12
THUN 2
THUNERSEE 2
INTERLAKEN 1
THE SIMMENTAL 25
LAUTERBRUNNEN
MÜRREN 18
OESCHINENSEE 6
GSTAAD 21
ADELBODEN 19
KANDERSTEG 20
LEUKERBAD 38
CRANS-MONTANA 34
SIERRE 28
SION 27
ST-PIERRE-DE-CLAGES 26
VAL D'ANNIVIERS 32
VAL D'HÉRENS 31
MARTIGNY 22
VERBIER 23
BARRAGE DE LA GRANDE DIXENCE 29
TRIENT VALLEY 30
ZERMATT 4
THE MATTERHORN 4
MONTE ROSA 33
GRAND ST BERNARD PASS 24
WESTERN SWITZERLAND
p130
SOLOTHURN
BERN
VALAIS
FRANCE
Jura
Lac de Neuchâtel
Lake Geneva
Bieler See
Niesen 2,362 m (7,749 ft)
Wildhorn 3,248 m (10,656 ft)
Grand Muveran 3,051 m (10,010 ft)
Mont Blanc de Cheilon 3,870 m (12,696 ft)
Grand Combin 4,314 m (14,150 ft)
Dom 4,545 m (14,911 ft)
Lötschberg-tunnel
Bern International Airport
Ferrette
Liestal
Dornach
Porrentruy
Delémont
St-Brais
Balsthal
Bévilard
Langenthal
Grenchen
Herzogenbuchse
St. Imier
Bätterkinden
La Chaux-de-Fonds
Twann
Huttwil
La Neuveville
Lyss
Burgdorf
Morteau
Erlach
Aarberg
Neuchâtel
Zollikofen
Hasle-Rüegsau
Ittigen
Bern
Murten
Köniz
Worb
Langnau
Fleurier
Trubschachen
Münsingen
Champagne
Schwarzenburg
Payerne
Fribourg
Yverdon-Les-Bains
Steffisburg
Oberhofen
Moudon
Erlenbach
Spiez
Echallens
Frutigen
Gruyères
Zweisimmen
Lausanne
Vevey
Lenk
Blatten
Évian-les-Bains
Villeneuve
Gsteig
Aigle
La Baume
Monthey
Visp
St-Luc
Stalden
St. Maurice
Grimentz
Montriond
Euseigne
Saxon
Zinal
Taninges
Tasch
Orsières
Arolla
Cluses
Bourg-St-Pierre
Ferret
Sallanches
Chamonix-Mont-Blanc
Emme
Simme
Rhône

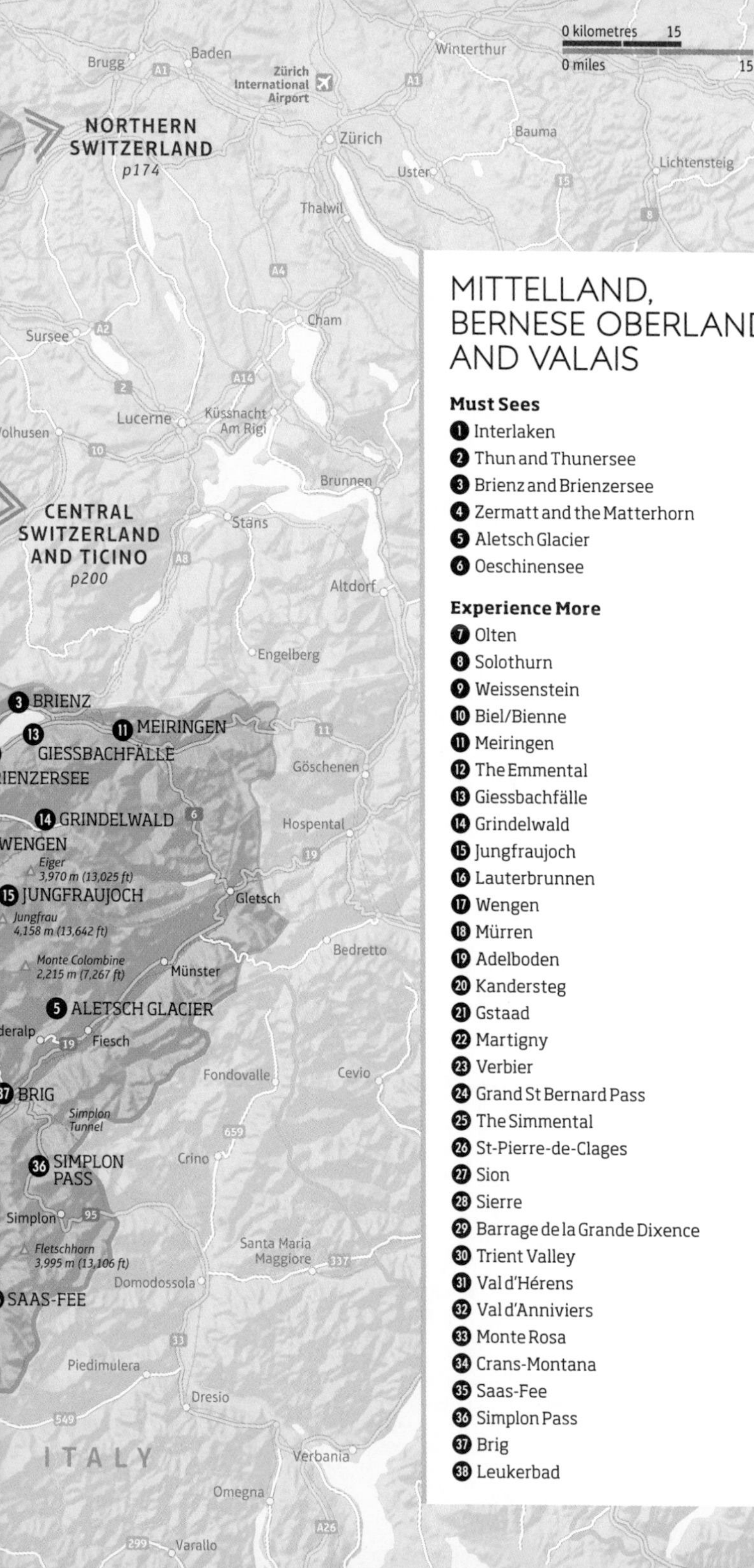

MITTELLAND, BERNESE OBERLAND AND VALAIS

Must Sees

1. Interlaken
2. Thun and Thunersee
3. Brienz and Brienzersee
4. Zermatt and the Matterhorn
5. Aletsch Glacier
6. Oeschinensee

Experience More

7. Olten
8. Solothurn
9. Weissenstein
10. Biel/Bienne
11. Meiringen
12. The Emmental
13. Giessbachfälle
14. Grindelwald
15. Jungfraujoch
16. Lauterbrunnen
17. Wengen
18. Mürren
19. Adelboden
20. Kandersteg
21. Gstaad
22. Martigny
23. Verbier
24. Grand St Bernard Pass
25. The Simmental
26. St-Pierre-de-Clages
27. Sion
28. Sierre
29. Barrage de la Grande Dixence
30. Trient Valley
31. Val d'Hérens
32. Val d'Anniviers
33. Monte Rosa
34. Crans-Montana
35. Saas-Fee
36. Simplon Pass
37. Brig
38. Leukerbad

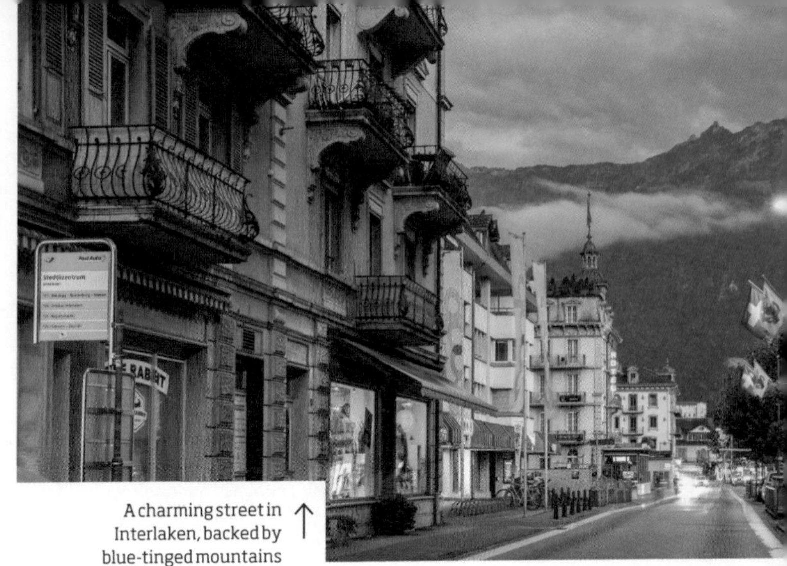

A charming street in Interlaken, backed by blue-tinged mountains

INTERLAKEN

C4-D4 Bern Interlaken Ost, Interlaken West
Marktgasse 1; www.interlaken.ch

Sitting on a narrow strip of land between Thunersee *(p86)* and Brienzersee *(p88)*, Interlaken owes its name to the 12th-century monastery founded here, named Inter Lacus, meaning "between lakes" in Latin. Today a popular resort, the town makes an excellent base for skiers in winter and for mountaineers and hikers in summer, as well as for visitors looking to make the most of the surrounding lakes.

Heimwehfluh

Därligenstrasse 32
Apr-Oct: 8:30am-4:30pm daily Nov-Mar
heimwehfluh.ch

The Heimwehfluhbahn, one of Switzerland's oldest funiculars, has been transporting view-point chasers to the top of Heimwehfluh hill since 1906. The funicular takes just a couple of minutes to reach an altitude of 680 m (2,230 ft), and rewards passengers with splendid views along the way.

At the top of the hill, there is a huge adventure playground, a model railway and a restaurant appropriately named Panorama, which overlooks Interlaken and the surrounding villages.

Between April and October, visitors can take the Rodelbahn, a summer sledging run through the Rugen forest, to get back to town from the hill. It's a thrilling ride.

GREAT VIEW
On High

The Eiger, Mönch and Jungfrau peaks can be seen from the summit of Harder Kulm mountain, which overlooks Interlaken. The Two Lakes Bridge offers stunning views from a glass-floored platform.

Kunsthaus Interlaken

Jungfraustrasse 55
2-5pm Mon-Sat, 11am-5pm Sun kunsthaus interlaken.ch

Interlaken's most important art museum opened in 2009 and is housed in a striking, modern gallery. Inside, the Kunsthaus hosts a variety of temporary exhibitions focused primarily on the Swiss Alps. The programme explores how local and international artists interpret the Alps' landscape, way of life and history. Aside from art, the gallery hosts regular film screenings, workshops and concerts.

Unspunnen Castle

The ruins of Unspunnen Castle loom over Interlaken and the nearby village of Wilderswil. Dating from the early 13th century, the ruins have become a popular destination for hikes and

excursions owing to their beautiful forested setting and sublime views over the Jungfrau massif. The castle was owned by several noble families – including the lords of Weissenberg and, later, the lords of Scharnachtal – before falling into disrepair in the early 16th century. In its state of ruin, the castle became an icon of Alpine Romanticism; it is even said to have inspired Lord Byron to write the poem "Manfred". The Castle Trail walking route leads from the ruins to the picturesque village of Wilderswill.

Unterseen

Separated from Interlaken by the Aare, Unterseen (literally meaning Lower Lake) was an important fortified town in the Middle Ages, controlling trade in the Lütschin valleys and over the passes towards central Switzerland and Italy. Today, Unterseen has a far more serene atmosphere than Interlaken, and its pretty Old Town makes for a glorious stroll at any time of day.

At the centre of the Old Town lies Stadthausplatz, where the imposing Stadthaus houses a café and restaurant. Just off the square is the **Reformierte Kirche** with its 15th-century clock tower. Nearby, a 17th-century rectory is now home to the quirky **Tourismuseum**, which traces the history of tourism in the Jungfrau region. Exhibitions explore the history of the Alpine railways and the development of winter sports from their beginnings (look out for the early examples of ski lifts and bobsleighs) to the challenges posed by climate change today. The highlight of the museum is the exhibition on the history of mountaineering, which includes feats by the earliest mountaineers, who climbed the Eiger in little more than a suit and tie.

Reformierte Kirche
Kirchgasse 3
Summer: 9am-6pm daily; winter: 9am-5pm daily

Tourismuseum
Obere Gasse 26
Apr-Oct: 2-5pm Wed-Sun; Nov-Mar: 2-5pm Wed & Sun
tourismuseum.ch

Today, Unterseen has a far more serene atmosphere than Interlaken, and its pretty Old Town makes for a glorious stroll at any time of day.

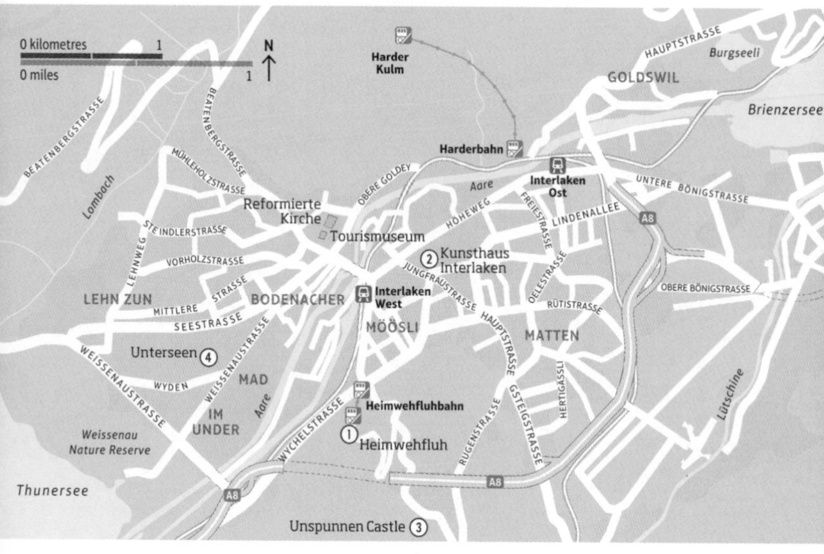

2

THUN AND THUNERSEE

C4 Bern Bahnhof; www.thunersee.ch

Famed for its turquoise waters, Thunersee is the larger of the two lakes that surround Interlaken, and offers many watersports, including sailing and diving. At its northern end, on the River Aare, lies the market town of Thun, whose origins go back to 1191, when Berthold V, Duke of Zähringen, built a hilltop castle here.

Thun Altstadt

Thun's Old Town spreads out beneath Schloss Thun, along the right riverbank. Obere Hauptgasse, its main street, runs parallel to the river, and is split into two levels. The upper walkway is built on the roofs of the arcaded buildings lining the lower street, so pedestrians must step down to enter the shops below. Alleys off Obere Hauptgasse lead up to the castle.

Schloss Thun

Schlossberg 1 Feb & Mar: 1-4pm daily; Apr-Oct: 9:30am-5:30pm daily; Nov-Jan: 1-4pm Sun schlossthun.ch

Perched on a hill above Thun, this castle has impressive views of the town and the Bernese Oberland. Inside the castle's massive turreted keep is a museum that traces the town's history. Other rooms in the castle contain collections of household objects, weapons and uniforms. Also on the hill is Stadtkirche, the town's church.

Did You Know?

In 1969, the Swiss government dumped more than 6,500 munitions in Thunersee.

Schadau Park

Set on the river's left bank, Schadau Park is a beautiful English garden, where you can admire seasonal plants and dine in Schloss Schadau, a mid-19th-century palace that has been transformed into a restaurant. There's also a Neo-Gothic folly and a pavilion, which houses the **Wocher Panorama**, an 1814 painting by Marquard Wocher that records daily life in 19th-century Thun. It's the oldest such panorama in the world.

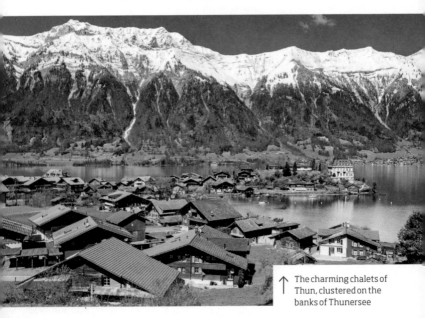

↑ The charming chalets of Thun, clustered on the banks of Thunersee

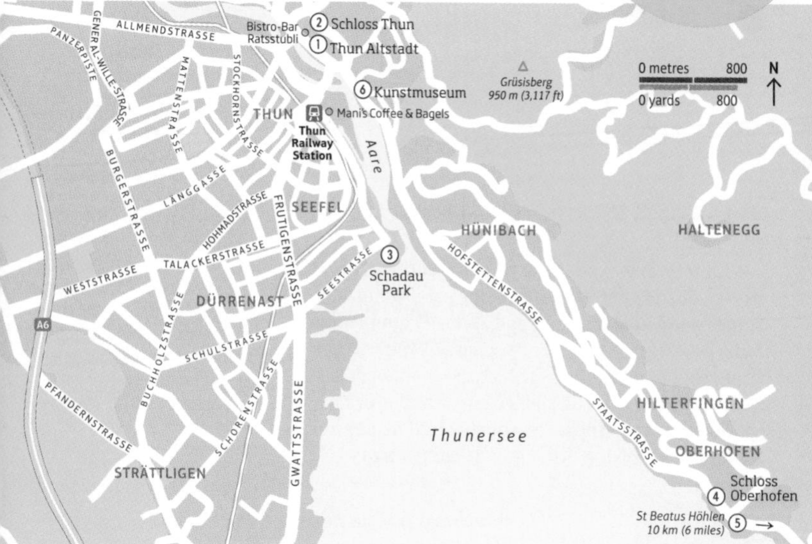

Wocher Panorama
Seestrasse 45 Mar-Jun, Sep & Oct: 11am-5pm Tue-Sun; Jul & Aug: 10am-6pm daily thun-panorama.ch

④ Schloss Oberhofen

Oberhofen 21 May-Oct: 11am-5pm Tue-Sun schlossoberhofen.ch

On Thunersee's northern shore is Schloss Oberhofen, once the castle-home of the von Oberhofen family. Originally built in the early 13th century, it has been remodelled many times over the years. The most extensive renovations were made in the mid-19th century when it was given its present Romanesque appearance.

The castle has served as a museum dedicated to its previous residents since the 1950s. Highlights include the 15th-century chapel, which has some beautiful murals, the smoking room at the top of the keep and the exhibition dedicated to the legions of staff who kept the castle running over the years. Don't miss the gardens.

⑤ St Beatus Höhlen

Seestrasse 30, Sundlauenen 21 Mar-Oct: 9am-6pm Mon-Thu & Sun (Fri & Sat: to 9pm) Nov-Feb beatushoehlen.swiss

Legend has it that a terrifying dragon once lurked inside the St Beatus caves. Look out for the creature yourself as you explore the 1 km (0.5 miles) of the cave system that is open to the public. Discover grottos, stalagmites and stalactites, and limestone formations along the way. The temperature in the caves is around 8°C, so dress appropriately.

Above ground, there is an on-site restaurant with lake views and a museum tracing the caves' natural history.

⑥ Kunstmuseum

Hofstettenstrasse 14 10am-5pm Tue-Sun (Wed: to 7pm) kunstmuseumthun.ch

Built in the French Renaissance style that was popular in the 1870s, the former Grand Hotel Thunerhof sits on the River Aare. Since the 1970s, it has housed the Kunstmuseum's collection of Swiss artworks, ranging from 18th-century Bernese landscapes to 20th-century Dada and Pop Art pieces. The museum does not display a permanent collection; three or four themed exhibits are usually on at any one time.

DRINK

Bistro-Bar Ratsstubli
This café-meets-pub serves a range of local beers. Expect DJs and occasional live music in the evenings.

Rathausplatz 6, Thun ratsstuebli.ch

Mani's Coffee & Bagels
Vegans and vegetarians are spoiled for choice at this café serving great coffee, bagels and cakes.

Panoramastrasse 1A, Thun manis.ch

3

BRIENZ AND BRIENZERSEE

D4 Bern Hauptstrasse 143, Brienz; 033 952 80 80

East of Interlaken *(p84)*, the clear waters of Brienzersee stretch out beneath forested slopes and waterfalls. Some 14 km (9 miles) long and almost 3 km (2 miles) wide, Brienzersee is smaller and less developed than Thunersee *(p86)*, making it much more appealing to some visitors. At the lake's eastern end is Brienz, the main town on the lake's shore, which makes a good base for hiking, fishing and watersports.

1 

Rothorn Bahn

Hauptrasse 149, Brienz May-Oct: 8am-6pm daily Nov-Apr brienz-rothorn-bahn.ch

Since 1892, steam locomotives have been pushing the little red carriages of the Brienz-Rothorn rack railway up to the 2,350-m (7,710-ft) summit of the Rothorn, the highest peak in the Emmental Alps. While on board, passengers are treated to panoramic views of Brienzersee; there are also several intermediate stops on the route, allowing visitors to hike part of the way. At the top of the Rothorn is Gipfel, a good restaurant, with a large terrace where you can dine alfresco and enjoy breathtaking views of no fewer than 693 other mountain peaks.

Reservations for seats aboard the Rothorn Bahn should be made in advance, as numbers are limited.

2 

Trauffer World of Experiences

Holzkuhplatz 1 10am-6pm daily trauffer.ch

The Trauffer family has been making high-quality wooden toys and souvenirs for generations. With its two on-site restaurants, the World of Experiences visitor centre shows how these items are crafted through workshops and demonstrations. Learn more about the history of this unique craft and discover how the artisans ensure the sustainability of their practice.

3 

Geigenbauschule

Oberdorfstrasse 94 033 951 18 61 By appointment

Another speciality of Brienz is violin-making. Aspiring violin-makers learn their craft at the Geigenbauschule, a training school. Sign up for a guided tour or visit the on-site exhibition, which showcases some of the violins that have been made here over the years.

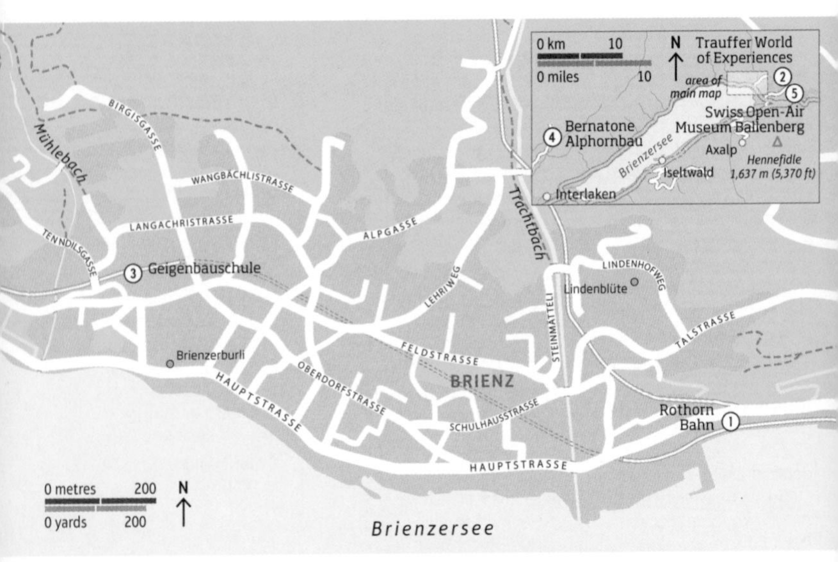

↑ The enchanting town of Brienz, nestled along the lake

Bernatone Alphornbau

Habkern 8am-noon & 1-5pm daily (workshop visits by appointment only) bernatone.ch

One of the most recognizable cultural symbols of the Swiss Alps, a traditional alphorn, or alpenhorn, is carved from a single piece of softwood (usually spruce but sometimes pine). Discover how alphorns are made at the Bernatone Alphornbau, a workshop and educational centre located in the village of Habkern. Here, members of the Tschiemer family will take you through the age-old process of crafting alphorns and tell you about the history of this instrument, which dates back to at least the 15th century, as well as of Swiss cattle herding, a practice that is entwined with the alphorn's past. You can even try your hand at playing the instrument yourself and, should you discover that you have a natural talent, you can purchase one from the family's shop on site.

HIDDEN GEM

Spring in your Step

Behind Haupstrasse, Brienz's main street, is Brungasse, a narrow cobbled street lined with pretty 18th-century wooden chalets. Come spring, their balconies overflow with flowers.

Swiss Open-Air Museum Ballenberg

3 km (2 miles) E of Brienz Apr-Oct: 10am-5pm daily (grounds: from 9am) ballenberg.ch

From simple Alpine chalets to entire farmsteads, about 100 historic rural buildings and 250 farmyard animals fill this 66-hectare (160-acre) open-air museum. The buildings here are mainly constructed from wood, although some brick and stone examples can also be found, and come from several regions of the country. Some of the houses at the museum have workshops, where crafters using authentic tools and original machinery demonstrate various crafts and trades, including weaving, spinning and cheesemaking.

EAT

Brienzerburli

Local food, including beef sourced from nearby farms, fresh perch, raclette and rösti, is served by cheerful staff at this restaurant on the shore of the lake.

Hauptsrasse 11, Brienz brienzerburli.ch

Lindenblüte

With a large sun terrace and a winter garden, this elegant option is perfect for every season. The set menus also change with the time of year as dishes are made using only local ingredients.

Lindenhofweg 15, Brienz hotel-lindenhof.ch

The Matterhorn rising dramatically above snowy ridges, reflected in a lake

Did You Know?

The Matterhorn is the tenth highest mountain in Switzerland.

4

ZERMATT AND THE MATTERHORN

C6 Valais Bahnhofplatz, Zermatt; www.zermatt.ch

At 4,478 m (14,692 ft), the Matterhorn is Switzerland's most famous mountain. The small pastoral village of Zermatt, located at its base, grew quickly at the end of the 19th century to serve climbers tackling the peak. Today, it is a major ski resort and is home to one of the largest piste networks in Europe. Opportunities for climbing, hiking, glacier skiing and snowboarding abound, too.

1 Gornergratbahn

Bahnhofplatz 7am-9:50pm gornergrat.ch

Climbing to an altitude of 3,089 m (10,135 ft), the Gornergratbahn was the country's first electrified, and Europe's highest, rack railway when it opened in 1898. It operates year-round, transporting skiers to the pistes in winter and hikers to the trails in summer. Along the 9-km (6-mile) route, passengers are rewarded with magnificent views of the Matterhorn, many glacial lakes, and dense forests from its specially designed carriages. At the top, there are both short trails and fauna and flora trails (wild ibex are a common sight), as well as longer hikes. The summit is also home to the Kulmhotel Gornergrat, one of Europe's highest hotels, which serves sunset suppers in its restaurant.

2 Matterhorn Museum Zermatlantis

Kirchplatz 3-6pm daily zermatt.ch/museum

Underneath Zermatt's central Kirchplatz, and accessed via a glass hut, Zermatlantis chronicles the brave yet often tragic story of the early attempts to conquer the Matterhorn. Alongside a reconstruction of the first successful ascent in 1865 are personal effects of some of the climbers who did not make it. The collection also shows you how 19th-century mountaineering expeditions transformed the town.

INSIDER TIP

Take a Hike

Hikers of all abilities are spoiled for choice by the scores of trails around Zermatt. The pick of the lot is a four-hour walk to the top of Gornergrat (3,089 m/10,135 ft). A cog railway carries you back down to Zermatt.

 Glacier Express

Zermatt station **Summer: 8:50am & 9:50am; winter: around 8:50am** **glacierexpress.ch**

Dubbed the world's slowest express, this train service from Zermatt to St Mortiz is not to be hurried. The full trip takes 7.5 hours, carrying passengers over 291 bridges and through 91 tunnels, granting unrivalled views of the Swiss Alps. If you don't have time for the full route, the section from Zermatt to Brig is the most dramatic.

 Pfarrkirche St Mauritius

Englischer Viertel 8 **pfarrei.zermatt.net**

The oldest church in Zermatt, St Mauritius dates back to the 13th century, although the current church building, with its soaring spire, was built in 1913. The stunning painting on the ceiling of the central nave, *Noah's Ark*, was added in 1980.

In the church's courtyard is the Mountaineers' Cemetery. A poignant reminder of just how many lives have been lost on the Matterhorn and nearby peaks, it contains the graves of more than 50 climbers. Most of the simple yet moving tombstones carry an explanation of how the respective climber died – avalanche, rockfall, crevasse – but one memorial to a young American climber carries the striking message: "I chose to climb".

CLIMBING THE MATTERHORN

The extreme difficulty involved in reaching the Matterhorn's summit made it the last of the great Swiss mountains to be conquered. In 1865, a team led by the British explorer Edward Whymper made it to the top, but four of the climbers died during the descent. Even so, the Matterhorn remains a huge draw for experienced climbers across the world to this day.

 Matterhorn Alpine Crossing

The Matterhorn Alpine Crossing project, and specifically the Matterhorn Glacier Ride II, opened in July 2023, allowing walkers and skiers to travel by cable car from Breuil-Cervinia to Zermatt through the highest border crossing in the Alps.

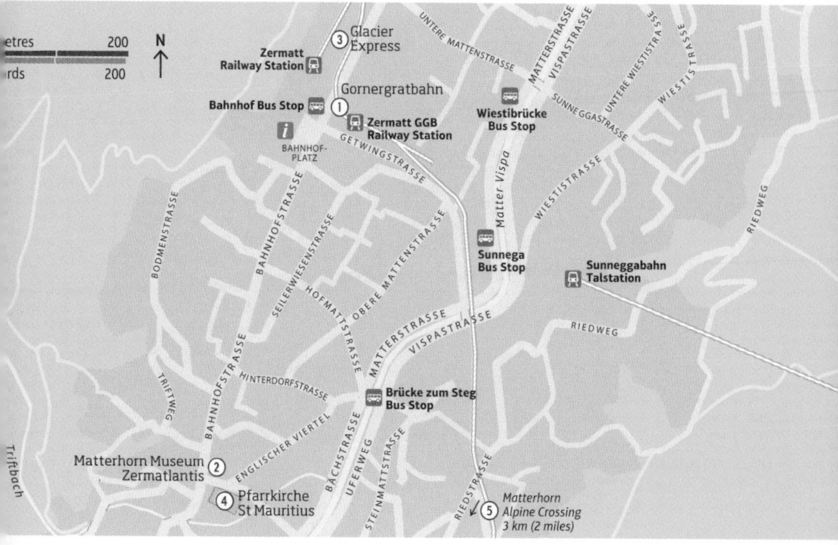

THE SWISS ALPS

About two-thirds of Swiss territory consists of Alpine and sub-Alpine areas, giving the country diverse landscapes. At lower elevations up to 1,500 m (5,000 ft), agricultural land and deciduous trees predominate. These give way to coniferous forests, which above 2,200 m (7,200 ft) in turn give way to scrub and Alpine pastures. At altitudes above 3,000 m (9,800 ft), mosses and lichens cover a desolate rocky landscape, above which are snowfields, glaciers and permanently snow-covered peaks.

FORMATION OF THE ALPS

About 70 million years ago, the Adriatic Microplate began to drift northwards, colliding with the rigid European Plate. While the oceanic floor that lay between them was forced downwards, the Adriatic Microplate was thrust upwards, creating the Alps. This upheaval, which continued until 2 million years ago, caused the upper strata of rock to fold over on themselves. The older metamorphic rocks, thrust up from the substratum, thus form the highest part of the Alps, while the more recent sedimentary and igneous rocks make up the lower levels. The action of glaciers during successive ice ages then scoured and sculpted the Alps, giving them their present appearance.

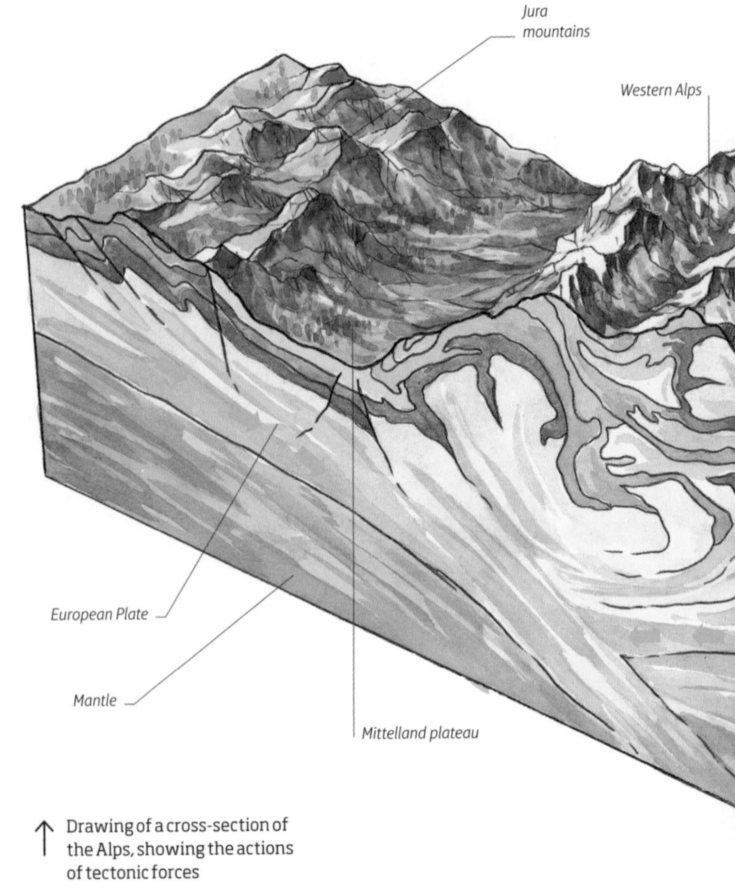

↑ Drawing of a cross-section of the Alps, showing the actions of tectonic forces

ALPINE GLACIERS

Vestiges of the Ice Age, Alpine glaciers continue their erosive action. As they advance, they scour valley floors and sides, carrying away rocks, which are ground and then deposited as lateral and terminal moraines. Glacial lakes fill basins scooped out by glaciers. Hanging valleys were created when glaciers deepened the main valley.

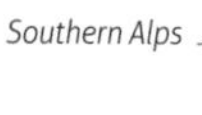

Alpine plants and animals

Edelweiss

▶ With many ballads sung in its praise, star-shaped edelweiss is the country's most famous flower. It grows among rocks at altitudes up to 3,500 m (11,500 ft). A symbol of purity and love, the woolly-leafed plant has become increasingly rare and is now a protected species.

The Alpine ibex

A species of wild goat with backward-curving horns, the Alpine ibex lives above the treeline for most of the year. It is extremely agile over mountainous terrain.

Gentian

◀ Intensely blue in colour and trumpet-like in shape, this flower grows in rock crevices and in woodlands. Its roots are used in the pharmaceutical industry.

The chamois

This goat-like antelope lives between wooded mountainsides and the snowline. Agile and shy, it is seldom seen at close range. It was once hunted for its hide, which makes a very soft leather, but hunting quotas are now imposed.

Alpenrose

◀ An evergreen species of rhododendron, alpenrose - also known as snow-rose - grows mostly at altitudes of 2,500 m (8,200 ft). Its pink-red blossoms create large clusters of dense colour. The plant and its seeds can be poisonous if ingested.

The marmot

▶ Difficult to spot but easy to hear, this rodent lives in burrows high on the valley slopes. Found throughout the Alps, marmots are particularly abundant in Graubünden and Ticino. When disturbed, they emit a piercing, high-pitched whistle.

5

ALETSCH GLACIER

D5 Valais Jungfraujoch Bahnhofstrasse 7, Riederalp; www.aletscharena.ch

A vast river of ice that stretches for more than 23 km (14 miles) from the Jungfrau region down to the Massa Gorge, the Aletsch Glacier is the longest in the Alps and the most spectacular of all Switzerland's ice fields.

The result of a vast accumulation of snow around 18,000 years ago, the glacier is part of the Jungfrau-Aletsch Protected Area, which was declared a UNESCO World Heritage Site in 2001. The best way to experience the Aletsch Glacier is to take one of the guided walks that traverse its expanse. These tours can vary in length from a couple of hours to long hikes that run over two days. Setting off from the cable car station above the ski resort of Riederalp, these walks allow visitors to explore the glacier, and its caves and tunnels, some of which are stunningly lit when the light of the sun penetrates the walls of ice. Special night excursions into these caves and tunnels can be arranged with experienced guides. The glacier is encircled by 32 dramatic peaks, accessible by cable car; the summits of Eggishorn and Bettmerhorn – both well over 2,500 m (8,200 ft) high – offer awe-inspiring panoramic views of the glacier from above.

A mountaineer making a night-time descent into one of the glacier's caves

The spectacularly located Jungfraujoch Station, high above the Aletsch Glacier

A group of walkers standing back to admire a section of the glacier

CLIMATE CHANGE

Although the sheer size of the Aletsch Glacier means that it is reacting more slowly to climate change than smaller glaciers, since around 1870 this ice mass has lost over 3 km (2 miles) in length; in 2022 alone, it lost around 6.2 per cent of its ice. By 2100, it is estimated that around 90 per cent of the ice will have disappeared. In 2007, the American photographer Spencer Tunick had hundreds of people pose naked for a photoshoot on the glacier in order to draw attention to the negative effects of global warming.

Did You Know?

The glacier contains over a fifth of the total ice volume in the Swiss Alps.

Panoramic view over the icy path formed by the Aletsch Glacier ↑

6

OESCHINENSEE

C5 Bern Kandersteg From Kandersteg
oeschinensee.ch/en

Cradled between glaciers and ancient pine woods and surrounded by fiercely steep mountains, Oeschinensee is one of Switzerland's most stunning glacial lakes. It is also the western gateway to the Jungfrau Aletsch UNESCO World Heritage Site.

Few places in the country are as picture perfect as Oeschinensee, nestled between the sheer drop of the Blüemlisalp and a prettily wooded shore. Set at a height of 1,578 m (5,177 ft), the lake is usually frozen in winter. Ice skating is possible some years, while ice fishing is a popular activity from January to March; the lake is home to delicious rainbow trout and Arctic char. Some gentle skiing is also available on the slopes surrounding the lake. The lake is at its best during the summer, when its crystal-clear, turquoise waters beckon brave swimmers; fed by a series of mountain creeks, the water remains ice-cold all year. Kayaking and hiking lure outdoorsy types, while thrill-seekers make a beeline for an exhilarating *via ferrata* (protected climbing route) and the epic summer toboggan run. Most visitors just come to relax and enjoy the peaceful surroundings with a picnic hamper full of tasty local produce. The easiest way to access the lake is via the cable car from the village of Kandersteg *(p105)*, followed by a short shuttle ride or a pleasant 25-minute walk.

VIA FERRATA

The mountain village of Kandersteg is the starting point of the Kandersteg-Allmenalp *via ferrata*. Starting at the railway station, this tough climb soon becomes vertical, and requires the use of iron cam hooks drilled into the rock. The Allmibach river itself is crossed using two rope bridges.

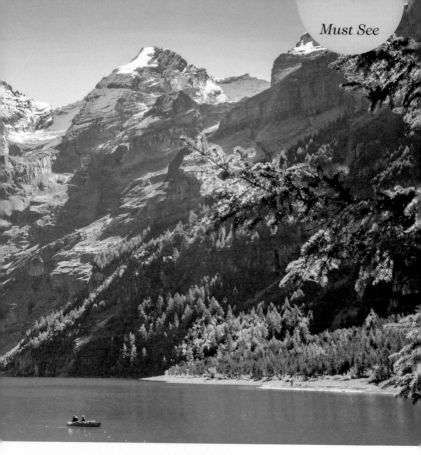

↑ Boating on the sparkling waters of Oeschinensee against an awe-inspiring backdrop of snowy peaks

1 In winter, visitors and locals come out to ice skate and walk on frozen Oeschinensee.

2 Wooden chalets are dotted around the shores of the lake.

3 The Kandersteg-Allmenalp *via ferrata* goes through stunning mountain landscapes, passing a 350-m- (1,150-ft-) high vertical wall and crossing four lovely waterfalls created by the Allmibach river.

EXPERIENCE MORE

Olten

D3 Solothurn
Frohburgstrasse 1; www.oltentourismus.ch

The small town of Olten is set in a picturesque location on the banks of the River Aare. Pedestrian access to the old part of the town is provided by the Alte Brücke, a covered bridge dating from 1802.

The Old Town is dominated by the tall Gothic belfry of a church that was demolished in the 19th century. There are many fine historic houses, particularly on Hauptgasse and along the Old Town's riverbank. Also of interest are the 17th-century monastery church and the Neo-Classical Stadtkirche, which dates from 1806–12 and is decorated with detailed paintings by draughtsman and caricaturist Martin Disteli. Many works by this local artist, along with 19th- and 20th-century paintings, installations and sculpture, are exhibited in the **Kunstmuseum**.

Kunstmuseum

Kirchgasse 8
Noon-5pm Tue-Fri, 10am-5pm Sat & Sun kunstmuseumolten.ch

Solothurn

C3 Solothurn
Hauptgasse 69; www.solothurn-city.ch

Acclaimed as Switzerland's most beautiful Baroque city, Solothurn was founded by Celts but later became the second-largest Roman town north of the Alps. From here, boats depart for Biel/Bienne, and explore a particularly scenic stretch of the Aare.

Solothurn's monumental Neo-Classical **St Ursus Kathedrale** was built from 1763 to 1773, and is flanked by friezes depicting the city's patron saints, Ursus and Victor, martyred by the Romans. The treasury in the crypt is open for guided tours only. The climb up to the bell tower is worth it for the sweeping views over the rooftops to the surrounding countryside.

Nearby is the former arsenal, the **Altes Zeughaus**, now a museum of militaria, including arms and uniforms used by Swiss mercenaries who served as bodyguards to popes and French kings. The town's small art gallery, the **Kunstmuseum**, contains some fine Old Masters, including the *Madonna of Solothurn* (1522) by Hans Holbein the Younger. Ferdinand Hodler's dramatic depiction of William Tell emerging from the clouds, painted in 1897, is iconic.

St Ursus Kathedrale

Seilergasse 4 032 626 46 46 Church: 8am-6:30pm daily; tower: Apr-Oct: 9:30am-5:30pm Mon-Sat, noon-5:30pm Sun

Altes Zeughaus

Zeughausplatz 1
1-5pm Tue-Sat, 10am-5pm Sun museum-alteszeughaus.so.ch

Kunstmuseum

Werkhofstrasse 30
11am-5pm Tue-Fri, 10am-5pm Sat & Sun
kunstmuseum-so.ch

9

Weissenstein

C3 Solothurn From Oberdorf Hauptgasse 69, Solothurn; www.solothurn-city.ch

Some of the most spectacular views of the Mittelland can be enjoyed from the summit of the Weissenstein, a ridge of the Jura that rises like a

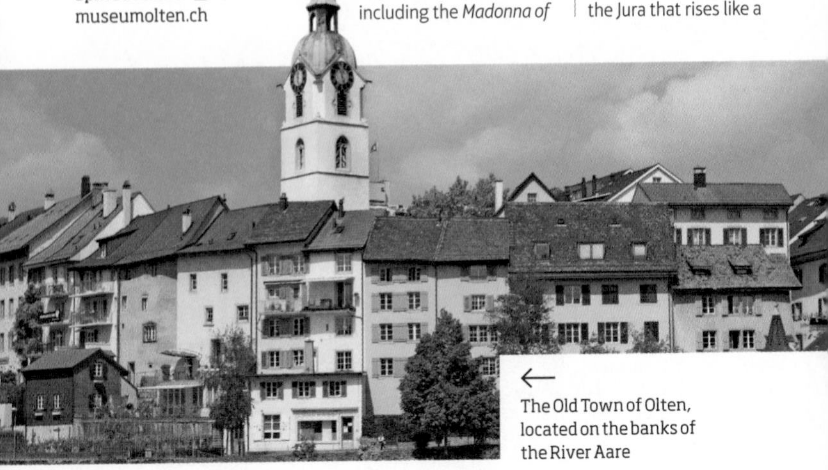

←
The Old Town of Olten, located on the banks of the River Aare

The stunning Jura mountains dotted with high Alpine meadows

rampart 1,284 m (4,213 ft) high. It is situated 10 km (6 miles) north of Solothurn. It is accessible by road or rail to Oberdorf, from where you can either hike to the summit or take a telecabine (closed on Monday and Tuesday).

On the ridge is the Hotel Weissenstein, with a restaurant. This is a good base for hiking, rock climbing and paragliding in summer, and for sledging in winter. Among the area's other attractions are a botanical garden and the Nidlenloch, a limestone cave.

Biel/Bienne

C3 Bern
Bözingenfeld/Champ; www.biel-seeland.ch

Biel, known as Bienne in French, is the second-largest town in the canton of Bern. Founded in the 13th century, it was ruled by the prince-bishops of Basel until the 19th century. Biel/Bienne's principal industry is watchmaking and its factories produce some of the world's leading brands, such as Omega and Rolex. It is Switzerland's largest bilingual town: three-fifths of its inhabitants speak French, and the rest German.

The town is set on the shores of the Bielersee (or Lac de Bienne) at the point where the River Schüss (or Suze) flows into it. Set on a hill, the Old Town has narrow cobbled streets and fountains. Its nucleus is a square known as the Ring, which is surrounded by fine arcaded houses. One of them is the house of the guild of foresters. It has a 16th-century circular turret topped by an onion dome. Also on the square is the 15th-century church of St Benedict, with impressive late-Gothic stained-glass windows.

At the intersection of Burggasse and Rathausgasse, west of the Ring, stands the Rathaus, the Gothic town hall, which dates from the 1530s. It is fronted by a Fountain of Justice. The late 16th-century Zeughaus, or arsenal, nearby is now used as a theatre.

In two adjacent buildings, Schwab and Neuhaus, the **Neues Museum Biel** imagines 19th-century bourgeois life with displays of domestic interiors. Other sections are devoted to industry, archaeology, and 19th- and early 20th-century paintings by local artists. Further down Seervorstadt the dynamic **Centre Pasquart** stages a programme of changing exhibitions of contemporary art and photography.

There are boat trips on the lake, including services to Solothurn, medieval Twann and pretty La Neuveville.

Neues Museum Biel
Seervorstadt 52
11am-5pm Tue-Sun
nmbiel.ch

Centre Pasquart
Seervorstadt/Faubourg du Lac 71-73
Noon-6pm Wed & Fri, noon-8pm Thu, 11am-6pm Sat & Sun pasquart.ch

Some of the most spectacular views of the Mittelland can be enjoyed from the summit of the Weissenstein, a ridge of the Jura that rises like a rampart.

The valley of Emmental, with its unspoiled meadows and mountain backdrop

Meiringen

D4 Bern
Bahnhofplatz 12; www.haslital.ch

This small town lies in the heart of the Hasli Valley, the Upper Aare Valley to the east of Brienzersee. It is a historic settlement, dating back to 1234, and has always been the political capital of the surrounding valley due to its strategic location at the foot of several Alpine passes. Today, Meiringen is a snow-sports resort in winter, and a base for hiking and mountain biking in summer.

Meiringen lies near the **Reichenbachfälle Falls**, the waters chosen by the writer Arthur Conan Doyle as the scene of Sherlock Holmes's death after a struggle with Professor Moriarty. The town's quirky **Sherlock Holmes Museum**, which is found beneath the deconsecrated English Church, features a representation of the famous detective's drawing room at 221B Baker Street, London. From Meiringen a funicular takes visitors to the top of the Reichenbachfälle. From here there is a stunning view of the cascading waters.

Also of interest in Meiringen is the little church of St Michael at the top of the town, built in 1684 over a Romanesque crypt. It replaced the original village church, which was built in the 9th or 10th century and destroyed by a flood. Close by, to the east of the town, is the ruined castle of Restiturm, which was originally built in the 13th century to protect and control trade through the mountainous passes. Information boards around the site tell the castle's history.

Between Meiringen and Innertkirchen is the impressive **Aareschlucht**, a deep gorge cut by the River Aare.

A statue of Sherlock Holmes in Conan Doyle Place, Meiringen

Did You Know?

Switzerland produces more than 450 varieties of cheese, with Emmental the most exported.

Reichenbachfälle Falls
033 972 90 10 (funicular)
May-Oct: 9am-5:30pm daily (last ascent 5:15pm)
Nov-Apr grimselwelt.ch

Sherlock Holmes Museum
Bahnhofstrasse 26
May-Oct: 1:30-6pm daily (Jul & Aug: to 9pm Thu); Nov-Apr: 4:30-6pm Wed & Sun
sherlockholmes.ch

Aareschlucht
Apr-mid-Jun & mid-Sep-Nov: 8:30am-5:30pm; mid-Jun-mid-Sep: 8:30am-6:30pm Dec-Mar
aareschlucht.ch

The Emmental

C3 Bern
Schlossstrasse 3, Langnau; www.emmental.ch

The Emmental, the long, wide valley of the River Emme,

has a beautiful landscape of green meadowland, grazed by cows. The valley, criss-crossed with excellent cycling and hiking routes, is dotted with traditional wooden chalets with high roof eaves that brush the ground.

Farming and traditional customs are central to the valley's local culture. This is also where the famous Emmental cheese is made, most of it by hand. At the **Schaukäserei** (show dairy) in Affoltern, visitors can see every stage in the process of producing this holey, nutty-tasting cheese. It is on sale in the dairy's shop and on the menu in its restaurant, and is also available in inns up and down the valley.

Burgdorf is a small town located in the north of the Emmental. The old part of the town is perched on top of a hill. It features arcaded houses, a Gothic church, and a 7th-century castle founded by the Zähringers. Further up the valley, the quiet village of Trubschachen has pottery workshops where colourful local wares are made and offered for sale.

The Emmental also has the longest arched wooden bridge in Europe. Built in 1839, the Holzbrücke spans the Emme just downstream of the village of Hasle-Rüegsau.

Schaukäserei
Schaukäsereistrasse 6, Affoltern 9am-5pm daily emmentaler-schaukaeserei.ch

---

13

Giessbachfälle

C3 Bern

At 400 m (1,312 ft) high, this waterfall thunders down a verdant hillside into the valley below. It's at its most impressive during late spring and early summer, when the sheer volume of meltwater means that it can be heard from some distance away.

The best way to reach Giessbachfälle is via a ferry ride across Brienzersee from Brienz *(p88)*. From the jetty, take Switzerland's oldest **funicular**, dating from 1879, up to the Grandhotel Giessbach. Once a stately home, it's now a hotel that marks the starting point of a circular hiking route to the falls. The highlight of the two-hour route is when the path passes behind the water.

The falls are illuminated at night, proving a lovely sight for those dining or staying at the hotel.

Funicular
Jun-Oct: 10am-9pm daily Nov-May

STAY

Hotel Bären
An 18th-century village coaching inn near Wilderswil station. Ask for a room overlooking the Eiger.

C4
Oberdorfstrasse 1, Wilderswil baeren.ch

Chalet zum Steg
A gorgeous chalet in the hills above Meiringen. Large apartments are available for families.

D4 Balmstrasse 69, Meiringen chalet zumsteg.ch

Grandhotel Giessbach
Ideal for romantic getaways, this opulent hotel offers lovely views of both Brienzersee and Giessbachfälle.

D4 Brienz giessbach.ch

↑ The waters of the dramatic Giessbachfälle, gushing down a hillside

↑ Grindelwald, a popular destination in the Swiss Alps

Grindelwald

**D4 Bern
Dorfstrasse 110; www.grindelwald.ch**

The road and railway lines into the mountains diverge just south of Interlaken. One branch carries into the Lauterbrunnen Valley towards Mürren; the other heads east along the Lütschen Valley to Grindelwald. From here, many visitors immediately jump onto the Eiger Express cable car up to Kleine-Scheidegg, from where the Jungfraubahn train climbs up to Jungfraujoch, the highest railway station in Europe, granting breathtaking views at the summit and along the way. But Grindelwald rewards those who stop here. Nestled beneath the Eiger, Wetterhorn and Mettenberg, this lively resort village has long been one of the most popular destinations in the Alps. In winter it offers plenty of snow sports, with excellent pistes and the opportunity to try the ubiquitous *velogemel*, and in summer great hiking. A one-hour walk east of the village leads to a wooded trail up to the Oberer Gletscher, a glacier inching its way down the Wetterhorn. Another popular hike takes walkers from the cable-car station at First (a minor summit on the slopes of the Schwarzhorn) to Bachsee, a gorgeous lake set amid pretty Alpine meadows.

The First summit is also home to the spectacular **First Cliff Walk** – a raised metallic structure bolted onto the rock face that snakes above the summit. This narrow walkway leads to a viewing platform that affords unrivalled panoramic views of the Eiger. When it's time to descend from First, you can either ride a mountain cart or take the **First Flyer Zipline**, which speeds downhill at 80 km/h (50 mph) to the Schreckfeld intermediate cable car station.

First Cliff Walk
Bergstation First
Dec-Oct: 8:30am-5:30pm daily Nov

First Flyer Zipline
Bergstation First
May & Jun: 11am-3:15pm daily; Jul-mid-Aug: 10am-4:30pm daily; mid-Aug-Oct: 11am-4pm daily Nov-Apr

GRINDELWALD'S VELOGEMEL, OR BIKE-SLEDGE

Have a go on the unique Swiss bike-sledge for the ride of a lifetime. A local woodworker invented the wooden contraption, called a "*velogemel*", to get around in deep snow back in 1911. And it is still used today by the local mail carrier in Grindelwald. It looks like a bike, with skis in place of wheels. You can rent one at the train station at Grindelwald and *velogemel* down from Bussalp above Grindelwald. Every year the Velogemel World Championships are held here, around Bussalp.

Jungfraujoch

**D5 Bern and Valais
Höheweg 37, Interlaken; www.jungfrau.ch**

South of Interlaken lies the Bernese Oberland's most impressive mountain scenery, centred on a triple-peaked ridge: the Eiger (3,970 m/ 13,025 ft), the Mönch (4,099 m/ 13,448 ft) and the Jungfrau (4,158 m/13,642 ft). An efficient network of rail and cable car routes from Interlaken *(p84)* makes it easy to travel around this ridge.

One of the best-known rail excursions takes you up to the

Jungfraujoch. This icy saddle, lying just below the summit of the Jungfrau, is dubbed the "Top of Europe", and at 3,454 m (11,332 ft) above sea level, the train station here is the highest on the continent.

As there are two different routes up to the Jungfraujoch, this excursion can easily be done as a circular journey. Trains head from Interlaken to Lauterbrunnen. Here, you can change to the rack railway that climbs up through the village of Wengen *(p104)* and on further up to the dramatic station at Kleine-Scheidegg, directly beneath the famous north face of the Eiger.

Different trains head from Interlaken up to Grindelwald, where you again change, this time to the rack railway, which climbs up to Kleine-Scheidegg from the other direction. From Kleine-Scheidegg, a separate line heads up through tunnels and along the mountain face to the Jungfraujoch itself. From April to September seat reservations are recommended. The cogwheel railway stops twice, at the Eismeer and at the Eiger Wall, from where visitors can enjoy magnificent views.

Lauterbrunnen

D4 Bern
lauterbrunnen.swiss

Unspoiled Lauterbrunnen is the world's deepest U-shaped valley, a rough-hewn glacial valley hemmed in by steep walls cut by 72 waterfalls. A local legend claims that, in 1911, the 19-year-old J R R Tolkien found inspiration for the fictional landscape of Middle-Earth, the setting for *The Lord of the Rings* (1954), here. Similarly, the German poet Johann Wolfgang von Goethe is said to have broken into verse, namely the *Song of the Spirits over the Waters* (1779), on seeing the 297 m (974 ft) Staubbach Falls, Switzerland's highest free-falling waterfall.

During summer, Staubbach Falls are accessible via a narrow yet easy path from Lauterbrunnen village to a natural rock balcony. Information panels along the route explain the various natural phenomena that led to the fall's formation. The round trip takes about three hours to complete.

In winter, skiers descend on Lauterbrunnen to tackle the 2,000-m (6,562-ft) ski run from the summit of Schilthorn to Lauterbrunnen. The village is also one of Switzerland's most popular destinations for cross-country skiers. One 16-km (10-mile) route passes several frozen waterfalls along the way.

↓ Lauterbrunnen village, set in a magnificent wild valley gorge

EAT

Bergrestaurant Bussalp

Climb through cow-dotted fields for hearty mountain fare.

D4 Bussalp, Grindelwald bergrestaurant-bussalp.ch

Piz Gloria

A revolving restaurant offering good food and down-to-earth prices.

C5 Schilthorn, Mürren schilthorn.ch

C UND M Café Bar

Great pastries in a former ski school chalet with views to the Eiger.

D5 Almisgaessli 1, Grindelwald cundm-grindelwald.ch

17

Wengen

D4 Bern
Dorfstrasse; www.wengen.ch

At an altitude of 1,274 m (4,180 ft), the car-free resort of Wengen overlooks the pretty Lauterbrunnen Valley. This is classic Swiss Alpine scenery, with snowy peaks, sheer cliffs, cascading waterfalls and verdant, rolling meadows where the cows graze.

Mountain trains heading from Lauterbrunnen climb towards the Jungfraujoch *(p102)*, stopping en route at Wengen. A village of chalets and large hotels tucked on a shelf of southwest-facing pasture, Wengen is blessed with long hours of sunshine even in winter and has a long history of being a popular mountain holiday destination, just like its neighbours Mürren and Grindelwald *(p102)*.

Skiing terrain is extensive and especially suited to families, and in summer the countryside around Wengen offers superb hiking. Trails lead down to the flower-filled meadows around Wengwald, and up to Männlichen (which can also be reached by cable car). From here visitors can enjoy spectacular views down over Grindelwald on one side and the Lauterbrunnen Valley on the other.

Did You Know?

There are over 500 km (310 miles) of sign-posted hiking trails around Wengen.

Mürren

D5 Bern
Höhemaate 1074B, Mürren; www.muerren.ch

From Lauterbrunnen *(p103)* there are two ways of reaching the small car-free village of Mürren, on the opposite side of the valley from Wengen. Both routes are spectacular. A cable car rises to Grütschalp, from where a tram takes a scenic route along the cliff edge to reach Mürren. Alternatively, buses travel along the valley-floor road (past a striking series of waterfalls at Trümmelbach) to Stechelberg, from where a cable car climbs to Mürren, perched 1,638 m (5,374 ft) above sea level. The views, down the valley and up to a dazzling panorama of snowy crags, are astounding. Another cable car heads further up, to the ice-bound summit of the Schilthorn (2,970 m/9,744 ft), where there is a revolving restaurant, Piz Gloria *(p103)*, famously featured as the villain's lair in the James Bond film, *On Her Majesty's Secret Service* (1969).

Adelboden

C5 Bern
Dorfstrasse 23; www.adelboden.ch

Located at the head of the Engstligenalp, a wide valley, Adelboden is an attractive village with chalets, pleasant streets and well-kept gardens.

↑ The charming mountain village of Mürren set amid spectacular Alpine scenery

The mountain village of Kandersteg, an ideal base for skiing or hiking

The small 15th-century parish church here is of interest for its frescoes and stained-glass windows created by Augusto Giacometti. The village also has an interesting museum documenting local history and daily life in the Engstligenalp.

Adelboden is primarily a resort, with 72 ski lifts and some 210 km (130 miles) of pistes in the Adelboden-Lenk ski-pass region. The town also offers facilities for extreme sports, as well as ice rinks for skating and curling. In summer it's a base for mountain biking and hiking.

The Engstligen Falls, spectacular waterfalls tumbling from Engstligenalp, 4 km (2.5 miles) above Adelboden, are accessible by cable car. There are several hiking trails, which lead to higher altitudes, including Ammertenspitz (2,613 m/8,573 ft), and also down past the falls.

Kandersteg

D5 Bern
Äussere Dorfstrasse 26; www.kandersteg.ch

The village of Kandersteg stretches out along the valley of the River Kander, west of the Jungfrau massif. The village is located near the north entrance to the old Lötschberg Tunnel, through which trains run for 15 km (9 miles) under the Lötschberg to emerge at Goppenstein, in eastern Valais. In 2008, a 35 km (22 mile) tunnel opened beneath the old line, massively cutting travel times.

Apart from its attractive 16th-century parish church, Kandersteg's main interest to visitors is as a resort. In winter, the gentle slopes around the village make ideal skiing pistes for beginners. In summer the village turns into a popular base for hiking, biking and paragliding or simply for exploring the stunning lakes and soaring mountains.

Oeschinensee, a small lake surrounded by towering cliffs, can be reached by a chairlift from the eastern edge of the village. Fit hikers can take the trail back down to Kandersteg. Blausee, an enchanting small boating lake surrounded by a pine forest, is a ten-minute drive north of Kandersteg.

Nearby, the lofty peak of the Blüemlisalphorn (3,671 m/12,044 ft) and its impressive neighbour the Hockenhorn (3,297 m/10,820 ft) offer mountaineers a somewhat more demanding challenge. The Lötschenpass hut is a handy spot to overnight during multi-day treks.

STAY

Alpinhotel Bort

A small chalet hotel with simple, sparsely furnished rooms with lots of sunlight.

D4 Bortweg 44, Grindelwald
033 853 17 62

Landgasthof Ruedihus

Visit this large rustic house dedicated to tradition: no metal, no plastic and no Wi-Fi.

C5 Hinder de Büele 249, Kandersteg
doldenhorn-ruedihus.ch

Alpenruh

This cosy hotel, near Mürren cable car terminus, offers great views and large family rooms.

D5 Eggli 954B, Mürren alpenruh-muerren.ch

Hotel Belvedere Grindelwald

The swankiest spot in the village, Belvedere features a gorgeous gourmet restaurant.

D4 Dorfstrasse 53
belvedere-grindelwald.ch

Bellevue des Alpes

Unrivalled views and true comfort provided for seasoned climbers and casual walkers.

D4 Kleine-Scheidegg
scheidegg-hotels.ch

↑ The village of Gstaad, with its traditional Swiss architecture

21

Gstaad

C5 Bern i Haus des Gastes; www.gstaad.ch

Given it is one of Switzerland's most famous resorts, Gstaad is a surprisingly small village, its size out of proportion to its international prestige. At the junction of four valleys, it connects into a larger regional ski-pass network, including the Diablerets Glacier.

In summer, Gstaad attracts numerous visitors who come to enjoy rock climbing, hiking, cycling and rafting on the turbulent waters of the Saane. By remaining faithful to traditional architecture, the town has maintained its romantic character. Its main street, the Promenade, is lined with shops, cafés and galleries.

Martigny

B5 Valais i 6 Avenue de la Gare; www.martigny.com

Located where the Dranse and Rhône rivers meet, at the point where the latter curves to the north, Martigny was established by the Romans as Octodorus in about 15 BCE. Excavations have unearthed a complex of Roman buildings, among them baths, an amphitheatre and a temple dedicated to Minerva.

The town is dominated by the Tour de la Bâtiaz, a 13th-century fortress set on a promontory. In Martigny's old district are the 15th-century Maison Supersaxo and the Chapelle Notre-Dame-de-Compassion, built in the 1620s, both worth a visit.

Martigny's main attraction is the **Fondation Pierre Gianadda**, a museum built on the ruins of a Gallo-Roman temple. Among its several collections, the Musée Archéologique Gallo-Romain contains statues and artifacts uncovered during excavations. The Musée de l'Auto, in the basement, showcases vintage cars, including Swiss-made models. A small number of paintings, by Cézanne, Van Gogh and Toulouse-Lautrec and other artists, are shown in the Salle Franck, while important temporary exhibitions are staged in the main gallery.

Nearby is **Barryland**, a "living museum" dedicated to the famous St Bernard dogs that were once kept at the Grand St Bernard Pass monastery and who were trained by monks to sniff out travellers lost in snow or avalanches. The museum also keeps a number of dogs on site, which you are allowed to pet at certain times of day.

Fondation Pierre Gianadda

59 Rue du Forum
Jun–Nov: 9am–7pm daily; Dec–May: 10am–6pm daily
gianadda.ch

Barryland

34 Route du Levant
10am–6pm daily
barryland.ch

Verbier

B6 Valais i Place Centrale; www.verbier.ch

Verbier is Switzerland's most extensive ski area, with terrain to suit every skier, from gentle

Did You Know?

The International Alphorn Festival is held in July in Nendaz, near Verbier.

slopes to some of the most challenging pistes. That, plus its beautiful location, climate, cosmopolitan atmosphere and vibrant nightlife, have made it a celebrity favourite. At an altitude of 1,500 m (4,921 ft), the resort lies on a wide plateau with fine views of peaks in Switzerland, Italy and France. Just below Verbier lies the Val de Bagnes, a picturesque valley and one of the country's best kept secrets.

Verbier's ski-pass area covers more than 400 km (248 miles) of on- and off-piste runs. The highest point is Mont Fort, at 3,330 m (10,925 ft). From there are far-reaching views as far as Mont Blanc. In summer, there are two golf courses and good hiking trails.

Xtreme Verbier is a winter event in which skiers and snowboarders swoop down steep mountain faces studded with cliffs. In summer, the town hosts the Verbier Festival, an international festival of classical music with free workshops. August sees the world's best horse riders compete in a prestigious dressage event.

Grand St Bernard Pass

B6 Valais
Grand-St-Bernard; www.saint-bernard.ch/en

Situated on the border with Italy at an altitude of 2,469 m (8,100 ft), the St Bernard Pass is the oldest of all Alpine pass routes, in use since 800 BCE.

The pass is named after Bernard of Menthon, Bishop of Aosta, who built a hospice for travellers here in 1049. It has been inhabited by monks ever since. It welcomes travellers all year round – access in winter is by skis or snowshoes. There is also an interesting museum that documents the history of the pass.

The St Bernard Pass is closed to vehicles all winter, with snow common in June. However, the St Bernard Tunnel provides a year-round route between Switzerland and Italy.

The Simmental

C4 Bern
3 Rawilstrasse, Lenk; www.lenk-simmental.ch

The Simmental, the beautiful long valley of the River Simme, is divided into two sections. Nieder Simmental, the lower section, runs from the town of Spiez – where the River Simme enters Thunersee (Lake Thun) – westwards to Boltigen. Here the valley veers to the south, becoming Obere Simmental, the upper section. This part stretches up a little above the valley to the holiday resort and spa town of Lenk, near the source of the Simme.

Several charming villages lie along the Simmental, among them Erlenbach, the starting point for whitewater rafting down the Simme.

INSIDER TIP
The Simmental Cycle Route

Head out on this enjoyable flat-terrain bike route, which winds its way over tarmacked and natural paths from Lenk to Erlenback *(lenk-simmental.ch)*.

→ The 17th-century church within the Grand St Bernard Pass hospice

26

St-Pierre-de-Clages

B5 Valais

The tiny medieval village of St-Pierre-de-Clages is set on the southern, vineyard-covered slopes of the Rhône Valley. Apart from an annual book festival and some well-stocked antiquarian bookshops in the village, its main attraction is a beautiful Romanesque church with an octagonal bell tower. Dating from the late 11th to the early 12th century, it was originally part of a Benedictine priory. The rib-vaulted interior is almost entirely devoid of decoration, and this pleasing austerity is accentuated by the unadorned stonework of the walls and columns. The stained glass dates from 1948.

Sion

C5 Valais
Place de la Planta; www.siontourisme.ch

The capital of the canton of Valais sits along the Rhône, at the foot of two hills. Four castles stand guard over the town of Sion: Valère, Tourbillon, Majorie and Montorge, each dating back to the 13th century or earlier. The surrounding Rhône Valley is renowned for its apricots and indiginous Fendant vineyards.

Four castles stand guard over the town of Sion: Valère, Tourbillon, Majorie and Montorge, each dating back to the 13th century or earlier.

The **Château de Tourbillon** itself is now in ruins, but many of the ramparts remain. The chapel, with ribbed vaulting and carved capitals, contains medieval wall paintings. The nearby **Château de Valère** is a 12th-century fortified church with 15th-century murals and the world's oldest working organ, dating from 1430.

Château de Tourbillon
Mid-Mar-Apr & Oct-mid-Nov: 11am-5pm daily; May-Sep: 10am-6pm daily
Mid-Nov-mid-Mar
tourbillon.ch

Château de Valère
Jun-Sep: 10am-6pm daily; Oct-May: 10am-5pm Tue-Sun
musees-valais.ch

Sierre

C5 Valais 10 Place de la Gare; www.sierretourisme.ch

Located in the Rhône Valley, Sierre (Siders in German) lies on an invisible linguistic border separating French-speakers from their German compatriots. The town enjoys a wonderfully sunny climate and is surrounded by vineyards. It contains several historic buildings, including a 16th-century castle, the Château des Vidomnes. The Baroque town hall contains a small museum of pewter objects.

The local winemaking tradition is documented by the **Wine Museum Sierre**, which has fascinating collections displayed in two places. One part occupies a wing of the 16th-century Château de Villa in Sierre, the other the 16th-century Zumofenhaus in Salgesch (Salquenen in French), a village east of Sierre. The scenic 6-km (4-mile) Sentier Viticole, or wine route, wends through villages and

HIDDEN GEM
Lac St Léonard

Between Sion and Sierre lies Europe's largest underground lake, Lac St Léonard *(www.lac-souterrain.com)*. You can visit it mid-March to November - in summer, concerts are staged on the water.

The Lac des Dix framed by Alpine peaks and the Grande Dixence dam

vineyards, with a number of wine-tasting stops along the way. The route connects the museum's two parts.

Wine Museum Sierre

Château de Villa, 6 Rue Ste-Catherine Mar-Nov: 2-6pm Wed-Fri, 11am-6pm Sat & Sun Dec-Feb museeduvin-valais.ch

Barrage de la Grande Dixence

C6 Valais Late Jun-mid-Oct grande-dixence.ch

The world's highest gravity dam and the greatest feat of modern engineering in Switzerland, this extraordinary hydroelectric dam towers 285 m (935 ft) high, across the River Dixence, at the head of the Val d'Hérémence.

The Lac des Dix, the stretch of water that fills the valley above the dam, is surrounded by mountains. Rising to the west is Rosablanche (3,336 m/ 10,945 ft); to the east soars Les Aiguilles Rouges (3,646 m/ 11,962 ft); and to the south climbs Mont Blanc de Cheilon (3,870 m/12,697 ft) and Pigne d'Arolla (3,796 m/12,454 ft). A cable car runs from the foot of the dam, where there is a restaurant, up to the lake. From here you can hike to the Cabane des Dix, a mountain refuge, walk around the lake or take the six-hour hike to the small resort of Arolla.

Val d'Hérémence joins the Val d'Hérens *(p110)* at the small town of Hérémence. The town is a good base for skiing on the eastern slopes of Mont Rouge, and also for hiking in the mountains.

Trient Valley

B6 Valais 3 Rue de la Poste, Martigny; www.valleedutrient.ch

Connecting Martigny to Chamonix in France over the narrow Forclaz Pass, Trient is an almost forgotten valley of tranquillity and pastoral life. A rack-railway train, the "Mont Blanc Express", carries passengers along the edge of the valley, offering views car drivers will never see on the road. Especially spectacular is the journey up to the lake and dam at **VerticAlp Emosson** on the Swiss border, involving three types of funicular.

Hikers can walk all the way up to the permanent ice of Trient Glacier. Along the way are the village of Le Trétien, famed for its centuries-old wooden buildings, and the natural rock swimming pool at Les Marécottes. Hikers can spend the night in one of the Swiss Alpine Club's mountain huts dotted across the terrain.

VerticAlp Emosson

6 Route du Châtelard, Le Châtelard Jun-mid-Oct: 9am-5pm daily Mid-Oct-May verticalp-emosson.ch

Did You Know?

One of the funiculars up the Trient Valley to Emosson climbs at an incline of 87 per cent.

Sion, capital of the French-speaking Valais, dramatically set amid rocky outcrops

The unspoiled Val d'Anniviers, a side valley in the Valais, popular with hikers

Val d'Hérens

C5 Valais 13 Rue Principale, Euseigne; www.valdherens.ch

Stretching southeast from Sion, the tranquil Val d'Hérens (Eringertal in German) reaches into the Pennine Alps. This pretty valley has enchanting scenery and is home to charming villages with wooden chalets.Traditions are kept alive here, making it seem a world away from modern life.

A striking geological feature of the Val d'Hérens is a cluster of rock formations known as the Pyramides d'Euseigne. Visible from the valley road, these sawtoothed outcrops of rock jut out of the hillside like fangs. They were sanded into shape during the Ice Age by the erosive action of wind, rain and ice. Each point is capped by a rock, which protected the softer rock beneath from erosion, thus producing these jagged formations.

The village of Evolène, 15 km (9 miles) south of the village of Euseigne, is a good base for hiking. At the head of the valley, amid lush Arolla pine forests and flowery meadows, is the hamlet of Les Haudères, where there is a Geology and Glacier Centre with an interesting museum. Beyond this small outpost, the Val d'Hérens extends into tree-lined Val d'Arolla. At the end of the road sits the small resort of Arolla.

The dramatic jagged rocks that form the Pyramides d'Euseigne

Val d'Anniviers

C5 Valais valdanniviers.ch

A popular destination in the summer for hikers, the rugged Val d'Anniviers begins across from Sierre and runs up to the glaciers of Zinal to the south. Surrounded by the high peaks of the Pennine Alps and cut by the River La Navisence, the valley is dotted with villages which offer visitors skiing in the winter, and hiking and cycling in the summer.

Near the entrance to the valley perches the unspoiled mountain village of Vercorin. From Soussillon you can journey to medieval Chandolin, a village of quaint wooden chalets and fantastic views. From Vissoie it is worth going to sun-drenched Saint-Luc at 1,650 m (5,413 ft) for a breathtaking view of the Val d'Anniviers. From there you can proceed up to the top of Bella Tola (3,025 m/9,925 ft).

INSIDER TIP

Hike the Valais Bisses

The *bisses* are irrigation channels that run throughout Valais. Some of them have been there for centuries, and many are now restored and make excellent hiking paths. Some are vertigo-inducing, set along a cliff edge; others are more gentle.

Grimentz is a fascinating village, full of traditional tall wooden chalets built on the underlying bedrock. From here, hiking trails lead up to the Moiry dam and the Glacier de Moiry. The highest village in the valley is Zinal at 1,670 m (5,479 ft). This resort is a ski centre in winter and a good base for summer hiking. From Zinal, guides can be hired for the climb to the summit of the Zinal-Rothorn (4,221 m/ 13,848 ft), the Pyramide des Besso, Oberes Gabelhorn and Pointe de Zinal. There are also many easier peaks and highly scenic rambling routes.

Monte Rosa

C6 Valais
Gornergrat

The Monte Rosa massif spans Swiss and Italian territory, and possesses the highest peak in Switzerland and the second highest in the Alps after Mont Blanc: the Dufourspitze, which peaks at 4,634 m (15,203 ft). Because of its shape, Monte Rosa is easier to climb than the Matterhorn.

Situated on its Italian side, near the summit at 4,556 m (14,947 ft), is the Capanna Regina Margherita, the highest mountain shelter in Europe, built in 1893. The Monte Rosa massif is encircled by the Gornergletscher, a vast glacier and the second-largest glacial system in the Alps; stretching lower down are the usually deserted slopes of Stockhorn and Gornergrat.

Crans-Montana

C5 Valais
cransmontana.ch

The fashionable ski and golf resort of Crans-Montana lies on a plateau north of the Rhône Valley, with a clear view of the Valais Alps to the south. In the late 19th century, as the fashion for mountain holidays grew, Crans and Montana expanded and merged into one legal entity.

Crans-Montana can be reached by road from Sion, and from Sierre either by a road that winds up through vineyards and pasture, or by funicular. This very sunny resort has a network of cable cars and ski lifts, accessing over 140 km (87 miles) of pistes and the glacier of Plaine Morte, a popular destination for cross-country skiing. The resort is best known, however, for high-altitude golf. Two nine-hole courses, plus the legendary Swiss Masters links, with views over the Rhône Valley, make Crans-Montana Switzerland's premier golf centre. And at this altitude, balls fly an incredible 20 per cent further than at sea level.

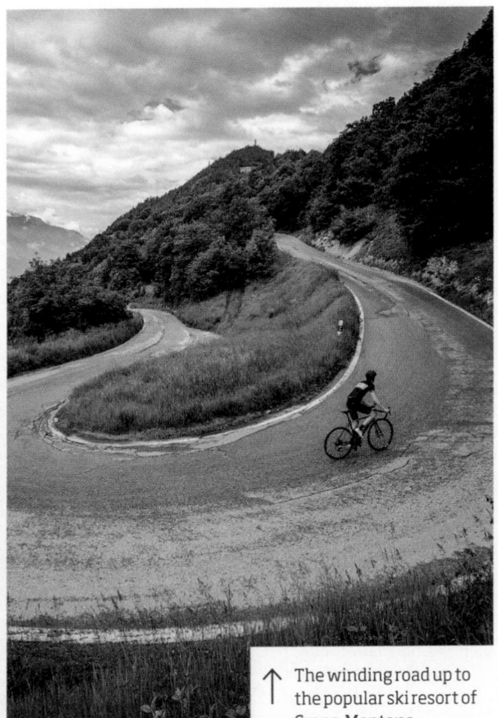

↑ The winding road up to the popular ski resort of Crans-Montana

EAT

La Brentaz

A family-friendly spot in the Val d'Anniviers serving hearty comfort food, with plenty of fresh fish on the menus.

C5 2 Place Centrale, Vercorin 027 455 17 01
Tue, Wed

L'Étable du Marais

Traditional Swiss food and an excellent wine list, served in a lovingly restored barn. The rösti Marais is a speciality.

C5 3 Route des Amis de la Nature, Grimentz
027 476 20 18

A roadside rest stop amid the hills around Saas-Fee in springtime

Saas-Fee

D6 Valais
Obere Dorfstrasse 2; www.saas-fee.ch

A village dating back to the 13th century, Saas-Fee, in the Pennine Alps, has been a resort since the early 19th century. It is the main town in the Saas Valley, through which flows the River Saaser Vispa. It has a magnificent setting at the foot of the Dom (4,545 m/ 14,911 ft) and is surrounded by other tall peaks.

The car-free resort has many traditional wooden chalets, which are built on high walls. Saas-Fee, more than many resorts in the area, cherishes its traditional rural culture, and several local traditions are enacted for visitors. These include processions marking Corpus Christi, cow fights and yodelling contests, folk festivals celebrating Swiss National Day, and the late-spring festival Alpaufzug, which marks the time when cows are taken up to their summer pastures. The Saaser Museum, with a reconstruction of a typical local house, and beautifully preserved crafts and costumes, is devoted to the region's folk traditions and culture.

All around the village, in winter or in summer, are vistas of mammoth glaciers and steep crevasses. Year-round skiing is possible on the Feegletscher (Fairy Glacier) in the Mischabel massif; it is the highest massif to lie entirely in Switzerland.

In summer, there is a range of hiking trails, from easy strolls to demanding treks, that lead into the surrounding peaks or to other sites, such as Mattmarksee, an artificial lake. A cable car also runs up to the rocky outcrop of Felskinn (3,000 m/9,800 ft). From here, the Alpine Metro makes the journey up to Mittelallalin, where you can savour the panorama from Allalin *(041 27 957 17 71)*, the highest revolving restaurant in the world at a height of 3,500 m (11,480 ft).

Simplon Pass

D5 Valais 631
Simplon Dorf; www.simplon.ch

The Simplon Pass is one of the most important routes between western and southern Europe. Connecting Switzerland and Italy, it also marks the border between the Pennine and Lepontine Alps. The route has been in use since the Stone Age, and so has played an essential role in trade since the Middle Ages.

The strategic importance of the pass was recognized by Napoleon, on whose orders a new road was built here in 1800–06. This road is about 64 km (40 miles) long and runs from Brig, over the pass and through the village of Simplon, down to the Italian town of Domodossola. Napoleon's road is passable virtually all year round. A railway tunnel under the pass was built in 1906, as an alternative crossing.

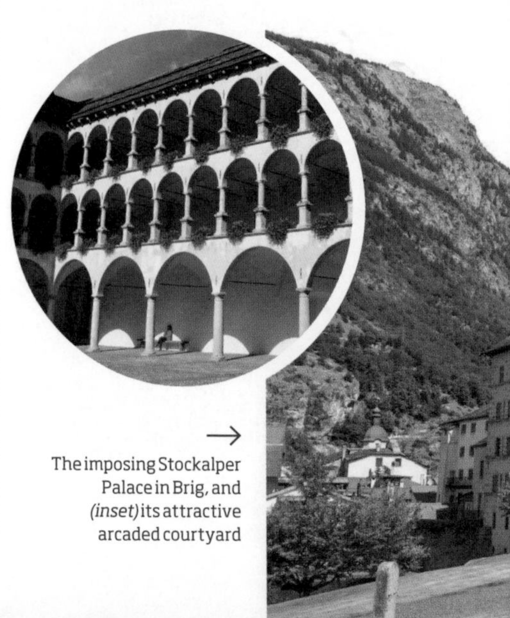

→

The imposing Stockalper Palace in Brig, and *(inset)* its attractive arcaded courtyard

Brig

D5 Valais
Bahnhofplatz 1; www.brig-simplon.ch

Built over a Roman settlement, Brig is the major town in the Upper Valais. It lies at the crossroads of the main alpine routes leading over the Simplon, Furka, Grimsel and Nufenen passes and through the Lötschberg Tunnel. Set on the Rhône, the bridges that span the river at this spot give the town its name. During the 17th century, the trade route to Italy, leading over the Simplon Pass, was controlled by the Stockalper family of merchants. Kaspar Jodok Stockalper von Thurm gave Brig its finest monument, a Renaissance-Baroque palace built between 1658 and 1678. The building is set with three tall square towers crowned by cupolas Caspar, Melchior and Balthazar. The palace has an arcaded courtyard and a chapel dedicated to the Three Kings, with an ornate silver altarpiece made by Samuel Hornung of Augsburg.

CUSTOMS OF THE LÖTSCHENTAL

The Lötschental is a remote valley just east of Leukerbad. For centuries the valley's inhabitants were isolated from the outside world during winter, and they have retained many ancient rituals, customs and traditions. One such custom is Tschäggättä, a festival that lasts from Candlemas until Shrovetide. Young bachelors don sheepskin coats, with the fleece on the outside and cowbells strapped to their waists, and wear garish masks *(left)*. Masked processions are held during the last week of the carnival.

Leukerbad (Loèche-les-Bains in French) is one of the highest spa resorts in Europe.

38 Leukerbad

C5 Valais
Rathausstrasse 8; www.leukerbad.ch

At the head of the Dala Valley, at an altitude of 1,400 m (4,595 ft), Leukerbad (Loèche-les-Bains in French) is one of the highest spa resorts in Europe. The therapeutic properties of its hot springs, which are rich in calcium, sulphur and gypsum, have been famed since Roman times.

Leukerbad has many public spa complexes, with pools and many other facilities, including treatments and rehabilitation programmes.

Above the resort, and accessible by cable car, lies the breathtaking Gemmi Pass, found on the hiking trail to Kandersteg *(p105)* and the Bernese Oberland.

Dusk setting over Geneva's Brunswick monument and fountain

GENEVA

The capital of Switzerland's westernmost canton, with which it shares its name, Geneva nestles against the shores of Lake Geneva (Lac Léman), where the Rhône and the Arve divide. It was settled by the Celtic Helvetii around 450 BCE, who were attracted by the fertile land and defensive position. The same appealed to the Romans, who swooped in to secure the city in 121 BCE. Fought over for centuries by different factions, the city gained its independence in 1536. By that point, the city of Geneva was established as a prosperous centre of trade, and on its way to becoming a stronghold of the Reformation. Known as the Protestant Rome, the city attracted Protestant refugees from across Europe. These newcomers both increased the city's wealth and boosted its cosmopolitan character. Artists and philosophers soon followed, adding to the city's culture. The city's reputation as a place of mediation and civility was cemented in 1864, when the International Red Cross was founded by a group of Genevois. In the century that followed, the League of Nations and later the United Nations made their home here. Now home to more than 200 international organizations, including CERN, one of the world's most advanced laboratories, it remains a centre of international cooperation.

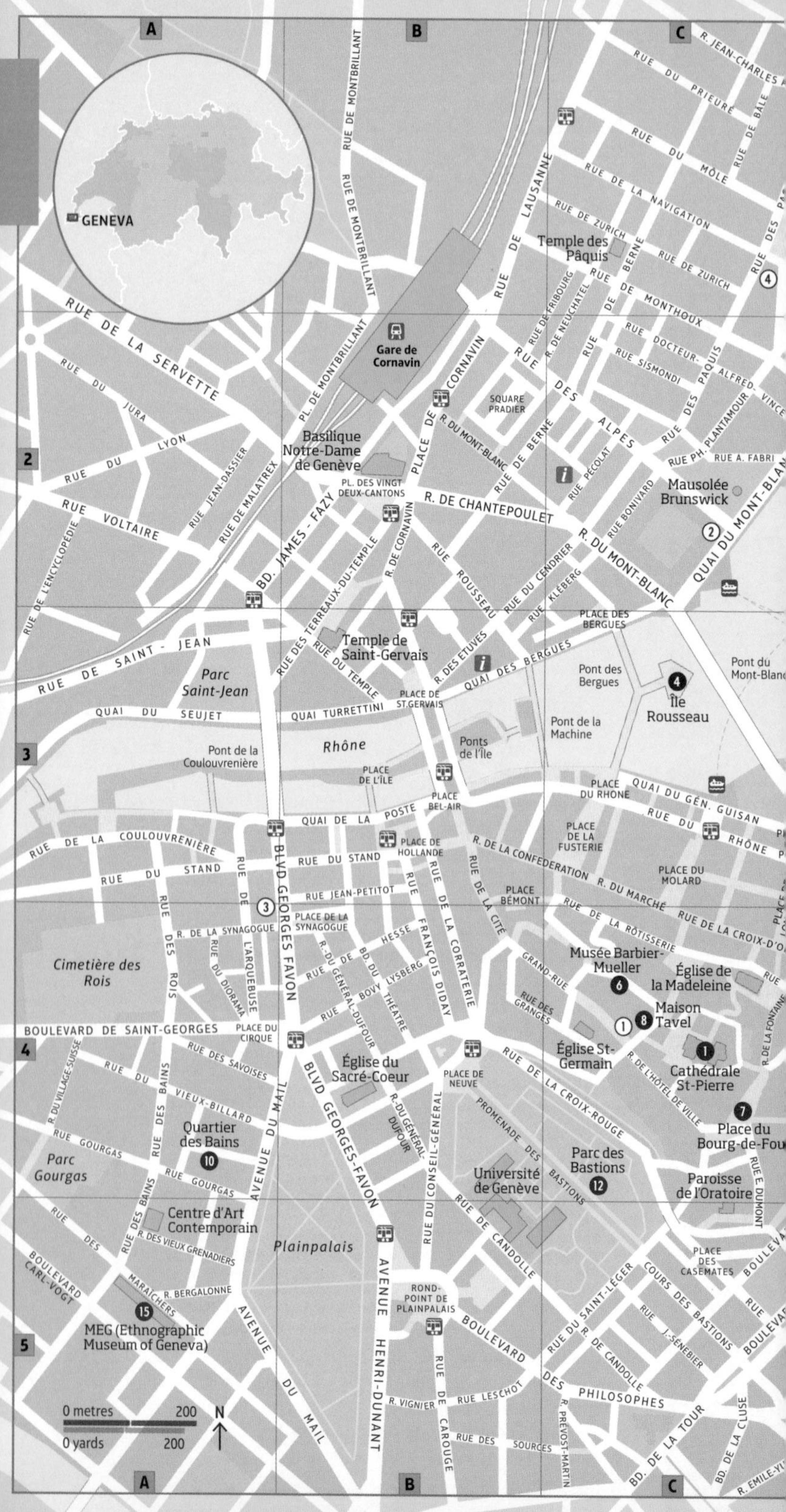

A
B
C
1
2
3
4
5
GENEVA
Gare de Cornavin
Basilique Notre-Dame de Genève
PL. DES VINGT DEUX-CANTONS
Temple des Pâquis
SQUARE PRADIER
Mausolée Brunswick
Temple de Saint-Gervais
Parc Saint-Jean
PLACE DES BERGUES
Pont des Bergues
Île Rousseau
Pont du Mont-Blanc
Pont de la Machine
Ponts de l'Île
Rhône
Pont de la Coulouvrenière
PLACE DE L'ÎLE
PLACE BEL-AIR
PLACE DE ST.GERVAIS
PLACE DU RHONE
PLACE DE LA FUSTERIE
PLACE DE HOLLANDE
PLACE DU MOLARD
PLACE BÉMONT
PLACE DE LA SYNAGOGUE
Cimetière des Rois
Musée Barbier-Mueller
Église de la Madeleine
Maison Tavel
Église St-Germain
Cathédrale St-Pierre
Place du Bourg-de-Four
PLACE DU CIRQUE
Église du Sacré-Coeur
PLACE DE NEUVE
Parc des Bastions
Université de Genève
Paroisse de l'Oratoire
Quartier des Bains
Parc Gourgas
Centre d'Art Contemporain
Plainpalais
PLACE DES CASEMATES
ROND-POINT DE PLAINPALAIS
MEG (Ethnographic Museum of Geneva)
RUE DE LA SERVETTE
RUE DU JURA
RUE DU LYON
RUE VOLTAIRE
RUE DE L'ENCYCLOPÉDIE
RUE JEAN-DASSIER
RUE DE MALATREX
RUE DE MONTBRILLANT
PL. DE MONTBRILLANT
BD. JAMES - FAZY
RUE DES TERREAUX-DU-TEMPLE
R. DE CORNAVIN
PLACE DE CORNAVIN
RUE DE LAUSANNE
RUE DES ALPES
R. DU MONT-BLANC
RUE DE BERNE
R. DE CHANTEPOULET
RUE ROUSSEAU
RUE DU CENDRIER
RUE KLEBERG
R. DES ETUVES
QUAI DES BERGUES
QUAI DU MONT-BLANC
RUE BONIVARD
RUE PÉCOLAT
RUE DES PÂQUIS
RUE PH. PLANTAMOUR
RUE A. FABRI
RUE ALFRED-VINCENT
RUE DOCTEUR-ALFRED-VINCENT
RUE SISMONDI
RUE DE MONTHOUX
RUE DE ZURICH
RUE DE FRIBOURG
R. DE NEUCHATEL
RUE DE LA NAVIGATION
RUE DU MÔLE
RUE DU PRIEURÉ
R. JEAN-CHARLES
RUE DE BÂLE
RUE DE SAINT-JEAN
QUAI DU SEUJET
QUAI TURRETTINI
RUE DU TEMPLE
QUAI DE LA POSTE
QUAI DU GÉN. GUISAN
RUE DU RHÔNE
RUE DE LA COULOUVRENIÈRE
RUE DU STAND
RUE JEAN-PETITOT
RUE DE HESSE
R. DE LA CONFEDERATION
R. DU MARCHÉ
RUE DE LA RÔTISSERIE
RUE DE LA CROIX-D'OR
RUE DE LA CITÉ
RUE DE LA CORRATERIE
RUE FRANÇOIS DIDAY
RUE DU DIORAMA
RUE DE L'ARQUEBUSE
R. DE LA SYNAGOGUE
RUE DES ROIS
BLVD GEORGES FAVON
RUE DE BD. DU THÉATRE
R. DU GÉNÉRAL-DUFOUR
RUE BOVY LYSBERG
GRAND-RUE
RUE DES GRANGES
R. DE L'HÔTEL DE VILLE
R. DE LA FONTAINE
BOULEVARD DE SAINT-GEORGES
RUE DES SAVOISES
RUE DU VIEUX-BILLARD
R. DU VILLAGE-SUISSE
RUE GOURGAS
RUE DES BAINS
AVENUE DU MAIL
BLVD GEORGES-FAVON
R. DU GÉNÉRAL-DUFOUR
RUE DU CONSEIL-GÉNÉRAL
PROMENADE DES BASTIONS
RUE DE LA CROIX-ROUGE
RUE DE CANDOLLE
RUE DUMONT
BOULEVARD
RUE DES MARAÎCHERS
R. DES VIEUX GRENADIERS
R. BERGALONNE
BOULEVARD CARL-VOGT
AVENUE HENRI-DUNANT
BOULEVARD DES PHILOSOPHES
RUE DU SAINT-LÉGER
R. DE CANDOLLE
COURS DES BASTIONS
RUE J.-SÉNEBIER
R. VIGNIER
RUE LESCHOT
RUE DE CAROUGE
RUE DES SOURCES
R. PRÉVOST-MARTIN
BD. DE LA TOUR
BD. DE LA CLUSE
R. EMILE-YUNG
0 metres 200
0 yards 200
N

GENEVA
Must Sees
1 Cathédrale St-Pierre
2 Musée d'Art et d'Histoire
Experience More
3 Jet d'Eau
4 Île Rousseau
5 Jardin Anglais
6 Musée Barbier-Mueller
7 Place du Bourg-de-Four
8 Maison Tavel
9 International Red Cross and Red Crescent Museum
10 Quartier des Bains
11 Palais des Nations
12 Parc des Bastions
13 Fondation Martin Bodmer
14 CERN
15 MEG (Ethnographic Museum of Geneva)
Eat
① Café-Restaurant de l'Hôtel de Ville
② Fiskebar
Drink
③ L'Apothicaire Cocktail-Club
④ Qafe Guidoline
D
E
F
1
2
3
4
5
QUAI WALD-WILSON
RUE JEAN-JAQUET
RUE L'ANCIEN-PORT
R. DU LÉMAN
QUAI DU MONT-BLANC
Rade de Genève
3 Jet d'Eau
QUAI GUSTAVE ADOR
Parc La Grange
AVENUE WILLIAM-FAVRE
RUE MERLE D'AUBIGNÉ
RUE DES EAUX-VIVES
RUE DE MONTCHOISY
RUE DES VOLLANDES
RUE DU NANT
RUE ERNEST-BLOCH
RUE MAUNOIR
RUE DU-31 DÉCEMBRE
RUE DE LA MAIRIE
RUE DU SIMPLON
RUE DU LAC
R. DES PIERRES-DU-NITON
RUE MUZY
R. DE LA SCIE
PROMENADE DU LAC
5 Jardin Anglais
QUAI DU GÉNÉRAL-GUISAN
RUE DU RHÔNE
RUE F. VERSONNEX
RUE PIERRE FATIO
RUE D'ITALIE
R. DE LA TOUR-MAÎTRESSE
RUE DU PRINCE
RUE DE RIVE
ROND-POINT DERIVE
PLACE DES EAUX-VIVES
AVENUE PICTET-DE-ROCHEMONT
AVE DE FRONTENEX
ROUTE DE FRONTENEX
RUE DU NANT
BOULEVARD HELVÉTIQUE
CAPREFOUR DE RIVE
RUE DE LA TERRASSIÈRE
RUE DE LA CHAPELLE
RUE DE LA FLÈCHE
VILLEREUSE
RUE F. HODLER
DALCROZE
RUE DES GLACIS-DE-RIVE
RUE ADRIEN-LACHENAL
RUE DU MIDI
RUE DE
2 Musée d'Art et d'Histoire
ROUTE DE MALAGNOU
RUE C. STURM
Église Russe
PLACE EMILE GUVENOT
RUE EMILIE GALLAND
RUE ÉMILIE GOURD
TRANCHÉES
RUE DE-BEAUMONT
RUE DE CONTAMINES
RUE DU ST. VICTOR
BOULEVARD DES
ROUTE DE FLORISSANT
AVENUE JULES CROSNIER
Around Geneva
Geneva International Airport
A1
106
1
International Red Cross and Red Crescent Museum
11 Palais des Nations
Lake Geneva (Lac Léman)
105
107
14 CERN 4 km (2.5 miles)
13 Fondation Martin Bodmer
109
GENEVA
area of main map
104
111
0 km 1
0 miles 1
N

←

1 Old Town in Geneva.

2 A paddle steamer docking on Lake Geneva.

3 The Jet d'Eau, seen from Geneva's cathedral.

4 Touring Maison Tavel.

2 DAYS

in Geneva

Day 1

Morning Start the day discovering early Geneva at the city's oldest house, 12th-century Maison Tavel *(p125)*. Spend a couple of hours diving into Geneva's fascinating history, then, once you've worked up an appetite, swing by one of the lively local markets to choose picnic treats from stalls crammed with fresh produce.

Afternoon Visit the home of the Large Hadron Collider at CERN *(p127)* for a fascinating tour. If you'd rather be out in the fresh air, hop on bus 8 for an easy outing up "Geneva's mountain", Mont Salève, instead. Get off at Veyrier-Douane, where it's a mere ten-minute walk across the Swiss-French border (remember your passport) to the foot of the cable car that ascends the mountain. Travel to the top and pop into the summit restaurant for coffee with a stupendous view over the city and Lake Geneva. Follow the paths that cling to the rockface. There are glorious views to be found round every corner.

Evening Return to the city for an atmospheric dinner aboard the *Savoie* paddle steamer, built in 1914. As you dine, the boat passes numerous landmarks, including the impressive Jet d'Eau *(p124)*, a powerful water fountain that has become symbolic of the city.

Day 2

Morning Enjoy a leisurely morning croissant by the river, then take a walk through the university campus to the International Red Cross and Red Crescent Museum *(p126)*, where the well-curated three-part permanent exhibition takes visitors on an emotional journey to highlight humanitarian efforts around the world. From there, head over the Arve river via the cross-hatched Hans-Wilsdorf bridge and make your way to Carouge, Geneva's very own Little Italy. Towards the neighbourhood's southern end is Café La Clemence *(www.laclemence.ch)*. Serving up an excellent coffee, it's the perfect spot for a *petite pause*.

Afternoon Allow some time to take in the sights, sounds and delicious smells of this dynamic neighbourhood. Once a hamlet built in the Sardinian style, it is now an urban enclave, filled with artisan boutiques, crafters' workshops and quaint streets lined with independent bistros and cosy cafés.

Evening Stroll back along the river towards the Old Town and dine at the three-Michelin-starred Café-Restaurant de l'Hôtel de Ville *(p127)*. Dating from 1764, it is steeped in the old-fashioned charm of a neighbourhood bistro, serving up classic Genevois dishes such as traditional *fricassée de porc* (spiced pork stew).

CATHÉDRALE ST-PIERRE

C4 6-8 Cour St-Pierre 36 Archaeological site: 10am-5pm daily; church: hours vary, check website cathedrale-geneve.ch

Built over a span of some 70 years from 1160 to 1230, with later additions, Geneva's vast cathedral is a mish-mash of styles, from the Gothic to the Neo-Classical, with a mix of Catholic and Protestant symbolism.

Archaeological evidence, unearthed in the 1970s, shows that there has been a Christian church on this site since at least 360 CE. A complex of 4th-century ecclesiastical buildings were erected here – and subsequently built over repeatedly until the 1100s, when the complex was razed and work began on the present Gothic-Romanesque cathedral. While the cathedral faced a programme of reinvention, as religious aesthetic principles changed, the original structure remained largely untouched until 1976, when excavations under and around the cathedral were started. Today, beneath the cathedral, an archaeological museum displays remains from some of the 4th-century buildings, as well as the findings of excavations from the surrounding area.

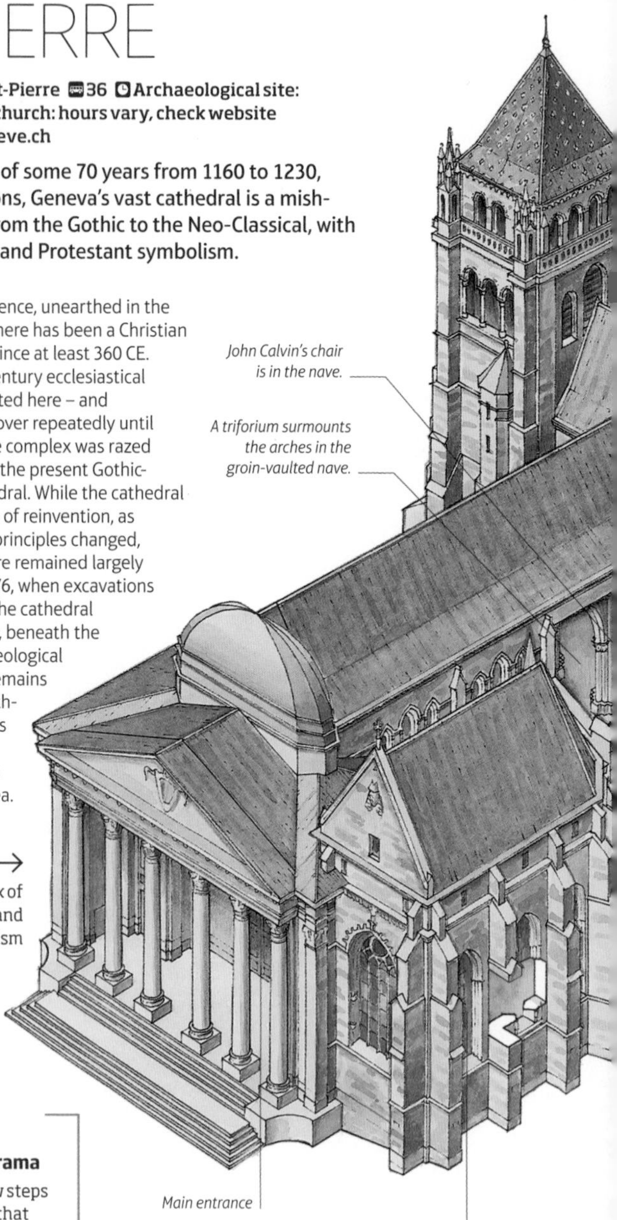

John Calvin's chair is in the nave.

A triforium surmounts the arches in the groin-vaulted nave.

→

The cathedral, a mix of architectural styles and religious symbolism

Main entrance

The flamboyant 15th-century Chapelle des Macchabées

GREAT VIEW
City Panorama

Climb the narrow steps (all 157 of them) that wind up the north tower to enjoy the spectacular panoramic views over the city.

The tall spire was added in the 19th century.

Tomb of Henri de Rohan

Romanesque and Gothic stonework capitals survived the Reformist purge.

With intricately carved back panels and canopy, the stalls originally stood near the choir.

1 A riot of colour fills the presbytery, from the stained-glass windows to the brilliantly painted ceiling.

2 An exquisitely carved animal in the stalls is a survivor of the purge of the Reformation.

3 A bas relief of St Pierre stands outside Geneva's austere cathedral.

Timeline

360s

▼ A Christian church consecrated on this site.

1160–1230

▼ Construction of original cathedral.

1500s

▼ Flamboyant interiors removed by Reformers in favour of austerity.

1970s

▼ Remains of the 4th-century church uncovered during renovations.

2

MUSÉE D'ART ET D'HISTOIRE

D4-D5 2 Rue Charles-Galland 7 11am-6pm Tue-Sun mahmah.ch

Geneva's impressive Museum of Art and History, presenting paintings, sculpture and artifacts covering prehistory to the present day, is the city's largest art museum. Visitors can easily spend several hours here perusing the vast collection, which consists of over half a million items.

The museum is divided into sections: the large archaeological section contains around 70,000 pieces from Egypt, Greece, Rome and other ancient cultures. The displays of applied arts feature furniture (including side chairs, armchairs, table and a bookcase designed by Josef Hoffmann of the Vienna Workshops for the 19th-century Swiss painter Ferdinand Hodler), textiles, stained glass, musical instruments and other fine objects. The fine arts collections cover major artistic movements and key artists in the history of Western painting, from the 15th to the 21st century. Look out for works by Monet, Picasso and Rubens, as well as Konrad Witz's 1444 *Miraculous Draft of Fishes*, arguably the highlight of the museum. Excellent temporary exhibitions are frequently held, which are free for children, though there is usually an admission charge for adults.

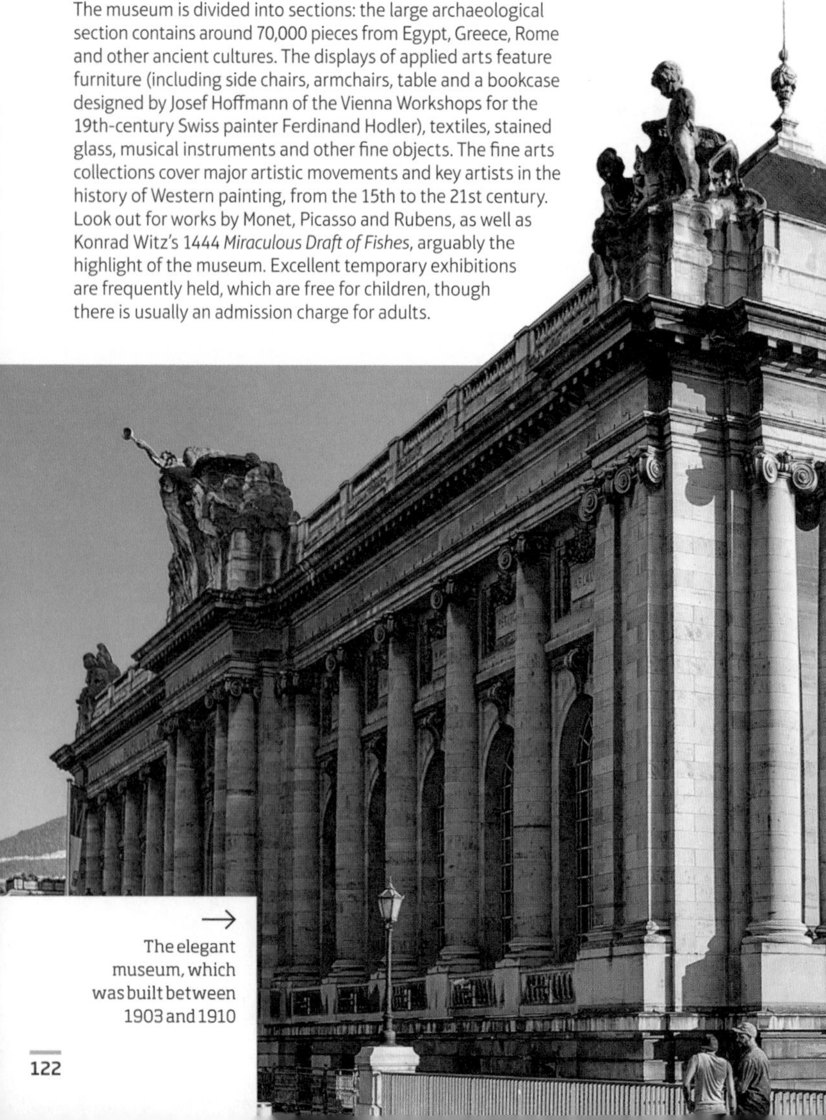

→ The elegant museum, which was built between 1903 and 1910

GALLERY GUIDE

In the basement are displays of archaeological discoveries found in the Geneva region, while archaeological exhibits from ancient civilizations occupy the lower ground floor. Also on the ground floor are rooms devoted to the applied arts; temporary exhibitions are hosted here too. The first floor is closed to the public, but paintings and sculptures are displayed on the second floor, representing artists from across Europe who lived and worked from medieval times to the modern age.

1 In his 1907 *Le Bain Turc* Swiss artist Félix Vallotton (1865-1925) pays homage to Neo-Classical painter Jean-Auguste-Dominique Ingres's masterpiece *The Turkish Bath*.

2 Venus bids farewell to Adonis before he sets off on a fatal hunt in this marble statue carved by Antonio Canova (1757-1822); Venus is based on one of Canova's most famous models.

3 The *Miraculous Draft of Fishes* is part of the altarpiece that Konrad Witz made for the Cathédrale St-Pierre *(p120)* in 1444. In the background is a view of Geneva.

Did You Know?

A huge renovation for the museum was postponed after Genevans rejected the idea in 2016.

EXPERIENCE MORE

Geneva's spectacular Jet d'Eau shooting water into the sky

Jet d'Eau

E2 Off Quai Gustave-Ador 2, 6, E, G

Located on a jetty on the south bank of Lake Geneva, the Jet d'Eau is one of the world's highest fountains, shooting a plume of water 140 m (460 ft) into the air, at a rate of 500 litres (110 gallons) per second and a speed of 200 km/h (125 mph). It came into existence almost by accident.

In the late 19th century a purely functional fountain was set up to relieve excess water pressure while a reservoir system was being installed. The fountain was so popular that the authorities decided to construct a permanent fountain, which became more spectacular as more powerful pumps were installed. Visible from afar and floodlit after dark, the Jet d'Eau is the pride of Geneva and has been adopted as the city's emblem.

Île Rousseau

C3 Pont des Bergues 6, 8, 9, 25

A walkway jutting out from the centre of the Pont des Bergues leads to a medieval bastion in the Rhône. Now known as the Île Rousseau, it is named after Jean-Jacques Rousseau (1712–78), the writer and philosopher of the Enlightenment who was one of Geneva's most distinguished citizens.

Jardin Anglais

D3 Quai du Général-Guisan 2, 6, 7, 8, 9, 10, 12

Laid out on the lakeside at the foot of the Old Town, the Jardin Anglais (English Garden) offers an open view of the harbour and quayside buildings. At its entrance is the Horloge Fleurie, a large floral clock. This tribute to Switzerland's clockmaking tradition, created in 1955, has eight intersecting wheels and features 6,500 flowering plants.

Protruding from the lake at a point just north of the Jardin Anglais are two stones brought down by glaciers during the Ice Age. They are known as the Pierres du Niton (Neptune's Stones); the larger of the two was once used as the reference point from which altitude was measured in Switzerland.

Musée Barbier-Mueller

C4 10 Rue Jean-Calvin 36 11am-5pm daily barbier-mueller.ch

Hidden away in a back street near the Cathédrale St-Pierre *(p120)*, this art museum features stunning works from a range of cultures dating back to classical antiquity. It was founded in 1977 to preserve a collection begun in 1907 by the Muellers, a family of art collectors. On display are sculptures, masks and other artifacts from Africa, Asia and Oceania.

Place du Bourg-de-Four

C4 36

Probably overlying Geneva's Roman forum, the Place du Bourg-de-Four was the city's marketplace in the Middle Ages. Today, lined with 16th-century houses, art galleries and antiques shops, and with busy cafés and restaurants, the square is still the hub of Geneva's Old Town.

The imposing Palais de Justice on the southeastern side of the square was built in 1707–12 and has been used as the city's law courts since 1860. Nearby, on Rue de l'Hôtel-de-Ville on the southwestern

The Île Rousseau and Quai des Bergues on the River Rhône

↑ Place du Bourg-de-Four, the bustling heart of Geneva's Old Town

side of the square, stands the Hôtel de Ville. Built in the 15th century, it was originally the city hall and now serves as the seat of the cantonal authorities. The Tour Baudet, a tower dating from 1455 and the oldest part of the city hall, once housed the cantonal archives. On the ground floor of the Hôtel de Ville is the Alabama Room, where the Geneva Convention was signed in 1864 and where the International Red Cross was recognized as a humanitarian organization. It was also here that the League of Nations assembled for the first time, in 1920.

Maison Tavel

C4 6 Rue du Puits-St-Pierre 36 11am-6pm Tue, Wed & Fri-Sun, midnight-9pm Thu mahmah.ch

Built by the Tavel family, this fine limestone building is the oldest house in Geneva. The Gothic façade, with three tiers of windows and a turret at one corner, is decorated with the Tavel coat of arms, as well as with curious stone sculptures of animal and human heads. Although it was rebuilt after the fire of 1334, which destroyed much of Geneva, the earliest record of the house goes back to 1303.

Maison Tavel now houses the Musée du Vieux Genève, a museum devoted to daily life in Geneva from the 14th to the 19th centuries. While the basement is reserved for temporary exhibitions, the rest of the house is filled with exhibits, including coins, ironwork, tiles, wooden doors and other elements of ancient houses. Twelve rooms on the second floor illustrate urban life in the 17th century. In the attic is a huge model of Geneva, made in 1850, before the city's medieval fortifications were demolished. A *son-et-lumière* presentation highlights points of interest on the model.

A separate section is devoted to Général Dufour (1787–1875), the son of a Genevan clockmaker who created a 1:100,000-scale topographic map of the country. As commander of the Federal forces during the civil war of 1847, he managed to defeat the separatists. He was also a founder of the International Red Cross – the neutral organization that assists victims of war and violence – which has its headquarters nearby *(p126)*.

DRINK

L'Apothicaire Cocktail-Club

Perfectly balanced wines and hand-mixed cocktails in an industrial-chic setting.

B3 16 Blvd Georges-Favon Sun & Mon apothicairecocktailclub.ch

Qafe Guidoline

A large bar, with a terrace, which serves a wide range of craft beers and cocktails. DJs spin discs here on the weekends.

C1 24 Rue des Pâquis qafeguidoline.ch

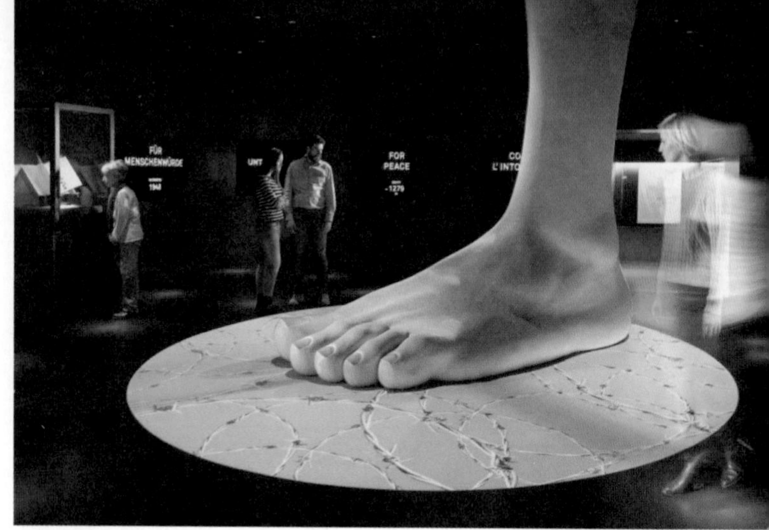

International Red Cross and Red Crescent Museum

E5 17 Avenue de la Paix 8, 20, 22, F Apr-Oct: 10am-6pm Tue-Sun; Nov-Mar: 10am-5pm Tue-Sun redcrossmuseum.ch

Moving and harrowing yet inspiring hope, this museum within the headquarters of the International Committee of the Red Cross is devoted to documenting human kindness and compassion, as well as the cases of cruelty and suffering that the Red Cross has sought to alleviate since its foundation in 1863. The building, a glass-and-concrete bunker, is designed to allow natural light to illuminate the rooms.

The museum educates visitors about contemporary humanitarian action with an interactive exhibition designed around three zones, each by an internationally renowned architect: *Defending Human Dignity* (Gringo Cardia, Brazil), *Reconstructing the Family Link* (Diébédo Francis Kéré, Burkina Faso) and *Refusing Fatality* (Shigeru Ban, Japan). Within each zone, visitors live through an intense emotional experience, with the aim of raising awareness of an issue. Historical and background information is then provided. The "On the Spot" area shows the latest news from the field on an interactive globe.

Quartier Des Bains

A4 2, 19, 35 quartierdesbains.ch

This vibrant district in the city's west end centres on an independent and private grouping of 18 galleries and photography studios. Set in a stretch between the Rhône and the Arve, the collective frequently shares themed exhibitions, and is dedicated to promoting the latest in contemporary art, ranging from installations to sculpture. A number of cool bars and restaurants are nearby.

HIDDEN GEM

Bains des Pâquis

Jutting out into Geneva's lake are the Bains des Pâquis *(www.bains-des-paquis.ch)*, public baths with hot tubs, Turkish baths, good food and enough shoreside towel space for (almost) everyone in the city.

Palais des Nations

F5 14 Avenue de la Paix Apr-Jun: 10am-noon & 2-4pm daily; Jul & Aug: 10am-4pm daily; Sep-Mar: 10am-noon & 2-4pm Mon-Fri ungeneva.org

Built in 1929–36, the Palais des Nations is the focal point of Geneva's international area. It began as the headquarters of the League of Nations, which had been founded in 1920. In 1946 the League was replaced by the United Nations and in 1966 the Palais des Nations became the official Geneva headquarters of the UN. Some 3,000 people from all over the world now work here.

Parts of the palace are open to the public, with guided tours (bring identification) available in 12 languages. Tours take in the Salle du Conseil (Council Chamber), with walls and ceiling decorated with allegorical paintings by the Catalan artist Josep Maria Sert, depicting, among other things, a vision of a future free of conflict. Visitors can also see the Salle des Assemblées (Assembly Hall). With seating for 2,000 people, it is the largest of the United Nations Office's 30-something conference rooms.

International Red Cross and Red Crescent Museum exhibit

The Parc des Nations, which surrounds the UNO, is planted with trees and decorated with interesting sculptures.

Parc des Bastions

C4 12, 17 3, 5, 20, 25

Created in the 18th century, Parc des Bastions lies just outside the ramparts on the south side of the city. Along the eastern edge of the park is the Mur des Réformateurs (Reformation Wall), which was erected in 1909 to mark the 400th anniversary of the birth of Jean Calvin and the 350th anniversary of the foundation of Geneva's Academy, the city's famous Protestant school. The monument takes the form of a wall 100 m (330 ft) long, on which stand 5-m- (16-ft-) tall statues of four of the leaders of the Reformation in Geneva: Guillaume Farel, Jean Calvin, Théodore de Bèze and John Knox. Flanking the monument are memorials to Martin Luther and Ulrich Zwingli.

Fondation Martin Bodmer

F5 19-21 Route Martin Bodmer, Cologny A 2-6pm Tue-Sun fondationbodmer.ch

Just north of the city centre is a large villa with a unique mission: to be a museum of the human mind. The 150,000 items include ancient Egyptian papyrus books of the dead and pages bearing the handwritten scribblings of William Shakespeare. Also on view are a Gutenberg Bible and Gottfried Liebnitz's copy of Sir Isaac Newton's *Principia Mathematica*, complete with his cramped margin notes.

CERN

E5 1 Esplanade des Particules, Meyrin 18 8am-6pm Mon-Sat home.cern

The European Organization for Nuclear Research, better known by its French acroynm, CERN, has since 1954 been trying to explore all laws and theories related to particles, which make up the entire universe. In 2010, it first opened its doors to visitors.

The research centre's various exhibitions look at the origins of the universe. The highlight is the Big Bang show, a multimedia extravaganza that takes place every hour in a futuristic globe known as the Universe of Particles. Other exhibits include a scale model of CERN's Large Hadron Collider (LHC), the world's largest particle accelerator, which includes real pieces of equipment. This model explores the technical challenges and ingenious engineering solutions that went into the LHC's construction.

EAT

Café-Restaurant de l'Hôtel de Ville

Exceptional traditional Genevois fare.

C4 39 Grand-Rue hdvglozu.ch

Fiskebar

Expect fabulous, seasonal seafood here.

C2 11 Quai du Mont-Blanc geneva-fiskebar.com

MEG (Ethnographic Museum of Geneva)

A5 65 Blvd Carl-Vogt 2, 19 11am-6pm Tue-Sun ville-ge.ch/meg

MEG has won numerous awards, both for its innovative architecture and for its theme of human diversity – amply exhibited with a range of costumes, folk music and workshops.

The sleek modern building of the MEG (Ethnographic Museum of Geneva)

A SHORT WALK
OLD TOWN

Distance 1.5 km (1 mile) **Nearest bus stop** Place de Neuve **Time** 25 minutes

Set on elevated ground on the south bank of the Rhône, the Old Town (Vieille Ville) clusters around the cathedral and Place du Bourg-de-Four. This atmospheric district, whose main thoroughfare is the pedestrianized Grand-Rue, has narrow cobbled streets lined with historic limestone houses. While the southern limit of the Old Town is marked by the Promenade des Bastions, laid out along the course of the old city walls, its northern side slopes down to the quay, which is lined with wide boulevards and the attractive Jardin Anglais.

Maison Rousseau, *the birthplace of the 18th-century writer and philosopher Jean-Jacques Rousseau, is at 40 Grand-Rue.*

START

RUE

GRAND-RUE

RUE DES GRANGES

FINISH

RAMPE DE LA TREILLE

PROM.

The Hôtel de Ville *is where the first Geneva Convention was signed in 1864.*

Did You Know?

Place du Bourg-de-Four is the oldest square in Geneva, dating back to Roman times.

Outdoor cafés in Place du Bourg-de-Four in Geneva ↓

↑ The ornate interior of Geneva's majestic Cathédrale St-Pierre

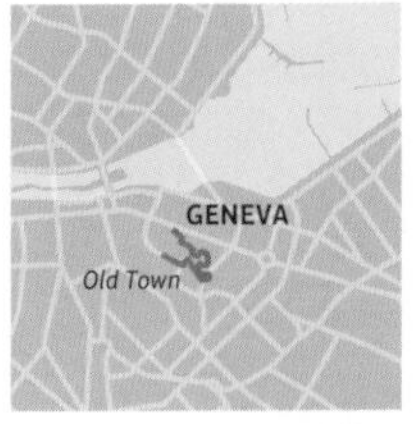

Locator Map
For more detail see p116

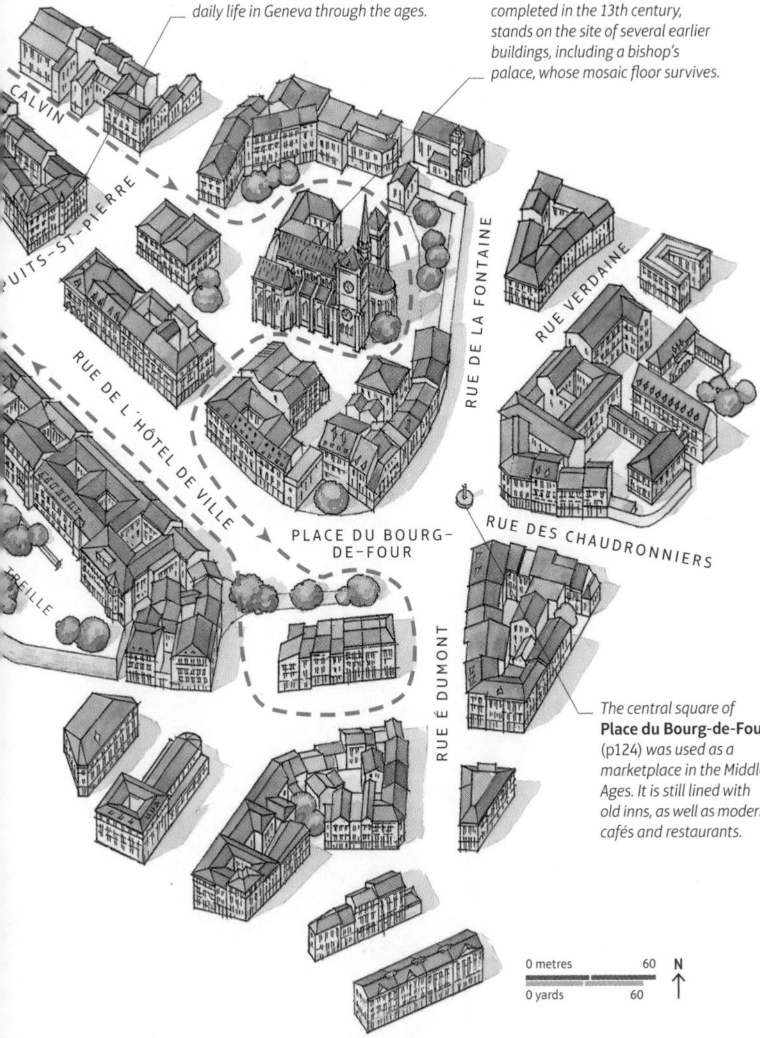

Maison Tavel (p125), *the oldest house in the city, was built in 1334. It is now a museum documenting daily life in Geneva through the ages.*

Cathédrale St-Pierre (p120), *completed in the 13th century, stands on the site of several earlier buildings, including a bishop's palace, whose mosaic floor survives.*

CALVIN

PUITS-ST-PIERRE

RUE DE LA FONTAINE

RUE VERDAINE

RUE DE L'HÔTEL DE VILLE

PLACE DU BOURG-DE-FOUR

RUE DES CHAUDRONNIERS

TREILLE

RUE É DUMONT

The central square of **Place du Bourg-de-Four** (p124) *was used as a marketplace in the Middle Ages. It is still lined with old inns, as well as modern cafés and restaurants.*

0 metres 60
0 yards 60
N ↑

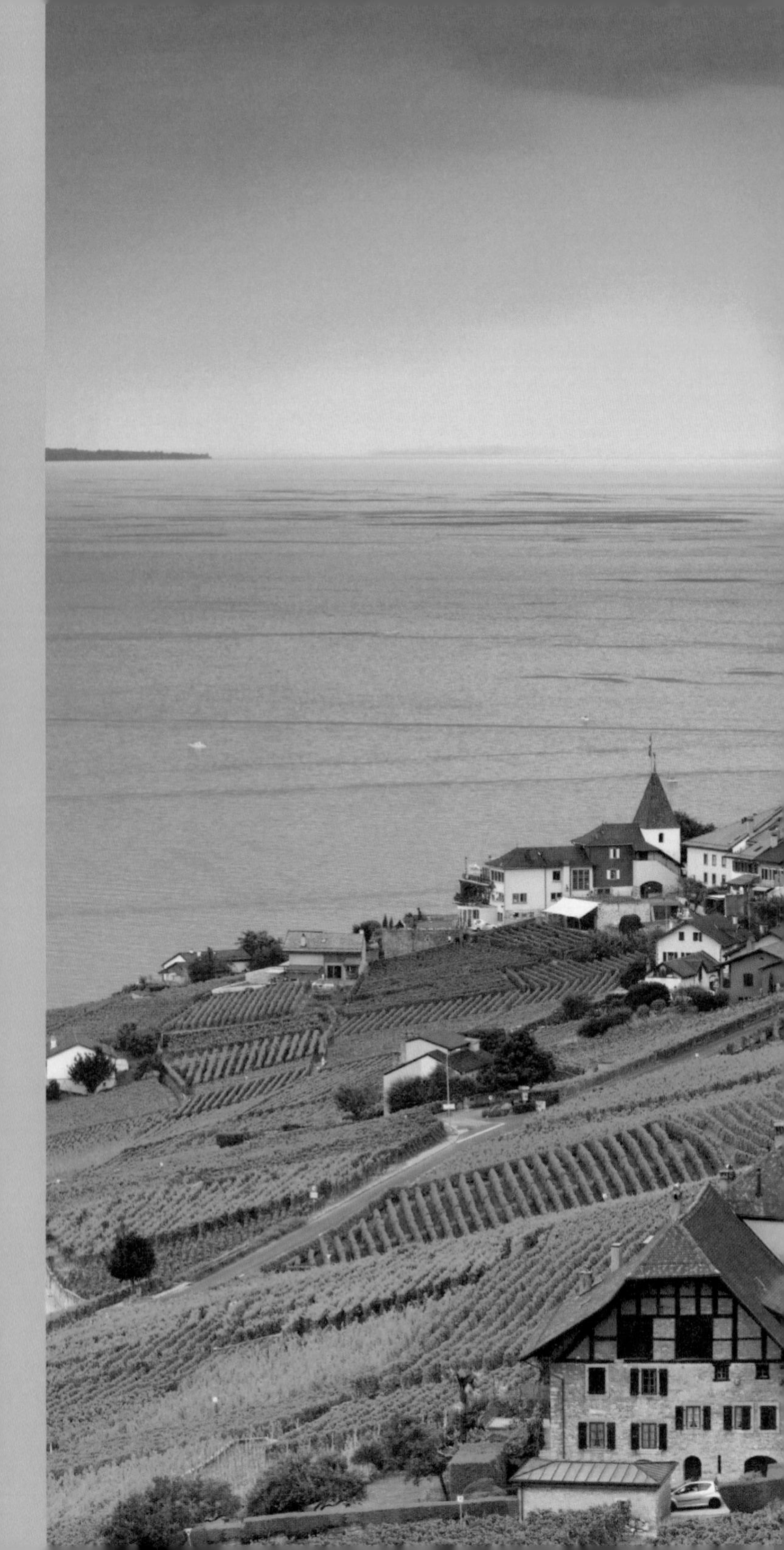

The sun rising over a verdant vineyard overlooking Lake Geneva

WESTERN SWITZERLAND

Bordered by France, French-speaking western Switzerland is known as Suisse Romande, or Romandie. The region was settled by Gallic Celts, around 450 BCE, and annexed by the Christianized Burgundians in the 5th century CE. The Burgundians' language, customs and architecture were swiftly adopted throughout the region, and the French-Swiss cultural identity remains strong to this day. Although western Switzerland was taken over by the German Savoy in the 1100s, the French connection was such that the borderlands region of Vaud was placed under the protection of the governing body in Paris following the French Revolution. It was only in 1806 that Vaud become a canton of Switzerland, with Lausanne as its capital. With relatively easy countryside to navigate, western Switzerland has attracted those escaping European conflict. During the Protestant Reformation, refugees fled to Jura, bringing in talent, which set in motion the country's now world-famous watchmaking industry. During the two world wars, the region again became a safe harbour for refugees who made it across Kilometre Zero at the Franco-Swiss border. Today, those same sunny hillsides serve as a gateway into this wine-making region's more mountainous landscapes.

WESTERN SWITZERLAND
FRANCE
NEUCHÂTEL
VAUD
GENÈVE
Jura
Montbéliard
Fahy
Baume-les-Dames
Saint-Hippolyte
Laviron
Passavant
Saignelég
Le Noirmar
Pierrefontaine-les-Varans
Bonnétage
Doubs
Valdahon
LA CHAU DE-FONI
LE LOCLE
Chouzelot
Omans
Saint-Gorgon-Main
NEUCHÂTEL
Peseu
Noiraigue
Boudry
Lac de Neuchâtel
Lavier
Les Verrières
Fleurier
CREUX DU VAN
Pontarlier
ESTAVAYE LE-LAC
Frasne
SAINTE-CROIX
Concise
Cheyres
Malbuisson
L'Auberson
GRANDSON
Payerne
YVERDON-LES-BAINS
Champagnole
La Broye
Orbe
Lucens
Mouthe
VALLORBE
Thierrens
Romont
Romainmôtier
Le Pont
La Sarraz
Moudon
Lac de Joux
Echallens
VALLÉE DE JOUX
Cossonay
Cheseaux
Morez
Le Brassus
Bussigny
Essertes
Châtel-St-Denis
Bière
Vufflens-le-Château
LAUSANNE
Pully
Morges
Cully
Blor
Vevey
Saint-Cergue
Rolle
LAKE GENEVA
Montreux
Gland
Saint-Claude
Nyon
Thonon-les-Bains
Rhône
Gex
Tannay
Douvaine
AIGLE
Versoix
La Baume
Geneva International Airport
Monthey
Meyrin
Geneva
Lancy
Annemasse
Montriond
Collonges
Neydens
Valleiry

0 kilometres 15
0 miles 15
N
NORTHERN SWITZERLAND
p174
oncourt
Porrentruy
JURA
23 ST-URSANNE
Delémont
Bassecourt
21 FRANCHES-MONTAGNES
Balsthal
Zofingen
Langenthal
Grenchen
Sursee
St. Imier
Biel/Bienne
Huttwil
Bieler See
Lyss
Burgdorf
Wolhusen
Aare
Erlach
Aarberg
Kerzers
Bern
12 MURTEN/MORAT
Köniz
Lac de Morat
Bern International Airport
AVENCHES
Saane
Münsingen
3 FRIBOURG
Schwarzenburg
Marly
BERN
Rossens
Lac de la Gruyère
Erlenbach
FRIBOURG
Bulle
Jaun
11 GRUYÈRES
MITTELLAND, BERNESE OBERLAND AND VALAIS
p80
Sarine
Rougemont
7 CHÂTEAU D'OEX
Gstaad
Lenk
Gsteig
YSIN
6 LES DIABLERETS
Les Diablerets 3,210 m (10,531 ft)
Sierre
5 VILLARS-SUR-OLLON
Sion
Euseigne
Saxon
Martigny
WESTERN SWITZERLAND
Must Sees
1 Lausanne
2 Lake Geneva
3 Fribourg
Experience More
4 Leysin
5 Villars-sur-Ollon
6 Les Diablerets
7 Château d'Oex
8 Vallorbe
9 Aigle
10 Estavayer-le-Lac
11 Gruyères
12 Murten/Morat
13 Yverdon-les-Bains
14 Grandson
15 Sainte-Croix
16 Neuchâtel
17 Vallée de Joux
18 Le Locle
19 Avenches
20 La Chaux-de-Fonds
21 Franches-Montagnes
22 Creux du Van
23 St-Ursanne

1922

The year T S Eliot completed the poem *The Wasteland,* while under psychiatric care in Lausanne.

↑ The terracotta-coloured rooftops of Lausanne's hilltop Old Town

LAUSANNE

B4 Vaud 9 Place de la Gare; www.lausanne-tourisme.ch

Nestled on the outstandingly beautiful north shore of Lake Geneva, Lausanne is one of Switzerland's finest cities. A Roman lakeshore settlement in the 1st century, it was later moved to higher ground. This area is now the city's Old Town. Lausanne became a bishopric in the late 6th century, and its Fondation Académie was founded here in 1537. Today, the city remains a centre of the cultural and economic life of French-speaking Switzerland. Its importance is evident – it is the location of the Federal Supreme Court and the International Olympic Committee.

← The figure of Justice crowning the 16th-century Fontaine de la Justice

Place de la Palud

M Riponne M Béjart
1, 2, 7, 8

Lausanne's 17th-century town hall, a fine arcaded building, dominates the south side of this square. On 10 April 1915, the founder of the modern Olympics, Pierre de Coubertin, ratified the establishment of the International Olympic Committee here and moved the headquarters to the city.

At the centre of the square is the 16th-century Fontaine de la Justice, with a figure of Justice. The covered wooden stairs beyond, known as the Escaliers du Marché, lead to Rue Viret, from where further steps lead up to the cathedral.

The square is a popular meeting area. A street market takes place here twice a week on Wednesday and Saturday, and once a month the square is filled with a crafts fair.

Tour Bel-Air and Salle Métropole

1 Place Bel-Air
Lausanne-Flon
1, 2, 3, 4, 6, 7, 8, 9, 16, 17
021 345 00 29

Set on a steep slope, at the foot of the Old Town, the Tour Bel-Air was Switzerland's first high-rise structure. It contains offices, residential apartments and the Salle Métropole theatre. Completed in 1931, the building was initially considered an insult to good sense and taste, but quickly became a beloved landmark. Inspired by the cityscape of New York, the building gives the town's skyline a touch of metropolitan verve.

The theatre has become one of the city's cultural hubs and has hosted some of the best in the performing arts. In its heyday, audiences flocked here to see dancer Josephine Baker and trumpeter Louis Armstrong. These days, the Métropole's programme still features highly acclaimed talents, among them the Ukrainian Classical Ballet and the musician Alain Chamfort. The Lausanne Symphony Orchestra also makes its home here.

GREAT VIEW
Across the Rooftops

Built on a hill, the lower and higher parts of the city are connected by a series of steps. Take the market stairs up to the cathedral, then climb all the way into the belfry, which is the highest point in the city, to soak up stunning views across the roofs of old Lausanne to the green steeple of St-François church, the lake and the mountains beyond.

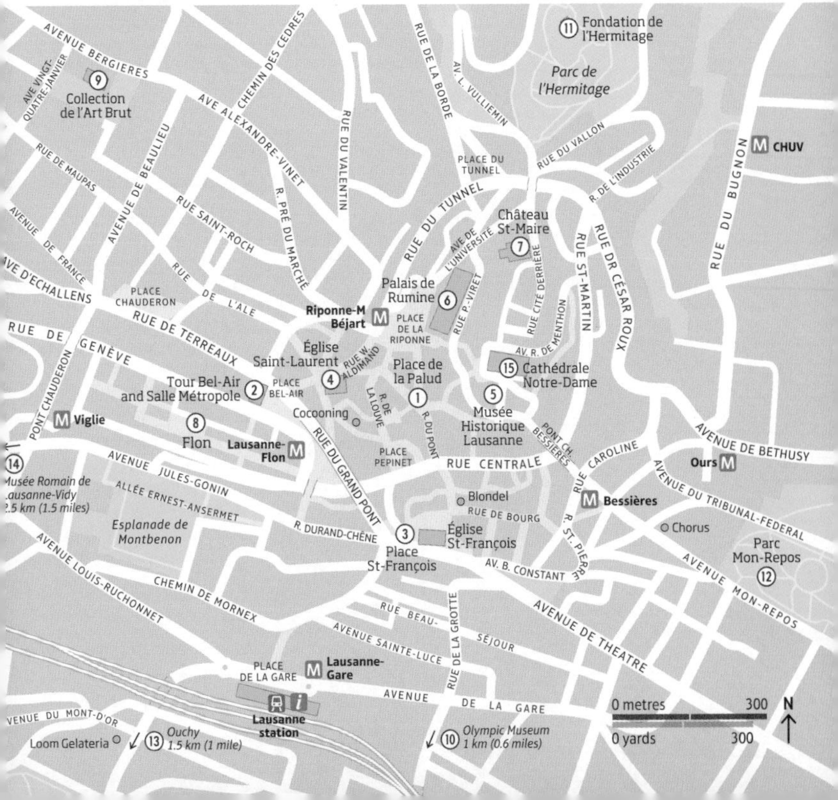

Avenue Bergieres
Ave Vingt-Quatre-Janvier
9 Collection de l'Art Brut
Rue de Maupas
Avenue de France
Ave d'Echallens
Avenue de Beaulieu
Ave Alexandre-Vinet
Chemin des Cedres
Rue Saint-Roch
R. Pré du Marché
Rue du Valentin
Rue de la Borde
Av. L. Vulliemin
11 Fondation de l'Hermitage
Parc de l'Hermitage
Place du Tunnel
Rue du Vallon
R. de l'Industrie
CHUV
Rue du Bugnon
Rue du Tunnel
Ave de l'Université
Château St-Maire 7
Rue Cité Derrière
Rue St-Martin
Rue Dr César Roux
Place Chauderon
Rue de l'Ale
Rue de Terreaux
Rue de Genève
Palais de Rumine 6
Riponne-M Béjart
Place de la Riponne
Rue P.-Viret
Av. R. de Menthon
Église Saint-Laurent 4
Rue W. Haldimand
Place de la Palud 1
15 Cathédrale Notre-Dame
Tour Bel-Air and Salle Métropole 2
Place Bel-Air
Pont Chauderon
Viglie
8 Flon
Lausanne-Flon
Cocooning
R. de la Louve
R. du Pont
5 Musée Historique Lausanne
Pont Ch. Bessières
Rue Caroline
Avenue de Bethusy
Ours
14 Musée Romain de Lausanne-Vidy 2.5 km (1.5 miles)
Avenue Jules-Gonin
Allée Ernest-Ansermet
Rue du Grand Pont
Place Pepinet
Rue Centrale
Blondel
Rue de Bourg
Bessières
Avenue du Tribunal-Fédéral
Esplanade de Montbenon
R. Durand-Chêne
3 Place St-François
Église St-François
R. St-Pierre
Chorus
Parc Mon-Repos 12
Avenue Louis-Ruchonnet
Av. B. Constant
Avenue Mon-Repos
Chemin de Mornex
Rue Beau-Séjour
Rue de la Grotte
Avenue de Theatre
Avenue Sainte-Luce
Place de la Gare
Lausanne-Gare
Lausanne station
Avenue de la Gare
Avenue du Mont-d'Or
Loom Gelateria
13 Ouchy 1.5 km (1 mile)
10 Olympic Museum 1 km (0.6 miles)
0 metres 300
0 yards 300
N

Place St-François

Lausanne-Flon 1, 2, 4, 6, 7, 8, 9, 12, 13, 16, 17

At the centre of this square stands the Église St-François, built in the 13th and 14th centuries as the church of a Franciscan monastery that was later dissolved during the Reformation. The streets leading off Place St-François are among the city's smartest. Rue du Bourg, which is lined with old houses, contains swanky jewellers' shops and bijou boutiques, as well as bars and jazz clubs.

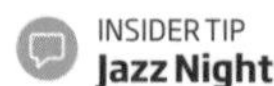

INSIDER TIP

Jazz Nights

You can catch the latest young talents from Lausanne's renowned jazz school performing at various venues across the city. Chorus, an atmospheric cellar near the city centre *(www.chorus.ch)*, is one of our favourites. Some gigs are free.

Église Saint-Laurent

Rue Saint-Laurent
Riponne M Béjart
1, 2, 3, 4, 6, 7, 8, 9, 16, 17
lausanne.ch

Amid the well-preserved houses of the Old Town stands the Protestant Église Saint-Laurent. It was completed in 1719, on the ruins of a 10th-century church, and its façade was added in the latter half of the century. Free choral concerts, with an aperitif, are offered year-round.

5

Musée Historique Lausanne

4 Place de la Cathédrale
Bessières 22, 60
11am-6pm Tue-Sun
lausanne.ch/vie-pratique/culture/musees/mhl

Lausanne's museum of history fills the restored rooms of the former bishop's palace, which dates from the 11th century. The museum's collections provide a detailed account of the city's history from its inhabitation by Celtic tribes to the present day. Don't miss the small-scale model of Lausanne as it was in 1638.

The streets of the popular Flon district pulsing with energy after dark ↑

Palais de Rumine

6 Place de la Riponne
Riponne M Béjart 1, 2, 7, 8 10am-5pm Tue-Sun
palaisderumine.ch

Built from 1896 to 1906, the Neo-Renaissance Palais de Rumine once housed the University of Lausanne. It now contains several museums covering archaeology and history, fine art, geology, zoology and numismatics (the study of currency) – all with the same hours and a shared admission fee. Of particular

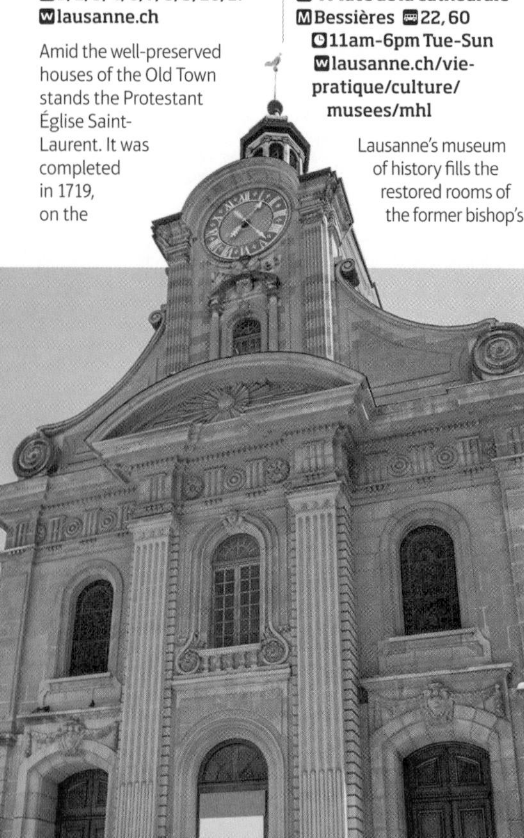

The imposing façade of the Église Saint-Laurent on a sunny day

interest is the Musée Cantonal des Beaux-Arts, on the ground floor, which has a fine collection of Swiss paintings from the 18th to the 20th centuries. The museum of history and archaeology, on the sixth floor, displays artifacts unearthed in local excavations. The exhibits date from the Bronze Age to the medieval period, and one of the finest is a gold bust of Marcus Aurelius, discovered at Avenches in 1939.

Château St-Maire

Place du Château
Riponne M Béjart
7, 22, 60

Although it's closed to visitors, you should still seek out this former bishop's palace. The massive edifice was built from 1397 to 1427 for the bishops of Lausanne, who ruled the city. When they were overthrown by Bernese forces, the château became the residence of new overlords, the bailiffs of Bern. The fight for the independence of Lausanne and the canton of Vaud was led by the notary turned soldier Jean Davel, who was beheaded in 1723 on the orders of the Bernese authorities after he led an abortive separatist movement. A monument to his memory stands in front of the château. The building is now the seat of the cantonal authorities of Vaud.

Flon

Lausanne-Flon 18

Once the city's main industrial district, Flon was built on a river of the same name that was filled over in the 19th century. If you look down, you can still see water running in a narrow channel under the pavement. These days the area has thrown off its grubby past to become an entertainment district, its former warehouses converted into shops, bars, restaurants, galleries, a cinema complex and the buzzing MAD nightclub. The main pedestrian square hosts a jungle-themed pop-up bar in summer and an ice rink in winter.

SHOP

Blondel

An institution since 1850, Blondel's sumptuous window displays and the delectable whiff of chocolate wafting out the door make it impossible to pass by this shop without going in.

5 Rue de Bourg
blondel.ch

Cocooning

Pick up soaps, creams and other cosmetics here. They are handmade using natural ingredients - you can buy a body butter made with the Swiss national flower - edelweiss - for instance.

16 Rue Grand-Saint-Jean cocooning.ch

⑨

Collection de l'Art Brut

11 Avenue des Bergières 2, 21 Jul & Aug: 11am-6pm daily; Sep-Jun: 11am-6pm Tue-Sun; free adm 1st Sat of the month artbrut.ch

Art Brut ("Raw Art") is the name the French painter Jean Dubuffet (1901–85) gave to art created by people living on the fringe of society, such as criminals, patients at psychiatric hospitals or institutions, and spiritualist mediums, who had no artistic training. The ideas behind their art were free from established cultural influences and the history of fine arts tradition. In 1945 Dubuffet began to amass a private collection, which he presented to the city in 1971. The Collection de l'Art Brut opened in 1976.

The exhibits are laid out over four floors in converted stables at the 18th-century Château de Beaulieu, north-west of the city centre. These works have a striking force and spontaneity. Alongside each exhibit is a short biography of the artist, providing insights into the circumstances in which these works were created.

EAT

Loom Gelateria 1900

Join the queue out the door to sample delicious artisanal ice cream. Among the more adventurous offerings here are lapsang souchong sorbet and curry ice cream.

45 Blvd de Grancy loom-gelateria.ch

Run Up by Nag Arnoldi at the Olympic Museum, overlooking Lake Geneva

⑩

Olympic Museum

1 Quai d'Ouchy Jordils 24 9am-6pm Tue-Sun olympics.com/museum

Set in peaceful parkland planted with Mediterranean trees and shrubs, the well-presented Olympic Museum illustrates the fascinating history of the Olympic movement. Everything from the athletes of Ancient Greece to the Olympic Games of today is explored via interactive stations, photographs, videos, archive film footage and multimedia presentations. With its excellent facilities for school groups, the museum draws over 200,000 visitors a year. There are many displays specifically geared towards younger visitors, such as "All Different, All Winners" where games investigate themes such as fair play and diversity.

⑪

Fondation de l'Hermitage

2 Route du Signal 16 10am-6pm Tue-Sun (to 9pm Thu) fondation-hermitage.ch

The imposing Neo-Gothic villa set in magnificent grounds north of Lausanne was built in 1842–50 by Charles-Juste Bugnion, a wealthy banker, and donated to the city by his descendants. Now known as the Fondation de l'Hermitage, it is a gallery with an impressive collection of Impressionist and Post-Impressionist paintings, as well as the works of Vaudois artists from the 20th century. Every year the Fondation also stages two or three large-scale temporary exhibitions.

The Parc de l'Hermitage, the extensive grounds in which the villa is set, is landscaped with rare trees. Towards its northern extremity is the Signal de Sauvabelin, a hill which rises to a height of 647 m (2,120 ft) and offers views of Lake Geneva and the Alps. Beyond the hill are woodland and the Lac de Sauvabelin,

where there is a reserve for ibexes, marmots and other Alpine animals.

Parc Mon-Repos

Avenue Mon-Repos M Ours 13

This landscaped park is the most elegant of all the city's gardens. At its centre is a Neo-Classical villa, once inhabited by the 18th-century French writer Voltaire. The villa was later home to the Olympics revivalist Baron Pierre de Coubertin (1863–1937), who believed that sport plays an essential role in the development of citizens and nations. In 1894, he established the International Olympic Committee (IOC), and two years later the first modern Olympic Games were held in Athens. Until the 1970s this was also the IOC's headquarters. At the north end of the park stand Switzerland's supreme court buildings.

INSIDER TIP
Lakeside Pop-ups

All throughout the summer, lively pop-up bars and restaurants take over the lakeshore. Join the locals by taking a dip in the lake followed by an *apéro* and some tasty nibbles at Jetée de la Compagnie *(www.jeteedelacompagnie.ch)*.

13   

Ouchy

On Lake Geneva, 2 km (1 mile) S of central Lausanne M Ouchy Olympiade

Once a fishing village, Ouchy is now a popular lakeside suburb of Lausanne. It has a beautiful setting with views of the surrounding mountains, and a tree-lined promenade. Cruises on the lake depart from here.

A tower is all that remains of the 12th-century castle that once defended the harbour. It forms part of the Neo-Gothic Château d'Ouchy, which was built in the 1890s. The château is now a hotel and restaurant. A short walk along the lakeshore will take you to the Hôtel d'Angleterre. This is the house where Lord Byron stayed during his visit to Lausanne and where he wrote *The Prisoner of Chillon,* a poem which details the imprisonment of a Genevois monk, François Bonivard.

14  

Musée Romain de Lausanne-Vidy

24 Chemin du-Bois-de-Vaux 25 Jul & Aug: 11am-6pm daily; Sep-Jun: 11am-6pm Tue-Sun W museeromain.ch

About ten minutes' walk west of Ouchy are the remains of Lousonna and Vidy, two Roman towns that flourished from 15 BCE to the 4th century CE. Finds uncovered during an excavation here are on show in the Musée Romain nearby.

Beyond the hill are woodland and the Lac de Sauvabelin, where there is a reserve for ibexes, marmots and other Alpine animals.

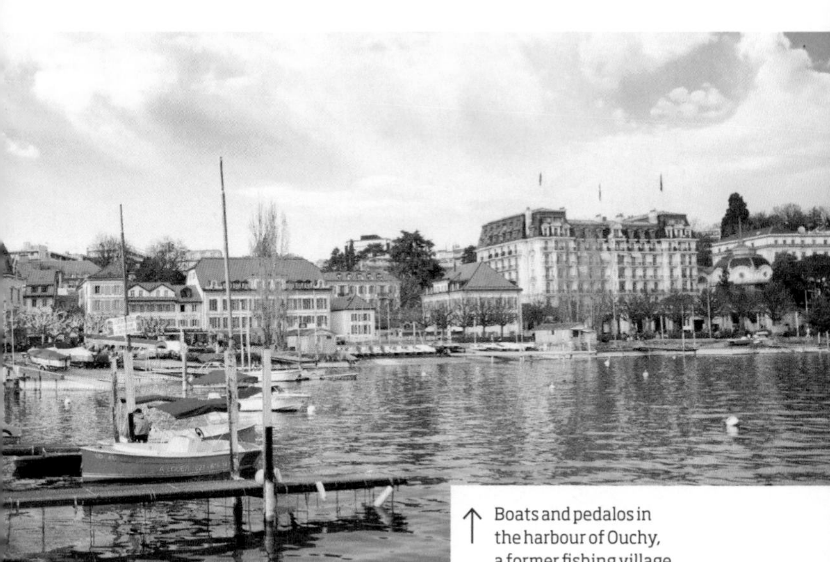

↑ Boats and pedalos in the harbour of Ouchy, a former fishing village

⑮

CATHÉDRALE NOTRE-DAME

1 Place de la Cathédrale Riponne M Béjart 16
Church: 9am-5:30pm daily (Apr-Sep: to 7pm); tower: hours vary, check website cathedrale-lausanne.ch

At the centre of Lausanne towers the magnificent Cathédrale Notre-Dame. Begun in the mid-12th century and completed in the 13th, it is the finest Gothic building in Switzerland.

The cathedral is built on the site of a Roman camp and overlies the foundations of Carolingian and Romanesque basilicas. With a central nave flanked by aisles, an ambulatory and a transept over which rises a tower and an apse, the cathedral's design and decoration show the influence of the French Gothic style. The southern arm of the transept is lit by a 13th-century rose window with stained glass depicting the seasons, the elements and signs of the Zodiac. Consecrated by Pope Gregory X in 1275, Notre-Dame has been a Protestant cathedral since the Reformation. The top of the southwest tower provides a spectacular view of the city and Lake Geneva.

Did You Know?

A nightwatchman calls the hour from 10pm to 2am from each of the cathedral's towers.

Illustration of Lausanne's majestic Gothic Cathédrale Notre-Dame ↓

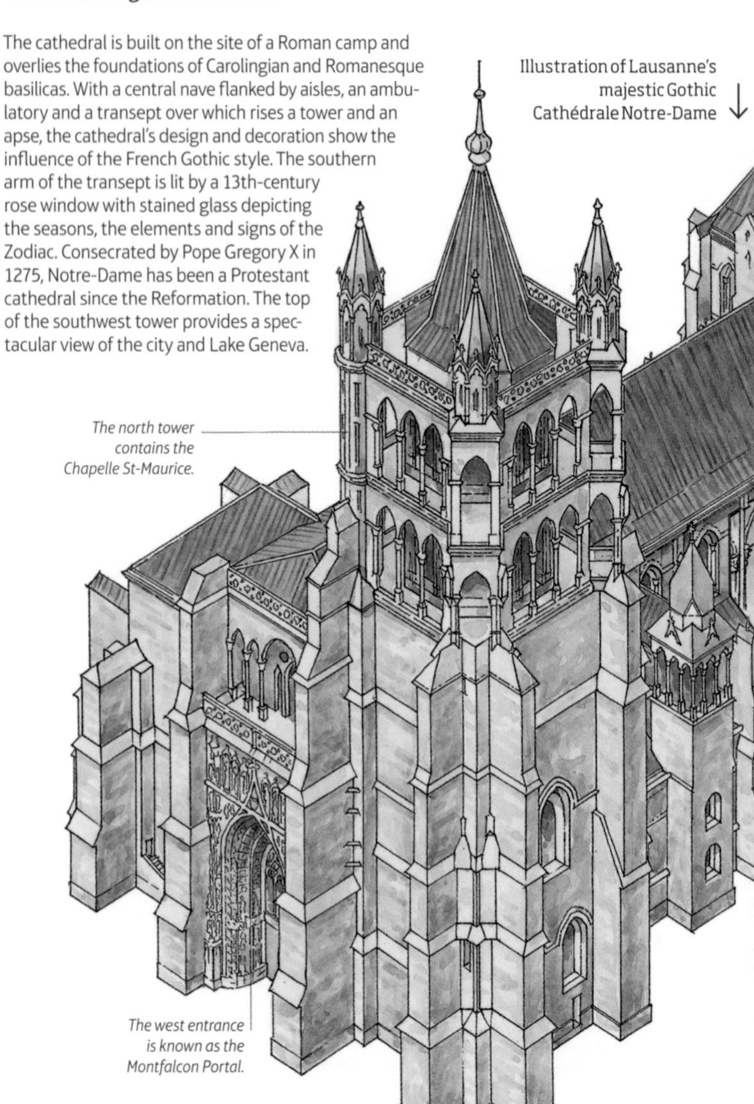

The north tower contains the Chapelle St-Maurice.

The west entrance is known as the Montfalcon Portal.

The tower was completed in the 19th century.

Rose window

Carved decorative details, including human figures, fill the vaulting.

The vestibule is decorated with late-Gothic murals dating from the early 16th century.

This Bernese pulpit is topped by a canopy with intricate wooden tracery from 1666.

1 One of Switzerland's most visited sights, the Cathédrale Notre-Dame attracts over 400,000 visitors every year.

2 The cathedral has multiple decorative stained-glass windows, such as this one.

3 An ornate cross, standing in the cathedral's central nave. Notre-Dame is a working cathedral with regular services.

1

2

3

INNOVATIVE ORGAN

The cathedral's striking organ was the first in Europe to be built by an American, although it was made to Italian Giorgetto Giugiaro's design, and the first to feature four styles: Romantic, Classical French, Symphonic French and Baroque. Most impressive is that it can be played remotely, by any other organist playing an organ in another part of the world, thanks to a cutting-edge interface system.

2

LAKE GENEVA

A5-B5 Geneva and Vaud 60 Avenue d'Ouchy, Lausanne myvaud.ch

Lying in an arc bordered by the Jura mountains to the west, the French Alps to the south and the Mittelland to the northeast, Lake Geneva is the largest lake in the Alps. While most of the lake's southern shore is French territory, the greater part of the lake lies within Switzerland. With the mountains reflected in its still blue waters, it is one of Switzerland's most spellbinding sights. Pretty towns dot the shores and many of these serve as departure points for boat trips – an ideal way to experience the lake's serenity. Another way to take in the sights is to walk the shore path, a 42-km- (26-mile-) long trail that meanders along the lakeshore.

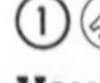 

Vevey

Vaud Théâtre, Montreux 5 Rue du montreuxriviera.com

With Montreux, Vevey is one of the two best-known holiday resorts of the Swiss Riviera – the stretch of land on the shore of Lake Geneva between Lausanne and Villeneuve. The region's climate and culture attracted English Romantics Lord Byron and Mary Shelley in the 19th century, and later Charlie Chaplin, who spent the last 25 years of his life in Vevey.

Known in Roman times as Viviscus, Vevey was once Lake Geneva's main port. By the 19th century it was the first industrial town in the Vaud canton. It was here, in 1867, that Henri Nestlé set up the powdered milk factory that revolutionized baby foods. Nestlé still has its international headquarters in Vevey.

→ A statue of Charlie Chaplin in Vevey

One of the most attractive parts of Vevey is its Grande Place (also known as Place du Marché). On Tuesday and Saturday mornings this square is filled with a market, and in summer regional growers offer wine tastings. A folk arts market is also held here on Saturday mornings in July and August.

Chaplin's World, a museum dedicated to the comedian's life and work, is in Le Manoir-de-Ban, Chaplin's former home. It features personal items, an interactive studio and re-created film sets.

East of the train station is the **Musée Jenisch**, housing paintings and sculptures by Switzerland's prominent 19th- and 20th-century artists, as

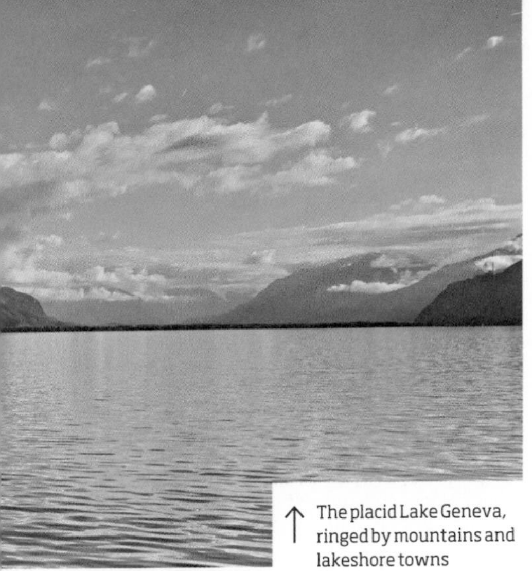

The placid Lake Geneva, ringed by mountains and lakeshore towns

well as the vast Fondation Oskar Kokoschka, which contains 800 paintings by the Austrian artist. Also here is Europe's largest collection of lithographs by Rembrandt.

Did You Know?

The bottled water brand Evian is sourced from Évian-les-Bains, on Lake Geneva.

Chaplin's World

2 Route de Fenil, Le Manoir-de-Ban Jan-mid-Apr, Nov & Dec: 10am-5pm daily (mid-Apr-Jun, Sep & Oct: to 6pm; Jul & Aug: to 7pm) chaplinsworld.com

Musée Jenisch

2 Avenue de la Gare 11am-6pm Tue-Sun museejenisch.ch

EAT

Denis Martin

This Michelin-starred restaurant serves inventive fare. Opt for the tasting menu.

2 Rue du Château, Vevey denismartin.ch

$$$

Le Brasserie J5

Locally sourced ingredients feature on the French menu here. Order the beef tartare.

32 Avenue de Casino, Montreux brasseriej5.ch

$$$

Restaurant l'Oasis

A cheap and cheerful spot in Villeneuve. Try the local fish.

6 Rue de Quai, Villeneuven restaurantoasis.ch

$$$

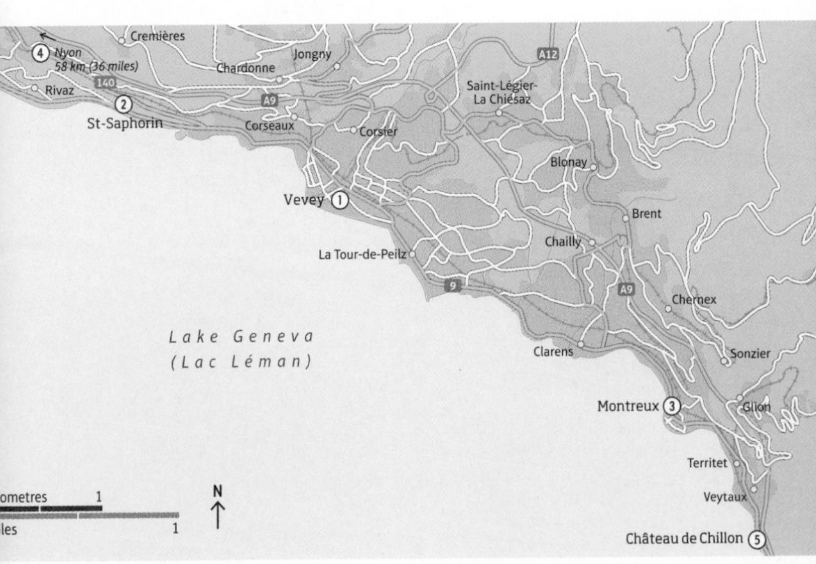

St-Saphorin

Vaud

Overlooked by vineyards, this picturesque winemaking village's cobbled streets have little changed over the centuries. Its landmark church was founded around 590 CE and is dedicated to Symphorian of Autun, an early Christian martyr for whom the village is now named. The current Gothic church, featuring a bell tower, dates from the 1520s, but the ruins of a Roman villa can still be seen in the church grounds.

Today, St-Saphorin is best known for its wine, producing everything from dry, white chasselas to fruity, red pinot noirs. Many footpaths wind their way from the village to the vineyards set above it.

Montreux

Vaud 5 Rue du Théâtre; www.montreuxriviera.com

The jewel of the Swiss Riviera, Montreux is famous for its annual jazz festival. The town began to develop as an international tourist resort in around 1815, and its peak period lasted until the outbreak of World War I in 1914.

Montreux has several Belle Époque hotels. The most well known of them is the Fairmont Le Montreux Palace on Grand Rue, located west of the town centre. Opposite this hotel is the Centre des Congrès, housing the Auditorium Stravinsky, a concert hall built in 1990 and dedicated to Igor Stravinsky (1882–1971), who composed *The Rite of Spring* while in Montreux. Montreux's other famous musical connection is to Freddie Mercury, vocalist in the band Queen, who made the town his second home and famously proclaimed that "if you want peace of mind, come to Montreux". On the lakeshore, you'll see a bronze statue of the singer.

250,000

The average number of people who attend the annual Montreux Jazz Festival.

Nyon

Vaud
8 Avenue Viollier
lacote-tourisme.ch

Surrounded by vineyards, the small town of Nyon is best known today as the home of European football's governing body, UEFA. The town was founded by the Romans as the settlement of Noviodunum around 30 CE, and three columns from the original Roman forum, found during construction work in the 1950s, still stand on the leafy Esplanade des Marronniers.

A short walk away is the town's defining feature, its Romanesque castle. First built in the 12th century, and greatly extended between 1574 and 1583, the **Château de Nyon** is now home to a museum displaying exquisite porcelain, produced in the town between 1781 and 1813, as well as contemporary ceramics. The collection also

Narrow street lined with boutiques and alfresco café tables in Nyon

includes works by local artists and the extensive Louis and August Kunz collection, two pioneers of early photography. The pedestrian streets behind the castle are packed with rows of elegant shops, cafés and restaurants.

The **Leman Lake Museum** in the lower town tells the story of the lake's formation, its wildlife and the lives of those who live on its shores.

Château de Nyon
5 Place du Château
Apr-Oct: 10am-5pm Tue-Sun; Nov-Mar: 2-5pm Tue-Sun chateaudenyon.ch

Leman Lake Museum
8 Quai Louis-Bonnard Apr-Oct: 10am-5pm Tue-Sun; Nov-Mar: 2-5pm Tue-Sun
museeduleman.ch

DRINK

Lavaux Vinorama, Rivaz

Sample some of Switzerland's finest wines, including the locally grown and subtly fruity chasselas blanc, at this terraced vineyard and tasting room in Rivaz.

2 Route du Lac, Rivaz
lavaux-vinorama.ch

Le Vins de Pierre et Michel Anex

Take a two-hour guided walk through the Ollon vineyards of Pierre and Michel Anex, tasting a range of their splendid white, rosé and red wines along the way. Tours by appointment only.

2 Chemin de la Monnaie, Ollon
anexvins.ch

Domaine des Faverges

Soak up the views of Lake Geneva, framed by terraced vines, at this St-Saphorin winery, before taking a tour of the domain's 19th-century stately home, the Grande Maison. By appointment only.

11 Route de Vevey, St-Saphorin
vignoblesdeletat.ch

Montreux, an idyllic waterside town on Lake Geneva

5

CHÂTEAU DE CHILLON

B5 21 Ave de Chillon, Veytaux, Vaud Veytaux-Chillon From Montreux Apr, May, Sep & Oct: 9am-6pm daily (Jun-Aug: to 7pm); Nov-Mar: 10am-5pm daily chillon.ch

This enchanting medieval castle, set on a rocky spur on the eastern shore of Lake Geneva, is one of Switzerland's most evocative sights and attracts hordes of visitors each year.

Built for the dukes of Savoy, the castle's origins probably go back to the 11th century; however, its present appearance dates from the 13th century. In 1536, the castle was captured by the Bernese, and from then until 1798 it was the seat of the region's Bernese bailiffs. Following the Vaudois Revolution of 1798, the castle became national property and has belonged ever since to the canton of Vaud. Throughout its history the castle was the centre of court life, and it was also used as a prison. Its most famous captive was François Bonivard, imprisoned here from 1530 to 1536. Today, the castle's many guided tours (by reservation only) are a great way to explore its history.

IMPRISONMENT OF FRANÇOIS BONIVARD

Born in 1493, François Bonivard was the prior of St Victor, a monastery just outside Geneva. Following his opposition to the Duke of Savoy's infringements against the liberties of the city of Geneva, he was held prisoner at Chillon for six long years. Bonivard was finally freed in 1536, when the Bernese attacked and gained control of the castle. He was later immortalized by Lord Byron in the long narrative poem *The Prisoner of Chillon*, which he wrote in Ouchy while travelling with fellow authors Percy Bysshe and Mary Shelley, in 1816.

Two bedchambers are located here.

Aula Nova, a former banqueting hall, now contains a museum.

The spectacular Castellan's Hall has a wooden ceiling resting on columns that support arches. The walls are richly decorated with paintings.

The covered bridge was originally a drawbridge.

Illustration of the Château de Chillon, a popular historical sight

Did You Know?

The castle's damp, dark dungeons are cut into the bedrock of the island itself.

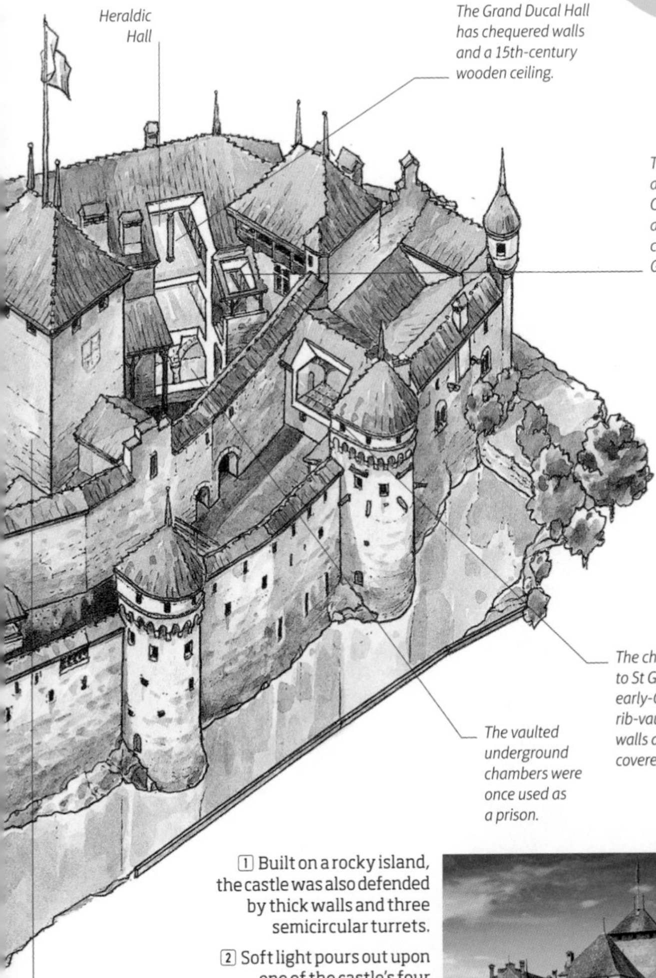

Heraldic Hall

The Grand Ducal Hall has chequered walls and a 15th-century wooden ceiling.

The Ducal Chamber, also known as the Camera Domini, has a wooden beamed ceiling and contains Gothic furniture.

The chapel, dedicated to St George, is in the early-Gothic style, with a rib-vaulted ceiling. The walls and ceiling are covered with frescoes.

The vaulted underground chambers were once used as a prison.

Bergfrieg, the tower that was the castle's final defence, is one of its oldest elements.

1 Built on a rocky island, the castle was also defended by thick walls and three semicircular turrets.

2 Soft light pours out upon one of the castle's four cobblestoned courtyards.

3 This bedroom, named the Bernese Chamber, features wall paintings and period-appropriate furnishings.

Did You Know?

The Pont de Berne, built in 1653, is the city's last remaining covered wooden bridge.

The River Sarine flowing under the Pont de Berne in Fribourg ↑

3

FRIBOURG

B4 Fribourg 1 Place Jean-Tinguely; www.fribourg.ch

With steep cobbled streets, immaculately preserved Gothic houses and numerous fountains, Fribourg (known as Freiburg in German) is one of the most attractive towns in Switzerland.

The city's 1899 funicular, one of the last in Europe to run on waste water

Set on a rocky peninsula within a bend of the River Sarine (the Saane in German), Fribourg was founded in 1157 by Berthold IV of Zähringen, and joined the Swiss Confederation in 1481. Despite the Reformation, Fribourg remained Catholic, and a Catholic university was founded here in 1889. The town's historic core has plenty to interest visitors. Just north of the Gothic Cathédrale St-Nicolas is the Éspace Jean Tinguely–Niki de Saint Phalle, a vast gallery with works by Fribourg-born Jean Tinguely and his wife, Niki de Saint Phalle. Next to it, set in a restored granary, is the Gutenberg Museum, showcasing the history of printing. South of the cathedral is the short Rue d'Or, worth a quick visit for its row of Gothic houses. The peninsula is connected to the river's south bank by the Pont de Berne, which leads to the Place des Forgerons, with a pretty Renaissance fountain and vestiges of the old town fortifications.

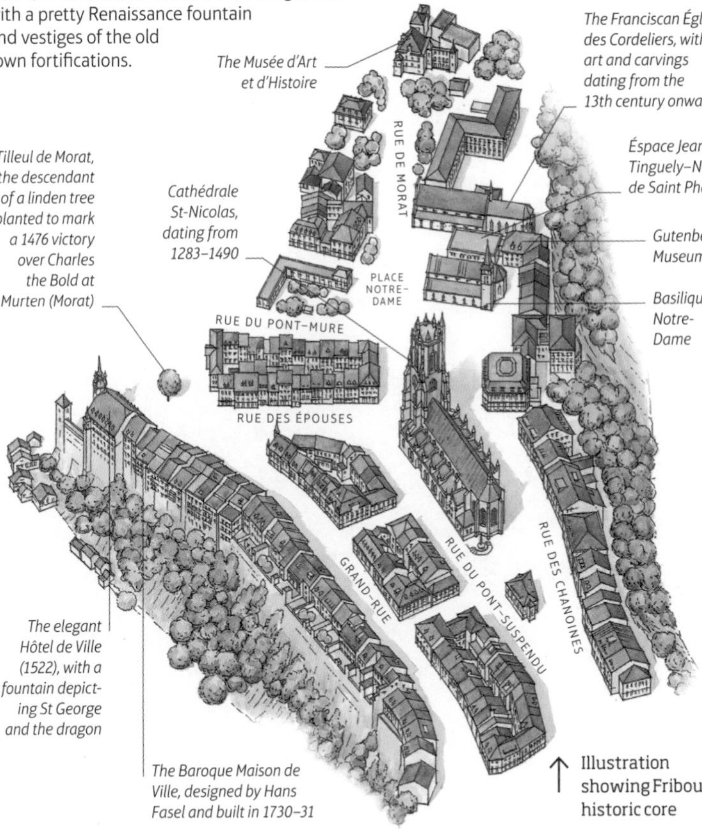

The Musée d'Art et d'Histoire

The Franciscan Église des Cordeliers, with art and carvings dating from the 13th century onwards

Tilleul de Morat, the descendant of a linden tree planted to mark a 1476 victory over Charles the Bold at Murten (Morat)

Cathédrale St-Nicolas, dating from 1283–1490

Éspace Jean Tinguely–Niki de Saint Phalle

Gutenberg Museum

Basilique Notre-Dame

RUE DE MORAT

PLACE NOTRE-DAME

RUE DU PONT-MURE

RUE DES ÉPOUSES

GRAND-RUE

RUE DU PONT-SUSPENDU

RUE DES CHANOINES

The elegant Hôtel de Ville (1522), with a fountain depicting St George and the dragon

The Baroque Maison de Ville, designed by Hans Fasel and built in 1730–31

Illustration showing Fribourg's historic core

EXPERIENCE MORE

Leysin

B5 Vaud Place Large; www.leysin.ch

Lying at an altitude of 1,260 m (4,135 ft), Leysin enjoys an unusually dry and sunny climate. Once a centre for the treatment of tuberculosis, the village is now a ski resort. Cable cars carry visitors up to the Tour de Mayen (2,326 m/ 7,631 ft) and to Berneuse (2,037 m/6,683 ft).

Villars-sur-Ollon

B5 Vaud 144

Popular with families, the ski resort of Villars-sur-Ollon sits on a sunny plateau, from where a cogwheel train transports visitors to Col-de-Bretaye at 1,800 m (6,000 ft).

Up here, golfers can enjoy an 18-hole course with a view of Mont Blanc; come winter the whole area is taken over by skiers. There are gentle slopes, making it a decent resort for beginners, while the chairlift links to nearby Gryon and Les Diablerets mean more experienced skiers have plenty of challenging runs to keep them entertained.

↑ The revolving panoramic restaurant at the top of Berneuse, above Leysin

Les Diablerets

B5 Vaud and Valais Rue de la Gare; www.diablerets.ch

Set among meadows in the Ormonts Valley, the ski resort of Les Diablerets offers many attractions including the Alpine Coaster, the highest situated toboggan run in the world, and the Monster Snowpark. There's also the narrow Peak Walk – the world's first suspension bridge to link two mountain peaks, the Scex Rouge and Glacier 3000. At 2,987 m (9,800 ft), it is also one of the highest suspension bridges in the world, alongside Titlis Cliff Walk in Obwalden.

Château d'Oex

B5 Vaud 175 6 Place du Village

Pretty Château d'Oex is immediately identifiable from

→ The popular winter resort of Villars-sur-Ollon, with gentle slopes, ideal for beginners

INSIDER TIP
Night Sledging

For a thrilling and magical experience, try sledging in the dark. Take the cable car up Les Diablerets three evenings a week to sledge down its 7-km (4.5-mile) sledge run, one of the longest in the country.

its 15th-century church, which sits on a hill in the centre of the village. An attractive place, the village is known for its special microclimate which is favourable to hot-air ballooning. Flights are available all year, and it's especially worth visiting in late January when it hosts the nine-day International Balloon Festival.

Vallorbe

A4 Fribourg 11 Rue des Grandes-Forges; www.vallorbe-tourisme.ch

This small industrial town lies near the Franco-Swiss border. From the Middle Ages until recently, the town was an iron-smelting centre. It was also at Vallorbe that the tunnel under the Jura was built, thus creating the Paris–Istanbul rail route.

The history of both the Swiss iron and railway industries is reflected in the **Musée du Fer et du Chemin de Fer** (Iron and Railway Museum), which sits on the bank of the River Orbe.

About 3 km (2 miles) southwest of Vallorbe are the **Grottes de Vallorbe**. These are caves with spectacular stalactites and stalagmites. The caves form a tunnel over the Orbe's passage, which surges through a gorge.

Musée du Fer et du Chemin de Fer

11 Rue des Grandes-Forges Apr-Oct: 10am-5pm Tue-Sun; Nov & Jan-Mar: 1-5pm Tue-Fri, 10am-5pm Sat & Sun Dec (except 26-29) museedufer.ch

Grottes de Vallorbe

Apr & May: 9:30am-4:30pm daily; Jun-Aug: 9:30am-5:30pm daily; Sep & Oct: 9:30am-4:30pm daily Jan-Mar, Nov & Dec grottesdevallorbe.ch

Aigle

B5 Vaud 5 Rue Colomb; www.aigle-tourisme.ch

Aigle is the capital of the Chablais, a winegrowing region that lies southeast of Lake Geneva and produces some of Switzerland's best wines. Set among vineyards covering the foothills of the Alpes Vaudoises, the town is dominated by the turreted Château d'Aigle. Built in the 12th century by the Savoyards, it was severely damaged in the 15th century and later rebuilt as the residence of the region's bailiffs. The castle now houses the **Musée de la Vigne et du Vin**, whose exhibits illustrate the age-old methods of vine cultivation and winemaking. Opposite this museum is the **Musée International de l'Etiquette**, which documents the history of wine labels.

Musée de la Vigne et du Vin and Musée International de l'Étiquette

Château d'Aigle, 1 Place du Château 024 466 21 30 Jan-Mar, Nov & Dec: 10am-5pm Tue-Sat; Apr-Jun & Sep-Oct: 10am-6pm Tue-Sat; Jul & Aug: 10am-6pm daily museeduvin.ch

→ The turreted Château d'Aigle, now a museum of wine and winemaking

10

Estavayer-le-Lac

B4 Fribourg
16 Rue de l'Hôtel de Ville; www.estavayerpayerne.ch

On the southern shore of Lake Neuchâtel, this town lies within an enclave of the canton of Fribourg. A popular yachting centre, Estavayer-le-Lac is also a pleasant medieval town with arcaded streets. Its focal point is the Château de Cheneaux, a fine Gothic castle that is now the seat of local government.

The **Musée des Grenouilles** (Frog Museum), housed in a 15th-century mansion, features an unusual curiosity, namely a collection of 108 stuffed frogs *(grenouilles)* and other animals arranged in poses that parody the social life of the mid-19th century. The scenes, including dinner parties and games of pool, were created by François Perrier, an eccentric resident of Estavayer who served in the Vatican's Swiss Guard and who put together this somewhat bizarre display in the 1860s.

Musée des Grenouilles
13 Rue du Musée
Mar-Dec: 1-6pm Tue-Sun
Jan & Feb
museedesgrenouilles.ch

Gruyères

B4 Fribourg
26 Place des Alpes, Bulle; www.la-gruyere.ch

The well-preserved medieval village of Gruyères is a popular destination for visitors, and is often crowded in summer. As its only street is pedestrianized, vehicles must be left in the parking areas below.

The village has medieval-era houses and is crowned by an 11th-century castle, the **Château de Gruyères**. It was inhabited by the counts of Gruyères until the mid-16th century, when the bankrupted 19th count fled and his lands were divided between the lords of Bern and Fribourg.

Gruyères is also famous for its cheese. At the dairy La Maison du Gruyère *(www.lamaisondugruyere.ch)*, visitors can watch it being made.

Château de Gruyères
8 Rue du Château
Apr-Oct: 9am-6pm daily; Nov-Mar: 10am-5pm daily
chateau-gruyeres.ch

ALPINE CATTLE DESCENTS

Each autumn after several happy months munching on Alpine flowers on the high mountain pastures, it's time for the cows to come home to the valley for the winter. Many villages, including Charmey, near Gruyères, host a day-long celebration with plenty of local wine, cheese and bell-ringing as the cows and their farmers parade through the streets.

Murten/Morat

B4 Fribourg
Französische Kirchgasse 6; www.murten-morat.ch

The resort town of Murten (Morat in French) lies on the eastern shore of Murtensee (Lac de Morat). It has strong historical associations. It was

→ Sampling cheesy dishes at La Maison du Gruyère's restaurant, Pringy

at Murten, on 22 June 1476, that the forces of the Swiss Confederation crushed the army of Charles the Bold, Duke of Burgundy, killing 12,000 of his soldiers, while losing only 410 of their own. According to legend, a messenger ran 17 km (10 miles) from Murten to Fribourg with news of the victory, dropping dead with exhaustion on his arrival. His sacrifice is commemorated by an annual run between Murten and Fribourg that takes place on the first Sunday in October.

The town was founded by the Zähringer dynasty in the 12th century, and is still encircled by walls dating from the 12th to the 15th centuries. Hauptgasse, the main street through the old town, is lined with 16th-century arcaded houses with overhanging eaves. The rampart walk, reached from several points along Deutsche Kirchgasse, offers views of Murtensee, the castle and of the Old Town's brown-tiled houses. At the western end of the town is a 13th-century castle, with a courtyard that provides a fine view over the lake. At the eastern end stands Berntor (or Porte de Berne), a striking Baroque gatehouse with a clock dating from 1712. The **Musée Historique**, in a disused mill on the lakeshore, displays prehistoric finds from local archaeological excavations, and Burgundian War artifacts. It also stages frequent temporary exhibitions.

↑ The château at Estavayer-le-Lac seen from Lake Neuchâtel

Musée Historique
4 Ryf, Murten
Apr-Dec: 2-5pm Tue-Sat, 10am-5pm Sun Jan-Mar
museummurten.ch

Yverdon-les-Bains

B4 Vaud 1 Avenue de la Gare; www.yverdonlesbainsregion.ch

Situated at the southwestern extremity of Lake Neuchâtel, Yverdon-les-Bains is Vaud's second town after Lausanne. The Romans built thermal baths here to take advantage of the hot sulphurous springs. Yverdon's town centre overlies the Roman settlement. The focal point is the **Château d'Yverdon-les-Bains**, a 13th-century castle built by Peter II of Savoy. Part of the castle now houses a museum of local history, with a collection of Gallo-Roman finds and other exhibits.

Place Pestalozzi, opposite the castle, is dominated by the Hôtel de Ville, the town hall built in 1768–73 on the site of a former market hall. The collegiate church on the west side of the square dates from 1757. The arched pediment of its Baroque façade features an allegory of Faith. To the east, the otherworldly **Maison d'Ailleurs** (House of Elsewhere) is of interest to science fiction fans. This museum presents temporary exhibits related to science fiction, utopian worlds and fantasy.

Yverdon's thermal bath complex, the **Centre Thermal**, is one of Switzerland's largest and most modern spa centres, with indoor and outdoor pools, saunas and physiotherapy.

Château d'Yverdon-les-Bains
Jun-Sep: 11am-5pm Tue-Sun; Oct-May: 2-5pm Tue-Sun

Maison d'Ailleurs
14 Place Pestalozzi
11am-6pm Tue-Sun
25 Dec & 1 Jan ailleurs.ch

Centre Thermal
22 Avenue les Bains 9am-8pm Mon-Sat, 9am-6:30pm Sun bainsyverdon.ch

14

Grandson

B4 Vaud 13 Rue Haute; www.yverdon lesbainsregion.ch

Dominated by its medieval castle, the town of Grandson is associated with a momentous event in the history of the Swiss Confederation: the defeat of Charles the Bold, Duke of Burgundy, at the Battle of Grandson on 2 March 1476.

In February 1476, the duke's army laid siege to Grandson and its castle, eventually securing the surrender of the garrison, which was put to death. After raising an army of 18,000, the Confederates marched on Grandson to wreak revenge on the duke and his army. The Burgundians fled, abandoning their arms and horses, as well as the ducal treasury. The trove is now displayed in Bern's Historisches Museum *(p77)*.

Built between the 11th and 14th centuries, the **Château de Grandson** rises proudly from the magnificent shores of Lake Neuchâtel. It contains a model of the battlefield and a diorama illustrating the town's history from the Middle Ages to the present day. In the basement is an automobile museum with a white Rolls-Royce that belonged to Greta Garbo and Winston Churchill's Austin Cambridge.

Château de Grandson
Place du Château
024 445 29 26 Apr-Oct: 10am-6pm daily; Nov-Mar: 10am-5pm daily

GREAT VIEW
Sea of Fog

The elevated terrace at Sainte-Croix enjoys panoramic views from Santis, in the Alpstein massif, to Mont Blanc on clear days, but even on cloudy days it's worth the trip here for the chance to see the Swiss plateau blanketed in a thick sea of fog.

Sainte-Croix

A4 Vaud 10 Rue Neuve; www.sainte-croix-les-rasses-tourisme.ch

Appropriately known as the Balcony of the Jura, the town of Sainte-Croix lies at an altitude of 1,092 m (3,583 ft) and commands a wide view of the Alps, the Swiss Upland and the Jura mountains.

Since the early 19th century Sainte-Croix has been the world capital of musical-box manufacture. Two local museums are devoted to this art. In the town centre, the **Musée du CIMA** (Centre International de la Méchanique d'Art) has plenty of mechanical toys and devices, while the **Musée Baud**, in the village of L'Auberson, features music boxes collected by the Baud family, as well as singing birds and animated figures.

← An exhibit from the museum of mechanical devices in Sainte-Croix

Musée du CIMA
2 Rue de l'Industrie
Until 2024 for renovation
musees.ch

Musée Baud
23 Grand-Rue, L'Auberson By guided tour and reservation only at 2pm & 3:30pm daily; call 024 454 24 84 museebaud.ch

Neuchâtel

B3 Neuchâtel Hôtel des Postes; www.j3l.ch

Lying on the northwestern shore of Lake Neuchâtel, Neuchâtel is a graceful town with a strikingly Gallic atmosphere. Its main attractions are its castle, early-Gothic church (the Église Collégiale) and Renaissance market hall. It also has two museums of note. The Musée d'Art et d'Histoire displays paintings by some of the Swiss and French Impressionists, as well as fascinating automata.

Once a year the town's century-old Grape Harvest Festival celebrates the bounty from the region's vineyards.

↑ The Fête des Vendanges (Grape Harvest Festival), in late September, Neuchâtel

Vallée de Joux

A4 Vaud

The Jura may not be as dramatic as the Alps, but its moderate peaks and valleys offer a more accessible way to make the most of the great outdoors. One of the loveliest places in the Swiss Jura is the Vallée de Joux and its centrepiece, Lac de Joux, the largest lake in the Jura.

At 1,004 m (3,300 ft) altitude, the lake sometimes freezes in the coldest weeks, creating one of the largest natural ice rinks in Europe. In summer, the lake is a playground for boaters, swimmers and windsurfers, while hikers and cyclists take to the surrounding trails, including the hike up Mont Tendre – at 1,679 m (5,500 ft) it's the highest peak in the region, but a mere hillock compared to the Alps.

Le Locle

B3 Neuchâtel lelocle.ch

The town of Le Locle is renowned the world over as being the birthplace of Swiss watchmaking, and has been awarded World Heritage status by UNESCO. In 1705 the young watchmaker Daniel Jeanrichard arrived from Neuchâtel to settle in Le Locle, where he set up a workshop. The apprentices that he trained then established workshops of their own in La Chaux-de-Fonds, thus launching the now-famous Swiss watchmaking industry.

The Musée d'Horlogerie, which occupies a stately 18th-century mansion (the elegant Château des Monts), presents a large collection of timepieces from around the world, as well as several elaborate automata.

Avenches

B4 Vaud 3 Place de l'Église; avenches.ch

Originally the capital of the Helveti, the Celtic tribe that once ruled this part of the country, Avenches was captured by the Romans in the 1st century BCE. Named Aventicum, it became the capital of the Roman province of Helvetia. Vestiges of the Roman city can still be seen to the east of the medieval town centre. The most complete of these remains is the amphitheatre, with seating for 6,000. Other features include the Tornallaz, a tower that is the only surviving part of the old city walls, the forum, the baths and a 12-m (40-ft) Corinthian column known as the Tour du Cigognier. The **Musée Romain**, set within the amphitheatre, contains an impressive display of Roman artifacts discovered during excavations at Aventicum. The exhibits range from items of daily life to statues of Roman deities, mosaics and wall paintings. Avenches is famous for its music festivals, including an eclectic rock festival that has drawn international artists for nearly 30 years to perform in the Roman amphitheatre each August.

Musée Romain

Tour de l'Amphithéâtre
Apr-Sep: 10am-5pm Tue-Sun; Oct, Feb & Mar: 2-5pm Tue-Sun; Nov-Jan: 2-5pm Wed-Sun aventicum.org

EAT

Ananda Café-Boutique

Himalayan food in a vintage setting.

31 Fbg de l'Hôpital, Neuchâtel ananda-online.ch

KJU

Mediterranean dishes served with a twist.

22B Quai Perdonnet, Vevey q-vevey.ch

Ornate clocks at the Musée International d'Horlogerie at La Chaux-de-Fonds

La Chaux-de-Fonds

B3 Neuchâtel 1 Rue Espacité; 032 889 68 90

If Le Locle is the birthplace of the Swiss watchmaking industry, La Chaux-de-Fonds may be regarded as its cradle. The largest town in the canton of Neuchâtel, La Chaux-de-Fonds lies in the Jura at an altitude of 1,000 m (3,280 ft). Introduced to the town in the early 18th century, watchmaking was initially a cottage industry. In time it was industrialized, and La Chaux-de-Fonds became the leading centre of Swiss watchmaking. The industry reached its peak in the late 18th and 19th centuries.

After it was destroyed by a fire in 1794, the town was rebuilt to a grid pattern, with long, wide avenues. It is now dotted with a number of Modernist buildings.

The illustrious past of La Chaux-de-Fonds is celebrated in the magnificent **Musée International d'Horlogerie**. The museum's collection of some 3,000 pieces from around the world illustrates the history of timekeeping from its beginnings in antiquity to state-of-the-art instruments able to record time lapses of infinitesimal fractions of a second. Many of the most impressive-looking pieces on display were made in La Chaux-de-Fonds during the town's apogee. Musical, astrononomical, atomic and quartz clocks are also on display. The museum has audiovisual facilities, a library and a restoration workshop for antique clocks and watches. At the entrance is a tubular steel carillon that sounds every 15 minutes.

La Chaux-de-Fonds is also the birthplace of the Modernist architect Charles-Édouard Jeanneret (1887–1965), known as Le Corbusier, from the French word "le corbeau" or "the raven". Before he moved to Paris in 1917, Le Corbusier built several houses here, and an itinerary taking in buildings that he designed and places associated with him is available from the town's tourist office.

Did You Know?

Watches produced in Switzerland account for 53 per cent of the worldwide market by value.

Musée International d'Horlogerie

29 Rue des Musées
10am-5pm Tue-Sun
chaux-de-fonds.ch/musees/mih

→

The Creux du Van, western Switzerland's "Grand Canyon"

Franches-Montagnes

B3 Jura 6 Place du 23 Juin, Saignelégier; www.j3l.ch

The part of the Jura mountains that lies within the canton of Jura itself is known as the Franches-Montagnes. The area received its name in the 14th century, when the prince-bishop of Basel, who owned the territory that now makes up the canton of Jura, granted its inhabitants a *franchise*, or exemption from taxation, to encourage migration to this sparsely populated region.

The Franches-Montagnes lies at an altitude of 1,000–1,100 m (3,300–3,600 ft). With spruce and fir forests, undulating pastures and prettily picturesque low houses, this outstandingly beautiful plateau has extensive hiking trails, and cycling and cross-country skiing routes. It is also famous for its sturdy breed of horses.

The region's principal town is Saignelégier. Every year, on the second week of August,

it hosts the Marché-Concours National de Chevaux, a showpiece for the area's unique breed of Franches-Montagnes horses.

Creux du Van

B4 Neuchâtel

This horseshoe-shaped rock formation in the Jura is sometimes nicknamed western Switzerland's "Grand Canyon" (the Rhine gorge stakes its claim for the east of the country). That may be a bit of a stretch, but still, the 160-m- (525-ft-) high cliffs are impressive and offer far-reaching views of the Jura mountains and the lush valley below – if you dare look over the vertigo-inducing edge. The easiest way to access it is to drive up the road to the restaurant near the top, though it's much more satisfying to earn the views by hiking up the steep path through the woods from the village of Noiraigue. To descend, take an alternative path down through the centre of the horseshoe. You'll pass by the *fontaine froide*, a natural spring where the water is a chilly 4° C (39° F) year-round. It's a peaceful, isolated spot with a mythical status – during the century that absinthe was banned in Switzerland, covert drinkers would come here to enjoy it in secret, preparing it in the traditional way, by slowly adding water, a process known as "troubling".

St-Ursanne

B3 Jura
Place Roger Schaffter; www.j3l.ch

A charming medieval walled town with fortified gates, St-Ursanne is set in a deep canyon washed by the River Doubs. The town grew up around the hermitage that Ursicinus, a disciple of St Columba, established here in the early 7th century.

The focal point of the town is its beautiful Romanesque and Gothic church. It has an ornate Romanesque portal, with statues of the Virgin and St Ursicinus. There are many fine old medieval houses, as well as a graceful arched stone bridge, built in 1728 across the River Doubs on the south side of St-Ursanne, which provides a good view of the town and its setting. The bridge features a statue of St John Nepomucene, who is often considered the patron saint of bridges.

ABSINTHE

Absinthe may be the preferred tipple of anguished poets and painters in Paris, but the Green Fairy *(right)* actually comes from the canton of Neuchâtel *(p154)*. The spirit was banned for a century, though many continued to distil it in secret, creating colourful anecdotes of clandestine activity that are told in the Maison de l'Absinthe in Môtiers *(www.maison-absinthe.ch)*. Walk or cycle the Absinthe Trail, which connects distilleries, restaurants and even a chocolate shop that uses absinthe in its products.

A rooftop bar at sunset overlooking Zürich's Old Town

ZÜRICH

Capital of the densely populated canton of the same name, the city of Zürich lies on the north shore of Zürichsee at the point where the River Limmat flows north out of the lake. By the 1st century BCE, a Celtic settlement, Turicum, had been established on the Lindenhof. A Carolingian palace was built on this hill, now in the heart of the old city, in the 9th century, and a trading settlement developed at its base. Briefly under the control of the Zähringen dynasty, Zürich passed to the Holy Roman Empire in 1218 and joined the Swiss Confederation in 1351.

By the early Middle Ages, the silk, wool, linen and leather trades had already brought Zürich's merchants great wealth. This merchant class was overthrown and replaced by disgruntled guilds, who in turn held power until the late 18th century.

In the 16th century, Zürich embraced the Reformation, thanks to Ulrich Zwingli, who preached from the Grossmünster, the city's great cathedral. The city then fell into a period of relative obscurity until the 19th century, when Zürich underwent rapid industrial growth. As a result of Switzerland's neutrality, the city emerged from the aftermath of both world wars as a major centre of finance, which it continues to be to this day.

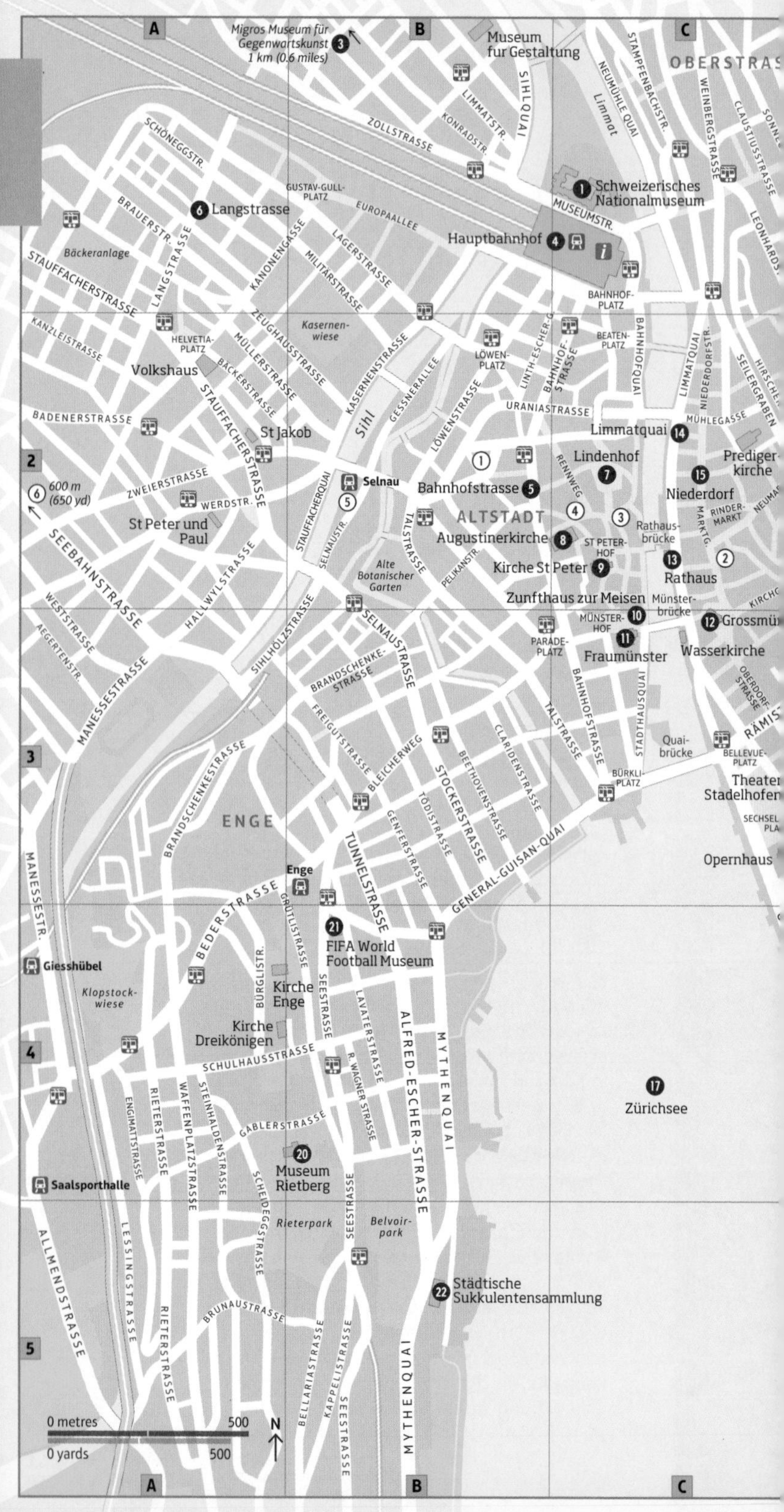

Migros Museum für Gegenwartskunst 1 km (0.6 miles)
Museum fur Gestaltung
OBERSTRASS
Schweizerisches Nationalmuseum
Langstrasse
Hauptbahnhof
Volkshaus
St Jakob
Selnau
600 m (650 yd)
St Peter und Paul
Limmatquai
Lindenhof
Predigerkirche
Bahnhofstrasse
Niederdorf
ALTSTADT
Augustinerkirche
Kirche St Peter
Rathaus
Zunfthaus zur Meisen
Grossmünster
Fraumünster
Wasserkirche
Theater Stadelhofen
Opernhaus
ENGE
Enge
FIFA World Football Museum
Giesshübel
Kirche Enge
Kirche Dreikönigen
Zürichsee
Museum Rietberg
Saalsporthalle
Städtische Sukkulentensammlung
0 metres 500
0 yards 500

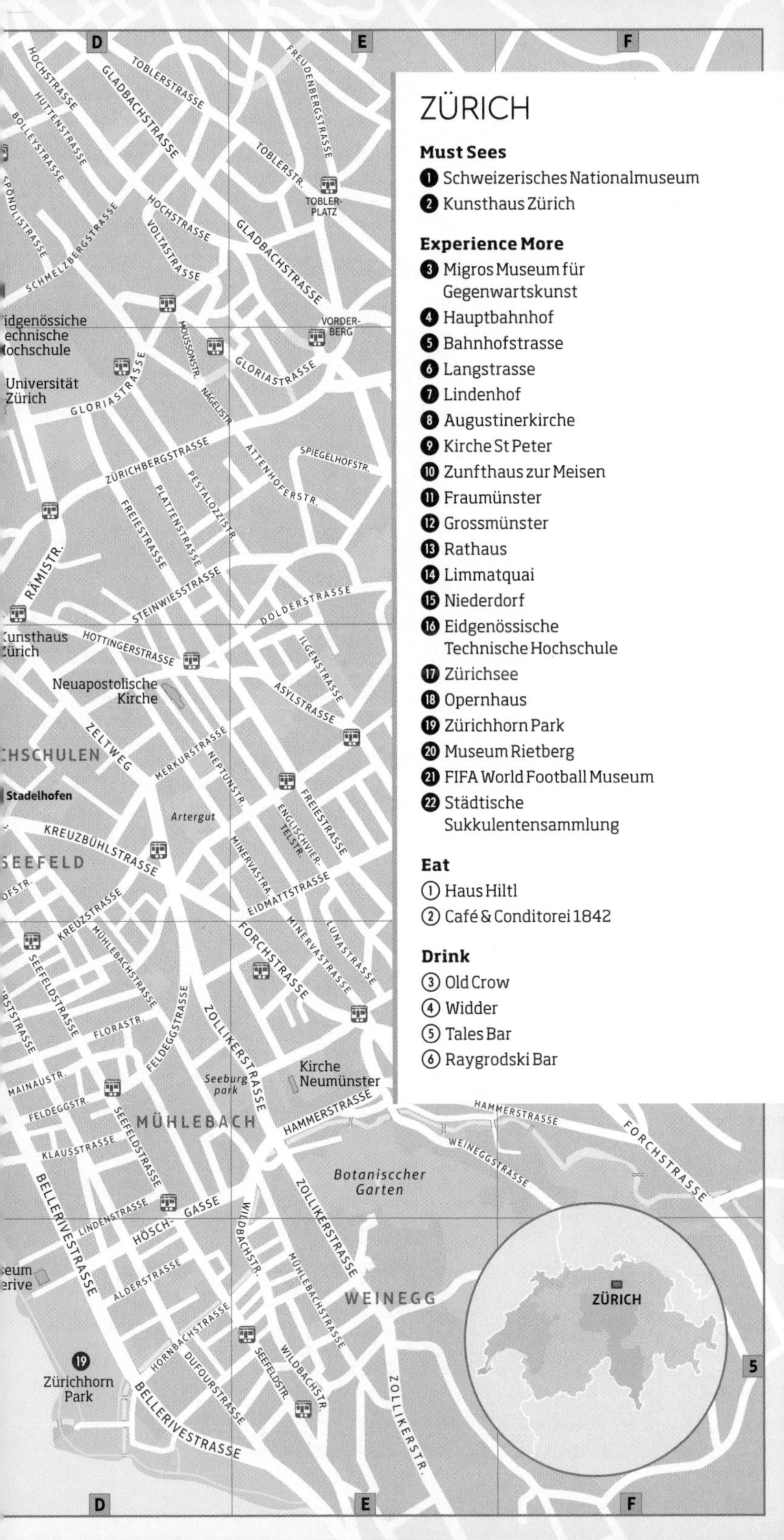
ZÜRICH
Must Sees
1 Schweizerisches Nationalmuseum
2 Kunsthaus Zürich
Experience More
3 Migros Museum für Gegenwartskunst
4 Hauptbahnhof
5 Bahnhofstrasse
6 Langstrasse
7 Lindenhof
8 Augustinerkirche
9 Kirche St Peter
10 Zunfthaus zur Meisen
11 Fraumünster
12 Grossmünster
13 Rathaus
14 Limmatquai
15 Niederdorf
16 Eidgenössische Technische Hochschule
17 Zürichsee
18 Opernhaus
19 Zürichhorn Park
20 Museum Rietberg
21 FIFA World Football Museum
22 Städtische Sukkulentensammlung
Eat
① Haus Hiltl
② Café & Conditorei 1842
Drink
③ Old Crow
④ Widder
⑤ Tales Bar
⑥ Raygrodski Bar
D
E
F
5
Universität Zürich
Kunsthaus Zürich
Neuapostolische Kirche
Stadelhofen
SEEFELD
MÜHLEBACH
WEINEGG
Artergut
Seeburg park
Kirche Neumünster
Botanisccher Garten
19 Zürichhorn Park
TOBLER-PLATZ
VORDER-BERG
ZÜRICH
HOCHSTRASSE
GLADBACHSTRASSE
TOBLERSTRASSE
FREUDENBERGSTRASSE
GLORIASTRASSE
ZÜRICHBERGSTRASSE
RÄMISTR.
STEINWIESSTRASSE
DOLDERSTRASSE
HOTTINGERSTRASSE
ASYLSTRASSE
ZELTWEG
KREUZBÜHLSTRASSE
FORCHSTRASSE
ZOLLIKERSTRASSE
HAMMERSTRASSE
SEEFELDSTRASSE
BELLERIVESTRASSE
FELDEGGSTRASSE
WEINEGGSTRASSE
MÜHLEBACHSTRASSE
WILDBACHSTR.

1 People sitting in Bürkliplatz

2 A yacht on Lake Zürich.

3 Mechanical sculpture in Zürichhorn Park.

4 The Grossmünster looming over Zürich.

3 DAYS

in Zürich

Day 1

Morning Jump straight into the city's (and Switzerland's) past with a visit to the Schweizerisches Nationalmuseum *(p164)*, where local history is revealed through fascinating exhibits on home design and fashion. Mull it all over with lunch at Spitz, the museum restaurant.

Afternoon Cross the Walchbrücke and explore the pedestrianized warren of Niederdorf *(p171)*. Detour down narrow Napfgasse and into Café & Conditorei 1842 *(p169)* for irresistible pastries and drinking chocolate made by Lindt. Meander on to the city's largest church, the Grossmünster *(p171)*, where the Protestant reformer Ulrich Zwingli preached.

Evening Stroll down Bahnhofstrasse *(p168)*, which ends at Bürkliplatz, then nip into the Arboretum and Belvoirpark with its huge collection of irises and daylilies. After, enjoy fresh fish dishes at a restaurant overlooking the water.

Day 2

Morning Have breakfast at Confiserie Sprüngli *(www.spruengli.ch)*. A meeting place for Zürich's well-to-do since 1859, it is now renowned for its chocolate truffles and "Luxemburgerli" macarons. Cross the Limmat to visit Zürich's Kunsthaus *(p166)*, home to the city's most important collection of art. Its highlight is Rudolf Koller's *Gotthard Post* (1873), a vivid painting of a postal coach scattering cows; it was voted Switzerland's most popular piece. Stop for lunch at Haus Hiltl *(p169)*, the world's first vegetarian restaurant, opened in 1898.

Afternoon Take in another side of the city with a train trip, from Hauptbahnhof *(p168)* to Üetliberg, Zürich's "mountain". A path from the station leads through the woods to Hotel Uto Kulm's *(www.utokulm.ch)* delightful café terrace. After a coffee, climb the 179 steps of the communications tower for splendid views over the city.

Evening Return to the city centre for an evening cruise on Zürichsee *(p172)* from the pier at Bürkliplatz. Afterwards, walk along the riverside into the Old Town for cocktails at Old Crow *(p170)*.

Day 3

Morning Dip into the city's best-known area of urban regeneration, Zürich West. This former *Industriequartier* has been transformed into a vibrant area of independent bars, restaurants and shops selling everything from Tunisian textiles to electric bikes. Nearby is the iconic Freitag shop *(www.freitag.ch)*, housed inside a stack of 19 shipping containers.

Afternoon After a lunch of pan-Pacific cuisine at hip Brauerei Steinfels microbrewery *(www.brauerei-steinfels.ch)*, wander south to Zürichhorn Park *(p173)*, which stretches all the way to Zürichsee. The park is dotted with sculptures by modern artists, including *Heureka*, a kinetic sculpture created by artist Jean Tinguely for Expo 64 in Lausanne *(p134)*.

1

SCHWEIZERISCHES NATIONALMUSEUM

C1 Museumstrasse 2 Zürich HB 4, 6, 8, 11, 13, 14 46
10am-5pm Tue-Sun (Thu: to 7pm) landesmuseum.ch

Housed in an 1898 fairy-tale mansion and an adjoining contemporary wing on the banks of the River Limmat, the Swiss National Museum's eclectic collections take visitors on a time-travelling turn through the highlights of Switzerland's history.

The collections of the Swiss National Museum illustrate the country's history and culture from prehistoric times to the present day. The museum has outposts at various locations around the country – the Château de Prangins in Vaud and the Forum of Swiss History in Schwyz – but its headquarters, in Zürich, have the largest collection of objects illustrating the cultural history of Switzerland.

Highlights include artifacts from Switzerland's rich archaeological past, displays of costumes and Swiss handicrafts. There is a wing of exposed concrete, connected to the original 1898 building and designed by Swiss architects Christ & Gantenbein. This striking, angular edifice houses a permanent collection of Swiss archaeology, temporary exhibition spaces, a library and an auditorium.

The museum was extensively renovated in 2020 and new attractions were added. These include "A Magic Carpet Ride Through History", which transports children into the past through interactive exhibits.

↑ A globe by Jost Bürgi (1552-1632), one of the scientific instruments on display at the museum

The stark exterior of the museum's extension, and *(inset)* the exhibition "Ideas of Switzerland" ↑

GALLERY GUIDE

The west wing houses the Collections Gallery, which showcases a cross-section of objects from the museum's collection and focuses on their history and how they were made. Items include altarpieces and tapestries from the Middle Ages, and fashion and jewellery. The first and second floors contain the History of Switzerland galleries, taking you on a tour of the nation's past. The southern wing has Swiss archaeology on the first floor. There are temporary exhibition spaces on all floors.

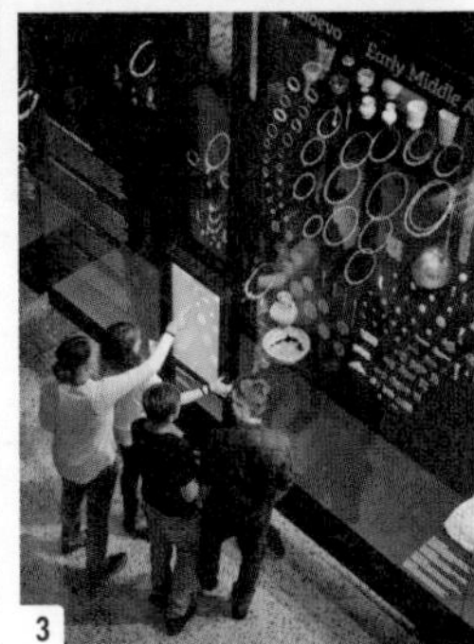

1 The altarpiece with St Eligius in the smithy was painted around 1495, by Hans Leu the Elder.

2 Visitors take in a Renaissance bust in the extension wing.

3 Young people engage with interactive displays in the Middle Ages section.

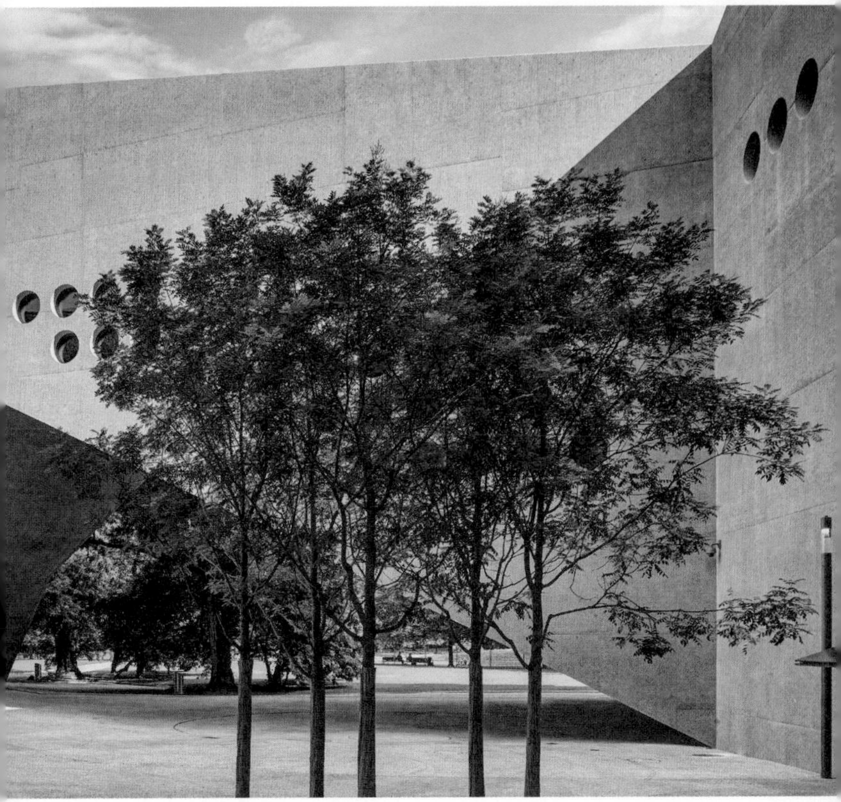

2

KUNSTHAUS ZÜRICH

D3 Heimplatz 1 Stadelhofen 3, 5, 8, 9, 11 31, 33 10am-6pm Tue & Fri-Sun, 10am-8pm Wed & Thu kunsthaus.ch

One of Switzerland's greatest art galleries, the Kunsthaus Zürich holds major works of art, from medieval religious paintings and Dutch Old Masters to Impressionist and Post-Impressionist artworks. The gallery's holdings also showcase the art movements of the 20th century.

Highlights of this superb collection include paintings by the 19th-century Swiss artists Ferdinand Hodler and Albert Anker, the largest assemblage of work by Edvard Munch outside Scandinavia, paintings by Marc Chagall, and paintings and sculpture by Alberto Giacometti. In 2021, the Sammlung E G Bührle collection of Impressionist and Post-Impressionist paintings moved into an extension of the Kunsthaus.

HIDDEN GEM

The Gates of Hell

Before you go into the museum, take a moment to admire *The Gates of Hell*, next to the entrance. Created by French sculptor Rodin, this intricate pair of bronze doors depicts a version of hell inspired by Dante's *Inferno*. It features almost 200 figures all clustered around a single man – a small-scale version of Rodin's famous *Thinker*.

GALLERY GUIDE

The first and second floors of the gallery are dedicated to the museum's permanent collections, while the ground floor houses a shop, café, cloakroom and information desk. On the first floor, European, American, Swiss and contemporary works are exhibited. The second floor has displays of early 19th-century French art, modern art and photography. The museum's temporary exhibitions are usually situated on the ground and first floors of the museum.

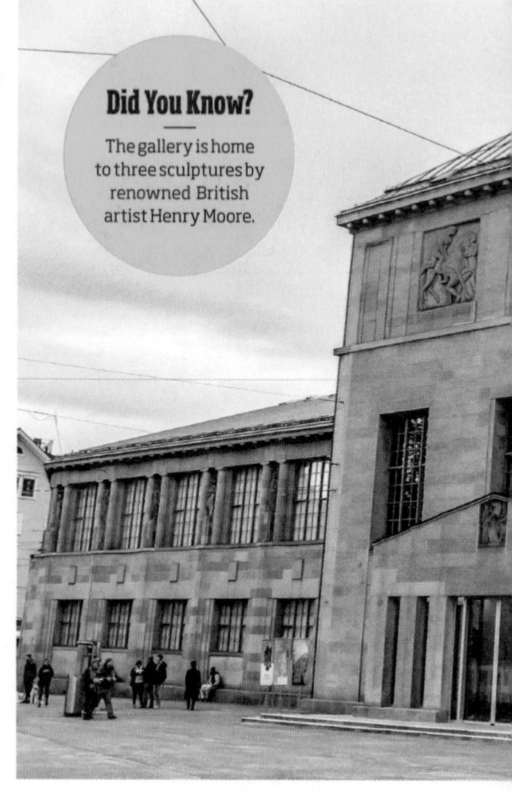

Did You Know?

The gallery is home to three sculptures by renowned British artist Henry Moore.

1 Visitors admire the work of German artist Sigmar Polke on display at the gallery.

2 *Wilhelm Wartmann* (1923) is one of several works by Edvard Munch on display in the permanent collection.

3 *Falstaff in the Laundry Basket* was painted by Swiss artist Johann Heinrich Füssli in 1792.

↑ The grand building within which sits the impressive fine arts gallery

EXPERIENCE MORE

Migros Museum für Gegenwartskunst

B1 Limmatstrasse 270 Wipkingen 4, 6, 8, 13 11am-6pm Tue-Sun (Thu: to 8pm) migros museum.ch

Several galleries with dynamic programming have made Zürich a leading international centre of contemporary art. One such gallery is the Migros Museum für Gegenwartskunst, which is located in the former Löwenbräu brewery. It specializes in organizing exhibitions of current art by Swiss and foreign artists. The museum provides an interactive space for reflection and viewing the works on display.

Hauptbahnhof

B1 Bahnhofplatz Zürich HB 4, 6, 8, 11, 13, 14 46

Zürich's Neo-Renaissance train station is one of the city's greatest icons. Completed in 1871, it is well preserved and the original structure of the main hall remains unaltered. The clean, well-kept concourse is filled with stalls throughout the year, and it is also used for seasonal fairs and markets. Beneath the concourse is a modern shopping centre.

From the concourse ceiling hangs an eye-catching sculpture, its vibrant, almost garish colours contrasting with the sobriety of the surroundings. This is *Guardian Angel* by the French sculptor Niki de Saint Phalle (1930–2002).

Bahnhofstrasse

B2 6, 7, 10, 11, 13

Running north to south from Bahnhofplatz to the edge of Zürichsee, Bahnhofstrasse is a long avenue that lies on the course of the medieval city's moat. Mostly pedestrianized, with tramlines running along it, this the centre of Zürich's commercial activity. It is lined with restaurants and shops, as well as the headquarters of several major Swiss banks.

Between Bahnhofstrasse (east) and Löwenstrasse (west) and Schweizergasse and Sihlstrasse (to the north and south) are Zürich's main department stores, Globus and Jelmoli, offering exclusive brands and upscale cafeteria-style dining. Beneath Beyer, a watch and jewellery shop, is the Uhrenmuseum Beyer, a clock museum containing a collection of timepieces ranging from simple sundials to elegant modern watches.

At Fraumünster, the street opens onto Paradeplatz on its western side. Once a military parade ground, the square is now lined with large buildings, including the headquarters of Sprüngli, the Swiss chocolatier. Bahnhofstrasse ends at Bürkliplatz. Facing onto Zürichsee, this square is the departure point for boat trips on the lake.

Did You Know?

Singer-songwriter Tina Turner lived in Zürich and was a Swiss citizen from 2013.

Langstrasse

A1 8 31, 32

Once a seedy red light district, "Long Street" is today a trendy area that features inexpensive boutiques and Zürich's best selection of global food stands. In July the four-day Latin music festival Caliente!, Europe's biggest Latin festival, takes over the street.

Parallel to the main railway line, and intersected by Langstrasse, is Europaallee, a vibrant and vivacious new district of

Trams plying along the Bahnhofstrasse, Zürich's main shopping street

↑ Panoramic views from the Lindenhof over the River Limmat and the Old Town

Zürich. The area has quickly become awash with a heady mix of culture, cutting-edge technology and the kind of modish shops and restaurants already found on Langstrasse.

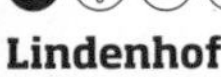

Lindenhof

C2 7, 10, 11, 13

This tree-covered hill rises on the west bank of the Limmat. Its strategic position made it an ideal location for a Celtic settlement and later for a Roman fort. In the 10th century, an imperial palace stood here. No buildings remain, but an observation platform offers a view of the surrounding rooftops and the university buildings. There's also a giant chess-board for open-air games.

Augustinerkirche

C2 Augustinerhof 8 7, 10, 11, 13 10am-7pm daily christkath-zuerich.ch

This beautiful early-Gothic church was built in the late 13th century for a community of Augustinian monks. When the monastery was dissolved during the Reformation, the church was deconsecrated and stood unused for almost 300 years. The interior was restored in the 1840s, and in 1847 the church was reconsecrated as a Roman Catholic church.

Kirche St Peter

C2 St-Peter-Hofstatt 6 4, 15 8am-6pm Mon-Fri, 10am-4pm Sat, 11am-5pm Sun st-peter-zh.ch

The most distinctive feature of the Church of St Peter is its clockface. With a diameter of 8.7 m (28 ft), it is the largest church clockface in Europe. This church stands on the site of a pre-Romanesque structure dating from the 9th century and its oldest surviving vestiges are those of a late Romanesque church erected in the early 13th century. They include the simple rectangular presbytery, which is lit by a semicircular window with an intricate frame. The presbytery is crowned by a mid-15th-century tower.

The main body of the church dates from 1705 to 1716. It takes the form of a galleried basilica with a striking Baroque interior. The dark panelling contrasts with the red columns of the nave and the brilliant white stucco decoration.

Zunfthaus zur Meisen

C3 Münsterhof 20 4, 15 By appt Mon-Sat zunfthaus-zur-meisen.ch

This elegant late Baroque house contains a collection of 18th-century faïence and porcelain, including pieces by Meissen and Sèvres. There are also locally made items produced by Schooren and other Swiss manufacturers.

EAT

Haus Hiltl

Try the saffron gnocchi at this pioneering vegetarian buffet.

B2 Sihlstrasse 28 hiltl.ch

Café & Conditorei 1842

Impossible-to-resist handmade chocolates tempt at this lavish cakebox of a café.

C2 Napfgasse 4 cafe1842.ch

The Fraumünster church and one of its Bodmer frescoes in the cloisters *(inset)* ↑

DRINK

Old Crow
Expertly mixed cocktails in an elegantly intimate setting.
C2 Schwanengasse 4 Mon & Sun oldcrow.ch

Widder
An extensive wine list served with an innovative menu.
C2 Rennweg 7 widderhotel.com

Tales Bar
Creative and bespoke cocktails, plus live music.
B2 Selnaustrassse 29 Mon & Sun tales-bar.ch

Raygrodski Bar
This cocktail bar buzzes with a hipsterish vibe.
A2 Sihlfeldstrasse 49 Sun raygrodski.ch

Fraumünster

C3 Am Münsterhofplatz 4, 15 Nov-Mar: 10am-5pm daily; Apr-Oct: 10am-6pm daily fraumuenster.ch

The history of the Women's Minster goes back to 853, when King Ludwig the German made his daughter Hildegard the abbess of a convent here. The convent was dissolved during the Reformation, and the site is occupied by the Stadthaus, a Neo-Gothic building that is now used for exhibitions.

The church, however, survives. It has a mid-13th-century presbytery in the late Romanesque style, an early-Gothic transept and a nave that has been remodelled several times. The Neo-Gothic façade was added in 1911.

The presbytery is lit by five stained-glass windows designed by Marc Chagall (1887–1985) and made in 1970. They depict biblical themes, and a different colour predominates in each. The central window, where green is the prevailing colour, depicts scenes from the life of Christ. It is flanked by a blue window with a design inspired by the visions of Jacob, and a yellow window known as the Zion Window, which features King David and the New Jerusalem. The rosette in the south transept, illustrating the Creation, was also designed by Chagall. The north transept has a window with a giant vision of Paradise created by Augusto Giacometti and installed in 1940.

The Romanesque cloisters on the south side of the church are decorated with frescoes executed by Paul Bodmer in 1923–32. They tell the story of the convent's foundation and illustrate the lives of Felix and Regula, the patron saints of Zürich, and of the city's legendary links with Emperor Charlemagne. The emperor is said to have founded Zürich when he discovered the graves of Felix and Regula, who deserted a Roman legion in the Valais and who were martyred for their Christian faith.

Grossmünster

C3 Grossmünsterplatz 4, 15 Mar-Oct: 10am-6pm daily; Nov-Feb: 10am-5pm daily grossmuenster.ch

The tall twin towers of the Grossmünster, or Great Minster, dominate Zürich's skyline from the east bank of the Limmat. According to legend, Charlemagne founded a church here in the late 8th to early 9th century, on the graves of Felix and Regula. After they were killed at the site of the Wasserkirche, these martyrs are said to have carried their heads up the hill to the spot now marked by the Grossmünster.

Construction of the present basilica began in about 1100, and the west towers were eventually completed in the late 15th century.

DADA

The avant-garde artistic movement Dada came to prominence in Zürich in around 1916, as an anarchic reaction to the senseless carnage of World War I. The focus of the movement was the Cabaret Voltaire in Zürich and among its main exponents were Tristan Tzara, Hans Arp and Francis Picabia. Dada's aim was to flout convention and the traditions of the artistic establishment through irony.

It was from the pulpit of the Grossmünster that the humanist Ulrich Zwingli preached the Reformation. In line with reformist ideals, the minster was stripped of its furnishings and decoration, so that the interior is now almost completely bare. However, vestiges of Gothic frescoes as well as the fine Romanesque capitals of the nave survive.

The Grossmünster's large crypt contains a 15th-century statue of Charlemagne, which originally graced the south tower. (The present statue on the tower is a replica.) Other notable features are its Romanesque portal, with a bronze door (1935), and stained-glass windows by Augusto Giacometti (1932).

Rathaus

C2 Limmatquai 55 4, 15 By guided tour only: Mon (book one month in advance) kantonsrat.zh.ch

Zürich's town hall was built on piles driven into the riverbed, and the waters of the Limmat flow beneath the platform on which it stands. The two-storey building dates from 1694–8.

The Rathaus's façade is ornamented with friezes featuring masks, the windows crowned with broken pediments filled with busts. The marble doorway has gilt decoration. One of its most impressive rooms is the Baroque council chamber.

Limmatquai

C2 4, 15

This pleasant riverside boulevard snakes along the east bank of the Limmat, running between the Bellevueplatz in the south and the Bahnhofbrücke in the north. The most interesting stretch of Limmatquai is its southern section, lined with guild houses, which have been converted into trendy shops or restaurants offering alfresco dining.

Among the finest of these houses are Haus zur Saffran at No 54, dating from around 1720; Haus zur Rüden at No 42, dating from the 17th century; and the adjoining Haus zur Zimmerleuten, an 18th-century building with a colourful oriel window.

Niederdorf

C2 4, 15

Consisting of a dense network of cobbled alleys leading towards Limmatquai, this small district constitutes the heart of the Old Town's eastern section. The main artery through this historic district is Niederdorfstrasse, a pedestrianized thoroughfare that turns into Münstergasse to the south. Niederdorf's narrow alleys are lined with antiques shops and art galleries, as well as small hotels, cafés, restaurants, beer halls and fast-food outlets.

↑ A narrow cobbled street in the picturesque old quarter of Niederdorf

Eidgenössische Technische Hochschule

D2 6, 9, 10
Rämistrasse 101
ethz.ch

The Federal Institute of Technology, or ETH, opened in 1855, and today it is one of the most highly regarded universities in the world. It occupies a Neo-Renaissance building designed by Gottfried Semper, a prominent German architect who was also the institute's first professor of architecture.

The architecture of the building is of interest in its own right, as are the displays from the eclectic Graphische Sammlung (Graphic Collection) of drawings and graphic art, and the temporary exhibitions that often fill its corridors. The ETH also owns the **Thomas-Mann-Archiv**, in a building nearby. The archive holds the entire literary legacy of this great German writer, who died in Zürich in August 1955.

The terrace of the ETH building commands a magnificent view of the city. Located just to the north of the ETH is the upper station of the Polybahn, a funicular that runs down to Central, a large square on the east side of the Bahnhofbrücke.

STREET PARADE

The city's single biggest event, drawing over a million fans, the Street Parade *(www.streetparade.com)* is the biggest techno music parade in the world. It takes place every second Sunday in August. The theme is "culture of tolerance". There are around 30 mobile stages and 8 concert platforms. There is even an "Antiparade" for techno fans who think the main festival has sold out music's core values.

Thomas-Mann-Archiv
Schönberggasse 15
10am–5pm Mon–Fri
tma.ethz.ch

Zürichsee

C4 2, 4, 5, 8, 9, 11, 15
912, 916

This beautiful glacial lake stretches in a 40-km (25-mile) arc from Zürich to the foot of the Glarner Alps, at its eastern tip. Many boat trips, run by such companies as **ZSG**, depart from the city. Ranging from short trips to half- and full-day cruises, they take in several lakeshore towns and villages. Zürichsee's clear blue waters are unpolluted and there are many beaches, lidos and swimming areas along the shoreline.

ZSG
Mythenquai 333 zsg.ch

18

Opernhaus

C3 Falkenstrasse 1
Stadelhofen 2, 4
opernhaus.ch

Zürich's Neo-Baroque opera house stages a world-class

The serene Zürichsee harbour lined with boats at sunset

programme of opera and ballet. It was designed by the Viennese architects Hermann Helmer and Ferdinand Fellner and completed in 1891. The elegant façade is fronted by two tiers of columns and a balcony framed by porticoes.

19 Zürichhorn Park

D5 912, 916

This pleasant park contains sculptures by well-known modern artists. At the southern end is a large kinetic sculpture that Jean Tinguely created for Expo 64 in Lausanne; entitled *Heureka*, it is set in motion from April to mid-October at 11:15am and 5:15pm daily.

In the eastern part of the park high walls enclose the **Chinagarten**. This Chinese garden, laid out in 1994, was a gift from the city of Kunming, and is filled with plants, buildings and objects typical of a Chinese formal garden.

Bordering the park, on Höschgasse, is the **Atelier Hermann Haller**, the studio of this Swiss sculptor. Designed by Haller (1880–1950), it is a rare example of wooden Bauhaus architecture. Next to it is the Pavillon Le Corbusier, which hosts exhibitions and concerts.

Chinagarten
Mid-Mar-mid-Oct: 11am-7pm daily.

Atelier Hermann Haller
Höschgasse 8a 044 383 42 47 Until 2025 for renovation

20 Museum Rietberg

B4 Gablerstrasse 15 5 10am-5pm Tue-Sun (Wed: to 8pm) rietberg.ch

The vast assemblage of ethnographic pieces and artifacts that make up the collections of this museum is displayed in two villas (covered by a single entry ticket) linked by extensive underground exhibition areas. Villa Wesendonck, a Neo-Classical mansion in which the composer Richard Wagner once stayed, houses the main collection. This consists of wooden, bronze and ceramic objects from Africa, India, China, Japan and other Southeast Asian countries. The neighbouring Park-Villa Rieter is devoted to Asian art. Two floors of the house are filled with changing selections of Indian, Chinese and Japanese prints and paintings.

21 FIFA World Football Museum

B4 Seestrasse 27 5, 6, 7, 8, 10 10am-6pm Tue-Sun fifamuseum.com

Zürich has been the home of FIFA, world football's governing body, since 1932. This excellent museum, which opened in 2016, offers an in-depth look at football's past and hints at its future. Exhibits here feature FIFA's founding documents, rare team shirts, unique photos, balls used in historic matches and the actual World Cup trophy. There is also a special kids' trail, with interactive games, and a cinema showing films on the game's history.

↑ Exhibits on display at the Villa Wesendonck, Museum Rietberg

22 Städtische Sukkulentensammlung

B5 Mythenquai 88 161, 165 9am-4:30pm daily stadt-zuerich.ch/sukkulenten

Comprising more than 8,000 species of cactuses, spurges, agaves, aloes and other succulents, this collection, founded in 1931, is one of the largest of its kind in Europe. Amazing succulents from every arid region of the world, from giant agaves to the tiniest cactuses, are found here in a fascinating display.

INSIDER TIP
Thermalbad and Spa Zürich

Bathe in wooden vats in this former brewery turned spa, not far from Museum Rietberg (*www.aqua-spa-resorts.ch*). The water is drawn from the legendary "Aqui" springs.

Looking across the Swiss plateau from Mount Rigi

NORTHERN SWITZERLAND

Bordered by the Rhine to the north and the Jura to the southwest, this relatively flat area was settled by the Celts around 450 BCE. By 44 BCE, the Romans, attracted by the trade opportunities opened by the Rhine, founded the town of Augusta Raurica, in the area east of what is now Basel, and soon spread westwards. On the banks of the Rhine, this port town soon became a centre of commerce, developing a wealthy merchant class. At the behest of a Papal bull, Basel Council established Switzerland's oldest university here, in 1460, to educate its wealthy sons. Around this time, Baden, to the east, had become an *ad hoc* capital city for the expanding Swiss Confederation, and the regular meeting place for the executive council. A popular spa town since Roman times, thanks to its natural thermal springs, Baden's reputation as a resort began to spread in the 15th century. Refugees of the War of Religion brought trade and industry to the flourishing northern cantons throughout the 1500s, and, by the 19th century, northern Switzerland was industrialized, and had become the country's most populated region.

NORTHERN SWITZERLAND

Must Sees

1. Basel
2. Baden
3. Winterthur

Experience More

4. Riehen
5. Augusta Raurica
6. Zofingen
7. Dornach
8. Aarau
9. Muri
10. Kloster Königsfelden
11. Wettingen
12. Regensberg
13. Kaiserstuhl
14. Eglisau

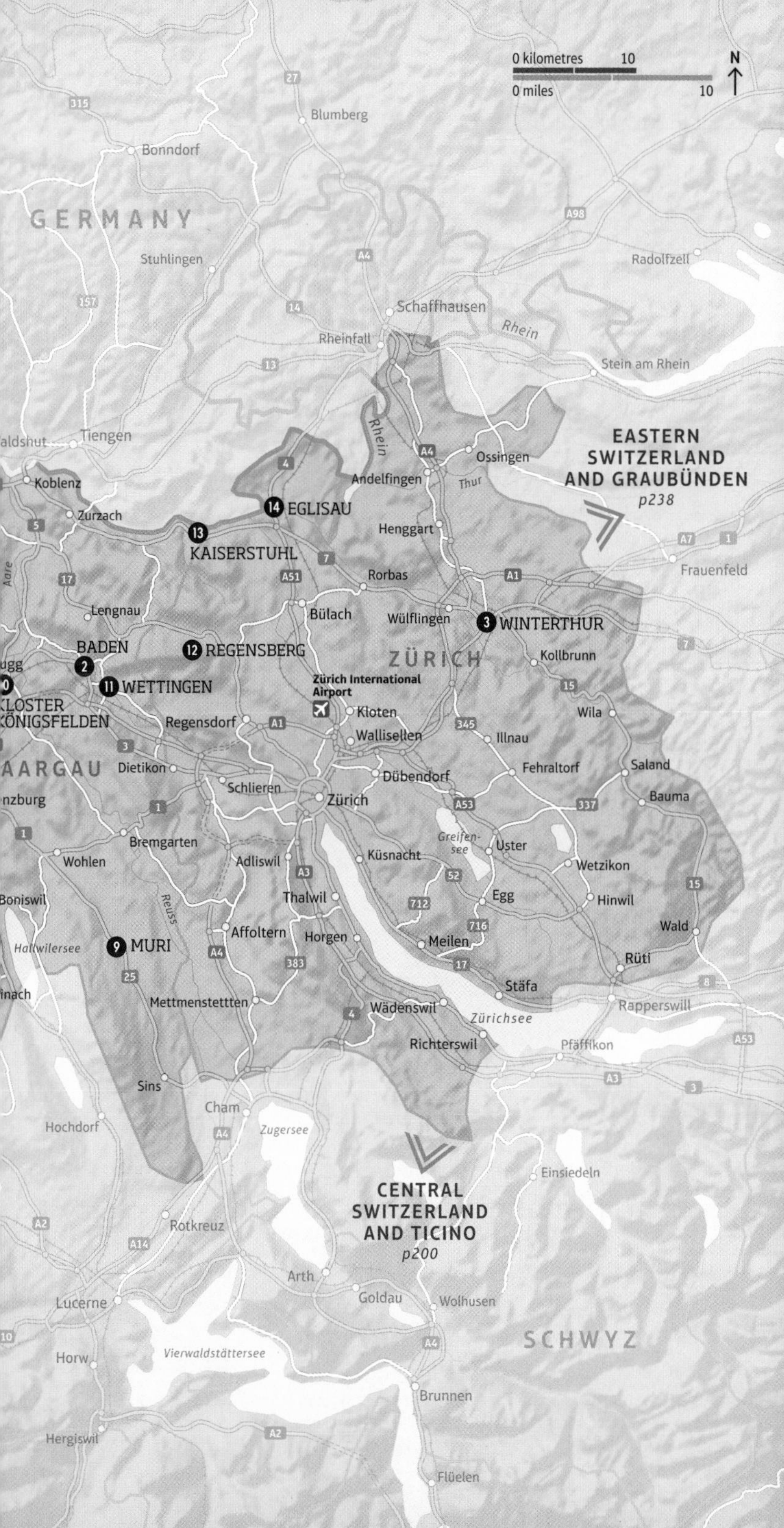

0 kilometres 10
0 miles 10
N
GERMANY
Blumberg
Bonndorf
Stuhlingen
Radolfzell
Schaffhausen
Rheinfall
Rhein
Stein am Rhein
Tiengen
Koblenz
Zurzach
Andelfingen
Ossingen
Thur
EASTERN SWITZERLAND AND GRAUBÜNDEN
p238
14 EGLISAU
13 KAISERSTUHL
Henggart
Frauenfeld
Rorbas
Lengnau
Bülach
Wülflingen
3 WINTERTHUR
BADEN
2
12 REGENSBERG
ZÜRICH
Kollbrunn
11 WETTINGEN
Zürich International Airport
KLOSTER KÖNIGSFELDEN
Kloten
Wila
Regensdorf
Wallisellen
Illnau
AARGAU
Dietikon
Dübendorf
Fehraltorf
Saland
Schlieren
Zürich
Bauma
Bremgarten
Greifensee
Uster
Wohlen
Adliswil
Küsnacht
Wetzikon
Thalwil
Egg
Hinwil
Reuss
Affoltern
Horgen
Meilen
Wald
Hallwilersee
9 MURI
Rüti
Mettmenstettten
Stäfa
Wädenswil
Rapperswil
Zürichsee
Richterswil
Pfäffikon
Sins
Cham
Hochdorf
Zugersee
CENTRAL SWITZERLAND AND TICINO
p200
Einsiedeln
Rotkreuz
Arth
Goldau
Wolhusen
Lucerne
SCHWYZ
Horw
Vierwaldstättersee
Brunnen
Hergiswil
Flüelen

↑ Basel's riverside Old Town under the towering presence of the cathedral

BASEL

C2 Basel Stadtcasino, Barfüsserplatz; Steinenberg 4, Bahnhof Basel SBB train station; www.basel.com

Mention the city of Basel and most people today will think of industry or art. Straddling the Rhine, this city is the country's only port and as such is a major centre of industry, with a long history of pharmaceutical expertise. The city is also one of Switzerland's most cultured, hosting Art Basel, the world's largest contemporary art fair. It is also famous for its festivals, the largest of which, Fasnacht, is an exuberant masked carnival.

① Jüdisches Museum der Schweiz

Kornhausgasse 8 3 30, 34 1-4pm Mon-Fri, 11am-5pm Sun juedisches-museum.ch

Through a variety of artifacts dating back to the 13th century, including liturgical objects, the museum illustrates Jewish religion and customs, and the history and daily life of this community. It is the only Jewish museum in Switzerland. The Jewish population in Basel is the second largest in Switzerland after Geneva. The first Zionist Congress took place in Basel, in 1897.

② Universität

Petersplatz 1 3 30, 34

Founded in 1460, Basel's university is the oldest in the country. Among the illustrious figures with whom it is associated are the humanist Erasmus of Rotterdam (1466–1536), the mathematician Jakob Bernoulli (1654–1705) and the philosopher Friedrich Nietzsche (1844–1900). The present university building is the Kollegienhaus, a great Modernist edifice on the east side of Petersplatz, completed in 1946. The entrance to the building is embellished with mosaics depicting the university's founders, and the main hall has stained-glass windows.

③ Spalentor

Spalenvorstadt 3 30, 33

This monumental Gothic gate stands at the entrance to

↑ The Gothic crenellated turrets framing the old city gate, the Spalentor

Spalenvorstadt, a narrow alley lined with picturesque shuttered houses, on the west side of the Old Town (Altstadt). Built in 1370, the Spalentor formed part of the defensive walls that once encircled Basel. The tower consists of a pair of crenellated turrets framing a square central section, which has a pointed roof laid with glazed red, black and white tiles. The gate, which has wooden doors and a portcullis, is embellished with sculptures and on its west side it bears the arms of the city.

④ **Spielzeug Welten Museum Basel**

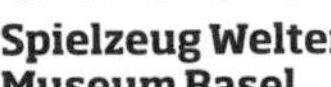

Steinenvorstadt 1 | 3, 6, 8, 11, 14, 15, 16, 17 | 10am-6pm Tue-Sun (daily in Dec) | spielzeug-welten-museum-basel.ch

With more than 6,000 items laid out on four floors, the Toy Worlds Museum in Basel is the largest of its kind in Europe. Most of the exhibits date from the late 19th to the early 20th centuries, although there are some contemporary pieces displayed as well. All the dolls' houses and miniature shops on display are meticulously decorated and furnished. The collection also includes mechanical models, teddy bears and a variety of other stuffed animals made by leading toymakers of today and yesterday.

Even if you don't have time to go in, the museum is always worth a visit – the spectacular window displays are an event in themselves.

↑ A mannequin and a bicycle on display in the Spielzeug Welten Museum Basel

Hebelstrasse · Bernoullistr. · Botanischer Garten · Petersplatz · ② Universität · ③ Spalentor · Jüdisches Museum der Schweiz ① · Pharmaziehistorisches Museum Basel ⑤ · Marktplatz ⑦ · ⑭ Rathaus · Martinskirche · Mittlere Rheinbrücke · Rhein · ⑯ Kleinbasel · Naturhistorisches Museum · Museum der Kulturen · ⑬ Augustinergasse · Münsterplatz · ⑱ Basel Münster · Wettsteinbrücke · Museum Tinguely 800 m (870 yd) ⑰ · Leonhardskirche ⑧ · ⑨ Historisches Museum · Antikenmuseum ⑥ · ⑲ Kunstmuseum Basel · St Alban ⑮ · St Alban Kirche · Spielzeug Welten Museum Basel ④ · ⑪ Schweizerisches Architekturmuseum · ⑩ Kunsthalle · Stadttheater · ⑫ Haus zum Kirschgarten · Aeschenplatz · Zoologischer Garten · Bahnhofplatz · Basel Station

0 metres 400 · 0 yards 400 · N

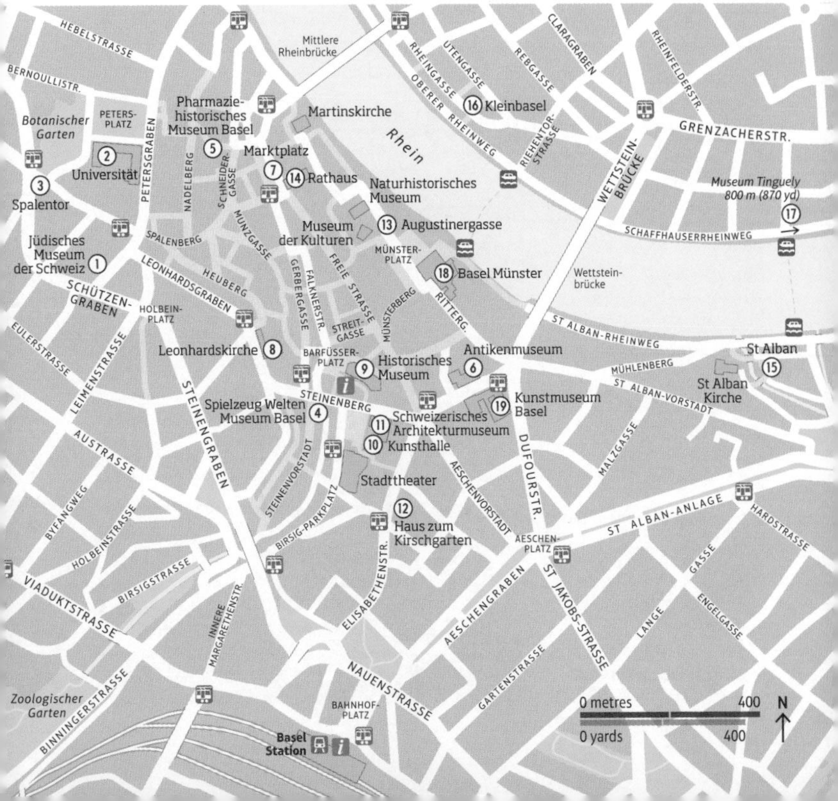

Pharmazie-historisches Museum Basel

Totengäslein 3 6, 8, 11, 14, 15, 16, 17 10am-5pm Tue-Sun pharmaziemuseum.ch

As befits one of the world's centres of the pharmaceutical industry, Basel has a museum devoted to the history of medicinal chemistry. It features instruments and medicines used by apothecaries through the ages, and is located in the house where Erasmus and Paracelsus once lived. There are also reconstructions of a pharmacy and a laboratory.

Antikenmuseum

St Alban-Graben 1, 2, 15 11am-5pm Tue & Wed (Thu & Fri: to 10pm), 10am-4pm Sat & Sun antikenmuseumbasel.ch

Basel's museum of antiquities covers over 5,000 years of history, and is devoted to the four great early civilizations of the Mediterranean basin – ancient Greece, Etruria, Rome and Egypt. The Greek pieces include a fine collection of vases from the Archaic to the Classical periods, marble sculpture, bronze figurines, pottery, coins and jewellery. The collections of Etruscan pottery and Roman and Egyptian art are equally impressive.

Marktplatz

Kornhausgasse 8 3, 6, 8, 11, 14, 15, 16, 17 061 261 95 14 7am-2pm Tue-Thu (Fri & Sat: to 6pm)

Every weekday morning, Marktplatz is filled with the stalls of a produce market, and on public holidays it becomes the hub of Basel's seasonal festivals. The square is lined with fine buildings dating from the late 19th to the early 20th centuries.

Just to the northeast of the Marktplatz is Mittlere Rheinbrücke. Near the bridge is a curious, bearded figure, the Lällekönig (Tongue King), which has become the symbol of Basel. It is a static replica of an amusing 19th-century mechanical figure that rolled its eyes and stuck out its tongue at passers-by. The original figure is in the Historisches Museum.

Leonhardskirche

Kohlenberg 3 9am-4pm Tue-Sun

The church of St Leonard overlooks the city from its hilltop location. It stands on the site of an 11th-century

Every weekday morning, Marktplatz is filled with the stalls of a produce market, and on public holidays it becomes the hub of Basel's seasonal festivals.

Basel's bustling Marktplatz, with stalls set up for market day ↑

church, whose Romanesque crypt survives. After the 1356 earthquake that destroyed much of Basel, the church was rebuilt in the Gothic style. The interior features 15th- and 16th-century Gothic paintings and a rood screen from 1455.

9 Historisches Museum

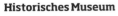

Barfüsserplatz 3, 6, 8, 11, 14, 15, 16, 17 10am-5pm Wed-Sun hmb.ch

The headquarters of three separate history museums, this collection occupies the Barfüsserkirche, a former Franciscan church. The Historisches Museum traces Basel's history from its beginnings as a Celtic settlement. Exhibits include pottery, silver-mounted vessels, wooden chests and Gothic, Renaissance and Baroque liturgical vessels, as well as other items from the cathedral treasury. There are also tapestries, altarpieces and weapons on display.

10 Kunsthalle

Steinenberg 7 1, 2, 3, 8, 10, 11, 14, 15, E11 11am-6pm Tue, Wed & Fri, 11am-8:30pm Thu, 11am-5pm Sat & Sun kunsthallebasel.ch

Thanks to the Kunsthalle, Basel is a well-established forerunner in the world of modern art. One of the city's most prominent cultural institutions, the Kunsthalle hosts a rolling programme of exhibitions of work by leading contemporary artists. The Kunsthalle is located opposite the Theater Basel, another institution in the city's cultural hub. Between the two buildings stands a fountain that incorporates several of Jean Tinguely's kinetic sculptures, created in a style known as metamechanics.

BASEL FASNACHT

Starting in early morning darkness, Basel gets turned upside down for *die drey scheenschte Dääg* ("the three most beautiful days") of the year. During Switzerland's biggest carnival, a sea of illuminated lanterns and thousands of costumed music-makers and masked *Fasnächtler* (participants) pour through the city streets for parties, parades and music.

11 Schweizerisches Architekturmuseum

Steinenberg 7 11am-6pm Tue, Wed & Fri, 11am-8:30pm Thu, 11am-5pm Sat & Sun sam-basel.org

The Kunsthalle also houses Switzerland's museum of architecture. This museum seeks to expand people's perceptions of architecture and urban development, concentrating primarily on the architecture of the early 20th century onwards, with an array of displays in Neo-Baroque rooms. The Architecture Museum also hosts temporary exhibitions, which showcase the work of Swiss architects, and of international architecture, as well as related subjects such as architectural photography, the effect of acoustics on a building's design and the links between art and architecture. There is also a programme of public workshops and lectures.

12 Haus zum Kirschgarten

Elisabethenstrasse 27-29 1,2 Summer: 11am-5pm Wed-Sun hmb.ch

This Rococo mansion, built in 1775–80, was the residence of J R Burckhardt, the owner of a silk mill. Furnished in period style, it now houses a museum that illustrates patrician life in the 18th and 19th centuries. On the first and second floors there are elegantly furnished drawing rooms, a dining room, a music salon and a kitchen. The top floor contains a display of rocking horses and other toys. The ground floor and basement are filled with a superb collection of ceramics, including Italian faïence, clocks and fine porcelain made at major European factories.

← Ornately decorated 18th-century clock in the Haus zum Kirschgarten

A visitor looking at a Papua New Guinean mask of initiation at the Museum der Kulturen

Augustinergasse

6, 8, 11, 14, 15, 16, 17

Augustinergasse is an alley that runs north from Münsterplatz, along the escarpment on the south side of the Rhine. As well as a Renaissance fountain with a figure of a basilisk, the street contains several 14th- and 15th-century houses.

The handsome Neo-Classical building at No 2 houses the **Naturhistorisches Museum**, which contains an extensive collection of minerals, and has sections devoted to zoology and palaeontology. Around the corner is the **Museum der Kulturen**, set in a building crowned with a shimmering fishscale roof that was designed by Basel architects Herzog & de Meuron. This anthropology museum examines cultures from around the world. Among the finest pieces are wooden reliefs from Tikal, the ancient Maya site in Guatemala.

Naturhistorisches Museum
Augustinergasse 2
10am-5pm Tue-Sun (1st Wed of month: to 8pm) nmbs.ch

Museum der Kulturen
Münsterplatz 20
10am-5pm Tue-Sun
mkb.ch

14

Rathaus

Marktplatz 9 6, 8, 11, 14, 15, 16, 17

The main feature of Basel's Marktplatz is the Rathaus, the Gothic town hall with a bright red façade. The central arcaded section of the building dates from 1504–21, while the tower and annexe date from the 19th century. The inner courtyard is painted with frescoes from the 16th century, though they are heavily restored. Tours in many languages, including English, can be arranged through the tourist office.

St Alban

3

The district of St Alban takes its name from the church of a former Benedictine monastery founded in the 11th century. The canal that runs through this attractive district was used to power the monastery's mills. One of these, the **Basler Papiermühle**, now houses a museum of paper, writing and printing. Visitors can watch paper being made by hand. The **Museum für Gegenwartskunst** (Museum of Contemporary Art), a short distance from the mill, showcases contemporary art.

Basler Papiermühle
St Alban-Tal 37
11am-5pm Tue-Fri & Sun, 1-5pm Sat baslerpapiermuehle.ch

Museum für Gegenwartskunst
St Alban-Rheinweg 60 11am-6pm Tue-Sun kunstmuseumbasel.ch

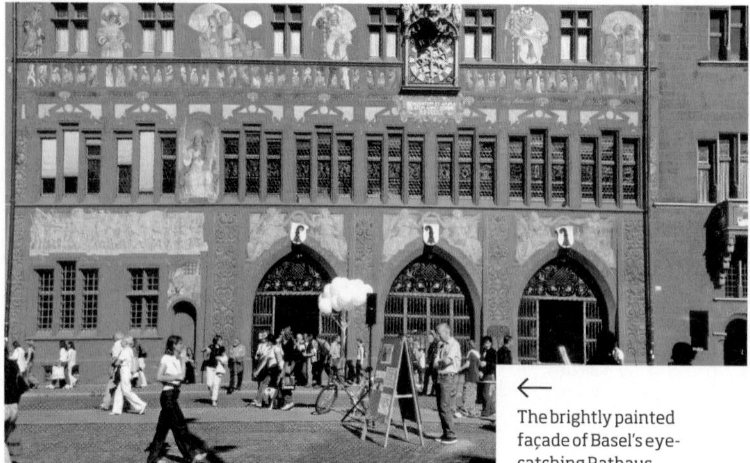

The brightly painted façade of Basel's eye-catching Rathaus

A visitor interacting with one of Jean Tinguely's kinetic sculptures

Kleinbasel

6, 8, 14, 15, 17 31, 34, 38

The first permanent bridge over the Rhine at Basel was built here in 1226. A small fortress was subsequently established on the north bank, and the settlement that grew up around it became part of the city in the late 14th century. For centuries, Kleinbasel – which translates as "Lesser Basel" – was inhabited mainly by the poorer sector of the city's population. In recent years, however, the area has been gentrified and it now buzzes with trendy galleries, cafés and restaurants.

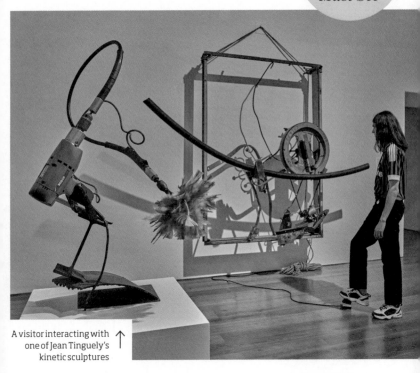

INSIDER TIP
Museum Pass

Valid for a full year, the Museum Pass is a good option if you plan to visit a few of Basel's 37 museums. The pass also gets you into castles, museums, gardens and parks across Germany, France and Switzerland.

Museum Tinguely

Paul-Sacher Anlage 2 31, 36, 38, 42 11am-9pm Thu tinguely.ch

This pale pink sandstone building, designed by the Swiss architect Mario Botta, stands in Solitude Park, on the banks of the Rhine. The museum is devoted to the work of Jean Tinguely, famous for his kinetic sculptures and interactive drawing machines.

Born in Fribourg in 1925, he was educated in Basel. He later settled in New York in 1960, but in 1968 he returned to his native country, where he lived until his death in 1991. The nucleus of the collection consists of works by Tinguely, donated by his wife, the artist Niki de Saint Phalle. These pieces, along with many later gifts, bequests and purchases, allow visitors to trace Tinguely's artistic development.

While various engine-driven contraptions that visitors can set in motion occupy the mezzanine, the upper floor is home to various items associated with Tinguely. The central exhibit on the ground floor is a huge sculpture, Tinguely's *Grosse Méta Maxi-Maxi Utopia* (1987). The museum also stages exhibitions concentrating on aspects of Tinguely's work, including its Dadaist roots.

Did You Know?

Jean Tinguely created his first piece of kinetic art when he was 12 years old.

18

BASEL MÜNSTER

Münsterplatz 9 1, 2, 15 Apr-Oct: 10am-5pm Mon-Fri, 10am- 4pm Sat, 11:30am-4pm Sun; Nov-Mar: 10am-4pm Mon-Sat, 12:30-4 pm Sun baslermuenster.ch

Set on a hill above the Rhine, Basel's monumental cathedral is a conspicuous and majestic presence in the city. With dark red sandstone walls and patterned roof tiles, it is a vivid monument to Romanesque and Gothic architecture.

The church that originally stood on this site was built in the 8th century, but the present cathedral was begun in the 12th century. Partly damaged by an earthquake in 1356, it was rebuilt in the Gothic style, although elements of the earlier building were also incorporated into the structure. In the 16th century, as a result of the Reformation, the cathedral was stripped of almost all its furnishings and decoration. However, some fine Romanesque and Gothic sculptures survive, as does the church's 19th-century stained glass and the beautiful 14th-century frescoes in the crypt. On the south side of the cathedral are peaceful Gothic cloisters, with several tombs and epitaphs that give this part of the complex its dignified, contemplative character.

The ambulatory is lit by 19th-century stained-glass windows depicting the Nativity, Crucifixion and Resurrection of Christ.
Carved elephants adorn the windows of the choir.
The magnificent Romanesque Galluspforte portal has carvings depicting Judgment Day and works of mercy.

↑ A fine Nativity scene among the frescoes on the ceiling of the crypt

↑ The cathedral's exterior, with its patterned roof atop sturdy sandstone walls

On the south side of the cathedral are peaceful Gothic cloisters, with several tombs and epitaphs that give this part of the complex its dignified, contemplative character.

Did You Know?

The hill on which the cathedral is located was a Celtic *oppidum* (fortified town) in the 1st century BCE.

The Georgesturm features a figure of St George. The whiter stonework at its lower levels formed part of the 11th-century church.
The Martinsturm culminates in a decorative fleuron completed in 1500.
Intricately carved, the 1486 font is an outstanding example of late-Gothic sculpture.
The roof is decorated with green and yellow tiles.
The late Romanesque Panel of the Apostles in the north aisle shows six of the apostles.

↑ The Basel Münster, a heritage site of national significance

19

KUNSTMUSEUM BASEL

St Alban-Graben 16 1, 2, 15 10am-6pm Tue-Sun (Wed: to 8pm)
kunstmuseumbasel.ch

The prestigious Kunstmuseum Basel is the largest art museum in Switzerland, with an impressive collection of paintings and sculpture spanning the early 15th century to the modern day.

Ranging from 17th-century Dutch and Flemish paintings through 19th-century works by Delacroix and Pissarro to 20th-century art, including works by Rousseau, Picasso and Dalí, the Kunstmuseum Basel's collection is vast. The galleries on the first floor of the museum's main building are hung with works of art from the 15th to 19th centuries, while the second floor is devoted to 20th-century art. Located across the street from the original 1930s building, a concrete minimalist extension (connected to the main building by an underground passageway) hosts special exhibitions and changing displays from the permanent collection.

Entry to the museum is free on the first Sunday of every month and also between 5 and 6pm on Tuesday, Wednesday, Friday and Saturday. There are regular guided tours, including some in English.

ART BASEL

Each year, members of the art world gather in the city for Art Basel. This internationally renowned art fair - and an absolute highlight of the art calendar - is a week-long celebration of top modern and contemporary works from around the globe.

1 Auguste Rodin's evocative bronze *Burghers of Calais* sculpture is on display in the Kunstmuseum's inner courtyard.

2 The Modernist façade of the Kunstmuseum Basel was designed by Basel-based architect Rudolf Christ.

3 Dating from 1627, *David Presenting Saul with the Head of Goliath* is a small-scale painting of the well-known biblical story; it is one of Rembrandt's earlier works.

Did You Know?

The museum holds the world's largest collection of paintings by Hans Holbein the Younger.

↑ Inside the Kunstmuseum Basel, with its colourful stained-glass windows

A SHORT WALK
OLD TOWN

Distance 2 km (1 mile) **Nearest tram** Schifflände **Time** 30 minutes

The nucleus of Basel's medieval Old Town, or Altstadt, lines the escarpment of the south bank of the Rhine. The hub of the Old Town is Barfüsserplatz, a buzzing square lined with cafés and crossed by trams, and its major landmarks are the Basel Münster, Basel's great Romanesque-Gothic cathedral, and the unmistakable Rathaus, the brightly painted town hall on Marktplatz. With shopping streets, several churches, steep alley-ways and leafy courtyards, this is Basel's busiest district. As many streets in the Old Town are closed to motor traffic, it is a pleasant area to explore on foot.

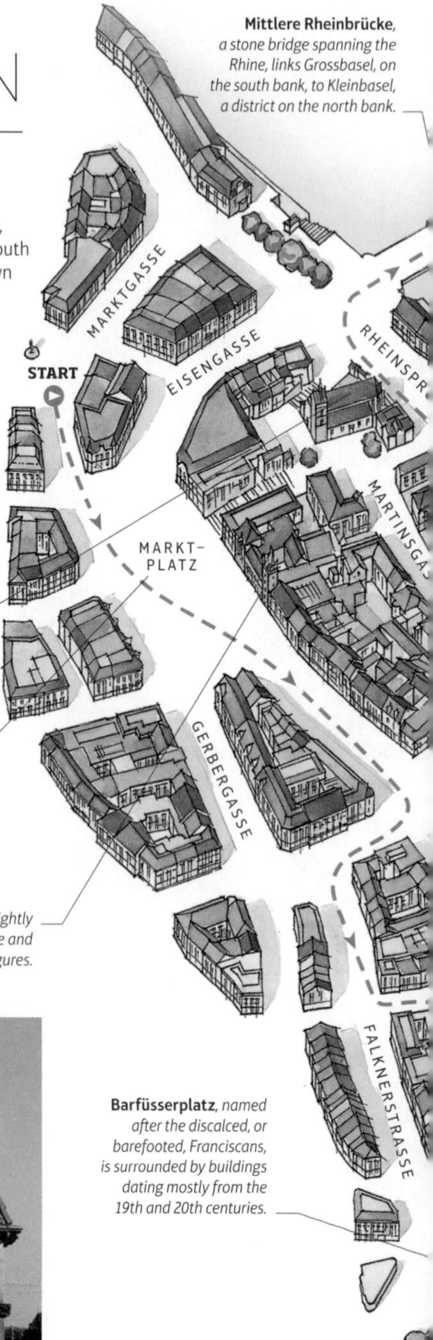

Mittlere Rheinbrücke, *a stone bridge spanning the Rhine, links Grossbasel, on the south bank, to Kleinbasel, a district on the north bank.*

MARKTGASSE

EISENGASSE

RHEINSPR

START

MARTINSGA

MARKT-PLATZ

GERBERGASSE

FALKNERSTRASSE

Dating from the 14th century, **Martinskirche** *is the oldest parish church in Basel.*

Marktplatz (p180) *has for centuries served as a market-place. It is also the hub of the city's festivals.*

The **Rathaus** (p182) *has a brightly and elaborately painted façade and a clock surmounted by figures.*

Barfüsserplatz, *named after the discalced, or barefooted, Franciscans, is surrounded by buildings dating mostly from the 19th and 20th centuries.*

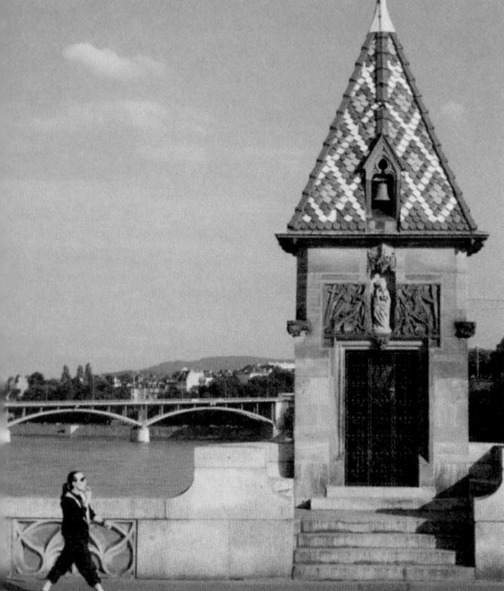

←

Walking along Mittlere Rheinbrücke, with its decorated towers

INISH

→ The medieval Basel Münster, looming over Munsterplatz

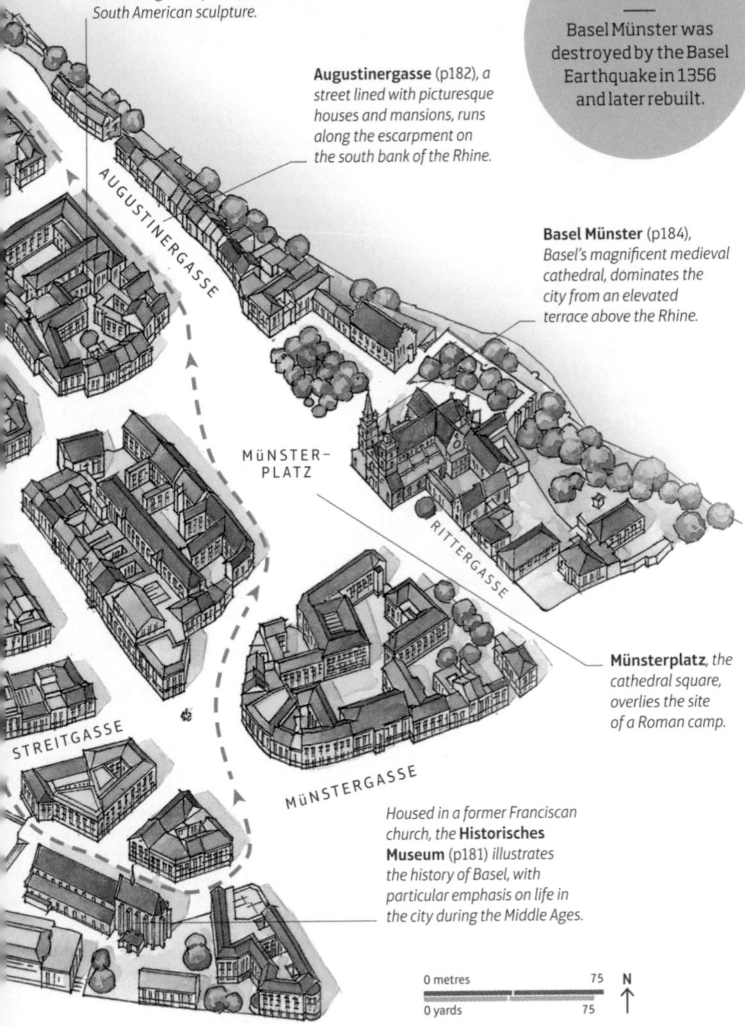

Basel's ethnographic museum, **Museum der Kulturen** *(p182), contains an extensive collection, including some oustanding examples of Pre-Columbian South American sculpture.*

Did You Know?

Basel Münster was destroyed by the Basel Earthquake in 1356 and later rebuilt.

Augustinergasse (p182), *a street lined with picturesque houses and mansions, runs along the escarpment on the south bank of the Rhine.*

AUGUSTINERGASSE

Basel Münster (p184), *Basel's magnificent medieval cathedral, dominates the city from an elevated terrace above the Rhine.*

MÜNSTER-PLATZ

RITTERGASSE

Münsterplatz, *the cathedral square, overlies the site of a Roman camp.*

STREITGASSE

MÜNSTERGASSE

Housed in a former Franciscan church, the **Historisches Museum** *(p181) illustrates the history of Basel, with particular emphasis on life in the city during the Middle Ages.*

0 metres 75
0 yards 75
N

Autumnal view across the terraces from the ruins of Baden's castle ↑

BADEN

D2 Aargau  Bahnhofplatz 1; www.baden.ch

One of Switzerland's oldest health resorts, Baden (meaning "baths") is a peaceful, stately town. The therapeutic properties of its hot sulphur springs, which the Romans knew as Aquae Helveticae, have been exploited since ancient times. From the Middle Ages, Baden's location on the River Limmat has contributed to it becoming an important centre of trade, and its beautiful Old Town is the legacy of this historical status. Today, Baden is still a popular spa centre, with facilities for large numbers of visitors, as well as a thriving industrial town. A good place to begin exploring Baden's Old Town is the east bank of the Limmat. From here, the rest of the Old Town is reached by crossing a wooden bridge.

Ruine Stein

The ruins of a castle look eastwards towards the Old Town from the top of a rocky promontory, beneath which runs a road tunnel. Originally built in the 10th century, the castle passed through the hands of several noble families before being inherited by the Habsburgs in 1264. It was rebuilt in the 13th century as an arsenal and fortress for Austrian forces, when Baden and the surrounding area fell under *Vorderösterreich* (Further Austria). In 1712, the castle was destroyed during conflicts between Protestant and Catholic cantons. Today these ruins are wreathed by green spaces, making it a pleasant place for a stroll. The hilltop offers a splendid view over the curving passage of the River Limmat and of the picturesque Old Town laid before it.

Stadtturm

Schlossbergplatz 3
056 200 87 87

This tall four-sided tower was built in the 15th century to guard the Old Town. It is set with four corner turrets, and its steep roof of red, black and white tiles is crowned by a belfry. The tower also features a clock framed by frescoes.

③

Pfarrkirche Mariä Himmelfahrt

Kirchplatz 056 222 57 15

Baden's parish church, the Church of the Assumption, was built in the centre of

INSIDER TIP
Spanisch Brötli

A light, flaky pastry, filled with a tasty mix of roasted and crushed hazelnuts and apricot jam, this baked treat is a Baden speciality. Enjoy it warm from the oven with a cup of coffee as a delicious morning snack.

Did You Know?

The Reformed church by Bahnhofplatz was built from the stones of the castle after it was destroyed.

the Old Town between 1457 and 1460. Although it was remodelled on several occasions, acquiring Baroque features in the 17th century and Neo-Classical elements in the early 19th, it retains its original Gothic outline, and is topped by a pointed spire. The church treasury, with a collection of liturgical objects, is open to visitors by appointment only.

④

Stadthaus

Rathausgasse 1 8am-noon Mon-Fri baden.ch

The Stadthaus, Baden's town hall, located north of the church, contains a thoughtfully restored council chamber, the Tagsatzungssaal. It was here that the Swiss Diet, an early version of Switzerland's parliament, sat from 1426 to 1712. This well-preserved chamber is lined with wood panelling and beautifully carved wooden adornments. The striking stained-glass windows, which feature the emblems of 13 of the Swiss cantons, are copies of those created by the Zürich glass painter Lukas Zeiner; each was donated to the Stadthaus by ten towns across the canton in 1500.

⑤    

Historisches Museum Baden

Landvogteischloss 1-5pm Tue, Wed, Fri & Sat, noon-7pm Thu, 10am-5pm Sun museum.baden.ch

The massive Gothic castle on the east bank of the Limmat was built in the 15th century, and from 1415 to 1798 was the residence of Baden's bailiffs. The castle keep now houses a museum of local history. Its archaeological section includes Roman pottery, coins and other objects found in Baden. There are also displays of weapons, traditional costumes of the Aargau region and rooms decorated in the style of different historical periods. A wing, which extends along the riverbank, contains displays of objects relating to Baden's more recent history. The interactive displays will keep older children busy, while younger visitors will love exploring the castle with Frank the Bat.

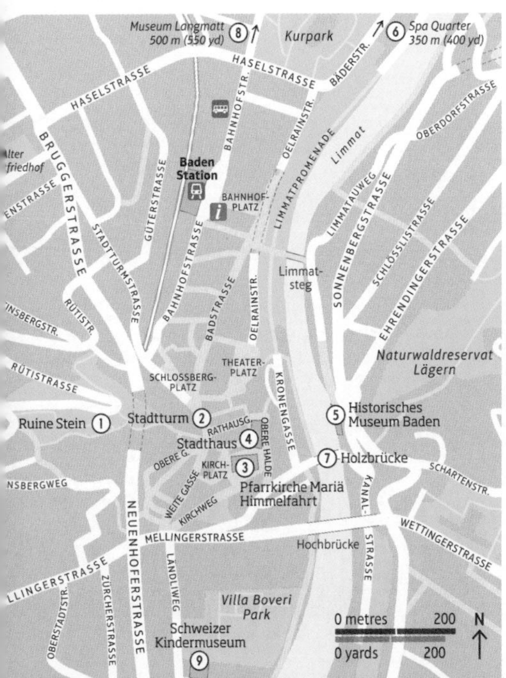

A bust of the Roman goddess Juno at the Historisches Museum

Spa Quarter

A short distance north of the Holzbrücke, along the Limmat's left bank, Baden's 18 thermal springs spout warm mineral-rich waters that are especially effective in curing rheumatism and respiratory ailments. The quarter has several hotels with their own pools and wellness areas. A public complex opened in 2018, with thermal pools and treatment areas.

Colourfully shuttered houses lining the streets of Old Town near the Holzbrücke

Holzbrücke

Spanning the Limmat from the base of the Historisches Museum Baden, this pretty wooden bridge is covered by a ridge roof. It was built across this narrow stretch of the river to connect the Landvogteischloss (Bailiff's Castle) to the lower-lying east bank in the 13th century. The current bridge, built in 1810 on 17th-century abutments, had at least five predecessors, each destroyed over the centuries either by natural calamity, such as flood, fire or ice drift, or in an effort to save the town in times of war.

14 CE

The year the Romans discovered the naturally warm springs in the bend of the Limmat.

The Holzbrücke stretching across the River Limmat towards the Old Town

Museum Langmatt

Römerstrasse 30 Mar-early Dec: 2-5pm Tue-Fri, 11am-5pm Sat & Sun langmatt.ch

On Römerstrasse, a short walk westwards from the spa area, stands a charming villa that was once the home of the industrialist and art connoisseur Sidney Brown-Sulzer (1865–1941) and his wife, Jenny. The Art Nouveau villa was built in 1900–01 by Karl Moser; a few years later a wing was added, which, like the house itself, contains an exquisite art collection. The nucleus of the collection consists of French Impressionist paintings, with works by Corot, Pissarro, Renoir, Monet, Sisley, Degas and Cézanne. The collection also includes rare ceramics and a series of 18th-century Venetian *veduta*, several works by Fragonard and Watteau, and paintings by Van Gogh and Gauguin. Some of the rooms contain 17th- and 18th-century French furniture.

The Brown-Sulzers filled their house with artists and musicians, and in keeping with this tradition, there are regular formal and informal events that bring together art, literature and music in interesting ways to discuss a selected theme. Also regularly held are special events to introduce children to Impressionist art.

↑ A display of toys engaging visitors of all ages at the Schweizer Kindermuseum

Schweizer Kindermuseum

Ländliweg 7 2-5pm Tue-Sat, 10am-5pm Sun kindermuseum.ch

Housed in an old mansion, this museum contains an expansive collection of toys and everyday objects from around the world that illustrate various aspects of childhood, including children's mental development and education. Younger visitors are actively encouraged to touch, examine and play with many of the exhibits.

BADENFAHRT

Taking place once every ten years, this themed party seems to defy what might be expected of a visit to Switzerland. The cobblestoned town swells to ten times its normal population as attendees flood in to chug beer, chow down on street food, dance to Swiss-German rap music till the early hours and go for a spin on carnival rides. It's an opportunity to see the Swiss really let their hair down.

WINTERTHUR

E2 Zürich Winterthur Hauptbahnhof; www.winterthur.com

Now associated chiefly with textiles and mechanical engineering, Winterthur is the second-largest city in the canton of Zürich. Despite its industrial character, this is a pleasant town, with leafy streets, open green spaces and a fully pedestrianized historic core. It also has several outstanding art galleries that can be explored via the museum bus, which circles the town every hour, stopping at the main museums and galleries.

Kunsthalle Winterthur

Marktgasse 25 Noon-6pm Wed-Fri, noon-4pm Sat & Sun kunsthallewinterthur.ch

The former Waaghaus (Weigh House) has been converted into a spacious exhibition hall, the Kunsthalle Winterthur, which organizes shows of contemporary art by local and internationally renowned artists every year. Marktgasse, the Old Town's pedestrianized main artery and its principal shopping street, is lined with several other historic buildings, including the 1717 Haus zur Geduld (Patience House).

Rathaus

Marktgasse 20 2-5pm Tue-Sat, 10am-noon & 2-5pm Sun stadt.winterthur.ch

Winterthur's Neo-Renaissance town hall was built in 1874 on the site of a former Gothic structure. In 1878, the ground floor was converted into a shopping arcade. The upper floors have remained intact and include the stuccoed Festsaal, and former offices and residential quarters. The town hall passage, which connects Marktgasse with Stadthausstrasse, is decorated with opulent ceiling frescoes and hosts shops and a café.

A two-minute walk away, at Stadthausstrasse 4a, stands the imposing Neo-Renaissance Stadthaus. It was designed by Gottfried Semper, who lectured at Zürich's Technical University, and completed in 1869. Once the seat of the city council, it now houses the town's main concert hall.

Fotomuseum

Grüzenstrasse 44 Until early 2025 for renovation fotomuseum.ch

This oustanding museum, set in a spacious and well-restored warehouse, is one of the finest of its kind in Europe. On display is a comprehensive range of images, from the early beginnings of photography to the most recent examples of the art, by international and local photographers. The museum also holds world-class exhibitions.

↑ Tubular undulation hanging above the foyer of Technorama

Technorama

Technoramastrasse 1
10am-5pm daily
technorama.ch

Featuring more than 500 fascinating interactive exhibits, Switzerland's only science and technology museum is a family-friendly affair, with indoor picnic rooms and barbecue areas in the leafy park. There are daily shows on various topics.

Kunst Museum Winterthur

Beim Stadthaus: Museumstrasse 52; Reinhart am Stadtgarten: Stadthausstrasse 6
10am-5pm Tue-Sun (Beim Stadthaus: Tue: to 8pm; Reinhart: am; Stadtgarten: Thu: to 8pm) **kmw.ch**

In 2017, the Kunstmuseum and Museum Oskar Reinhart merged to form the Kunst Museum Winterthur, with two main locations in town.

The Kunst Museum Beim Stadthaus has an excellent collection of 19th- and 20th-century works by a range of artists, including Monet, Van Gogh, Picasso, Rodin, Miró and Mondrian. The building also houses the Naturmuseum (a natural history museum) and the Kindermuseum.

Across Museumstrasse stands the Classical-style building of the Kunst Museum Reinhart am Stadtgarten. Oskar Reinhart (1885–1965), who was born in Winterthur, amassed one of the greatest private art collections of the 20th century. He bequeathed part of it to the town, and the rest to the Swiss nation.

The collection here has German, Austrian and Swiss Romantic and Realist works from the late 18th to the early 20th centuries.

Sammlung Oskar Reinhart am Römerholz

Haldenstrasse 95
10am-5pm Tue-Sun (Wed: to 8pm) **roemerholz.ch**

From 1926 until his death, the art collector Oskar Reinhart lived in this lovely country villa. It holds about 200 works from his extensive collection. Reinhart juxtaposed various styles, hanging Goya with Renoir, in an effort to establish continuities across time and to reveal the quintessence of art.

Did You Know?

The name of the town is thought to be a compound of the Celtic words *uito* (willow) and *durōn* (gate).

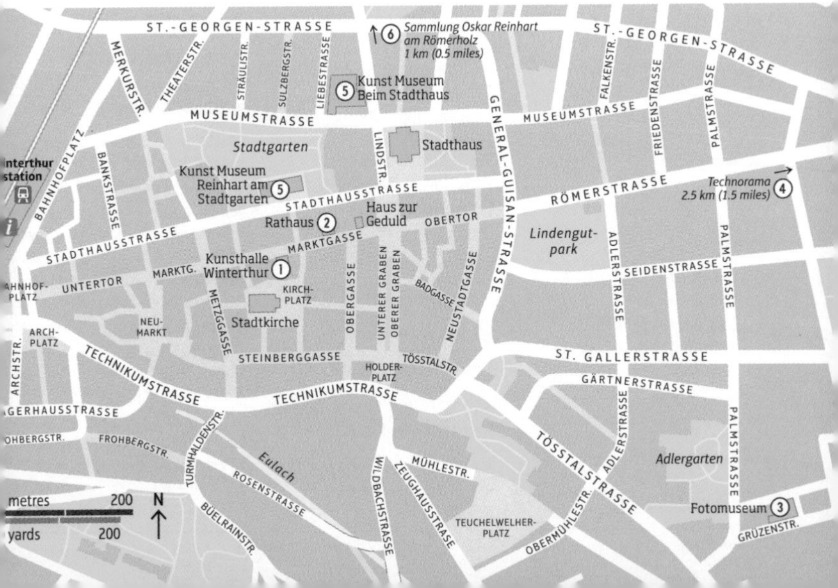

An exhibition at Riehen's modern-art museum, the Fondation Beyeler

EXPERIENCE MORE

Riehen

C2 Basel
riehen.ch

The charming town of Riehen, northeast of Basel, is filled with smart villas and old country houses, and has much to interest visitors.

Wettsteinhaus, once the home of a 17th-century mayor, now houses the **Muzeum Kultur & Spiel Riehen**. This superb toy museum contains exhibits ranging from toy trains and tin cars to dolls and board games, some dating from the 19th century. Also here are the Dorfmuseum, which documents daily life in Riehen in 1900, and the Rebbaumuseum, devoted to the local winemaking industry.

Riehen's largest museum is the exceptional **Fondation Beyeler**. It was set up by Hilda and Ernst Beyeler, prodigious art collectors who acquired some 200 pieces. These were put on public display in 1997, in a building designed by the Italian architect Renzo Piano. Most of the paintings in the collection date from the late 19th and 20th centuries. Among them are Impressionist paintings by Monet, works by Cézanne, Van Gogh, Picasso and Matisse, and canvases by Miró, Mondrian, Bacon, Rothko, Warhol and other major artists of the 20th century. A selection of artifacts from other parts of the world, including Africa and Oceania, complements the paintings.

INSIDER TIP
Take a Trip

Fancy a French break? Take tram 10, one of the few municipal transport routes in the world to cross an international border, from Dornach to Rodersdorf. The penultimate stop on the line, Leyman, is in France.

Muzeum Kultur & Spiel Riehen
Baselstrasse 34
11am-5pm Mon & Wed-Sun muks.ch

Fondation Beyeler
Baselstrasse 101
10am-6pm daily (Wed: to 8pm, Fri: to 9pm)
fondationbeyeler.ch

Augusta Raurica

C2 Augst, Basel
augustaraurica.ch

The Roman town of Augusta Raurica lies 11 km (7 miles) east of Basel, at the confluence of the Ergolz and the Rhine. It was founded in 27 BCE and at its height in about 200 CE it had a population of 20,000 people. By about 350 CE, the town had been largely destroyed by the Alemani, a northern tribe.

Carefully excavated, Augusta Raurica is now a large and fascinating open-air museum. The site includes restored temples, amphitheatres, baths and sewers, as well as a forum and numerous houses.

Some of the many objects unearthed during excavations are displayed in the excellent **Römermuseum**. They include a hoard of late antique silver discovered at the foot of the town's fortress. The reconstruction of a Roman house furnished with pieces found at the site illustrates daily life in the town.

Römermuseum
Giebenacherstrasse 17, Augst 061 816 22 22
10am-5pm daily

Zofingen

D3 Aargau
Kirchplatz 26; www.zofingen.ch

Zofingen, in the canton of Aargau, is a town with a history that goes back to the 12th century. Its well-preserved old town is surrounded by a green belt laid out along the course of the former fortifications. Almost all the town's sights are clustered around three neighbouring squares: Alter Postplatz, Kirchplatz and Niklaus-Thut-Platz.

In the centre of Alter Postplatz is a historic arcaded market hall that is still used for a weekly market today.

Kirchplatz (Church Square) takes its name from the Stadtkirche, a parish church built in the Romanesque style but with later Gothic and Renaissance elements added.

Niklaus-Thut-Platz is marked by a fountain with a statue of the eponymous Thut, a fearless mayor who fought during the Battle of Sempach in 1386, when the Confederates routed the Austrians. Among the fine buildings surrounding the square are the Metzgern-Zunfthaus (butchers' guild house), dating from 1602, and the Baroque town hall with a council chamber furnished in the Neo-Classical style.

Dornach

C2 Solothurn
dornach.ch

The small town of Dornach, on the southern outskirts of Basel, is the location of the world centre of anthroposophy. Founded in about 1912 by the Austrian-born social philosopher and educator Rudolf Steiner (1861–1925), anthroposophy holds that one's spiritual development, nourished by myth-making and other creative activities, is of prime importance to one's humanity. Steiner was strongly influenced by the writing of the German author Johann Wolfgang von Goethe and his ideas live on in the worldwide network of Waldorf schools.

The **Goetheanum**, a huge concrete building overlooking Dornach, is the seat of the Anthroposophical Society, which advocates the freedom of the individual. Constructed in line with the principles of this philosophy, it has no right angles, and is widely regarded as the epitome of Expressionist architecture.

Goetheanum
Rüttiweg 45
9am-8pm daily
goetheanum.ch

Aarau

D3 Aargau
Metzgergasse 2; www.aarauinfo.ch

Aarau has a scenic location on the River Aare. The old part of the town is built on terraces that rise steeply from the riverbank.

Briefly the capital of the Helvetic Republic, Aarau became the capital of the canton of Aargau in 1803. Its wealth is derived from the textiles industry.

The town's highest point is marked by Schlössli, a castle thought to date from the 11th century, which now houses a museum of local history. Other notable buildings are the 16th-century town hall with a Romanesque tower and the 15th-century Stadtkirche. Some houses lining the narrow streets of Aarau's old districts have stepped gables and are decorated with floral motifs.

The town also has a decent art gallery, the **Aargauer Kunsthaus**, with a collection of modern paintings, and a museum of natural history.

Aargauer Kunsthaus
Aargauerplatz
10am-5pm Tue-Sun (Thu: to 8pm) aargauerkunsthaus.ch

Did You Know?

Swiss poet Erika Burkart (1922-2010), winner of the Grosser Schillerpreis, was born in Aarau.

The Goetheanum in Dornach, seat of the Anthroposophical Society

Muri

D3 Aargau
Marktstrasse 10; www.muri.ch

The splendidly restored Benedictine monastery in Muri constitutes this town's main attraction. **Kloster Muri** was founded by Ita von Lothringen and Count Redebot von Habsburg in 1027 and was inhabited by a community of monks until 1841. It then fell into disrepair and was gutted by fire in 1889. In 1960, after it had been meticulously restored, a small group of Benedictine monks returned to the monastery, where they ran a hospice.

The oldest surviving parts of the monastery's church include its Romanesque presbytery, crypt and transept. Some Gothic elements also survive. The main body of the church, however, is in the Baroque style. Built to an octagonal plan and topped by a dome, it dates from the 17th century. Most of the church furnishings were made in the late 17th and 18th centuries.

The cloisters adjoining the church are the burial place of the hearts of Emperor Karl I and his wife, Zita. An exhibition of paintings by the Swiss artist Caspar Wolf and items from the monastery's treasury are also displayed here.

Kloster Muri
Marktstrasse 4 **Summer: 11am–5pm Tue–Sun; winter: 11am–4pm Tue–Sun**

Kloster Königsfelden

D2 Museumstrasse, Windisch, Aargau
Until 2025 for renovation
klosterkoenigsfelden.ch

The Franciscan Abbey of Königsfelden lies between the quaint villages of Brugg and Windisch. It was founded in 1308 by Elizabeth von Habsburg to mark the spot where her husband Albrecht I was murdered by Duke Johann of Swabia. The monastery was later given to a community of Franciscan monks and nuns of the Order of St Clare. After Elizabeth's death, building work on the abbey was continued by her daughter Agnes of Hungary.

During the Reformation these religious communities were dissolved and in 1804 the monastery buildings were converted into a psychiatric hospital. When the hospital moved to new premises later in the 19th century, most of the monastery buildings were dismantled.

The church, however, survives. Built in 1310–30, it takes the form of a monumental Gothic basilica with a wooden ceiling. In the aisles are wooden panels with depictions of knights and coats of arms. The 11 stained-glass windows in the presbytery are some of the country's finest. Made between 1325 and 1330 and restored in the 1980s, they show scenes from the lives of Christ, the Virgin Mary, the Apostles and various saints.

↓ The splendidly restored Kloster Muri *(inset)*, with its highly ornate Baroque interior

The medieval village of Regensberg attractively set on a hill among vineyards

Wettingen

D2 Aargau
Seminarstrasse 54; www.wettingen.ch

Set among hills bordering the Limmat Valley, Wettingen is a town with a stunning Cistercian abbey, **Zisterzienserkloster**. The monastery was dissolved in 1841, and now serves as a school. Its church and the cloisters are open to visitors.

The abbey church was founded in 1227. Although the Renaissance stalls survive, the church's interior is decorated in Baroque style. The Gothic cloisters now contain a display of stained glass.

Zisterzienserkloster
Klosterstrasse 11
056 437 24 03 Church: Mar-Oct: 10am-5pm Tue-Sun; cloisters: Mar-Oct: 9am-5pm Sat & Sun

Regensberg

D2 Zürich
From Dielsdorf

The attractive winegrowing village of Regensberg lies on a minor road off the highway between Zürich and Waldshut. Set on a hillside amid vineyards, it is one of the best-preserved medieval villages in Switzerland. Its main square and oldest streets are lined with half-timbered houses. The history of Regensberg goes back to 1245. The oldest building in the town is the castle's circular crenellated keep; the castle itself dates from the 16th and 17th centuries. Also of note is the 16th-century parish church, overlying the foundations of a medieval building.

13

Kaiserstuhl

D2 Aargau
aargautourismus.ch

Set on a hillside on the bank of the Rhine, Kaiserstuhl is a beautiful old town. Its historic centre, which is contained within an irregular triangle, is a listed conservation area.

The upper corner of the triangle is marked by Oberer Turm (Upper Tower), a medieval bastion that once formed part of the town's fortifications. From Kaiserstuhl, a bridge over the Rhine leads to Hohentengen, where there is a 13th-century castle, Schloss Rötelen.

Eglisau

E2 Zürich
Untergass 7; www.eglisau.ch

Eglisau straddles the River Rhine and is surrounded by gentle hills covered in vineyards. Its origins go back to medieval times, when it was established at what was then a ford across the river, on an ancient route south to Zürich.

When a hydroelectric dam was built across the Rhine, the picturesque houses that once stood on the riverbank were engulfed by water. Eglisau's historic covered bridge was also lost. The higher part of the old town, with its 18th-century domed church, now stands just above water level. This historic centre is filled with half-timbered houses, some of which are decorated with colourful murals.

EAT

Gasthof Hirschen
Bistro setting, gourmet dishes and splendid Rhine views.

E2 Untergass 28, Eglisau hirschen-eglisau.ch

PANINI Caffè
Hand-crafted *piadine* (Italian flatbread), with barista coffee.

D3
Laurenzentorgasse 14, Aarau panini aarau.ch

Sporrer
Home cooking at a family-friendly spot.

E2 Im Sporrer 1, Winterthur sporrer.ch

Dusk falling over breathtaking Lake Lugano

CENTRAL SWITZERLAND AND TICINO

The cradle of the Swiss Confederation and the birthplace of the legendary hero William Tell, central Switzerland is at both the geographical and the historical heart of the country. Bordering the east and south shores of Lake Lucerne, Schwyz, Uri and Unterwalde, known as the Waldstätte, or Forest Cantons, formed an alliance in 1291 that marked the foundation of the Swiss Confederation. Champion of the people William Tell became the stuff of legend by inciting the peasant rebellion, in 1307, that would go on to overthrow Habsburg rule, but it wasn't until the latter half of the 15th century that he appears in a collection of folk tales.

While William Tell was reputedly leading uprisings to the north, the dukes of Milan were fighting over what is now the southern canton of Ticino. Separated from its northern neighbours by the Alps, this Mediterranean-influenced region is bordered on almost all other sides by Italy. It was annexed by the Swiss Confederates in the early 16th century, but it only joined the Confederation as a free canton in 1803. This large, Italian-speaking canton in the sunny foothills of the southern Alps has a pace of life that's markedly more relaxed than elsewhere in Switzerland.

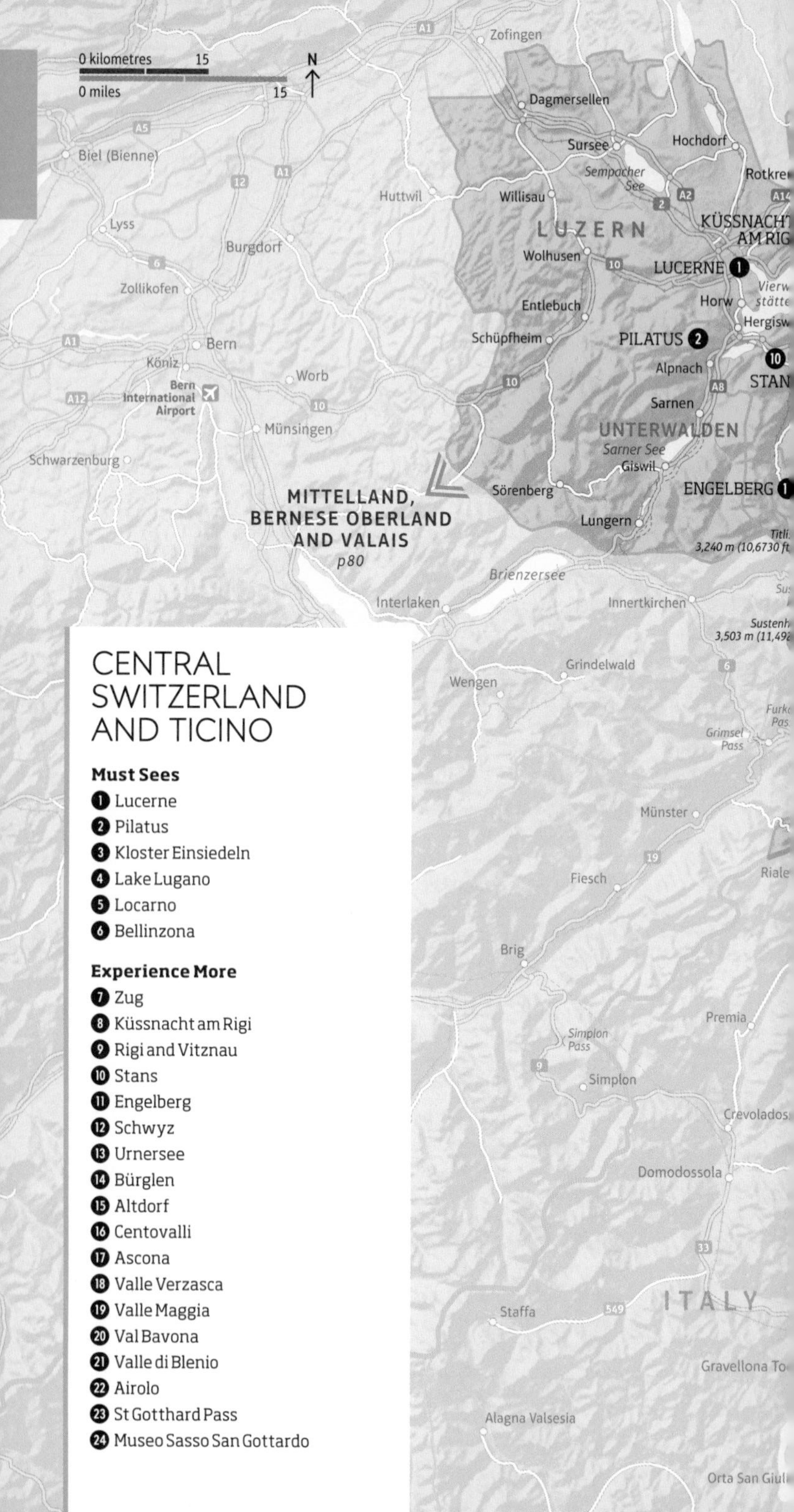

CENTRAL SWITZERLAND AND TICINO

Must Sees

1. Lucerne
2. Pilatus
3. Kloster Einsiedeln
4. Lake Lugano
5. Locarno
6. Bellinzona

Experience More

7. Zug
8. Küssnacht am Rigi
9. Rigi and Vitznau
10. Stans
11. Engelberg
12. Schwyz
13. Urnersee
14. Bürglen
15. Altdorf
16. Centovalli
17. Ascona
18. Valle Verzasca
19. Valle Maggia
20. Val Bavona
21. Valle di Blenio
22. Airolo
23. St Gotthard Pass
24. Museo Sasso San Gottardo

NORTHERN SWITZERLAND
p174
CENTRAL SWITZERLAND AND TICINO
EASTERN SWITZERLAND AND GRAUBÜNDEN
p238
7 ZUG
ZUG
3 KLOSTER EINSIEDELN
SCHWYZ
12 SCHWYZ
VITZNAU
RIGI
13 URNERSEE
ALTDORF 15
14 BÜRGLEN
URI
24 MUSEO SASSO SAN GOTTARDO
23 ST GOTTHARD PASS
22 AIROLO
21 VALLE DI BLENIO
AL BAVONA
20
TICINO
VALLE MAGGIA 19
18 VALLE VERZASCA
6 BELLINZONA
CENTOVALLI 16
5 LOCARNO
ASCONA 17
LAKE LUGANO 4
ITALY
Baar
Pfäffikon
Lachen
Rüti
Wattwil
Uznach
Sihlsee
Ägerisee
Näfels
Wägitaler See
Arth
Goldau
Glarus
Brunnen
Muotathal
Flüelen
Linthal
Klausen Pass
Gross Scharhorn 3,295 m (10,810 ft)
Erstfeld
Gross-Spannort 3,198 m (10,492 ft)
Gotthard Base Tunnel
Rhein
Chur
Flims
Breil
Ilanz
Lenzerheide
Thusis
Disentis
Wassen
Göschenen
Sedrun
Andermatt
Gotthard Tunnel
Zillis
Savognin
Olivone
Splügen
Quinto
Valle Leventina
Chiggiogna
San Bernardino
Madesimo
Fusio
Malvaglia
Mesocco
Giornico
Biasca
Soazza
Sonogno
Maggia
Bignasco
Cevio
Brione
Chiavenna
Stampa
San Vittore
Novate Mezzola
Vogorno
Ticino
Domaso
Palagnedra
Vira
Piantedo
Morbegno
Brissago
Mezzovico
Lago di Como
Fraccia
Bioggio
Lugano
Lago Maggiore
Luino
Verbania
Monte Generoso 1,704 m (5,590 ft)
Stresa
Mendrisio
Chiasso
Lecco
San Pellegrino Terme
Varese
Como

LUCERNE

D3 Lucerne Zentralstrasse 5; www.luzern.com

Central Switzerland's largest town, Lucerne (Luzern in German) lies on the western shore of Lake Lucerne. From its origins as a small fishing village, it grew into an important staging point when the St Gotthard Pass was opened in 1220. Easily explored on foot, the medieval Old Town lies on the north bank of the River Reuss and can be reached by crossing over the Chapel Bridge. The town's newer 20th-century suburbs climb the hills to the northeast and southwest, and stretch out along the banks of the lake.

Chapel Bridge

This 14th-century covered footbridge spanning the Reuss at an angle formed part of the town's early fortifications, protecting its citizens against attack from the direction of the lake. Near the centre of the river, the bridge joins the iconic Wasserturm, an octagonal tower that has served as a lighthouse, a prison and a treasury. In the 17th century, the bridge's roof panels were painted with scenes from the history of Lucerne and episodes in the lives of the martyrs St Leodegar and St Mauritius, who became the town's patron saints.

The oldest wooden bridge in Europe, Chapel Bridge (Kapellbrücke) has become the symbol of Lucerne. In 1993 the bridge was partly destroyed by a fire but it has since been rebuilt and most of its historic paintings have been restored.

KKL

Europaplatz 1 kkl-luzern.ch

With its cantilevered roof, the Kultur- und Kongresszentrum Luzern (Lucerne Culture and Convention Centre), or the KKL, is a strikingly Modernist glass-and-steel building that juts out over Lake Lucerne. It was designed by the French architect Jean Nouvel and was opened in 1998. The building contains both intimate and capacious theatres, concert and conference halls, and the Kunstmuseum, displaying contemporary art. Lounge areas, a range of restaurants and bars, and a seasonal ice rink also add to the appeal.

Did You Know?

The town hosts the Lucerne Festival of Classical Music with three annual events.

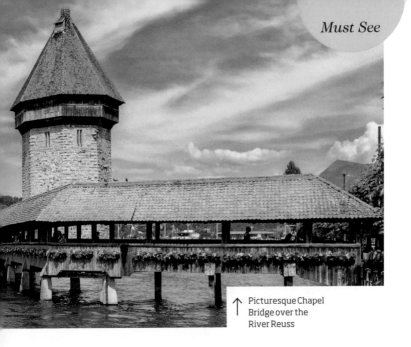

↑ Picturesque Chapel Bridge over the River Reuss

Kunstmuseum

KKL 11am-6pm Tue-Sun (Wed: to 7pm) kunstmuseumluzern.ch

The vast collections of the Kunstmuseum are displayed in about 20 rooms on the topmost floor of the KKL building. The gallery has a fascinating permanent collection of 18th- and early 20th-century Swiss painting, and presents a rotating programme of exhibitions of the work of international contemporary artists. On the same floor, and accessible to the general public, is the Kunstmuseum's Art Library, which has an interesting collection of various art books and magazines as well as an archive of previous exhibition catalogues.

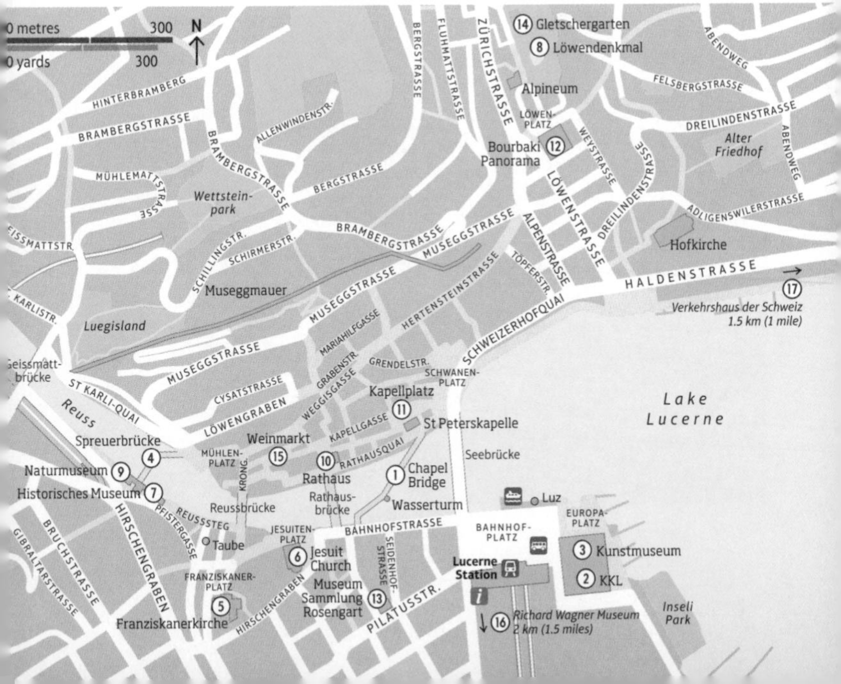

0 metres 300
0 yards 300
N
14 Gletschergarten
8 Löwendenkmal
Alpineum
12 Bourbaki Panorama
Alter Friedhof
Hofkirche
Wettstein-park
Museggmauer
Luegisland
17 Verkehrshaus der Schweiz 1.5 km (1 mile)
Lake Lucerne
Kapellplatz
11 St Peterskapelle
Seebrücke
Reuss
4 Spreuerbrücke
9 Naturmuseum
7 Historisches Museum
15 Weinmarkt
10 Rathaus
1 Chapel Bridge
Rathaus-brücke
Wasserturm
Reussbrücke
Luz
Taube
6 Jesuit Church
13 Museum Sammlung Rosengart
Lucerne Station
3 Kunstmuseum
2 KKL
5 Franziskanerkirche
16 Richard Wagner Museum 2 km (1.5 miles)
Inseli Park

Spreuerbrücke

This wooden covered bridge spans the Reuss at the western edge of the Old Town. It was built in 1408 and incorporates a small chapel. The bridge's roof is lined with panels painted by Kaspar Meglinger in 1626–35. Depicting the Dance of Death, they run in sequence from the north bank and culminate with Christ's triumph over Death at the south bank.

The Nadelwerk, a device that controls floods, stands downstream of the bridge.

Did You Know?

Of the original 67 paintings in the Spreuerbrücke Dance of Death, 45 are preserved on the bridge.

Franziskanerkirche

Franziskanerplatz

This Franciscan church was built in the Gothic style, but over the centuries has been transformed with ornate Renaissance choir stalls and Baroque ceiling paintings.

Jesuit Church

Bahnhofstrasse 11

A major landmark on the south bank of the Reuss, the great Jesuitenkirche, the Jesuit church of St Francis Xavier, was built in 1666–73; however, its onion-domed twin towers were not completed until the 19th century. The Baroque interior is richly and colourfully decorated with intricate stuccowork and beautiful ceiling paintings depicting the apotheosis of St Francis Xavier.

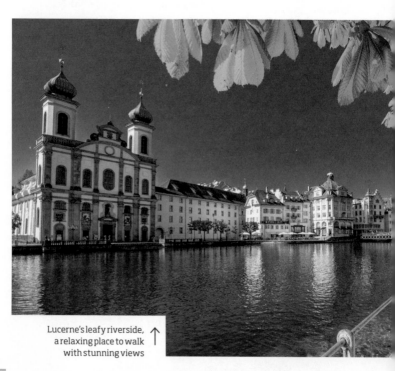

Historisches Museum

Pfistergasse 24 10am-5pm Tue-Sun historischesmuseum.lu.ch

Lucerne's history museum occupies the former arsenal, a Renaissance building dating from 1597. Also named the Depot, the museum has been brought up to date with interactive displays, barcodes and hand-held scanners in place of traditional information boards and audio guides.

Thousands of fascinating historical objects on display include weaponry, costumes, and folk art and crafts, as well as early advertising material from the Swiss manufacturing and tourism industries. Actors in period costume dramatize scenes from history in daily performances at the museum.

In the adjacent building is the Naturmuseum. Its displays focus on various aspects of natural history, in particular zoology and geology.

Lucerne's leafy riverside, a relaxing place to walk with stunning views ↑

The mournful Lion Monument, carved into the wall of a former sandstone quarry

Löwendenkmal

Denkmalstrasse

This massive figure of a dying lion pierced by a spear is a startling monument to the Swiss Guards of Louis XVI of France. On 10 August 1792, the guards defended the Palais des Tuileries, in Paris, when it was stormed by revolutionaries. Those who survived the attack were arrested and guillotined on the night of 2–3 September. The Löwendenkmal, or Lion Monument, was designed by the Danish sculptor Bertel Thorvaldsen, and carved out of the sandstone cliff face by Lukas Ahorn. The sculpture was unveileved in 1821 and is 10 m (33 ft) long and 6 m (20 ft) high. Reflected in the waters of a small pond, the monument has great drama and pathos.

Naturmuseum

Kasernenplatz 6
10am-5pm Tue-Sun
naturmuseum.ch

The Natural History Museum is an easy ten-minute stroll from the Old Town, southwest across the Spreuerbrücke. With a variety of animals and interactive displays, this is a popular choice with children and is one of the country's most family-friendly museums. Hallways are lined with taxidermy, and there is a full-time guide on hand to explain the exhibits in detail. There is plenty to keep adults engaged, too, such as the topographical representation of the Alps in prehistoric times. Various flora and fauna from central Switzerland, including a brightly coloured exhibit of butterflies, are displayed on rotating panels.

Rathaus

Kornmarkt 3 041 417 03 10 By arrangement

The present town hall, built in a grand Renaissance style, was completed in 1606. Of the 14th-century town hall that stood on the same site, only a tower remains. The council chamber inside is lined with finely carved wood panelling.

Kapellplatz

St Peterskapelle: 7:30am-6:15pm Mon-Wed & Fri, 7:30am-9pm Thu, 7:30am-5pm Sat, 8:30am-8pm Sun

This square buzzes with life, particularly on market days. In the centre lies the Fritschi Fountain, adorned with allegorical figures depicting Brother Fritschi, a figure of Swiss legend who features in Lucerne's Carnival tradition.

Kapellplatz takes its name from the 18th-century chapel, St Peterskapelle, which stands on the site of a 12th-century church, the earliest to be built in Lucerne. The chapel contains a 14th-century Gothic crucifix.

INSIDER TIP
Lucerne's Markets

Although a relatively compact town, the markets in Lucerne are dazzling in their array of goods. Small farmers markets generally occur on Tuesdays whereas on weekends you'll find a selection of unique handicrafts, locally produced food and vintage gems. The squares of Weinmarkt and Kapellplatz are two of the key hot spots.

EAT

Luz

A perfect pit-stop, this tiny coffee joint serves delicious snacks and fabulous lake views.

Landungsbrücke 1
luzseebistro.ch

Taube

The go-to place for delicious local Lucerne dishes, cooked just like a grandmother would do.

Burgerstrasse 3
taube-luzern.ch

12   

Bourbaki Panorama

Löwenplatz 11 Apr-Oct: 10am-6pm daily; Nov-Mar: 10am-5pm daily bourbakipanorama.ch

One of the world's few surviving panoramas, this giant circular mural depicts the march of the French army through Switzerland under General Bourbaki, during the Franco-Prussian War (1870–71). In a stone building now housed in a glass shell, it is 112 m (370 ft) long and 10 m (33 ft) high, and was painted by Edouard Castres. Sound effects, a spoken narrative (in several languages) and a smartphone app help bring the characters depicted to life and turn this form of storytelling into an incredibly immersive experience with a digital narrative. The building hosts a variety of cultural events and contains a museum, a cinema and a small art gallery, as well as bars and a restaurant.

↑ Admiring a rich selection of Picasso's work in the private Rosengart Collection

13 

Museum Sammlung Rosengart

Pilatusstrasse 10 Apr-Oct: 10am-6pm daily; Nov-Mar: 11am-5pm daily rosengart.ch

The Sammlung Rosengart is a private collection of over 300 modern paintings that was formed over several decades by the art dealers Siegfried Rosengart and his daughter, Angela. As well as 125 works by Paul Klee, the museum also has a fabulous collection of watercolours and sculptures by Pablo Picasso, many of them previously housed in the former Picasso Museum. The collection also includes Impressionist paintings, with canvasses by Cézanne and Monet, as well as artworks by Chagall, Matisse and Kandinsky.

Gletschergarten

Denkmalstrasse 4 Apr-Oct: 10am-6pm daily; Nov-Mar: 10am-5pm daily gletschergarten.ch

This attractive garden is an oasis of tranquillity, as well as being the setting for a fascinating natural phenomenon. In 1872 an enormous rock, complete with 32 potholes and well-sized holes, was excavated here. Formed by glacial abrasion, the rock was shown by research to date from the Ice Age. The garden was made to conserve this geological feature, which is protected by a tent-roof that allows visitors to view the rock from the sides.

The site includes a museum, an exhibition on the geological processes involved in creating

the holes and the fascinating Mirror Maze of more than 90 mirrors in the royal style of Granada's Alhambra fortress.

Weinmarkt

Lined with historic houses, this square is one of the most attractive features of the Old Town. In the centre stands the Weinmarktbrunnen, a Gothic fountain which is a close copy of the original that now stands in the quiet courtyard of the Ritterscher Palast on pretty Bahnhofstrasse. The houses around both this square and the adjacent Hirschenplatz have painted façades, ornate doorways and oriel windows. Many of these buildings were once guildhouses, and Passion Plays enacting Christ's last days were performed in this iconic location in the late Middle Ages. These plays grew famous across Europe.

PICTURE PERFECT
Fancy Frescoes

Each building lining the Weinmarkt is uniquely and intricately painted. Pay attention to the details of these beautiful frescoes that often tell a story and be sure to take a snapshot of the square.

(16)   

Richard Wagner Museum

Richard-Wagner-Weg 27 Apr-Nov: 11am-5pm Tue-Sun richard-wagner-museum.ch

The German Romantic composer Richard Wagner was a regular visitor to Lucerne. He wrote the third act of his opera *Tristan und Isolde* here. Two complete operas, *Die Meistersinger von Nürnberg* and *Siegfried*, date from this period, and Wagner also started work here on *Götterdämmerung*.

The tranquil Villa Tribschen, where Wagner and his wife and son lived from 1866 to 1872, is devoted to this particularly happy period. Its rooms, with original furniture, are filled with memorabilia of the composer's life, including paintings, letters and musical instruments. Overlooking the lake, the museum's setting is very tranquil and there is also a little café outside in the summer months.

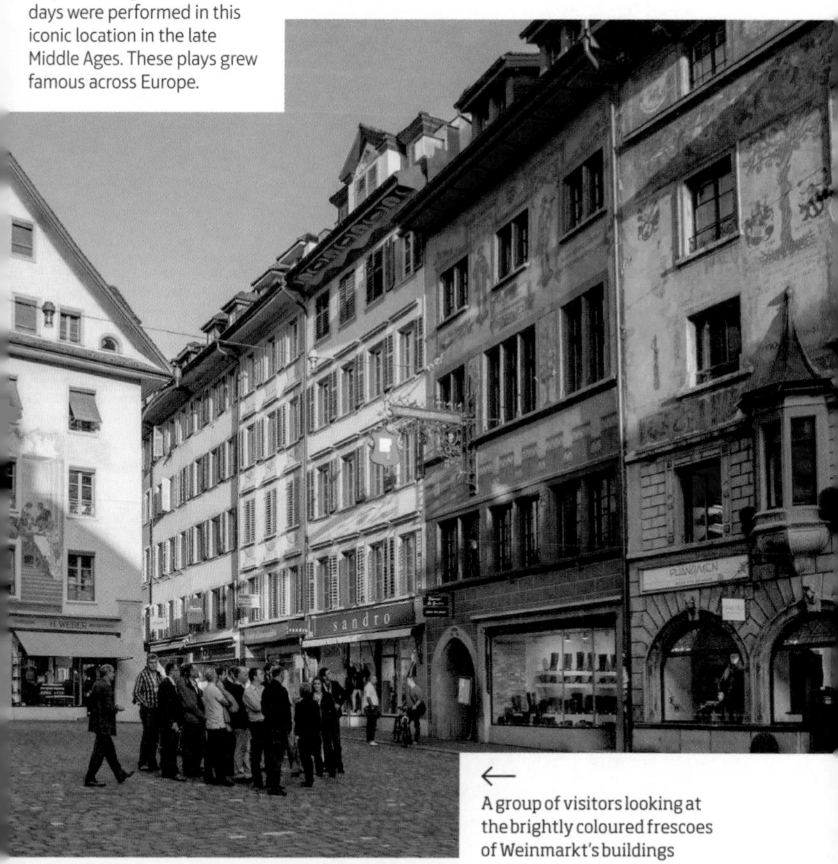

← A group of visitors looking at the brightly coloured frescoes of Weinmarkt's buildings

17

VERKEHRSHAUS DER SCHWEIZ

Lidostrasse 5 Apr-Oct: 10am-6pm daily; Nov-Feb: 10am-5pm daily verkehrshaus.ch

The Swiss Museum of Transport celebrates one of humankind's most fundamental longings: the urge to travel across our planet and beyond it. Planes and spacecraft hang overhead in its lofty galleries, while the floors are filled with more earthbound means of transport.

Almost every mode of mechanized transport, from the earliest bicycle to the latest spacecraft, is displayed at Lucerne's Swiss Museum of Transport, one of Switzerland's most visited museums. Vintage cars and steam locomotives are part of the exhibitions on road and rail transport, while the tourism section highlights the ingenuity of rack railways and cable cars. Water transport, aviation and space travel are also showcased. Among the museum's interactive features are three flight simulators, as well as a range of activities for young visitors. The museum also houses the country's largest planetarium and the Swiss Chocolate Adventure, which immerses visitors in the delicious world of one of Switzerland's principal exports.

Did You Know?

The first Swiss railway company was called Spanisch Brötli Bahn, literally "Spanish bread roll railway".

A hands-on exhibit that allows families to play a game involving Geneva Airport

GALLERY GUIDE

The rooms to the left of the main entrance are devoted to rail transport. Opposite the main entrance is the Road Transport Hall. The other main rooms contain aviation and space travel exhibits. The museum's Filmtheatre has the largest screen in the country, while the planetarium and the Swiss Chocolate Adventure are fun as well as educational.

Eye-catching transport signs covering the exterior of the museum

Exhibits, including a colourful paraglider, on display at the Swiss Transport Museum

A SHORT WALK
OLD TOWN

Distance 1 km (0.5 miles) **Nearest bus stop** Hirschengraben **Time** 20 minutes

Lucerne's historic Old Town (Altstadt) is set on a shallow bend of the Reuss at the point where the river turns from Lake Lucerne. From the Middle Ages the town was defended by ramparts on its northern side and by Chapel Bridge, which spans the river on its eastern side. The Old Town's ancient layout survives, and the façades of its fine historic houses, particularly around Hirschenplatz and along Weinmarktgasse, are painted with frescoes or covered with sgraffito decoration. This historic district of Lucerne is also a bustling urban centre, with plenty of shops, restaurants and cafés.

Did You Know?

The Chapel Bridge (Kapellbrücke) is the oldest covered wooden bridge in Europe.

Many of the paintings on the façades of the houses in Lucerne's Old Town are full of symbolism and allusions.

The central square of ***Weinmarkt*** *(p209), where wine was once sold, has several fine houses, many of which were guildhalls.*

The narrow alleys off Weinmarkt are lined with tall houses, some with colourfully painted shutters. Many of these houses have been converted into hotels, or contain boutiques and restaurants.

Completed in 1606, the late-Renaissance ***Rathaus*** *(p207) has an ornate façade.*

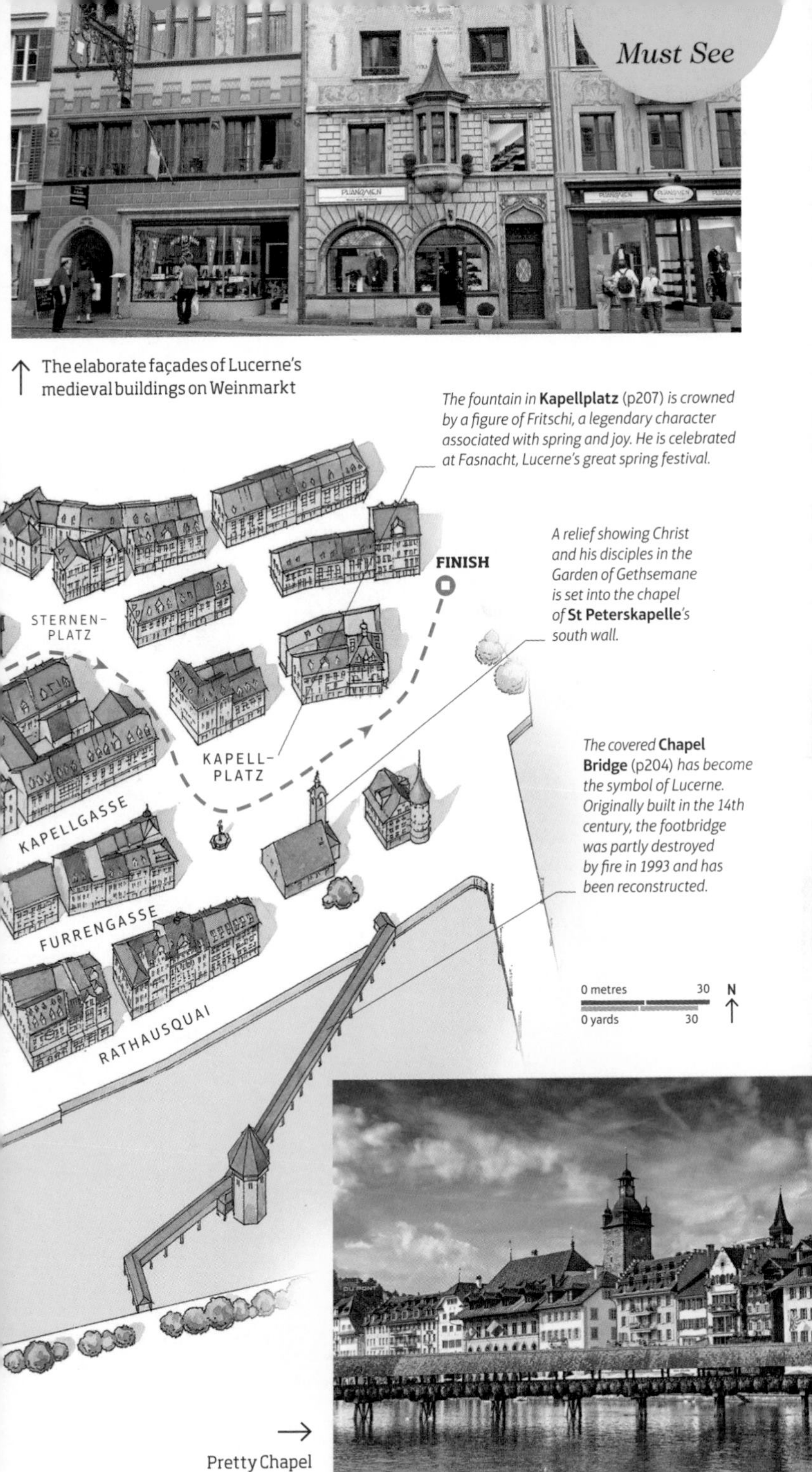

↑ The elaborate façades of Lucerne's medieval buildings on Weinmarkt

The fountain in **Kapellplatz** *(p207) is crowned by a figure of Fritschi, a legendary character associated with spring and joy. He is celebrated at Fasnacht, Lucerne's great spring festival.*

A relief showing Christ and his disciples in the Garden of Gethsemane is set into the chapel of **St Peterskapelle***'s south wall.*

The covered **Chapel Bridge** *(p204) has become the symbol of Lucerne. Originally built in the 14th century, the footbridge was partly destroyed by fire in 1993 and has been reconstructed.*

→ Pretty Chapel Bridge, stretching over the Reuss

2

PILATUS

D3 Obwalden, Nidwalden and Lucerne From Alpnachstad pilatus.ch

The rugged outlines of Pilatus, whose highest peak reaches an altitude of 2,132 m (7,000 ft), rise on the southwestern side of Lake Lucerne. Various legends shroud the mountain, including claims that it is both home to a dragon and that its heights are haunted by Pontius Pilate, who unleashes violent storms.

The massif has plenty to entertain visitors, including walking trails to its various peaks, a rope park and paragliding, as well as plenty of restaurants and two hotels. Getting to the summit is an adventure in itself. The first stage is a boat or train ride from Lucerne to Alpnachstad, near the foot of Pilatus, from where you can either take the cogwheel railway, a gondola or a cable car called the "Dragon Ride" from Schlossweg 1 to Pilatus Kulm, the upper station. The magnificent views from Pilatus' summit reward the journey.

← Walking up a signposted trail to the marker on Oberhaupt peak

COGWHEEL RAILWAY

Completed in 1889, the cog railway that climbs from Alpnachstad to Pilatus Kulm is, at an average gradient of 48 per cent, the steepest in the world. Designed by engineer Eduard Locher, the railway is almost 5 km (3 miles) long, and the journey takes 30 minutes. Originally driven by steam locomotives, the railway was electrified in 1937. One of the original steam railcars can be seen at the Swiss Museum of Transport in Lucerne *(p210)*.

1 Gondolas take visitors over the lush forest from Kriens to the top of Pilatus, offering panoramic views.

2 A variety of restaurants are found at Pilatus's summit.

3 Built in 1890, Hotel Pilatus-Kulm is a luxurious lodge with a beautiful restaurant.

INSIDER TIP
Flora Path

Follow the easy, well-marked flower trail at the top of Pilatus for an insight into the many colourful flowers that dot the hillside; some, like the Alpine dwarf orchid, can only be found at this altitude.

↑ A cable car descending from the Pilatus terminal, passing breathtaking scenery

KLOSTER EINSIEDELN

E3 Hauptstrasse 85, Einsiedeln, Schwyz Einsiedeln Church: 6am-8:30pm Mon-Sat, 7am-8:30pm Sun; Grosser Saal: 1:30-6pm daily; library: 2pm daily or by appointment kloster-einsiedeln.ch

Completed in 1735, the Benedictine abbey at Einsiedeln is one of the finest examples of Baroque architecture in the world. The abbey has been a place of pilgrimage since 948 when, according to legend, a miracle occurred during the consecration of the church, and now more than one million pilgrims come here each year.

Did You Know?

In the abbey's library is *Versus de scachis*, with the earliest known mention of chess in Western literature.

The history of the abbey goes back to 835, when Meinrad, a monk, chose the spot for his hermitage. In 934 a monastery was founded on the site, and it soon flourished as a place of learning, printing and music. Its library became renowned for its extensive collection of manuscripts. In the 13th century the pilgrimage to the abbey became known as the "Einsiedeln tradition". The abbey was left alone during the Reformation in the 16th century, despite the fact Protesant Reformist Ulrich Zwingli preached here during this time. The church and monastery were rebuilt in the 18th century, to a grand Baroque design. Most of the paintings, gilding and stuccowork are by the Bavarian brothers Cosmas Damian and Egid Quirin Asam. Today 60 monks continue to work and follow the Benedictine tradition.

The abbey library is a fine example of the Baroque style.

The confessional is located in the north transcept.

→ The statue of the Virgin crowning the Well of Our Lady

As they arrive, pilgrims drink the water from the Well of Our Lady.

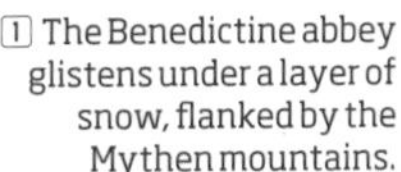

1 The Benedictine abbey glistens under a layer of snow, flanked by the Mythen mountains.

2 The 15th-century wooden figure of the Madonna, reputed to have miraculous powers, stands in gilt surroundings.

3 An intricately carved statue stands guard in front of the abbey.

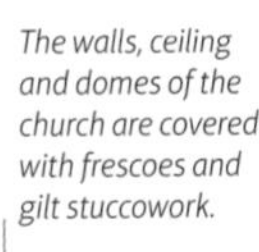

The walls, ceiling and domes of the church are covered with frescoes and gilt stuccowork.

← The 18th-century abbey complex, built in typically opulent Baroque style

The lavishly decorated Grosser Saal, or Great Hall, is still used for official ceremonies.

The organ is bedecked with figures of putti playing instruments.

The spacious nave is decorated with Baroque frescoes.

Figures of angels and the symbols of the Four Evangelists decorate the gilt pulpit.

INSIDER TIP
Christmas Time

Every December a Christmas market sets up along the town's main street and on the abbey square. With more than 150 stalls, it is one of the country's largest. Be sure to sample the gingerbread (it's a tasty local speciality).

4

LAKE LUGANO

E6 Ticino Lugano Lugano train station, Riva Giocondo Albertolli; 091 913 32 32

Nestling between steep Alpine slopes, this sheltered, glacial lake is one of Ticino's most beautiful natural features. Although most of it lies in Swiss territory, the southwestern shore, northeastern branch and a small central enclave belong to Italy.

A gateway to the Alps, Lake Lugano (Lago di Ceresio in Italian) endured a medieval tug-of-war between different Italian and, later, Swiss factions. It was only in 1752, when the Italian-Swiss border was fixed, that control of the lake was settled, and it remains largely unchanged to this day.

A road bridge crosses the lake at Melide, leading up to the St Gotthard Tunnel, but the best way of exploring it is by boat, from Lugano or several other points along the lakeshore. The lake's shape is unusual, twisting into branches dotted with villages and semitropical parks which cling to its rugged shoreline, and is best understood from above. Fortunately, a funicular from Lugano up Monte Brè and a cogwheel railway from Capolago up Monte Generoso allow just that, carrying passengers into the mountains that flank the lake.

Did You Know?

Fossils dating from the mid-Triassic (around 220 million years ago) have been found around the lake.

1 The restaurant atop Monte Generoso, designed by Mario Botta, commands stunning views of the southern shores of the lake.

2 Swissminiatur, the main attraction of Melide, displays 1:25 scale models of the country's landmarks.

3 The panorama of Lake Lugano and the mountains in the distance spills away from Monte Brè, which lies north of the lake.

PICTURE PERFECT
The Pearl of Ceresio

Set sail towards pretty Morcote, dubbed the Pearl of Ceresio. The postcard-ready terraced vineyards, with the domed Captain's Tower clinging to the slopes, are best viewed from the water.

The small church of Santa Maria del Sasso overlooking the lakeside hamlet of Morcote ↑

A SHORT WALK
LUGANO

Distance 1 km (0.5 miles) **Nearest funicular** Lugano Città **Time** 20 minutes

Lying in a shallow inlet on the north shore of Lake Lugano, this is the largest town in Ticino and one of the canton's great lakeside resorts. Lugano is also a centre of finance and banking. With piazzas, stepped streets and narrow, winding alleys, the Old Town (Centro Storico) has an Italianate character. Its hub is Piazza della Riforma, a square lined with tall shuttered buildings and filled with busy pavement cafés. Palm-fringed promenades line the quays, and the distinctive sugar-loaf outlines of Monte Brè and Monte San Salvatore rise to the east and south.

17

The number of heritage sites of national significance in Lugano.

The 18th-century **Palazzo Riva** *has decorated windows with wrought-iron balconies.*

START

The Renaissance façade of **Cattedrale San Lorenzo** *contains a rose window depicting the Madonna and Child.*

VIA SAN LORENZO

VIA PESSINA

VIA MOTTA

PIAZZA DELLA RIFORMA

RIVA GIOCONDO ALBERTOLLI

Palazzo Civico, *the Neo-Classical town hall built in 1844–5, features a statue of the architect Domenico Fontana from Melide.*

Filled with pavement cafés, **Piazza della Riforma** *is the social and geographical hub of Lugano's historic centre.*

← A pastel-coloured restaurant on the Piazza della Riforma

↑ The luxuriously decorated nave of Cattedrale San Lorenzo in Lugano, with intricate frescoes

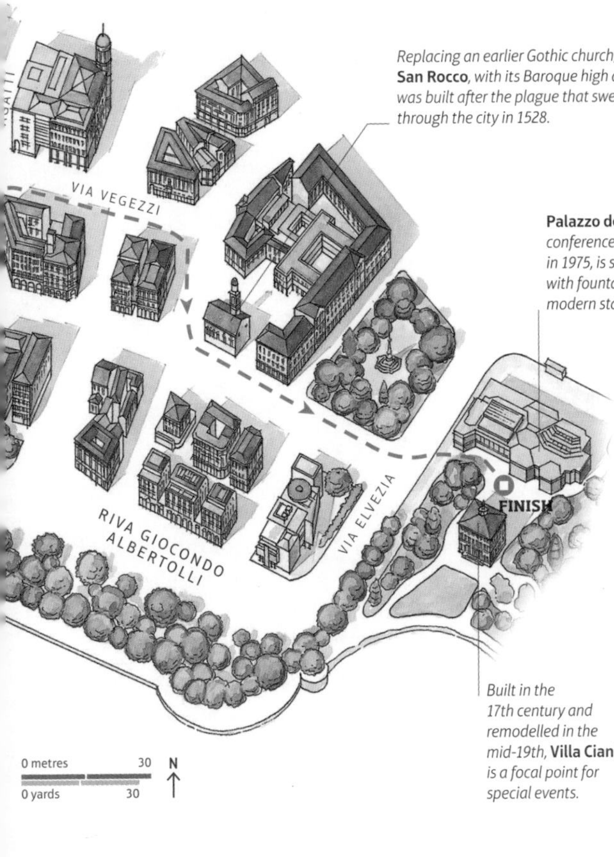

Replacing an earlier Gothic church, **San Rocco**, *with its Baroque high altar, was built after the plague that swept through the city in 1528.*

VIA VEGEZZI

Palazzo dei Congressi *conference centre, built in 1975, is set in a park with fountains and modern statuary.*

FINISH

VIA ELVEZIA

RIVA GIOCONDO ALBERTOLLI

Built in the 17th century and remodelled in the mid-19th, **Villa Ciani** *is a focal point for special events.*

0 metres 30
0 yards 30
N ↑

↑ A quiet sunny day in Piazza Grande, the core of the town of Locarno

5

LOCARNO

E5 Ticino Piazza Stazione; www.ascona-locarno.com

With an enchanting setting at the northern tip of Lake Maggiore, Locarno lies in a wide bay in the shelter of the Lepontine Alps. It is often said to be the sunniest of all Swiss towns, and date palm, fig, pomegranate and bougainvillea thrive in its mild climate. During the Middle Ages, Locarno was the centre of a dispute between the bishops of Como and the dukes of Milan, until the Swiss Confederation gained control in 1512. The capital of Ticino from 1803 to 1878, today Locarno is a resort that attracts visitors from north of the Alps who come to enjoy its Mediterranean climate.

1   

Piazza Grande

This rectangular paved square, one of Switzerland's biggest, is the focus of life in Locarno. Along its north side are 19th-century buildings with arcades of shops, cafés and restaurants. There is a weekly market here selling handicrafts and local produce on Thursdays, concerts are held in July, and during the renowned International Film Festival, a ten-day extravaganza held in early August, the square becomes an open-air cinema, lined with rows of seats and a huge screen.

2

Chiesa San Francesco

Via Cittadella 20

Completed in 1572, the church of St Francis stands on the site of a 13th-century Franciscan monastery. The eagle, ox and lamb on its Renaissance façade represent Locarno's aristocrats, ordinary citizens and country-dwellers respectively. The interior decoration dates mainly from the 18th century.

3 

Castello Visconteo

Piazza Castello 2 Apr-Oct: 10am-4:30pm Tue-Sun castellolocarno.ch

The origins of this castle go back to the 12th century, when it was built for the Orelli family. In 1342 ownership fell into the hands of the Milanese Visconti family. The dovetailed crenellation of the walls and the towers dates from a series of 15th-century expansions, as does the ravelin fortification, believed to be the work of Leonardo da Vinci. The surviving wing now houses an archaeology museum, which has a particularly good collection of Roman artifacts.

2,155

The average hours of sunshine Locarno enjoys every year.

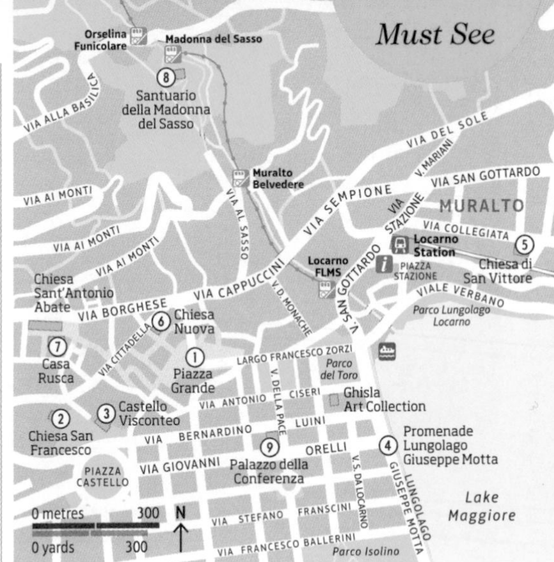

Promenade Lungolago Giuseppe Motta

Lined with trees, plants and shrubs from around the world, this lakeshore promenade resembles the seafront boulevards of the French Riviera. The promenade leads northwards to the end of the lake, where the Ghisla Art Collection, a small gallery, hangs an eclectic array of abstract art. To the south, the promenade leads towards the marina, beyond which is a sandy beach and an impressive public pool.

Chiesa di San Vittore

Via Collegiata, Muralto

Built in the 12th century, the Romanesque basilica of San Vittore stands on the site of a 10th-century church in Muralto, east of the train station. The basilica's belfry, begun in the 16th century but only completed in 1932, has a charming Renaissance relief of St Victor. The austere interior bears traces of medieval frescoes, and below, the crypt contains columns with carved capitals.

Chiesa Nuova

Via Cittadella

This church, also known as Chiesa Santa Maria Assunta, was completed in 1636. Its construction was funded by the architect Cristoforo Orelli. It has a splendid pastel-painted Baroque interior with sumptuous stuccowork and paintings depicting scenes from the life of the Virgin. Gracing the west front is a large statue of St Christopher with unusually tiny feet for a statue of its size. The Palazzo Cristoforo Orelli, next to the church, now serves as the canon's office.

Casa Rusca

Piazza Sant' Antonio
10am-4:30pm Tue-Sun
museocasarusca.ch

This elegant 18th-century residence houses an art gallery focussing on the work of modern and contemporary artists, many of whom have donated pieces of their work to the gallery. A highlight of the collection is a display of work by Hans Arp (1886–1966), the Dadaist artist who spent his final years in Locarno.

Santuario della Madonna del Sasso

Via Santuario 2, Orselina
Church: 7:30am-6pm daily; museum: Apr-Nov: 9:30am-12:30pm & 1-5pm Fri-Sun madonnadelsasso.org

The pilgrimage church of the Madonna of the Rock (Santa Maria Assunta) overlooks the town from the summit of a wooded spur. Dating from 1596, the church stands on the site of a 1487 chapel that marked the spot where legend claims the Madonna appeared before Bartolomeo da Ivrea, a monk in the Franciscan order. The present church features frescoes and oil paintings, including an altarpiece with the Flight into Egypt painted by Bramantino in 1522.

↑ Detail of the exquisite ceiling of Santuario della Madonna del Sasso

Palazzo della Conferenza

Via della Pace

It was in this *palazzo* that the Treaty of Locarno, drawn up between Germany and other European countries in the aftermath of World War I, was ratified in 1925.

→ The 270-m- (885-ft-) long suspension bridge above Sementina Valley

BELLINZONA

E5 Ticino Palazzo Civico; www.bellinzonaturismo.ch

Due to its strategic location between the great Alpine passes, Bellinzona was a fortress town from Roman times. During the Middle Ages, the dukes of Milan built the three castles here that now form a UNESCO World Heritage Site. The town was taken over by the Swiss Confederation in the 16th century, and became the capital of Ticino in 1803.

Castelgrande

Salita Castelgrande 18 Spring & summer: 10am-6pm daily; autumn & winter: 10:30am-4pm daily fortezzabellinzona.ch

Set on a high plateau, this is the oldest and grandest of Bellinzona's three castles. In the 12th century, the Roman fortress that already stood on the site was rebuilt and enlarged by the bishops of Como. The fortress was extended on several occasions until the late 15th century.

Today Castelgrande's main features are the Torre Bianca (White Tower) and the Torre Nera (Black Tower), which are joined by crenellated walls that form inner baileys. In the south wing, a museum traces Bellinzona's history, displaying 15th-century painted panels from the walls and ceiling of a villa from the town.

Old Town

Bellinzona's Old Town nestles in the wide Ticino Valley, in the shadow of its great medieval castles. With Italianate squares, Renaissance buildings and red cobblestones peppering its winding alleys, it is a typical Lombard town. Among the town's many fine buildings are the Palazzo Civico, an elegant town hall with an arcaded courtyard, and the Chiesa Santa Maria delle Grazie, a church with 15th-century frescoes. On Saturday mornings the Old Town fills with colourful market stalls heaped with fresh produce such as cheeses and bread, plus wines and local crafts.

Did You Know?

Bellinzona's annual Carnevale Rabadan (meaning "noise carnival") is over 150 years old.

Chiesa Collegiata dei Pietro e Stefano

Piazza Collegiata

This Renaissance monastery church stands at the foot of the ramparts of Castelgrande. The interior retains an earlier set of Gothic arches, and is sublimely decorated with stuccowork and lavish frescoes. Over the high altar is a depiction of the Crucifixion, painted by Simone Peterzano.

GREAT VIEW
The Tibetan Bridge

From the Bellinzona suburbs, a funicular will carry you through chestnut woods up to Monte Carasso. A pleasant circular hike leads to the spectacular Carasc wooden Tibetan bridge, anchored with flexible cables. It hangs above the Sementina Valley, and offers sweeping views over the treetops to the town.

④ 

Castello di Montebello

Via Artore 4 Apr-Oct: 10am-6pm daily Nov-Mar fortezzabellinzona.ch

A 13th-century keep and a 15th-century residential palace make up this complex fortress. The crenellated walls linking Castello di Montebello, to the east of the town, and Castelgrande, to the west, created a formidable defence system across the valley. The views from the castle are spectacular; on a clear day you can see as far as Lake Maggiore *(p234)*. A museum, in the keep, contains archaeological artifacts from the vicinity.

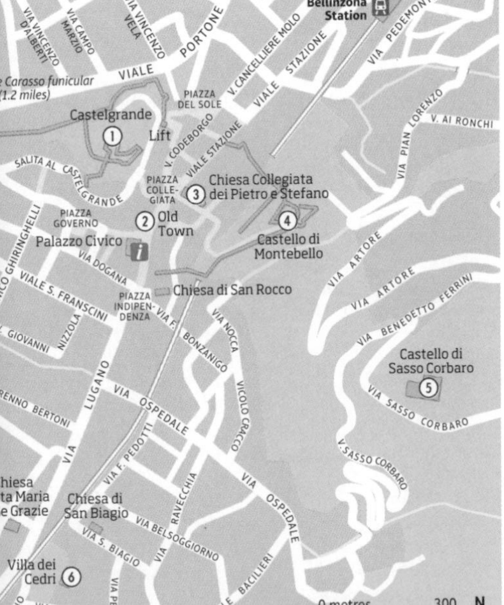

⑤   

Castello di Sasso Corbaro

Via Sasso Corbaro 44 Apr-Oct: 10am-6pm daily Nov-Mar fortezzabellinzona.ch

Castello di Sasso Corbaro is the youngest of the town's three fortresses. It was built in 1479 to the design of Benedetto Ferrini, after the Swiss had defeated the Milanese at the Battle of Giornico, thus increasing the threat to Ticino. The fortress, a quadrilateral residential tower and square ramparts, is set on an elevated headland and commands wide views across the Ticino Valley all the way to Lake Maggiore.

⑥ 

Villa dei Cedri

Piazza San Biagio 9 2-6pm Wed & Thu, 10am-6pm Fri-Sun villacedri.ch

Overlooking a vineyard, this Neo-Renaissance villa is the town's art gallery. On display are 19th- and 20th-century paintings and prints, including works by Giovanni Segantini.

A fountain standing in Zug's picturesque medieval Old Town

EXPERIENCE MORE

Zug

E3 Zug
Bahnhofstrasse; www.zug-tourismus.ch

Zug is set on the northeastern shore of Zugersee, in the wooded foothills of the Zugerberg. It is the capital of its namesake, Zug, the smallest but also the richest of all the Swiss cantons. Having the lowest taxation in Switzerland, Zug has become the headquarters of many multinational companies.

Substantial parts of the walls, set with towers, still encircle Zug's medieval Old Town. The main hub of the Old Town is Kolinplatz, which features a fountain with a statue of Wolfgang Kolin, a standard-bearer of the Swiss army. Nearby stands the Gothic Rathaus, built in 1509.

The former bailiff's castle houses the **Museum Burg Zug**, with small permanent collections of local history, as well as special exhibitions. Nearby is a 16th-century granary now converted into the **Kunsthaus**, a gallery with an important collection of Viennese modern art. The **Museum für Urgeschichte(n)** concentrates both on prehistory and antiquity.

Cruises on the Zugersee depart from the harbour jetty.

Museum Burg Zug
Kirchenstrasse 11
2-5pm Tue-Fri, 10am-5pm Sat & Sun burgzug.ch

Kunsthaus
Dorfstrasse 27
Noon-6pm Tue-Fri, 10am-5pm Sat & Sun
kunsthauszug.ch

Museum für Urgeschichte(n)
Hofstrasse 15
2-5pm Tue-Sun
urgeschichte-zug.ch

8

Küssnacht am Rigi

D3 Schwyz
Unterdorf 15; www.hohlgassland.ch

The small town of Küssnacht am Rigi lies at the foot of the Rigi. This massif rises to the east of Küssnachtersee, which extends as the northern arm of Lake Lucerne.

The town is a good base for hiking and other activities in the mountains and for exploring Lake Lucerne.

Buildings of interest in Küssnacht's historic district include the Baroque town hall and the Kirche St Peter und St Paul. Another is the Engel Hotel, a half-timbered building that dates from 1552 and has been an inn for over 400 years.

Rigi and Vitznau

D3 Lucerne
Bahnhofstrasse 7, Vitznau; www.rigi.ch

The Rigi massif, with views of 13 lakes and hundreds of peaks, is one of Switzerland's most popular holiday destinations. Instead of glaciers and crevasses, there are lavish resort hotels and hiking paths through woods and open pastures with more than 1,000

INSIDER TIP
Trotti Bike

Ride down prepared forest trails on these stand-up scooter-like bikes with fat tyres and no seat. They are suitable for anyone aged ten and up and can be rented in Engelberg *(www.titlis.ch)*.

Engelberg's thrilling Titlis Cliff Walk, a dizzying suspension bridge

species of flora. The highest of the summits is called Rigi-Kulm (1,798 m/5,900 ft), less than half the height of the Matterhorn, but a lot easier to climb with children.

A popular base is Vitznau, which lies in a sheltered bay on the north shore of Lake Lucerne. Vitznau is also the base station of the oldest rack railway in Europe, opened in 1871. It leads up to just below the summit of Rigi-Kulm, offering breathtaking views.

Stans

D4 Nidwalden Bahnhofplatz 4; www.nidwalden.com

Stans is a town on the banks of the River Engelberger Aa. Above the small town rises the Stanserhorn (1,900 m/ 6,234 ft), the summit of which can be reached from Stans by funicular and the world's first double-decker cable car with an open top.

The town's charming historic district revolves around Dorfplatz. This square is dominated by a Baroque parish church, Pfarrkirche St Peter und St Paul, with a Romanesque tower, the remains of an earlier church. In the centre of Dorfplatz stands a 19th-century monument to Arnold von Winkelried who sacrificed his life to help his Confederate comrades defeat the Austrians at the Battle of Sempach in 1386.

Also noteworthy in the town are the Höfli, a medieval turreted house that contains a museum of local history, and the Winkelriedhaus, a late-Gothic building that houses a museum of local folk crafts and traditions.

STAY

Rigi Kaltbad Spa Hotel

A designer retreat high on Mount Rigi with epic views.

D3 Zentum 4a, Rigi Kaltbad hotelrigikaltbad.ch

Hotel & Spa Internazionale

A powder pink confection with pleasant rooms in the town centre.

E5 Viale Stazione 35, Bellinzona hotel-internazionale.ch

Engelberg

D4 Obwalden Klosterstrasse 3, www.engelberg.ch

A popular mountain resort, Engelberg lies at an altitude of 1,000 m (3,280 ft), at the foot of Titlis, whose rocky peak reaches 3,239 m (10,627 ft) to a glacier.

The village nestles around the Kloster, a Benedictine monastery. Founded in the 12th century and rebuilt in the mid-18th, it has an exquisite Rococo church, built in 1735–40. The monastery, and its working cheese dairy, are open to visitors.

Engelberg has about 80 km (50 miles) of skiing pistes. It also offers tobogganing and ice-skating facilities. Marked trails in the vicinity lead up to the summits of Schlossberg Titlis, Urirotstock and Hutstock. There are also many cycling routes. The Rotair cable car, which rotates as it travels to give passengers an all-round view, runs from Stand, above Engelberg, over the Titlis glacier. Those with a head for heights can also inch across the Titlis Cliff Walk, one of Europe's highest suspension bridges, at 3,040 m (9,980 ft).

12

Schwyz

E3 Schwyz Zeughausstrasse 10; www.schwyz-tourismus.ch

This quiet town, capital of the canton of the same name, lies at the foot of the twin peaks of the Mythen. It has immense importance in Swiss history and culture.

The canton of Schwyz gave Switzerland both its name and its flag. Having sworn their mutual allegiance in 1291, the joint forces of Schwyz, Uri and Unterwalden united to defeat the Habsburgs at the Battle of Morgarten (1315). Thereafter they were known as Schwyzers, and by the late 1400s, the Swiss had adopted the name Schwyzerland.

The **Bundesbriefmuseum** (Museum of the Swiss Charters of Confederation) in Schwyz preserves a number of important historical documents. The most highly prized exhibit is the Charter of Confederation, written on parchment and stamped with the seals of the three Forest Cantons in 1291.

Schwyz's Old Town contains many 17th- and 18th-century buildings. Hauptplatz, the central square, is dominated by the Baroque Pfarrkirche St Martin and the Rathaus, the 17th-century town hall whose façade features a depiction of the Battle of Morgarten painted in 1891. The **Ital-Reding-Haus**, a mansion built in 1609, contains a suite of rooms with 17th- and 18th-century furnishings and decoration. Nearby is Haus Bethlehem, a wooden house built in 1287.

Did You Know?

Oscar-winning filmmaker Xavier Koller was born in Schwyz.

The calm waters of Urnersee, backed by steep-sided mountains

A former granary dating from 1711 houses the **Forum der Schweizer Geschichte**, a museum of daily life.

Bundesbriefmuseum
Bahnhofstrasse 20
10am-5pm Tue-Sun
bundesbrief.ch

Ital-Reding-Haus
Rickenbachstrasse 24
May-Oct: 2-5pm Tue-Fri, 10am-4pm Sat & Sun
irh.ch

Forum der Schweizer Geschichte
Zeughausstrasse 5
10am-5pm Tue-Sun
forumschwyz.ch

13

Urnersee

E4 Uri Bahnhof strasse 15, Brunnen; www.erlebnisregion-mythen.ch

Stunningly beautiful Urnersee forms the southeastern arm of Lake Lucerne. Surrounded on all sides by high, steep-sided mountains, Urnersee resembles a Norwegian fjord. On an elevated promontory below Seelisberg, on the west side of the lake, is Rütli Meadow (Bergwiese Rütli), where the alliance between the cantons of Schwyz, Unterwalden and Uri was sworn in 1291 *(p57)*.

The village of Seedorf, at the southern extremity of Urnersee, has a picturesque Gothic-Renaissance castle. It was built in 1556–60 and now houses a small geological museum. Flüelen, nearby, is the furthest port of call for any boats that sail across the lake from Lucerne.

Rathausplatz in the centre of Altdorf, in which stands the Telldenkmal

About 3 km (2 miles) north of Flüelen is the Tellsplate, a flat rock. According to legend, this is where William Tell made his leap to freedom during his journey across Lake Lucerne, on his way to imprisonment at Küssnacht. Near the rock stands the Tellskapelle, a 16th-century chapel remodelled in the 19th century.

WILLIAM TELL

Switzerland's national hero, or perhaps just a myth? Revisionist historians say William Tell *(right)* was invented more than a century after he allegedly freed his son, and his emerging country, from Habsburg feudal lords by shooting the evil bailiff Hermann Gessler in 1307. This emblematic act of courage and resistance has echoed down the ages and across the globe, thanks in part to Hollywood, Friedrich Schiller's play and Gioachino Rossini's opera. If, as now suggested, it was all a ploy designed to forge a sense of national unity, it worked.

14

Bürglen

E4 Uri uri.info

This small town at the mouth of the Schächen Valley is reputed to be the birthplace of William Tell, hero of Swiss legend. The supposed site of his house is marked by a chapel built in 1582. It is decorated with frescoes illustrating how Tell killed a Habsburg duke, triggering confederacy.

The legend of William Tell and the place it occupies in Swiss culture are illustrated through over 600 years' worth of paintings and chronicles at the fascinating **Tell Museum**. Also of interest in Bürglen are a 17th-century wooden tavern, the Adler Inn, which serves local beers, and an early Baroque church with a Romanesque tower.

Tell Museum

Postplatz May, Jun, Sep & Oct: 10-11:30am & 1:30-5pm daily; Jul & Aug: 10am-5pm daily tellmuseum.ch

15

Altdorf

E4 Uri
Tellspielhaus; www.uri.info

Altdorf is said to be the town where William Tell shot an apple from his son's head. The Telldenkmal, a statue of Tell, stands on Rathausplatz, and plays of the story are are regularly performed.

Centovalli

E5 Ticino Intragna; 091 780 75 00

The stunning Centovalli (Hundred Valleys) is so named for the many side valleys that cut into it. The **Centovalli Railway**, from Locarno to Domodossola in Italy, takes a spectacularly scenic route up the Centovalli. On this journey of about 40 km (25 miles), the train crosses 83 bridges or viaducts over deep canyons and passes through 24 tunnels. The first part of the journey leads along the vineyard-covered Val Pedemonte and then wends its way through rugged countryside and deep forests full of chestnut trees.

The train stops at several villages along the route. At Verscio, 4 km (2.5 miles) from Locarno, there is a performing arts school, founded by the famous Swiss clown Dimitri. Nearby Intragna has a Baroque church. Palagnedra has a small Gothic church decorated with 15th-century frescoes.

1995

The year Swiss clown Dimitri was inducted into the International Clown Hall of Fame.

Centovalli Railway
Via Franzoni 1, Locarno
vigezzinacentovalli.com

Ascona

E6 Ticino Via B Papio 5; www.ascona-locarno.com

A small fishing village for many centuries, Ascona developed in the early 20th century, when it became a fashionable health resort, attracting writers, painters and composers. Nearby Monte Verita (Hill of Truth) was established as a progressive colony around the same time, attracting some of Europe's leading thinkers, artists, revolutionaries and writers.

Ascona's exquisite Old Town (Centro Storico) is a maze of narrow cobbled streets, with small craft shops and art galleries. Many of the most picturesque of Ascona's historic buildings, the oldest of which date from the 14th century, line Contrada Maggiore. Piazza San Pietro is dominated by the 16th-century Chiesa dei Santi Pietro e Paolo, which has an altarpiece painted by Giovanni Serodine, a pupil of Caravaggio. Also notable are the Collegio Papio, which has a pretty Renaissance arcaded courtyard, and Santa Maria della Misericordia, a church with colourful 15th-century frescoes. The Museo Comunale d'Arte Moderna, in a 16th-century *palazzo*, contains work by artists who flocked to the town, including Paul Klee. Piazza Motta, a pedestrianized lakefront promenade, is home to cafés and restaurants.

Valle Verzasca

E5 Ticino Via ai Giardini, Tenero; www.ascona-locarno.com

Washed by the emerald waters of the River Verzasca, this is an exceptionally scenic valley lying north of Locarno. A gigantic dam, the Contra Dam, near the mouth of the valley has created the Lago di Vogorno, a large artificial lake.

The valley is lined with villages, whose stone houses cling to the mountainsides. Vogorno has a small church decorated with Byzantine frescoes. Near Lavertezzo, the river is spanned by the

INSIDER TIP
Bungee Jump

James Bond did it, so they call the 220 m (722 ft) bungee jump from the Contra Dam "the 007". It's one of the tallest bungees in the world; you can jump at night, or even go backwards.

← The handsome Italian-style buildings and cobbled streets of Ascona's Old Town

The Ponte dei Salti, a medieval double-arched bridge in Valle Verzasca ↑

Ponte dei Salti, a medieval double-arched bridge. A modern art trail, running for 4 km (2.5 miles) between Brione and Lavertezzo, is lined with works by 34 Italian, Swiss and German sculptors.

At Brione-Verzasca is a church with origins that go back to the 13th century. Its façade is decorated with a painting of St Christopher, and the interior features 15th-century frescoes.

Valle Maggia

E5 Ticino
www.vallemaggia.ch

This deep valley runs for about 50 km (30 miles) northwest of Ascona up to Cevio. At its lower levels, the valley is wide, though as it ascends it becomes increasingly rugged, with forests of pine and larch. The valley is also dotted with historical buildings and churches, and rugged stone houses. At Maggia, the largest village in the valley, you'll find the 15th-century Chiesa Santa Maria delle Grazie. The exterior is unremarkable but the interior is decorated with dazzling 16th- and 17th-century frescoes.

Past Giumaglio, where there are dramatic waterfalls, the road leads further up the valley to Cevio. A notable feature of this village is the 17th-century Palazzo Pretorio, its façade featuring the coats of arms of the bailiffs who successively occupied the building. Nearby stands the Palazzo Franzoni (1630), which houses a museum of regional history.

The hamlet of Mogno contains the serenely beautiful Chiesa di San Giovanni Battista. Designed by the Ticinese architect Mario Botta and completed in 1996, this extraordinary church is built of local stone. The interior is lined with white marble and grey granite arranged in stripes and chequer patterns. The light pouring in through the translucent ceiling only enhances the effect.

EAT

Grottos are shady, secluded outdoor restaurants with stone tables, typical of Ticino.

Grotto San Michele
A great choice, handy for the castle.

E5 Salita Castelgrande 18, Bellinzona
castelgrande.ch

Grotto Canvett
The epitome of tradition.

E5 Cà d'Varénzin 6, Semione
grottocanvett.ch

Grotto del Cavicc
Beloved of writer Hermann Hesse.

E6 19a Via ai Canvetti, Montagnola
grottocavicc.ch

The village of Foroglio, Val Bavona, a popular base for hiking

20

Val Bavona

D5 Ticino  Centro Commerciale, Maggia; 91 753 18 85; www.ascona-locarno.com

Said to be the steepest and rockiest valley anywhere in the Alps, the beautiful Val Bavona is very wild – almost a world apart from the lush meadows and hills found elsewhere in the country. It is deserted in winter and still not connected to the Swiss electricity grid, despite being under a hydroelectric plant. All the houses are made of grey stone, and massive boulders have been adapted into shelters for animals and humans alike. These structures, which are sometimes built into the rock, are called *sprügh*. In such precipitous terrain, waterfalls abound. The most impressive in all Ticino is the Cascata di Foroglio which falls 111 m (365 ft). The waterfall is an easy walk from the hamlet of Foroglio, which is on the Swiss postal bus route.

21

Valle di Blenio

E5 Ticino  Via Lavorceno, Olivone; 91 872 14 87; www.vallediblenio.com

This scenic valley, washed by the River Brenno, leads up to the Lucomagno Pass (1,916 m/ 6,286 ft). The road up the valley and over the pass leads into the canton of Graubünden. Val di Blenio lies in the heart of rural Ticino. One of the sunniest spots in the country, it has great scenery and is dotted with picturesque villages.

Biasca, at the foot of the valley, has a Romanesque church with Gothic frescoes. Just north of Biasca lies Malvaglia. The 16th- to 17th-century church here has a Romanesque tower and its façade features a large painting of St Christopher.

Negrentino is notable for its early Romanesque church of St Ambrose, whose tall belfry tower can be seen from afar. The interior of the church is decorated with frescoes dating from the 11th to the 16th centuries. Lottigna has an interesting museum of regional history (the Museo Storico della Valle di Blenio). The villages higher up the valley, such as Olivone, are good bases for mountain excursions and hikes.

22

Airolo

E5 Ticino  From Airolo station Casella Postale 145, Airolo; 091 869 15 33; www.airolo.ch

Located just below the St Gotthard Pass, Airolo lies at the point where the motorway and railway line through the St Gotthard Tunnel emerge. As it is bypassed by these major routes, Airolo is a quiet town. With several hotels, it is a convenient base for exploring the valley that stretches out

Negrentino's church with its beautiful Romanesque and late-Gothic frescoes

Did You Know?

The old road up to the St Gottard Pass has 37 bends, each with its own name.

below. A plaque in the town commemorates the 177 people who died during the tunnel's construction in the 1880s.

Valle Leventina, below Airolo, carries the motorway and main railway line that run from Zürich to Bellinzona and Lugano. The valley is dotted with small towns and villages, worth exploring for their interesting historic churches. Chiggiogna has a church with 15th-century frescoes, while Chironico has a 10th-century church with 14th-century frescoes. The 12th-century church in Giornico is one of the finest in Ticino. The interior is decorated with frescoes dating from 1478.

St Gotthard Pass

E5 passosan gottardo.ch

With the Reuss Valley in the canton of Uri to the north, and the Ticino Valley to the south, the St Gotthard Pass lies at an altitude of 2,108 m (6,916 ft). It is on the principal route from northern Europe to Italy and has been used as a major Alpine pass for over 700 years.

The pass is crossed by three tunnels. In 1882 the Gotthard Rail Tunnel opened, but it was not until almost a century later that a road tunnel followed, in 1980. In 2016, Switzerland inaugurated the world's longest rail tunnel here, the 57-km- (35-mile-) long Gotthard Base Tunnel, allowing for speeds of up to 200 km/h (124 mph) and reducing the journey time from Zürich to Milan to two hours and 40 minutes.

The old cobblestoned Tremola road, leading up to the St Gotthard Pass ↑

The 19th-century hospice on the St Gotthard pass houses the **Museo Nazionale del San Gottardo**, which reopened in 2022 after a complete refurbishment with new exhibitions and activities. The museum documents the history of the pass and describes the region's flora and fauna.

Marked trails lead up to the summit of many of the surrounding peaks, including Pizzo Lucendro, and to mountain terraces from which there are splendid views.

Museo Nazionale del San Gottardo

Jun-Oct: 9am-6pm daily
museonazionalesan gottardo.ch

Museo Sasso San Gottardo

E4 Passo del S Gottardo, Airolo
Jun & Jul: 10am-3pm Wed-Mon (Aug: daily; Sep & Oct: Wed-Sun)
sasso-sangottardo.ch

Located on the historic mountain pass of the same name, the Museo Sasso San Gottardo is set in a former secret military bunker buried deep in the mountains. Two museums in one, it is in part a natural history museum and in part a military museum. Visitors delve hundreds of metres into the mountains before taking the "Metro del Sasso", an underground cable car to the fortress. Inside, it is as if the 420 soldiers that once occupied it have only just left: dining hall, cannons, hospital, communications and map rooms are all as they were. The bunker was fully operational from 1943 to 1998, as dozens of Swiss mountain redoubts still are. In the natural history part of the museum is an exhibition on climate, ecology and the minerals that make up the Alps. Displays include enormous crystals – weighing over 1,360 kg – found near the St Gotthard Pass. Together, these two museums provide fascinating insight into the Swiss military mentality.

INSIDER TIP
Wrap Up at the Museum

Visiting the Museo Sasso San Gottardo? Then dress warmly. Even during summer, the underground tunnels and caverns are cold and damp.

A DRIVING TOUR
LAKE MAGGIORE

Locator Map

For more detail see p202

Length 40 km (25 miles) **Stopping-off points** Ascona and Locarno for a wide choice of restaurants

Only the northern tip of this long, slender pre-Alpine lake lies in Switzerland, with the remaining portion curving southwards into Italian territory. Some 60 km (40 miles) long and 6 km (4 miles) wide, Lake Maggiore is hemmed in by mountains to the north, south and west. Follow this route through beachy resort towns, mountainside vineyards and terraced villages with jaw-dropping views. Boats and hydrofoils cross the lake from Ascona, Locarno and Brissago, carrying passengers down to the resorts in its Italian section.

Did You Know?

According to legend, Napoleon Bonaparte declared the lake a "wellspring of happiness".

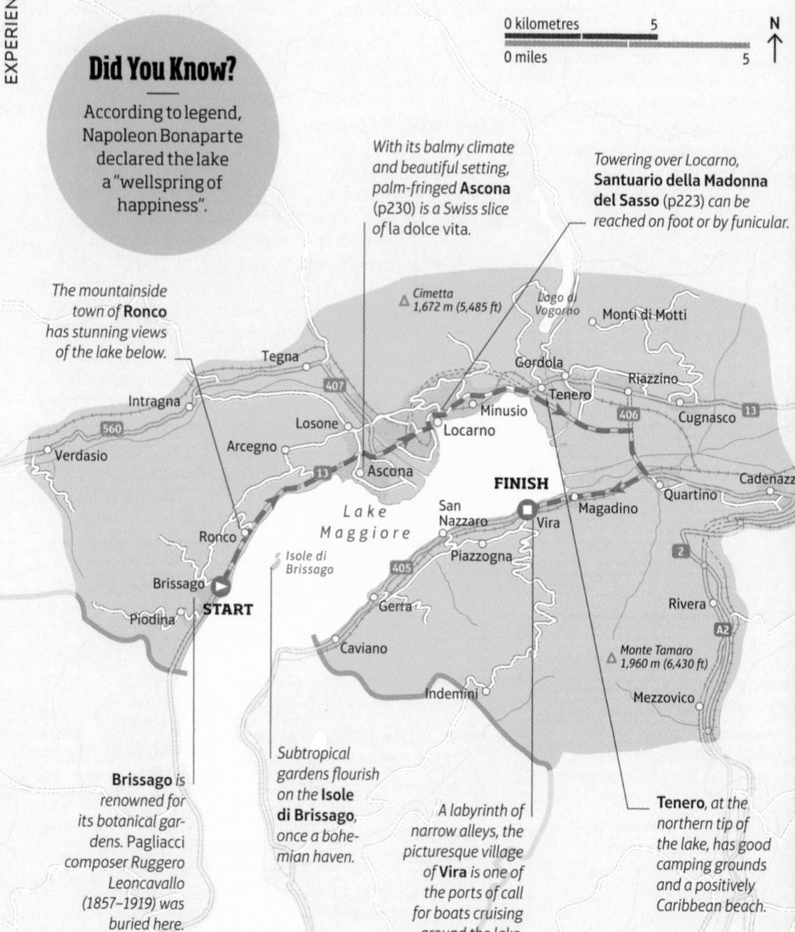

With its balmy climate and beautiful setting, palm-fringed **Ascona** *(p230) is a Swiss slice of* la dolce vita.

Towering over Locarno, **Santuario della Madonna del Sasso** *(p223) can be reached on foot or by funicular.*

The mountainside town of **Ronco** *has stunning views of the lake below.*

Brissago *is renowned for its botanical gardens. Pagliacci composer Ruggero Leoncavallo (1857–1919) was buried here.*

Subtropical gardens flourish on the **Isole di Brissago**, *once a bohemian haven.*

A labyrinth of narrow alleys, the picturesque village of **Vira** *is one of the ports of call for boats cruising around the lake.*

Tenero, *at the northern tip of the lake, has good camping grounds and a positively Caribbean beach.*

↑ The lofty Santuario della Madonna del Sasso rising from the town of Locarno

The town of Hospental dwarfed by snow-capped peaks in the distance ↑

A DRIVING TOUR
THREE PASSES

Length 120 km (75 miles) **Stopping-off points** Andermatt and Göschenen for small hotels and restaurants

CENTRAL SWITZERLAND AND TICINO
Three Passes

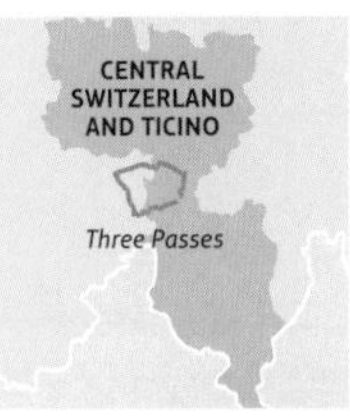

Locator Map
For more detail see p202

The circular route over the Uri Alps traverses some of the most spectacular Alpine scenery in Switzerland. On the route are three mountain passes – the Susten Pass, Grimsel Pass and Furka Pass – each of which marks cantonal borders. A feat of 19th-century engineering, the road twists and turns, makes tightly winding ascents and descents, crosses bridges over dramatically plunging valleys, and passes through tunnels cut into the rock. All along the route are spectacular views of snow-capped mountains, majestic glaciers and beautiful mountain lakes.

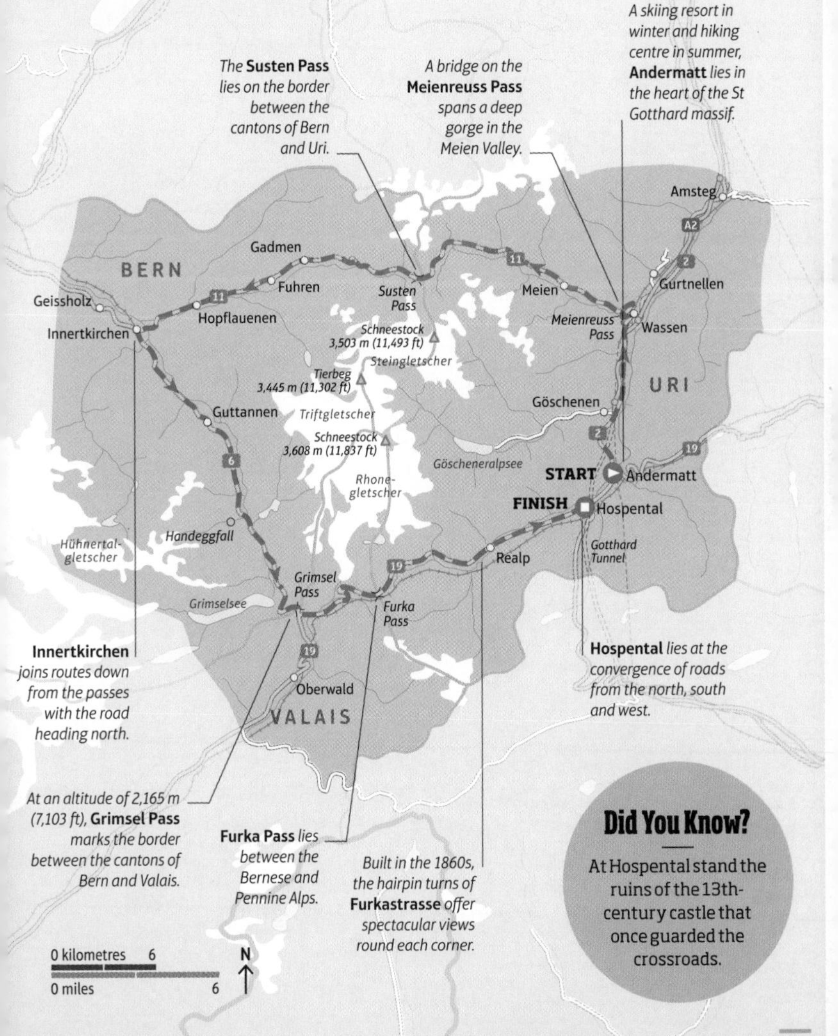

The Susten Pass lies on the border between the cantons of Bern and Uri.
A bridge on the Meienreuss Pass spans a deep gorge in the Meien Valley.
A skiing resort in winter and hiking centre in summer, Andermatt lies in the heart of the St Gotthard massif.
Amsteg
A2
2
Gurtnellen
Gadmen
BERN
Fuhren
11
Susten Pass
Meien
Meienreuss Pass
Wassen
Geissholz
Innertkirchen
Hopflauenen
Schneestock 3,503 m (11,493 ft)
Steingletscher
Tierbeg 3,445 m (11,302 ft)
URI
Göschenen
Guttannen
Triftgletscher
Schneestock 3,608 m (11,837 ft)
6
Göscheneralpsee
19
START
Andermatt
Rhonegletscher
FINISH
Hospental
Handeggfall
Hühnertalgletscher
Gotthard Tunnel
Realp
Grimsel Pass
Grimselsee
Furka Pass
Oberwald
VALAIS
Innertkirchen joins routes down from the passes with the road heading north.
Hospental lies at the convergence of roads from the north, south and west.
At an altitude of 2,165 m (7,103 ft), Grimsel Pass marks the border between the cantons of Bern and Valais.
Furka Pass lies between the Bernese and Pennine Alps.
Built in the 1860s, the hairpin turns of Furkastrasse offer spectacular views round each corner.
0 kilometres 6
0 miles 6
N

Did You Know?

At Hospental stand the ruins of the 13th-century castle that once guarded the crossroads.

The verdant rolling hills of Appenzell

EASTERN SWITZERLAND AND GRAUBÜNDEN

Traversed by the Rhine, which flows through Bodensee, eastern Switzerland is a relatively low-lying region of lush pastures and rural outposts, rising up into the high Alps at its most southerly extent. Known as Rhaetia in medieval times, much of the eastern part of Switzerland evolved strong German connections, in both trade and culture, while to the south, the rugged terrain increasingly cut communities off from would-be invaders.

As the Swiss Confederation spread its reach, most of the cantons to the east were partial members or subject territories, but following the defeat of Napoleon in 1815, two cantons were given full status: St Gallen and Graubünden. A university town, St Gallen has been a seat of learning since 747 when a Benedictine monastery was founded, requiring the contemplative study of books and the presence of a library. That library is now a UNESCO World Heritage Site, housing some 170,000 documents. Graubünden joined the Swiss Confederation in 1803, but it was in 1864 that it really came into its own – a hotelier in St Moritz lured summer residents back to stay for free that winter, and with this gesture, Swiss Alpine tourism was born. Home to some of the country's best ski slopes and greatest resorts, Graubünden is now a major centre for winter sports, and half of its population is involved in the tourist industry.

EASTERN SWITZERLAND AND GRAUBÜNDEN
Must Sees
1 Schaffhausen
2 St Gallen
3 Chur
4 Swiss National Park
Experience More
5 Rheinfall
6 Frauenfeld
7 Bodensee
8 Stein am Rhein
9 Appenzell
10 Toggenburg
11 Rapperswil
12 Walensee
13 Bad Ragaz
14 Maienfeld
15 Davos
16 Arosa
17 Engadine Valley
18 Müstair
19 Pontresina
20 Bernina Pass
21 Val Bregaglia
22 St Moritz
23 Sils
24 Zillis
25 San Bernardino Pass
26 Glarus
27 Klosters
28 Poschiavo
29 Mesocco
0 kilometres 15
0 miles 15
N
SCHAFFHAUSEN
RHEINFALL
STEIN AM RHEIN
FRAUENFELD
TOGGENBURG
RAPPERSWIL
GLARUS
NORTHERN SWITZERLAND
p174
CENTRAL SWITZERLAND AND TICINO
p200
Zürich International Airport
Bonndorf
Tengen
Singen
Stuhlingen
Waldshut
Rheinfelden
Rhein
Thur
Winterthur
Baden
Sissach
Aarau
Zürich
Olten
Zurichsee
Zug
Einsiedeln
Lichtensteig
Näfels
Altdorf
Piz Russein 3,611 m (11,847 ft)
Disentis
Vorderrhein
Sedrun
Andermatt
Airolo
Malvaglia
Biasca
Cevio
Someo
Bellinzona
Locarno
Ticino

EASTERN SWITZERLAND AND GRAUBÜNDEN
GERMANY
AUSTRIA
ITALY
LIECHTENSTEIN
SANKT GALLEN
GRAUBÜNDEN
BODENSEE
7
2 ST GALLEN
9 APPENZELL
12 WALENSEE
14 MAIENFELD
BAD RAGAZ 13
27 KLOSTERS
3 CHUR
15 DAVOS
16 AROSA
17 ENGADINE VALLEY
4 SWISS NATIONAL PARK
MÜSTAIR 18
24 ZILLIS
SAN BERNARDINO PASS
ST MORITZ 22
19 PONTRESINA
23 SILS
20 BERNINA PASS
29 MESOCCO
VAL BREGAGLIA
21
28 POSCHIAVO
St Gallen-Altenrhein Airport
Säntis 2,504 m (8,215 ft)
Piz Sardona 3,057 m (10,030 ft)
Weissfluhgipfel 2,845 m (9,334 ft)
Weisshorn 2,650 m (8,694 ft)
Piz Bernina 4,049 m (13,284 ft)
Maloja Pass
Silvrettagruppe
Rhein
Tamina
Hinterrhein
Inn
Ravensburg
Überlingen
Markdorf
Wangen im Allgäu
Konstanz
Kreuzlingen
Friedrichshafen
Romanshorn
Lindau
Arbon
Bregenz
Rorschach
Gossau
Herisau
Dornbirn
Gais
Altstatten
Riezlern
Au
Urnäsch
Damüls
Rankweil
Warth
Nesslau
Feldkirch
Wildhaus
Bludenz
Buchs
Vaduz
Landeck
Walenstadt
Sargans
Garfrescha
Jenaz
Martina
Scuol
Flims
Ardez
Susch
Lenzerheide
Thusis
Zernez
Vals-Platz
Savognin
Bergün
Zuoz
Valchava
Samedan
Livigno
Splügen
Bormio
San Bernardino
Silvaplana
Vicosoprano
Frontale
Stampa
Chiavenna
Ponte di Legno
Brusio
Tirano
Sondrio
Edolo
Marbegno

1

SCHAFFHAUSEN

E2 Schaffhausen Vordergasse 73; https://schaffhauserland.ch

Capital of the canton of the same name, the picturesque medieval town of Schaffhausen is set on the north bank of the Rhine, upriver from the spectacular cataracts known as the Rheinfall.

Thanks to its location at the point where the Rhine falls forced ships to unload their cargoes, the town was an important centre of trade from the early Middle Ages. The streets of its Altstadt (Old Town) are lined with Gothic, Renaissance, Baroque and Rococo buildings, such as the Haus zum Ritter, featuring frescoed façades and oriel windows. At the centre of its historic core lies Fronwagplatz, a square with two 16th-century fountains, the Metzgerbrunnen, topped by a statue of a mercenary, and the Mohrenbrunnen, with a statue of a Moorish king. A short walk to the southeast stands the austere Romanesque Münster, part of an 11th-century Benedictine abbey. The adjoining monastery is now home to a museum with prehistoric finds and Swiss art. The abbey cloisters hold the Schillerglocke, whose sound inspired German poet Friedrich Schiller to write the *Song of the Bell*. Above the town to the east lies the Munot, whose keep offers fine views of the town, the river and the countryside.

↑ The circular keep of the 16th-century Munot, now the symbol of Schaffhausen

↑ The Haus zum Ritter, with a façade covered in Renaissance frescoes dating from 1568–70

← Statue depicting a soldier at the Platz

Did You Know?

Schaffhausen has 171 oriel windows - more than any other Swiss town - built as status symbols.

The town and the 11th-century Kirche St Johann, seen from the Munot fortress

The beautiful Rococco reading hall of St Gallen Abbey's Stiftsbibliothek

ST GALLEN

F3 St Gallen Bankgasse 9; www.stgallen-bodensee.ch

The origins of St Gallen, eastern Switzerland's largest town, go back to 612, when Gallus, an Irish monk, chose the spot for his hermitage. A Benedictine abbey was founded here in 747 and soon became a centre of learning and culture; today, the abbey is a UNESCO World Heritage Site. By the 19th century, St Gallen was renowned for its textile industry. While the city's focal point is its magnificent cathedral, built in 1847, it also has a beautiful medieval centre.

Textilmuseum

Vadianstrasse 2
10am-5pm daily
textilmuseum.ch

Reflecting St Gallen's role as a centre of the European textiles industry, this museum is filled with a comprehensive array of pieces from Switzerland and abroad, including antique fabrics from Coptic graves in Egypt. The well-presented displays examine social questions through design and fashion, connecting Swiss history with the art of weaving, as well as intricate embroidery and exquisite handmade lace. Local patterns and products, and the implements that were devised to produce them, are also shown.

Stiftsbibliothek

Klosterhof 6d 10am-5pm daily stibi.ch

Although most of the abbey was destroyed during the Reformation, its important library, the Stiftsbibliothek, was spared. The main room, designed by Peter Thumb in 1758–67, is a stunning Baroque masterpiece, with elaborate Rococo touches. The wooden floor was intricately inlaid by Gabriel Loser, and the ceiling is decorated with stuccowork by Johann Georg and Mathias Gigl and trompe l'oeil paintings by Josef Wannenmacher.

The library contains more than 170,000 books and documents, including an important collection of Irish manuscripts dating from the 8th to the 11th centuries, and rare works dating from the 8th century.

HIDDEN GEM
Bierflaschen Museum

A must-visit for any beer lover, Switzerland's first beer bottle museum *(www.schuetzen garten.ch)* features more than 2,000 bottles from over 260 Swiss breweries - all empty. The well-curated exhibits are arranged by region, forming an impressive display of Swiss beer history.

Books printed after 1900 may be borrowed, but anything older can only be read on site in the reading rooms.

Marktplatz

Once the town's main market square, Marktplatz lies on the northern side of the old town. The square is surrounded by fine 17th- and 18th-century houses with intricately painted façades or decorated with delicate relief carving. Many also have attractive oriel windows, a feature typical of St Gallen's architecture.

On Marktgasse, the street leading off the southern side of Marktplatz, Labhart is a long-standing watchmaker's shop with a fascinating collection of musical boxes.

Did You Know?

St Gallen's university was decorated by some of the most innovative artists of the 20th century.

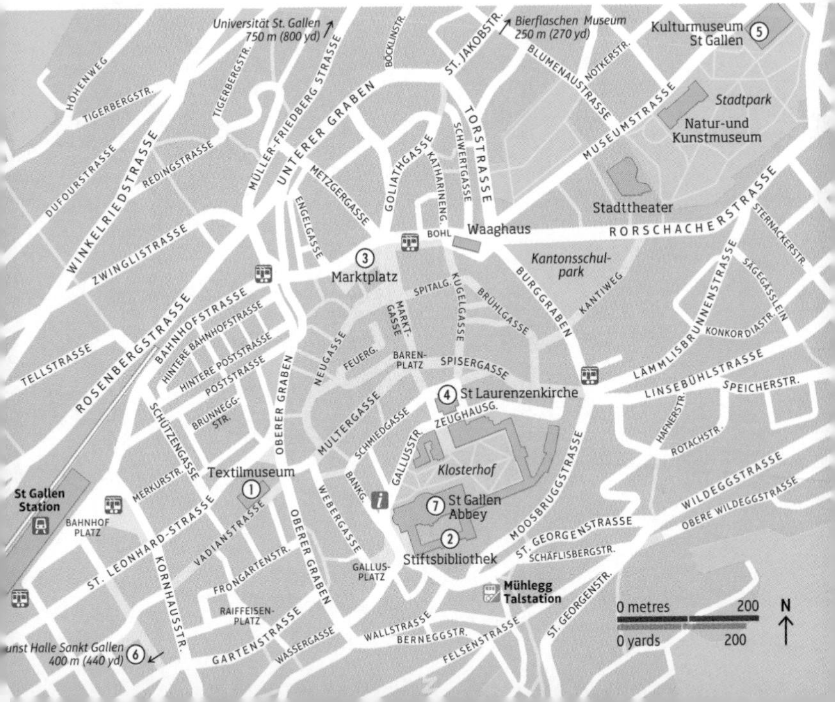

St Laurenzenkirche

Marktgasse 9:30-11:30am & 2-4pm Mon, 9:30am-4pm Tue-Sat (summer: to 6pm Tue-Fri) ref-sgc.ch

This church was originally part of the abbey complex. During the 16th century it became a centre of the Reformation in St Gallen. The building's present Neo-Gothic façade is the result of remodelling carried out in the mid-19th century.

Kulturmuseum St Gallen

Museumstrasse 50 10am-5pm Tue-Sun kulturmuseumsg.ch

The museum of history and ethnology focuses on the people and past of the town and region of St Gallen. As well as archaeological pieces, there are documents, mementos and reconstructions of domestic life from various periods, going back as far as prehistory. Highlights include a scale reconstruction of St Gallen's abbey and a model of the city as it was in the 17th century. The ethnographic collection also has Asian, African and South American artifacts.

Kunst Halle Sankt Gallen

Davidstrasse 40 Noon-6pm Tue-Fri, 11am-5pm Sat & Sun kunsthallesanktgallen.ch

This contemporary art hall sees itself as "a large small exhibitor", and an experimental space for artists to express themselves freely. The exhibits change regularly, keeping pace with developments in the world of contemporary art.

7

ST GALLEN ABBEY

170,000

The number of documents in the abbey library.

Klosterhof 6a Cathedral: 6am-6:30pm Mon-Wed, 7am-6:30pm Thu-Sat, 7:30am-8:30pm Sun; library, cellar & exhibition: 10am-5pm daily stiftsbezirk.ch

Nestled in the centre of the historic town, this abbey is one of the most spectacular examples of Baroque architecture in Switzerland. In addition to the elegant cathedral, there is a fascinating lapidarium with archaeological displays, as well as the magnificently decorated Stiftsbibliothek (abbey library), the oldest library in Switzerland.

The Benedictine abbey was established in 747 and was at the height of its importance from the 9th to the 11th centuries. The Romanesque church and monastery, built during that period, have not survived, their only remains being the crypt containing the tombs of the abbots. The present Baroque cathedral and monastery, designed by master architect Johann Michael Beer von Bildstein, were completed in 1767. The interior decoration was executed by the foremost artists of the day. Such is the importance of this sight, with its works of art and its renowned library *(p244)*, that it was made a World Heritage Site in 1983.

→ St Gallen Cathedral, with its Baroque architecture

← Frescoes by Josef Wannenmacher adorning the cathedral ceiling

The twin bell towers of St Gallen Cathedral on a sunny day ↑

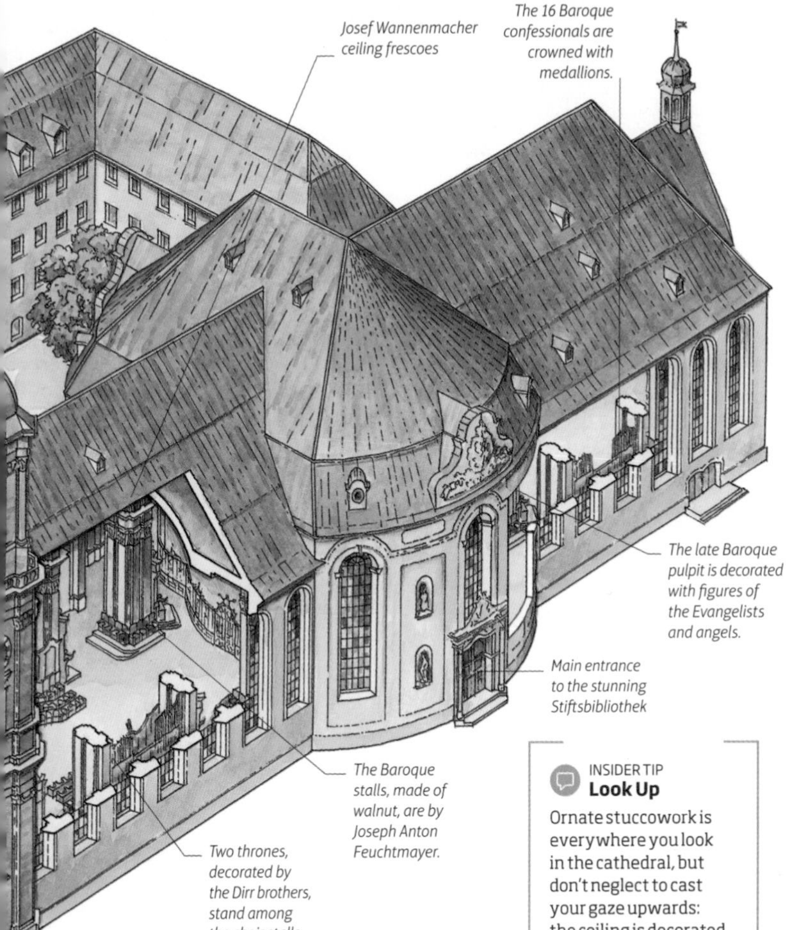

Josef Wannenmacher ceiling frescoes

The 16 Baroque confessionals are crowned with medallions.

The late Baroque pulpit is decorated with figures of the Evangelists and angels.

Main entrance to the stunning Stiftsbibliothek

The Baroque stalls, made of walnut, are by Joseph Anton Feuchtmayer.

Two thrones, decorated by the Dirr brothers, stand among the choir stalls.

INSIDER TIP
Look Up

Ornate stuccowork is everywhere you look in the cathedral, but don't neglect to cast your gaze upwards: the ceiling is decorated with dramatic and colourful frescoes by Josef Wannenmacher.

CHUR

F4 Graubunden Bahnhofplatz 3; www.churtourismus.ch

Located at the head of the Rhine Valley, Chur lies at the crossroads of ancient trade routes that linked the Alpine passes to the south and Bodensee to the north. Settled for over 5,000 years, today Chur calls itself the oldest Swiss city. The city prospered under the rule of prince-bishops from the 12th to the 16th centuries. Following the Reformation, Chur passed into secular rule, becoming the capital of the canton of Graubünden in 1803. The narrow streets and squares of the Old Town are quiet and pleasant to explore.

Rätisches Museum

Haus Buol, Hofstrasse 1
10am-5pm Tue-Sun
raetischesmuseum.gr.ch

Built in 1675 by patrician Baron von Buol Strassberg und Rieyberg, this Baroque patrician house in a quiet courtyard behind Reformierte Martinskirche is now home to this comprehensive local history museum. Although the information available in English is sometimes lacking, the displays at this museum neatly illustrate the history of Chur and its environs, with artifacts from prehistoric times to the 19th century. Among the exhibits are archaeological finds from the time of the Rhaetians – Alpine tribes who colonized the region in around 3000 BCE –and items from Graubünden's Roman period. Precious pieces from the cathedral treasury, including medieval reliquaries, are also showcased. Other exhibits include rooms of 17th-century furnishings and other domestic objects. The culture and folk arts of the Graubünden region from the 19th century through to the present day are also attractively documented.

Bischöflicher Hof

Hofplatz

The complex of buildings set on the terrace that rises to the east of the Old Town make up the oldest seated bishopric north of the Alps. Standing next to the cathedral, the bishop's palace was founded in the 6th century on the site of a Roman fort. The palace was extended on several occasions, and its thick walls reflect the ruling bishops' need for defence. The palace's present appearance is mainly the result of remodelling in the 18th and 19th centuries. Since it is still the residence of the bishops of Chur, it is not open to visitors.

Sunlight bathing the vineyards on the hills outside the city of Chur

UNDERGROUND CHUR

Subterranean remains of the city's 5th-century Kirche St Stephen were first discovered during the construction of a school in 1850. Once the cemetery church for the bishops of Chur, it lies next to Kirche St Luzi, which has a ring crypt. Both can be visited on a guided tour.

③

Reformierte Martinskirche

St Martinsplatz 081 252 22 92 8:30-11:30am & 2-5pm Mon-Fri

Since at least 769 CE there has been a church dedicated to St Martin on this spot. The late-Gothic church that stands here today was completed in 1491, replacing the earlier church that was destroyed by fire in 1464. The steepled tower, which dominates the city's landscape, was completed in 1534, and remained unaltered until 1917 when it was replaced by the tower seen today. According to local tradition, Protestant reformer Martin Luther himself delivered a sermon in the mid-1520s, which prompted the congregation's conversion.

Among the most notable features of its interior are the carved stalls and the stained-glass windows, on the right of the main doors, created by Augusto Giacometti in 1917–19, which depict the Nativity story. In the north and south façades is some of the original Carolingian masonry.

④ 

Kirche St Luzi

Alte Schanfiggerstrasse 9

This massive church, which is dedicated to the missionary who is said to have brought Christianity to the region, sits atop a vineyard-covered hill on the east side of the old town. Built in the 12th century as the church of a monastery, the building overlies the crypt of an 8th-century structure, including a ring crypt, where the relics of Saint Lucius were once displayed. Amid the church's soaring Carolingian arches and grand capitals, Romanesque carvings are visible. A seminary is on site.

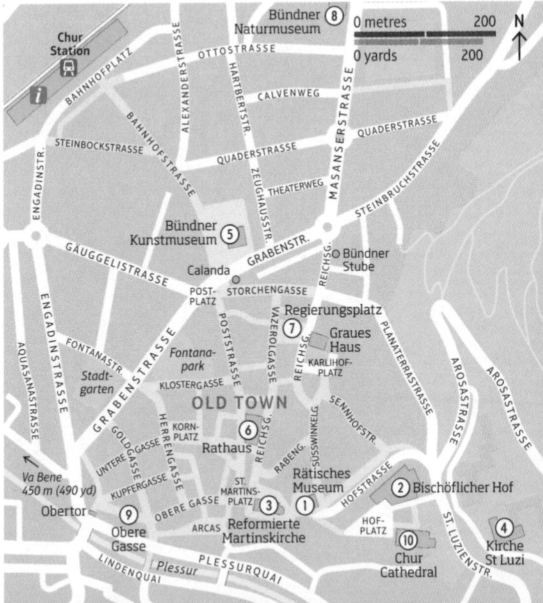

HIDDEN GEM

Alien Barscape

On the unassuming Comercialstrasse lurks the Giger Bar *(www.hrgiger.com)*. The bar is themed on the most famous (and Oscar-winning) work of Swiss artist H R Giger - the surrealistic creatures and nightmare landscapes of Hollywood blockbuster *Alien*. The entire bar, from the fittings to the roofs, are all designed in his iconic biomechanical style.

Bündner Kunstmuseum

Bahnhofstrasse 35 081 257 28 70 10am-5pm Tue-Sun (Thu: to 8pm) buendner-kunstmuseum.ch

Chur's museum of fine arts is spread across two buildings. One is a large, handsome Neo-Renaissance villa dating from 1874–5, built for Jacques Ambrosius von Planta, a merchant who traded in Egypt. This heritage accounts for the Middle Eastern character of the building's interior decoration. The exterior also reflects an affinity for Middle Eastern culture, with two sphinxes that greet visitors, flanking both sides of the front steps, and a golden dome designed in the Byzantine style. The pinnacle of this style takes the shape of the crescent moon that crowns the top of the dome. Next to the villa stands the award-winning annexe, designed by the Barcelona-based architect Barozzi Veiga. On the upper floors are airy public spaces, while the exhibitions are laid out on the lower floors underground. A pedestrian zone links the two buildings.

Most of the paintings and sculptures that fill the rooms of the two spaces are by artists who either were born or lived and worked in Graubünden between the 18th and 20th centuries. The impressive roster includes Angelica Kauffman, Giovanni Segantini, Ferdinand Hodler, Giovanni and Alberto Giacometti, and Ernst Ludwig Kirchner, as well as members of the Basel group of artists Rot-Blau (Red-Blue).

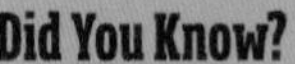

Did You Know?

Chur-born painter Angelica Kauffman was a well-known portraitist by the age of 12.

Rathaus

Poststrasse 33
By prior arrangement
081 254 41 13

Built in 1465, the Gothic town hall stands on the site of an earlier building that was destroyed by fire. At ground level is a handsome arcaded area that was once used as a marketplace. The upper floors of the town hall contain two finely decorated council chambers, one with a wooden ceiling and the other with Renaissance panelling. Both chambers have 17th-century tiled stoves.

The house that stands at Reichsgasse 57, nearby, is the birthplace of the Swiss painter Angelica Kauffman. Born in 1741, she later moved to London, where she became a well-known portraitist and painter of mythological figures, such as Cupid.

Regierungsplatz

Lining this square, on the north side of the Old Town, are several historic buildings, which now serve as the seat of the cantonal authorities. One of the finest is Graues Haus (Grey House), a stately three-storey residence dating from 1752. It is also known as the New Building, to distinguish

The gridded cube-shaped annexe of the Bündner Kunstmuseum

↑ One of the ornately decorated houses lining Obere Gasse

EAT

Bündner Stube
Candlelit meals of fresh, seasonal fare, much grown in the on-site kitchen garden.

Reichsgasse 11
stern-chur.ch

Calanda
A trendy spot with a popular lunch menu and new specials every day.

Grabenstrasse 19
calanda-chur.ch

Va Bene
Modern European fine dining, with a packed wine list to boot.

Gäuggelistrasse 60
restaurant-vabene.ch

it from the Altes Gebäu (Old Building), which stands on Fontanapark. In the centre of the square is the Vazerol-Denkmal, an obelisk installed to commemorate the free association formed by the communes of Graubünden in the 14th century, when the local population began to organize itself in an effort to ward off foreign domination.

Bündner Naturmuseum

Masanserstrasse 31 081 257 28 41 10am-5pm Tue-Sun natur museum.gr.ch

The displays of this modern museum showcases the beautiful natural environment of the canton of Graubünden. The well-presented displays include a large collection of minerals from the region's mountains, including gold, gemstones and microminerals which can be seen through a microscope, as well as plants and stuffed animals.

9

Obere Gasse

Chur's smartest shopping street, Obere Gasse runs from St Martinsplatz to Obertor, the Gothic city gate on the banks of the Plessur. All along this narrow, flag-hung street, the historic houses have been converted into boutiques, restaurants and cafés.

On Saturday mornings during the summer, a market is held in Obere Gasse and Untere Gasse.

→ A stonework ibex, which flanks one side of the city's coat of arms

⑩

CHUR CATHEDRAL

Hofplatz 6am-7pm Mon & Wed-Sat, 8am-7pm Tue, 7am-7pm Sun bistum-chur.ch

Officially known as the Cathedral of St Mary of the Assumption, Chur's Catholic church is a historic place of worship. During the Swiss Reformation, the town's Catholic community were confined to the cathedral and the surrounding bishop's court.

Begun in 1151 and completed in the mid-13th century, Chur Cathedral represents a mixture of the Romanesque and Gothic architectural styles. The earliest part of the basilica is its eastern section. The nave, with Romanesque columns and Gothic vaulting, and the bell tower, topped by a lantern, are later elements. The exterior was remodelled in the early 19th century, after the building was damaged by a fire that destroyed the original towers and roof. Peculiarly, the cathedral is built to an irregular plan, with the axis of the sanctuary and that of the nave being out of alignment. The sanctuary is home to one of the finest features of the cathedral – the renovated 15th-century golden altar triptych, which gleams in the light slanting through the small side windows.

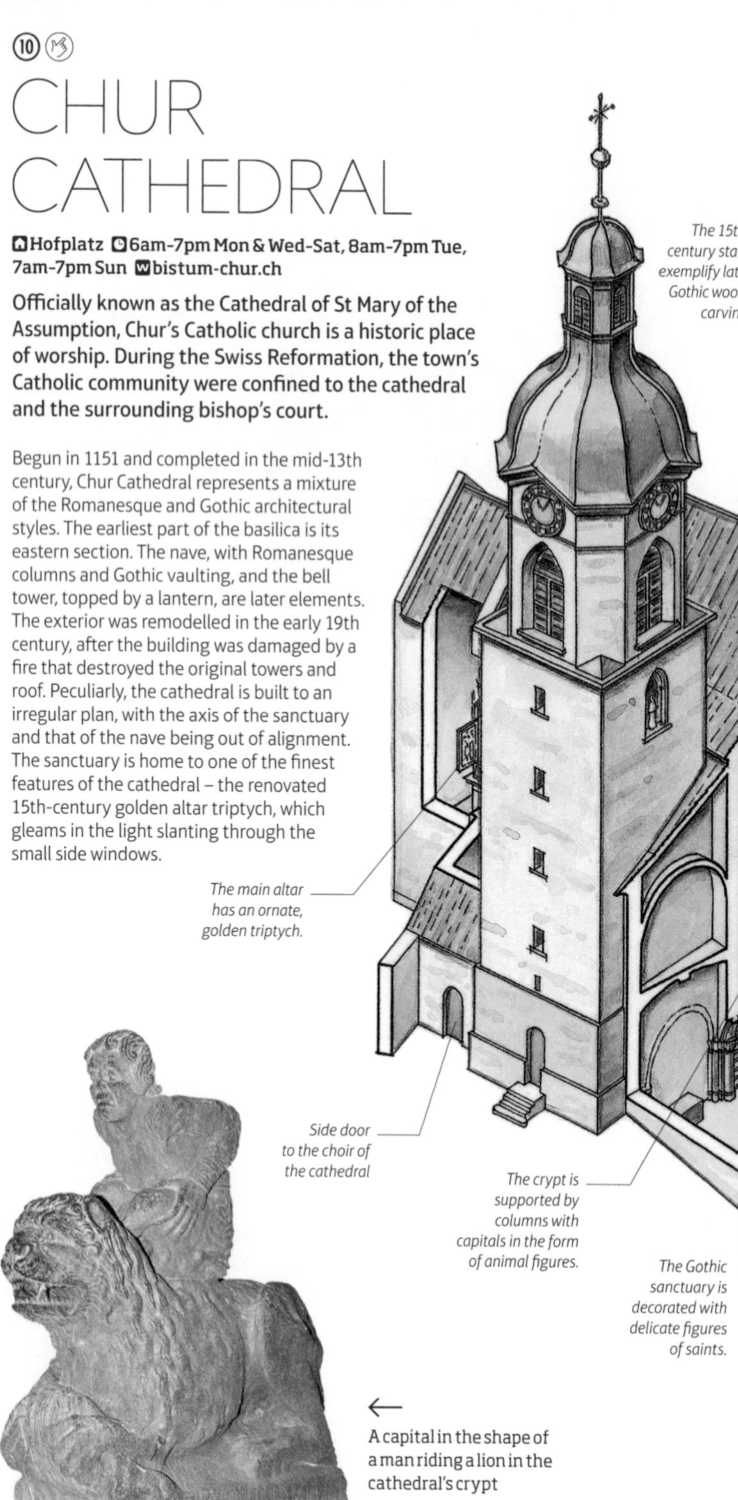

The 15th-century stalls exemplify late-Gothic wood-carving.
The main altar has an ornate, golden triptych.
Side door to the choir of the cathedral
The crypt is supported by columns with capitals in the form of animal figures.
The Gothic sanctuary is decorated with delicate figures of saints.

←

A capital in the shape of a man riding a lion in the cathedral's crypt

1
2
3
The capitals of the columns in the nave are outstanding examples of Swiss Romanesque stone carving.
Carvings of biblical scenes adorn the Baroque pulpit.
The west wall's magnificent stained-glass window
The cathedral is attached to other buildings in the bishop's court.
Main entrance

1 Chur Cathedral is easily recognized by its single bell tower, peeking through the town's trees.

2 The cathedral has an elaborate high altar, built in 1492 by Jacob Russ.

3 The stained-glass window in the west wall features scenes from the life of the Virgin Mary.

Did You Know?

The cathedral claims to house the relics of St Lucius, who brought Christianity to Britain.

↑ Chur's magnificent Cathedral of St Mary of the Assumption

4

SWISS NATIONAL PARK

G4 Graubünden Zernez Jun-Oct: 8:30am-6pm daily; Nov-May: 9am-5pm daily nationalpark.ch

Established in 1914, the Swiss National Park, or Parc Naziunal Svizzer in Romansch, was the first national park to be created in the Alps. This pristine nature reserve covers an area of 170 sq km (67 sq miles) and its topography ranges from sheltered valleys and dense forests to flower-covered meadows and rocky, snow-covered peaks.

The best way to appreciate the park is to follow its 80 km (50 miles) of well-marked hiking trails. Many of these start from parking areas off Ofenpassstrasse, the only highway through the park. A free app has detailed maps and park information, including where to find overnight accommodation in the park. Walkers are also reminded that they are forbidden to stray from these trails for conservation reasons. On the park's western border, Lai da Ova Spin reservoir overlooks rugged mountain terrain. To the east are magnificent snowy views of Piz Nair and Munt la Schera, while in the north the vista is of mountains blanketed in pine forests.

TOP FIVE ALPINE ANIMALS

Ibex
The Alps' iconic goats are instantly recognizable by their long horns.

Chamois
These skittish Alpine antelopes dart easily up and down cliffsides.

Golden Eagles
These regal birds spiral, disappear and swoop on the mountain wind.

Northern Vipers
The park's only snake, vipers are often found motionless in the grass.

Marmots
These adorable rodents thrive in the park's meadowlands.

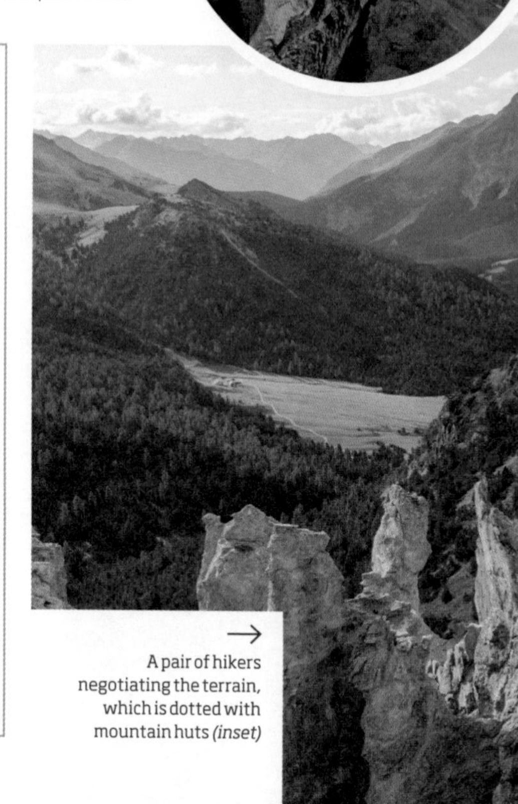

→ A pair of hikers negotiating the terrain, which is dotted with mountain huts *(inset)*

1 The *Aussichtplattform* (viewing platform) at Piz Nair offers incredible views over Silvaplanersee.

2 Throughout the park there are well-marked hiking trails, open from June to October.

3 A statue of an ibex, one of the park's most iconic animals, overlooks snow-capped Munt la Schera.

EXPERIENCE MORE

Rheinfall

E2 Schaffhausen Neuhausen, Rheinfallquai 3; www.rheinfall.ch

Creating a spectacle of rainbow-tinted spray, the waters of the Rhine tumble off a cataract at Neuhausen, 4 km (2.5 miles) downriver from Schaffhausen. The waterfall, Rheinfall, is the largest in Europe. Although it is only 23 m (75 ft) high, it is known for its width (about 150 m/492 ft) and its setting between tree-covered banks. Schloss Laufen, a turreted Renaissance castle overlooking the river from the south, has the best view of the falls. From the castle, steps lead down to viewing platforms. A fireworks display is staged at the Rheinfall during the evening of 31 July, the eve of National Day (1 August), each year.

PICTURE PERFECT
Behind the Falls

Capture the full majesty of the Rheinfall on a boat trip. Leaving from nearby Schaffhausen *(p242)*, tours stop at a mighty rock standing virtually in the middle of the falls, where platforms let you feel the vibration of the water as you snap the torrents up close.

Frauenfeld

E2 Thurgau Bahnhofplatz 75; www.frauenfeld.ch

Located on the River Murg, west of Bodensee, Frauenfeld is the capital of Thurgau canton. The town has burgher houses in its historic centre, the Baliere in Kreuzplatz that is now an art gallery, and the Naturmuseum Thurgau. The origins of Frauenfeld's castle go back to the 13th century. Its restored rooms house the Historisches Museum Thurgau, a museum of local history.

At Ittingen, located 4 km (2.5 miles) north of Frauenfeld, is the Kartause Ittingen, a Carthusian monastery founded in the 15th century. No longer inhabited by monks, the monastery is open to visitors. As well as a hotel, a restaurant and a farm shop, the monastery also has a museum illustrating monastic life and a gallery of 20th-century Swiss painting.

Bodensee

F2 St Gallen, Thurgau and Schaffhausen Hauptstrasse 39, Kreuzlingen; www.bodensee.eu

Bodensee, also known as Lake Constance, has become a summer playground for visitors attracted by the sailing, swimming and development of resort hotels along the shores. There is a wealth of watersports, including sailing and paddleboarding. There are 337 km (209 miles) of protected bike trails touching four borders: Switzerland, Austria, Germany and Liechtenstein.

The lake, which is both fed and drained by the Rhine, is 64 km (40 miles) long and 12 km (7 miles) wide. Its western and southern shores, which belong

→ Europe's largest waterfall, the Rheinfall, overlooked by pretty Schloss Laufen

→ The cobbled Rathausplatz, with its fine medieval buildings, in Stein am Rhein

to Switzerland, are lined with small resorts that have fishing and watersports facilities. Kreuzlingen is the principal Swiss town here, with the Baroque Kirche St Ulrich its finest building. Schloss Arenenberg and the medieval castle of Gottlieben are both on the Swiss shoreline, as is the 14th-century Turmhof fortification in Steckborn.

8

Stein am Rhein

E2 Schaffhausen
Oberstadt 3;
www.steinamrhein.ch

With its medieval half-timbered buildings and 16th-century houses with frescoed façades, Stein am Rhein is one of the country's most beautiful sights. Founded in Roman times, this small town began to prosper and expand in the late 11th century, when German emperor Heinrich II established a Benedictine monastery here. The outline of the town walls can be made out, and two of the town gates, Obertor and Untertor, still stand. The main square, Rathausplatz, is lined with handsome wood-framed houses painted with motifs reflecting their names, such as House of the Sun or House of the Red Ox. The **Lindwurm Museum** re-creates 19th-century middle-class life over four floors of a beautifully restored house in the historic Old Town.

Overlooking the Rhine stands Kloster St Georgen, a Benedictine monastery, and its 12th-century church. The well-preserved monastery rooms, decorated in the early 16th century, now house the **Klostermuseum St Georgen**, devoted to local history.

Lindwurm Museum

Understadt 18
Mar-Oct: 10am-5pm Tue-Sun Nov-Feb
museum-lindwurm.ch

Klostermuseum St Georgen

Fischmarkt 3
Apr, May & Sep-Nov: 11am-5pm Tue-Sun; Jun-Aug: 11am-6pm Tue-Sun Dec-Mar
klostersanktgeorgen.ch

THE RHAETIAN RAILWAY

Riding a mountain train when in Switzerland is essential. One of the most scenic lines is the private Rhaetian Railway, through nearly 100 tunnels and across 500 bridges. Its Albula/Bernina Line, climbing up the Albula Valley past the dramatic Landwasser viaduct, is now a UNESCO World Heritage Site and one of Europe's truly great rail journeys.

9

Appenzell

F3 Appenzell Hauptgasse 4, Appenzell; www.appenzell.ch

Surrounded on all sides by the canton of St Gallen, the region known as Appenzell consists of two half-cantons, Appenzell-Ausserrhoden in the north and west, and Appenzell-Innerrhoden in the south. From the 10th to the 15th centuries, Appenzell formed part of the territory owned by the abbey at St Gallen *(p246)*. Having gained its independence, Appenzell joined the Swiss Confederation in 1513.

While the bigger Appenzell-Ausserrhoden is Protestant and largely industrialized, Appenzell-Innerrhoden is Catholic and markedly more bucolic, with a farming economy and a developed tourist industry. It is renowned for its cattle-breeding and its dairy products, most especially its cheeses. Along with its rural character, Appenzell-Innerrhoden has strong folk traditions and a pristine natural environment.

Like many other towns in the region, Appenzell, capital of Innerrhoden, has a Landsgemeindeplatz, a square on which regular voting sessions are held. The well-preserved historic centre of this small town is filled with

INSIDER TIP
Appenzell Whisky Trek

Alpine paths connect 25 mountain inns across Alpstein. In each, barrels of individually distilled Alpine malts can be sampled and collected in bottles signed by the cask keeper *(www.appenzellerbier.ch)*.

colourfully painted wooden houses. Also of interest are the 16th-century town hall and the parish church, Kirche St Mauritius, which was built in the 16th century in the Baroque style and remodelled in the 19th century.

The history and culture of Appenzell is amply documented by the varied and extensive collections of the **Museum Appenzell**. These range from costumes and headdresses to embroidery and cowbells.

To the south of Appenzell lies the Alpstein massif. The highest peak here, the Säntis, rises to 2,504 m (8,215 ft). Popular with hikers and mountaineers, the Säntis can be reached by cable car from Schwägalp.

The picturesque village of Urnäsch, in Ausserrhoden, also has the **Appenzeller Brauchtumsmuseum**, a folk museum. Its collection includes reconstructed farmhouse interiors, as well as costumes and craft items.

North of Urnäsch lies Herisau, capital of the canton of Appenzell-Ausserrhoden. The town has attractive wooden houses and a church with Rococo furnishings dating from 1520.

A beautifully decorated bed on display in the Museum Appenzell

The impressive cascade of Thurwasserfälle at Unterwasser, Toggenburg

Stein, a quiet village east of Herisau, has an interesting folk museum and show dairy. While the displays at the **Appenzell Folklore Museum** illustrate the lives, culture and crafts of the local people, at the **Appenzeller Showcase Dairy (Schaukäserei)**, visitors can watch cheese being made using local methods.

The market town of Gais, at the centre of Appenzell, is of interest for its colourfully painted wooden houses, many of which have ornate gables. It is also an excellent base for exploring the region.

Museum Appenzell

Hauptgasse 4, Appenzell Apr-Oct: 10am-noon & 1:30-5pm Mon-Fri, 11am-5pm Sat & Sun; Nov-Mar: 2-5pm Tue-Sun museum.ai.ch

Appenzeller Brauchtumsmuseum

Urnäsch Apr-Oct: 9-11:30am & 1:30-5pm Mon-Sat, 1:30-5pm Sun; Nov-Mar: 9-11:30am Mon-Fri, 9-11:30am & 1:30-5pm Sat, 1:30pm-5pm Sun museum-urnaesch.ch

Appenzell Folklore Museum

Stein 10am-5pm Tue-Sun appenzeller-museum.ch

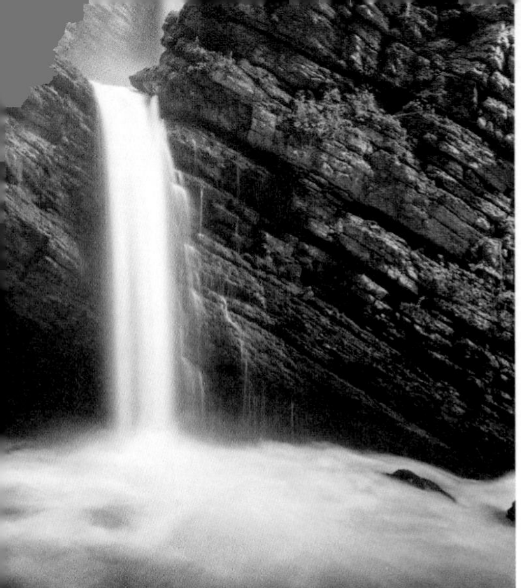

Appenzeller Showcase Dairy (Schaukäserei)
 Stein 9am-6:30pm (cheesemaking until 3pm) schaukaeserei.ch

10

Toggenburg

E3 St Galle
Hauptstrasse, Wildhaus; www.toggenburg.org

Washed by the River Thur, the Toggenburg is a long valley that lies on a north-south axis between Wil and Wattwil, then veers eastwards just above Alt St Johann, where it becomes Oberes Toggenburg, which then opens out onto the Rhine Valley.

The Toggenburg has more than 300 km (185 miles) of marked hiking and cycling trails, and its gentle slopes provide easy skiing pistes. The valley is dotted with attractive small towns and villages, among them Wil and Lichtensteig, which has historic houses.

Wildhaus, a pleasant resort at the eastern extremity of Oberes Toggenburg, is the birthplace of Ulrich Zwingli, the leader of the Reformation in Switzerland. The farmhouse where he was born in 1484 is open to visitors. Unterwasser is worth a visit too, for its impressive waterfall, the Thurwasserfälle.

11

Rapperswil

E3 St Galle
St Gallerstrasse 40; www.rapperswil.ch

This small town, in the canton of St Gallen, sits on a promontory on the north side of Zürichsee. Although the modern part of Rapperswil has nothing of great interest, the traffic-free medieval centre is a pleasant place to stroll. Behind the lakeside promenade lie narrow streets lined with houses fronted by arcades, and small squares with cafés and restaurants serving fresh locally caught fish. From May to October the air is filled with the delicate perfume of more than 15,000 roses. Known as the City of Roses, Rapperswil has more than 16,000 roses flowering in walled gardens, including one within a Capuchin monastery and a particularly serene one specially designed for the visually impaired and those with mobility issues.

Besides the 15th-century town hall and the parish church, Rapperswil's main feature is its looming Gothic castle, whose three forbidding towers rise above the town. From the castle there are views of Zürich to the north and of the Glarus Alps to the southwest. The village makes a good base for hiking in summer and skiing in winter.

Did You Know?

Rapperswil-born Marianne Ehrmann was one of the first German-speaking female writers.

↑ An attractive rose garden in a courtyard of Rapperswil's medieval castle

Walensee

E3-F3 St Gallen and Glarus Walenseestrasse 18; www.heidiland.com

This slender lake marks the border between the cantons of St Gallen and Glarus. About 15 km (9 miles) long and just 2 km (1 mile) across at its widest point, it lies in a steep-sided valley, with the rugged Churfirsten massif on its northern side and the Glarner Alps to the southeast. This lovely region is also known as "Heidiland" after Johanna Spyri's famous children's novel.

The railway line and the motorway linking Zürich and Chur run along the south side of the lake. Most of the towns and villages on the steep north shore are accessible only by boat or on foot. Cruises on the lake take in the charming town of Weesen.

A short distance south is Näfels, which is home to a late-Renaissance palace, the Freulerpalast. The building features a museum of local history. The neighbouring town of Mollis contains well-preserved burgher houses and fine 18th-century mansions, while Walenstadt, on the lake's eastern shore, is a convenient base for exploring the mountains, including Walenstadtberg and Berschis.

Bad Ragaz

F4 St Gallen resortragaz.ch Am Platz 1; www.heidiland.com

Bad Ragaz, set on the River Tamina, is one of Switzerland's foremost spa resorts, with grand old palace-style hotels and a golf course. Its natural thermal springs have been used to cure ailments since the 13th century. The resort has several indoor and outdoor pools – Tamina-Therme, in the centre of the resort, is the best known.

Bad Ragaz also has an early 18th-century parish church with Baroque wall paintings. The town hall contains a display of paintings and other works of art of Bad Ragaz and its environs.

1535

The year Swiss doctor Paracelsus recognized the healing powers of Bad Pfäfers' hot springs.

As well as skiing on the slopes of Pizol, Bad Ragaz offers golf, tennis and other sporting activities. It is also an excellent base for hiking in the surrounding hills.

About 5 km (3 miles) south of Bad Ragaz is Bad Pfäfers, a spa town with a beautiful Baroque church and a former Benedictine monastery that houses a local history museum.

Southwest of Bad Ragaz is the Taminaschlucht, a deep gorge carved out by the rushing waters of the Tamina. Also of interest is Sargans, which has beautiful Neo-Classical buildings and a Gothic castle.

> **Davos has some famous "off-piste" powder snow runs, but beginners are catered for, too: there are several ski and snowboarding schools.**

14

Maienfeld

F3 Graubünden
Bahnhofstrasse 1; www.heidiland.com

The village of Maienfeld, across the Rhine from Bad Ragaz, is also part of the Heidiland tourism area. It was this part of the Swiss Alps that Johanna Spyri chose as the setting for *Heidi* (1881), the story of an orphaned girl that has become a classic of children's literature. A very easy walking trail leads from Maienfeld up to the hamlet of Oberrofels and the Heidi-themed village of Heididorf. Here visitors can see Heidi's House, a wooden chalet and museum in which the fictional surroundings of Heidi's life with her grandfather are vividly re-created.

Davos

F4 Graubünden
Promenade 67; www.davos.ch

Originally a remote village, Davos developed into a health resort for tuberculosis sufferers in the 1860s, and was transformed into a winter sports resort in the 1930s. Today it is one of the largest Swiss resorts and hosts world leaders at the Davos World Economic Forum.

Davos has close associations with German writer and Nobel laureate Thomas Mann, who visited in 1911 and was inspired to write *The Magic Mountain*. The town is also associated with the German Expressionist painter Ernst Ludwig Kirchner, who settled here in 1917. The largest collection of his work in the world, including many of the Alpine landscapes that he painted during his years in Davos, are displayed in the **Kirchner Museum Davos** here.

Davos has some famous "off-piste" powder snow runs, but beginners are catered for, too: there are several ski and snowboarding schools, as well as some less demanding slopes. There are also toboggan runs and a large natural ice rink, where ice hockey is played.

Kirchner Museum Davos
Promenade 82
11am-6pm Tue-Sun
kirchnermuseum.ch

The small port of Weesen in an idyllic lakeside setting on Walensee

↑ The slopes of the Hörnli near Arosa, ideal for intermediate skiers

Arosa

F4 Graubünden
Poststrasse; www.arosa.ch

Set in a bowl in the narrow Schanfigg Valley, Arosa is one of Switzerland's most beautiful resorts. Although it lies at an altitude of 1,800 m (5,900 ft), it enjoys a gentle climate, with lots of sunshine.

The town is divided into two areas. Ausserarosa is the main resort and Innerarosa the original village. The crafts and folk art on display in the **Schanfigg Heimatmuseum** reflect mountain life in the days before the town became a popular winter holiday spot.

In winter, the neighbouring slopes of Weisshorn, Hörnli and Prätschli provide superb downhill pistes. There are also cross-country trails, a sleigh run and an ice rink. In summer, visitors can enjoy over 200 km (125 miles) of hiking trails and mountain biking routes, and the resort's two lakes offer a variety of watersports.

Schanfigg Heimatmuseum
Poststrasse, Innerarosa
Jun, Sep & Oct: 2:30–4:30pm Mon, Wed & Fri (Jul & Aug: Sun); Dec–Apr: 2:30–4:30pm Tue & Fri arosa-museum.ch

Hikers in the village of Ardez, notable for its houses painted with beautiful murals

17 Engadine Valley

G4 Graubünden
Via San Gian 30, St Moritz; www.engadin.stmoritz.ch

The Engadine Valley is generally acknowledged as one of Switzerland's most scenic. It begins at the foot of the Rhaetian Alps, near St Moritz, and extends north-eastwards as far as the border of Austria. It is named after the River Inn (En in Romansh), which runs along the valley and on into Austria, where it joins the Danube.

This deep valley between high cliffs is divided into an upper, southwestern section and a lower, northeastern section. The Upper Engadine (Oberengadin in German, Engiadin' Ota in Romansh) lies between the Maloja Pass and Zernez. With glaciers and snowy peaks on either side, the valley floor of the Upper Engadine lies at an altitude averaging 1,800 m (5,900 ft) and is dotted with several popular winter sports resorts, including Pontresina and St Moritz *(p264)*.

The Lower Engadine (Unterengadin in German, Engiadina Bassa in Romansh) lies between Zernez and Martina. Remote, unspoiled and very picturesque, this region is dotted with attractive villages set on either side of the River Inn. Many of these villages have houses with painted façades or sgraffito decoration, in which the upper layer of plaster is cut away to create a design. Particularly fine sgraffito decoration can be seen in Guarda, a village overlooking the River Inn. The village of Ardez is also notable for its painted houses, one of which has an exterior covered with a beautiful depiction of Adam and Eve in the Garden of Eden.

The principal town of the Lower Engadine is Scuol (Schuls in German), with a spa and a regional museum. On the opposite bank of the Inn lie the villages of Vulpera, which has picturesque houses and an 11th-century castle, and Tarasp, with a spa. Chaste Tarasp, a castle, perches on a rocky spur above the village. At S-charl, nearby, is a lead and silver mine, which is open to visitors.

Most of the towns and villages in the Lower Engadine make good bases for exploring the Silvretta mountain range to the north and the Swiss National Park *(p254)* to the south.

18 Müstair

G4 Graubünden
Chasa Cumünala, Tschierv; www.val-muestair.ch

Tucked away at the bottom of Val Müstair (Münstertal in German), and almost on the border with Italy, Romansh-speaking Müstair (Münster in German) takes its name from

CROSS-COUNTRY SKIING IN THE ENGADINE

Even more popular with Swiss families than downhill skiing is shuffling along the flats, through the woods and over the frozen lakes, on more than 230 km (142 miles) of trails in the Engadine Valley. The Engadine Skimarathon takes place every March, with many cross-country skiers racing over a 42-km (26-mile) course.

the Carolingian monastery founded here in about 780 CE. The working convent is one of the oldest buildings in the country.

The convent church, known in Romansh as the **Baselgia San Jon** and in German as Klosterkirche St Johann, is a working convent decorated with exceptionally well-preserved 12th- and 13th-century Romanesque frescoes. Because of these, the church has been declared a UNESCO World Heritage Site. While the frescoes on the side walls depict scenes from the life of Christ, those in the presbytery show scenes from the life of St John. A depiction of the Last Judgement covers the west wall. Some of the frescoes have now been moved to the Schweizerisches Nationalmuseum in Zürich *(p164)*. The church also has a 12th-century statue of Charlemagne and an 11th-century relief of the baptism of Christ. The small museum near the church contains Carolingian statuary and Baroque figures.

Baselgia San Jon

May-Oct: 9am-5pm Mon-Sat, 1:30-5pm Sun; Nov-Apr: 10am-noon & 1:30-4:30pm Mon-Sat, 1:30-4:30pm Sun muestair.ch

Pontresina

G5 Graubünden
Via Maistra 133; 081 838 83 00 pontresina.ch

A mountaineering resort since the 19th century, Pontresina, in the Upper Engadine, lies at the foot of Val Bernina at an altitude of 1,800 m (5,900 ft).

Among Pontresina's historic buildings are the Spaniola Turm, a Romanesque tower, and the chapel of Santa Maria, containing Romanesque frescoes, some of which depict scenes from the life of Mary Magdalene. Exhibits in the **Museum Alpin** illustrate the history of the town.

Pontresina is a year-round resort. In winter, the slopes of Diavolezza and Lagalb are linked into the 350-km (217-mile) network of the Engadine ski region. In summer, Pontresina offers gentle walking along wooded paths, as well as more demanding hiking and mountaineering up to the summits of Alp Ota and Munt della Bescha. The hiking trail up Val Roseg leads to a glacier at the foot of Piz Roseg. Experienced climbers can tackle Piz Bernina, at 4,049 m (13,284 ft) the highest peak in the Rhaetian Alps.

Did You Know?

Legend has it a red-haired siren lured mountineers to their doom on Diavolezza.

Museum Alpin

Via Maistra 199
081 842 72 73 Mid-Jun-mid-Oct & end Dec-mid-Apr: 3:30-6pm Mon-Sat

Bernina Pass

G5 Graubünden

At an altitude of 2,328 m (7,638 ft), the Bernina Pass is the highest point on the ancient route from St Moritz to Tirano, in Italy.

A road climbs up Val Bernina on the north side of the pass and descends Val di Poschiavo on its southern side. The pass is also served by ordinary trains and by the Bernina Express *(p274)*. The breathtaking view from the pass takes in the peaks of the Rhaetian Alps to the north and Lago Bianco, an artificial lake.

↑ The Bernina Express train making its dramatic ascent up to the Bernina Pass

21

Val Bregaglia

F5 Grisons Strada Principale 101, Stampa; www.bregaglia.ch

The western continuation of the Inn Valley culminates at the Maloja Pass (1,815 m/ 5,955 ft), which marks the western boundary of the Engadine. On the western side of the pass a road winds down the canton's predominantely Italian-speaking valleys.

Dotted with ruined castles and small churches, Val Bregaglia is popular with mountaineers for its many scenic hiking trails and extraordinary rock formations.

The main village in the valley is Vicosoprano, which has mansions and historic law courts. Further south lies Stampa, birthplace of the artists Augusto Giacometti and his son, Alberto. Their works can be seen in Stampa at the 16th-century Casa Granda, where there is also a museum of local history.

The charming hamlet of Soglio sits on the north side of the valley and is the starting point for numerous scenic hiking trails.

FOOD IN ST MORITZ

Known as a gourmet paradise in the snow, St Moritz has a buzzing culinary scene, with its share of celebrity chefs and Michelin stars. Central to its epicurean reputation is the town's Gourmet Festival *(late Jan-early Feb)*. At this festival gourmands get to sample elaborate and inventive dishes cooked by master chefs, taste local delicacies from around the world and quaff award-winning wines.

22

St Moritz

F5 Graubünden Via Maistra 12; www.stmoritz.ch

The birthplace of winter tourism, still celebrated for its champagne atmosphere at 1,800 m (5,900 ft), St Moritz (San Murezzan in Romansh) lies on a sunny terrace on the north shore of Moritzersee. Surrounded by mountains, it offers superb skiing and snowboarding, and is a base for hiking and mountaineering in summer. Visitors will also find the world's oldest and only natural-ice bobsled run here. It is also known for its curative springs, enjoyed at least since the Middle Ages.

75

The number of seconds it takes to zoom down the St Moritz bobsled run.

The town has two districts: St Moritz-Bad, the spa area on the southwestern side of the lake, and St Moritz-Dorf, on the northern side, with hotels, restaurants and boutiques.

Although little remains of the original village, St Moritz is an interesting place with two diverting museums. The **Giovanni-Segantini Museum**, on Via Somplaz, is devoted to the Symbolist painter, who spent the final years of his life in the Upper Engadine. On Via dal Bagn, just below Via Somplaz, is the **Museum Engiadinais**, which looks at life in the Engadine and the history of the spa.

Giovanni-Segantini Museum

Via Somplaz 30 Mid-May-Oct & Dec-mid-May: 11am-5pm Tue-Fri & Sun, 10am-5pm Sat Nov segantini-museum.ch

The traditional Engadine village of Sils on the north shore of Silsersee

Museum Engiadinais
 Via dal Bagn 39 Mid-May-Oct: 11am-5pm Thu-Sun museum-engiadinais.ch

23

Sils

F5 Grisons sils.ch

The village of Sils (Segl in Romansh) is set on the north shore of Silsersee. The village consists of two parts: Sils Baselgia, on the lakeshore, and Sils Maria, to the south. Many writers, painters and musicians have been drawn to Sils. From 1881 to 1889, Sils Maria was the summer residence of the German philosopher Friedrich Nietzsche. The house where he lived, and where he wrote *Also Sprach Zarathustra*, has been converted into a small museum, the **Nietzsche Haus**.

Nietzsche Haus
 Via da Marias 67 Mid-Jun-Oct & mid-Dec-Apr: 3-6pm Tue-Sun May-mid-Jun & Nov nietzschehaus.ch

24

Zillis

F4 Graubünden Thusis Poststelle Hauptstrasse; www.zillis-reischen.ch

In the village of Zillis (Ziràn in Romansh), a remarkable cycle of Romanesque frescoes adorn a small church on the east bank of the Hinterrhein.

The wooden ceiling of **Kirche St Martin** is covered with 153 square panels, painted between 1109 and 1114. The exterior panels depict an ocean filled with sea monsters; those in the interior show scenes from the life of Christ and of St Martin.

Kirche St Martin
Am Postplatz 10am-5:30pm daily zillis-st-martin.ch

Paintings displayed at the Giovanni-Segantini Museum, St Moritz

25

San Bernardino Pass

E5 Graubünden Strada Cantonàl 94; www.visit-moesano.ch

On the great transalpine route running from Bodensee, in the far northeast of the country, down to Lake Como, in Italy, San Bernardino is one of Europe's most important mountain passes, lying at an altitude of 2,066 m (6,778 ft). Although snow usually blocks the pass from November to May, the 7-km (4-mile) tunnel beneath it is permanently open. The village resort of San Bernardino, located on the south side of the pass, makes an excellent base for hiking and exploring the surrounding mountains.

STAY

Suvretta House St Moritz

Impeccable service and Alpine luxury perched high above the Engadine Valley.

F5 Via Chasellas 1, St Moritz May & Nov suvrettahouse.ch

SF SF SF

A spectacular waterfall near the Klausen Pass in the canton of Glarus

Glarus

E3 Glarus
Glarnerland Rätstätte A3, Niederurnen; www.glarnerland.ch

Capital of the canton of Glarus, this small town is also the urban centre of Glarnerland, a rather isolated and mountainous but beautiful region that lies between Walensee and the Klausen Pass. Largely rebuilt after it was destroyed by fire in 1861, the town is laid out on a grid pattern and as such is a classic example of 19th-century urban planning. Notable buildings here include the town hall, the Kunsthaus Glarus – an art gallery with a collection of 19th- and 20th-century Swiss paintings – and the Neo-Romanesque parish church with a treasury that contains a collection of liturgical vessels.

With beautiful lakes and valleys, the mountains around Glarus, particularly those of the Glärnisch massif, are popular with hikers.

With beautiful lakes and valleys, the mountains around Glarus, particularly those of the Glärnisch massif, are popular with hikers. Many of the slopes have excellent pistes. South of Glarus, the main road goes on to Linthal, from where a funicular climbs to Braunwald. This tranquil car-free resort is set on a plateau that offers superb hiking. Beyond Linthal the road leads through some spectacular scenery over the Klausen Pass (1,948 m/6,391 ft) and down to Altdorf *(p229)* and Lake Lucerne.

Did You Know?

Klosters is known as "Hollywood on the Rocks" because it attracts so many celebrities.

27

Klosters

G4 Graubünden
Alte Bahnhofstrasse 6; www.klosters.ch

Quieter and smaller than Davos *(p261)*, its neighbour to the south, the discreetly chic ski resort of Klosters has an intimate atmosphere. The only remaining trace of the medieval monastery from which it takes its name is Kirche St Jacob, which has beautiful stained-glass windows by Augusto Giacometti. The history of the village and its development into a resort are documented by displays in the **Nutli-Hüschi**, a 16th-century chalet.

Klosters shares a ski-pass region with Davos, encompassing 320 km (199 miles) of ski terrain. It is suitable for all levels of experience, from beginner to master skier.

Nutli-Hüschi
Monbielerstrasse 11
3-5pm Wed & Fri
museum-klosters.ch

Poschiavo's square with its town hall and church of San Vittore

Poschiavo

G5 Grisons
Stazione; www.valposchiavo.ch

The descent down Val di Poschiavo, the valley on the south side of the Bernina Pass, reveals a very different side of Switzerland. Here the climate and vegetation, as well as the language and the culture, are Mediterranean. Buildings show an Italian influence, the cuisine turns to pastas and antipasti, and cypress trees and palms grow in sheltered gardens.

Poschiavo (Puschlav in German) is the main town in the valley. At its heart is the Piazza Communale, a square lined with Italianate *palazzi* and two churches, a late 15th-century Catholic church and a 17th-century Protestant church. Other notable buildings include the Casa Torre, a Romanesque tower, and the Palazzo Albricci. The so-called Spaniolenviertel (Spanish Quarter) has imposing houses painted in a colourful Moorish style.

At nearby Cavaglia are remarkable geological features known as cauldrons. These are natural wells, up to 3 m (10 ft) in diameter, that were carved into the rock by the circular action of stones and water released by a melting glacier.

Mesocco

F5 Graubünden
mesocco.ch

The picturesque stone houses of Mesocco cluster on the banks of the River Moesa, which runs along the Valle Mesolcina. This valley stretches from the San Bernardino Pass southwards to Bellinzona and, although it is located in the canton of Graubünden, it has strong cultural links with Ticino.

The Castello di Misox, a ruined fortress set on a rocky outcrop above the town, commands a stunning view of the valley and the villages in it. Built for the counts of Sax von Misox during the 12th century, the castle was significantly extended in the 15th century and in 1480 it passed into the ownership of the Trivulizio family, from Milan. The slender campanile is a remnant of the castle complex, which was almost completely destroyed in 1526.

At the foot of the castle stands the Romanesque church of Santa Maria del Castello. Built in the 12th century, the church was partly remodelled in the 17th century. The nave has a coffered ceiling, and the walls are decorated with well-preserved 15th-century murals, which depict St George and the Dragon, St Bernard of Siena, patron saint of Valle Mesolcina, and scenes symbolizing the months of the year.

About 4 km (2.5 miles) south of Mesocco is Soazza, a village with an attractive 17th-century church. About 15 km (9 miles) south of Soazza is the village of San Vittore, where there is an 8th-century chapel. The Val Calanca, which runs into Valle Mesolcina, is also well worth exploring for its beautiful scenery.

EAT

Chesa Grischuna

Award-winning French cuisine in a grand chalet.

G4
Bahnhofstrasse 12, Klosters
chesagrischuna.ch

White Marmot

Fine wines and haute cuisine at high altitude.

F5 Corviglia, St Moritz 081 833 76 76 May-Nov

NEED TO KNOW

The scenic Langwieser viaduct, Arosa

Before You Go.....270

Getting Around.....272

Practical Information.....276

BEFORE YOU GO

Things change, so plan ahead to make the most of your trip. Be prepared for all eventualities by considering the following points before you travel.

AT A GLANCE
CURRENCY
Swiss Franc
SF
AVERAGE DAILY SPEND
SAVE
SF 250
SPEND
SF 400
SPLURGE
SF 650
BOTTLED WATER
SF 3.50
COFFEE
SF 4
BEER
SF 7
DINNER FOR TWO
SF 100
ESSENTIAL PHRASES
Hello
Guten tag/bonjour/ buongiorno
Goodbye
Auf wiedersehen/ au revoir/arrivederci
Please
Bitte/s'il vous plaît/ per favore
Thank you
Danke/merci/ grazie
Do you speak English?
Sprechen Sie Englisch?/ Parlez-vous anglais?/ Lei parla inglese?
ELECTRICITY SUPPLY
Power sockets are type J, fitting type J (3-pin) plugs and type C (2-pin) plugs. Standard voltage is 230V.

Passports and Visas

For entry requirements, including visas, consult your nearest Swiss embassy or check Switzerland's **Online Visa System**. EU nationals and citizens of the UK, US, Canada, Australia and New Zealand need a valid passport and, from 2024, must apply in advance for the European Travel Information and Authorization System (**ETIAS**).

ETIAS
W etiasvisa.com
Online Visa System
W swiss-visa.ch

Government Advice

It is important to consult both your and the Swiss government's advice before travelling. The **US Department of State**, the **UK Foreign, Commonwealth & Development Office**, the **Australian Department of Foreign Affairs and Trade** and the **Swiss Federal Council** offer the latest information on security, health and local regulations.

Australian Department of Foreign Affairs and Trade
W smartraveller.gov.au
Swiss Federal Council
W admin.ch
UK Foreign, Commonwealth & Development Office
W gov.uk/foreign-travel-advice
US Department of State
W travel.state.gov

Customs Information

You can find information on the laws relating to goods and currency taken in or out of Switzerland on the **Federal Customs Administration** website.

Federal Customs Administration
W ezv.admin.ch

Insurance

We recommend taking out a comprehensive insurance policy covering theft, loss of

belongings, medical care, cancellation and delays, and read the small print carefully.

UK and EU citizens are eligible for free emergency medical care in Switzerland provided they have a valid European Health Insurance Card (EHIC) or a UK Global Health Insurance Card (**GHIC**).

GHIC
W ghic.org.uk

Vaccinations

For information regarding COVID-19 vaccination requirements, consult government advice *(p270)*.

Booking Accommodation

Switzerland offers accommodation to suit all tastes and budgets. The **Swiss Hotel Association** offers a comprehensive list of accommodation. Advanced booking is essential in the mountain regions during ski season (December to April).

Swiss Hotel Association
W swisshotels.com

Money

Most establishments accept major credit, debit and prepaid currency cards. Contactless payments are widely accepted, but it's a good idea to carry cash for smaller items and tips. Cash machines are found in towns and city centres. Taxi drivers, hotel porters and concierges expect a tip of SF 5–10, housekeeping should be given SF 2–5 per day and you should round up restaurant bills to the nearest SF 5 or SF 10 for wait staff.

Travellers with Specific Requirements

Switzerland offers a high standard of facilities for travellers with specific requirements, but it is always worth calling ahead to check.

For assistance at train stations, phone the **SBB Call Centre Handicap** one hour before departure (or three working days beforehand for international travel). **Mietauto** has details on adapted hire vehicles.

Switzerland Tourism can provide full details of suitable hotel facilities for guests with specific requirements. The website of the **Swiss National Association of and for the Blind** advises travellers with visual impairments.

Mietauto
W mietauto.ch

SBB Call Centre Handicap
T 0800 007 102 (within Switzerland, toll-free), +41 51 225 78 44 (from abroad, subject to charge)

Swiss National Association of and for the Blind
W snab.ch

Switzerland Tourism
W myswitzerland.com

Language

Switzerland has four national languages – French, German, Italian and Romansh. Although English is not an official language, it is often used to bridge the language divides (especially in cities), and much official documentation is available in English. German is spoken mostly in the east, French mostly in the west, and Italian mostly in the southern canton of Ticino and the southern parts of neighbouring Graubünden. Romansh is spoken only in the canton of Graubünden.

Opening Hours

Situations can change quickly and unexpectedly. Always check before visiting attractions and hospitality venues for up-to-date opening hours and booking requirements.

Monday Some places are closed on Monday.
Thursday Cities, including Geneva and Zürich, have late-night shopping until 8pm.
Saturday Post offices and shops close at noon.
Sunday Most businesses are closed for the day.
Public holidays Shops, churches, museums and restaurants either close early or all day.

PUBLIC HOLIDAYS

1 Jan	New Year's Day
Mar/Apr	Good Friday
May	Ascension Day
1 Aug	National Day
25 Dec	Christmas Day

GETTING AROUND

Whether you are visiting for a short city break, a ski weekend or a rural retreat, discover how best to reach your destination and travel like a pro.

AT A GLANCE

PUBLIC TRANSPORT COSTS

BERN

SF 2.80

One-way
tram, bus, trolley bus

GENEVA

SF 3.00

One-way
tram, bus, ferry, local train

ZÜRICH

SF 2.70

One-way
bus, tram, local train

TOP TIP
Major cities offer travel passes, better value if you plan to use public transport often.

SPEED LIMIT

MOTORWAY
120 km/h (75mph)

DUAL CARRIAGEWAY
100 km/h (62mph)

SECONDARY ROAD
80 km/h (50mph)

URBAN AREA
50 km/h (31mph)

Arriving by Air

Zürich and Geneva airports are the main hubs for long-haul flights into Switzerland. Transatlantic flights are provided by SWISS, the national airline, as well as American Airlines, United Airlines, Delta and Air Canada. Both airports also offer flights to all major European cities with SWISS and a large number of carriers, including several budget airlines, such as easyJet, which has a hub at Geneva.

A number of smaller airports at Bern, Basel and Lugano also serve destinations within Europe. The airports of Sion, St Gallen and Engadin are used more for private business jets and internal flights than for scheduled international departures.

For information on distances and journey times between airports and cities, see the table opposite.

Train Travel

International Train Travel

Situated at the crossroads of major European routes, Switzerland has excellent international rail links. Regular high-speed trains connect the country to all major cities in the neighbouring countries of France, Germany, Austria and Italy, and beyond. Train journeys into the country can often compete with flights on price, and, for some short-haul routes, are not very much longer than flights door to door. Additionally, the opening of the 57-km- (36-mile-) long Gotthard Base Tunnel – the world's longest railway tunnel – in 2016 significantly reduced rail journey times for passengers transiting the Alps.

Making reservations early is strongly recommended, especially on overnight sleeper trains, as tickets get booked up quickly. **Eurail** and **Interrail** sell tickets for multiple international journeys and international rail passes for trips lasting from five days up to three months.

Eurail
W eurail.com

Interrail
W interrail.eu

GETTING TO AND FROM THE AIRPORT

Airport	Distance to City	Taxi Fare	Public Transport	Journey time
Euro Airport Basel-Mulhouse-Freiburg (MLH)	6 km (4 miles)	SF 50	Bus	18 mins
Bern Airport (BRN)	6 km (4 miles)	SF 50	Bus	35 mins
Geneva International Airport (GVA)	4 km (2 miles)	SF 35	Train	6 mins
Lugano -Agno Airport (LUG)	6 km (4 miles)	SF 35	Bus	15 mins
Engadin Airport St Moritz-Samedan (SMV)	7 km (4 miles)	SF 100	Bus	17 mins
Sion Airport/ Aéroport de Sion (SIR)	2.5 km (2 miles)	SF 46	Bus	4 mins
St Gallen-Altenrhein Airport (ACH)	20 km (12 miles)	SF 82	Bus	45 mins
Zürich Airport (ZRH)	10 km (6 miles)	SF 70	Train	10 mins

RAIL JOURNEY PLANNER

This map is a handy reference for intercity rail travel between Switzerland's main towns and cities.

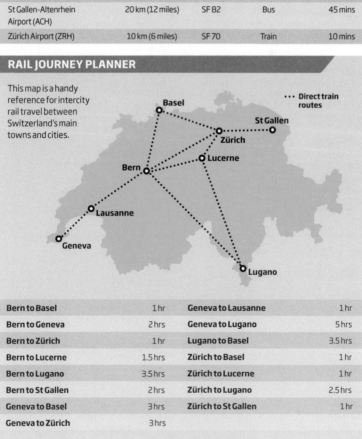

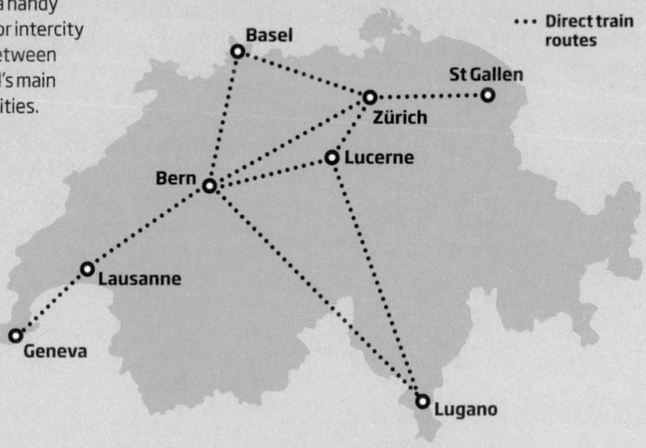

Bern to Basel	1 hr	**Geneva to Lausanne**	1 hr
Bern to Geneva	2 hrs	**Geneva to Lugano**	5 hrs
Bern to Zürich	1 hr	**Lugano to Basel**	3.5 hrs
Bern to Lucerne	1.5 hrs	**Zürich to Basel**	1 hr
Bern to Lugano	3.5 hrs	**Zürich to Lucerne**	1 hr
Bern to St Gallen	2 hrs	**Zürich to Lugano**	2.5 hrs
Geneva to Basel	3 hrs	**Zürich to St Gallen**	1 hr
Geneva to Zürich	3 hrs		

Domestic Train Travel

Travelling by train is one of the best ways to see the country. The comprehensive Swiss rail network is operated by Swiss Federal Railways or **SBB/CFF/FFS** (Schweizerische Bundesbahnen/Chemins de Fer Fédéraux Suisses/Ferrovie Federali Svizzere). Safety and hygiene measures, timetables, ticket information, transport maps, and more can be obtained from the SBB/CFF/FFS website.

All passengers must have a valid ticket before boarding – tickets are no longer sold on board and there are heavy on-the-spot fines for travellers caught with an unstamped ticket. **Swiss Travel System** (part of Switzerland Tourism) offers a range of discounted travel passes for use on all modes of transport. One of the most popular is the Swiss Travel Pass, which allows unlimited travel on most train, bus, tram and boat services, discounts on some funiculars and cable cars and entry to over 500 museums. There is also a Junior Travelcard for children aged 6 to 16 years. Most travel passes can be purchased in advance from travel agencies and Swiss tourist offices in your country.

Switzerland is known for its scenic railways, where visitors can enjoy the spectacular scenery in special trains with glass-roofed carriages. Among the most popular are the **Bernina Express** (Chur or Davos to Tirano, Italy), **GoldenPass Express** (Montreux to Lucerne), **Gotthard Panorama Express** (Lucerne to Lugano) and **Glacier Express** (St Moritz to Zermatt). It is essential to book in advance for these.

Bernina Express
W rhb.ch
Glacier Express
W glacierexpress.ch
GoldenPass Express
W gpx.swiss
Gotthard Panorama Express
W gotthard-panorama-express
SBB/CFF/FFS
W sbb.ch
Swiss Travel System
W swisstravelsystem.com

Long-Distance Bus Travel

Eurolines offers several coach routes between Swiss destinations and other European cities. Switzerland has an extensive network of routes covered by local buses and **Swiss Post**'s distinctive yellow postbuses. The latter vary in size depending on the remoteness of the destination and are useful for reaching Alpine locations inaccessible by rail. They also carry unaccompanied luggage, which is handy for hikers.

Eurolines
W eurolines.de
Swiss Post
W swisspost.ch

Boats and Ferries

In some cities, boats form an integral part of the transport system. Yellow *mouettes* (bus-boats) operated by **Mouettes Genevoises Navigation** shuttle foot passengers across Lake Geneva, while quirky *fähri* (cable-ferries) run by **Fähri-Verein Basel** have been ferrying people across the Rhine in Basel since the mid-19th century.

A cruise on one of Switzerland's lakes and rivers is a relaxing way to explore the country. Plying the waters of many of the major lakes are old-fashioned paddle steamers and other vessels, including those run by **SBS** across Bodensee, **CGN** on Lake Geneva, **SGV** on Lake Lucerne and **ZSG** across Zürichsee.

CGN
W cgn.ch
Fähri-Verein Basel
W faehri.ch
Mouettes Genevoises Navigation
W mouettesgenevoises.ch
SBS
W bodensee-schiffe.ch
SGV
W lakelucerne.ch
ZSG
W zsg.ch

Public Transport

S-Bahn and RER

Some cities, including Basel, Bern, Geneva and Zürich, have comprehensive urban rail networks (called S-Bahn in German and RER in French) which radiate out from the city centres to the suburbs and neighbouring towns. Some towns built on steep cliffs or hillsides, such as Lausanne and Fribourg, also have funicular railways.

Metro

Lausanne is the only Swiss city to have a metro. It has two lines and 30 stops, and operates from 5:30am to midnight, with trains every five to seven minutes.

Lausanne Metro
W t-l.ch

Buses and Trams

The quickest and easiest way of getting around towns and cities is by hopping on a bus or tram. These run at frequent intervals from around 5am to midnight. Larger cities also operate a reduced night-bus service at weekends.

Tickets are available from machines at every bus and tram stop, and are usually valid on all modes of transport. In most towns, the transport network is divided into zones; the more zones you traverse the higher the fare. Tickets valid for limited periods, from 30 minutes to a full day or more, are also available. These include

ZVV's ZürichCard and **TPG**'s GenevaPass; both of these also offer free entry to some city attractions. Tickets must be validated in the machine on the vehicle as you board.

TPG
W tpg.ch
ZVV
W zvv.ch

Taxis

In large cities, buses and trams are ubiquitous and inexpensive, and few people use taxis. They are expensive compared with public transport, and metered by distance; charges are higher at night and at weekends. If you do choose to travel by taxi, note that they cannot be hailed – they must be booked in advance or engaged at a taxi rank.

Driving

One of the best ways to explore Switzerland is by car. Driving here is pleasurable – the Swiss have a high regard for rules of the road and take pride in having the safest roads in Europe. EU driving licences are valid. If visiting from outside the EU, or if your licence is not in English, German, French or Italian, you may need to apply for an International Driving Permit (IDP).

Driving to Switzerland

If you bring your own overseas-registered car into the country, you must carry the vehicle's registration and insurance documents and a valid driver's licence.

Fuel is generally less expensive than in neighbouring countries. Bigger petrol stations are usually open from 7am to 8pm; smaller ones until 6pm. Outside these hours, petrol is widely available from automatic pumps. Some motorway service stations are open 24 hours.

To use Swiss motorways, which are indicated by green signs, drivers require a sticker called a vignette, which costs SF 40. It is sold at border crossings, petrol stations, tourist offices and post offices. Driving on a motorway without a valid vignette incurs a fine.

Driving in Switzerland

Well-maintained motorways and major roads link the major towns, and there are some spectacularly scenic routes over mountain passes and down Alpine valleys to more remote towns and villages. Most of the high Alpine passes are open between June and October; alternative ways of crossing the Alps include taking advantage of the Gotthard and San Bernardino road tunnels, which are open year-round (some have tolls), or driving your car onto a train to transit via the Lötschberg, Furka, Albula or Vereina tunnels.

Car Rental

To rent a car, you must be over 20 years of age and have held a valid driver's licence for at least a year. Drivers under 25 may incur a surcharge.

All major international car-hire companies have offices in the main cities and airports, and Swiss Railways also offers a **Mobility Click & Drive** online rental service with pick up from 400 railway stations.

Mobility Click & Drive
W mobility.ch

Rules of the Road

The legal car driving age in Switzerland is 18 (20 or 25 in a hire car). The Swiss drive on the right, and seatbelts are compulsory. It is illegal to use mobile phones while driving, or to drive under the influence of alcohol (the blood-alcohol content limit is 0.05 per cent). Children under 12 must travel in the back seat, and under-sevens must use a child seat. All vehicles must carry a warning triangle, a first aid kit and a reflective jacket, and full headlights should be on at all times. In winter, drivers are required by law to use snow tyres and/or chains on mountain roads when indicated by special warning signs.

Cycling

Environmentally conscious Switzerland encourages pedal power and, with the growing use of e-bikes, cycling has taken on a new popularity. Bike routes crisscross the entire country (marked by red signs with a white bicycle symbol) and include many long-distance paths.

Public bike-sharing schemes, such as **Züri rollt** in Zürich and **Genèveroule** in Geneva, are available in most major cities. **PubliBike** is a popular nationwide bike-sharing programme. Contact local tourist offices for details of schemes in their town. Bicycles can also be hired at main train stations (these need not be returned to the same station), and can be carried on most postbuses and trains for a fee.

Genèveroule
W geneveroule.ch
PubliBike
W publibike.ch
Züri rollt
W zuerirollt.ch

Walking

Laced with paths and trails, Switzerland is a hiker's paradise *(p43)*. Find your nearest walk on the **Switzerland Mobility** website. As well as detailed maps, guides and safety tips, it advises on the accessibility of each route.

Switzerland Mobility
W schweizmobil.ch

PRACTICAL INFORMATION

A little local know-how goes a long way in Switzerland. Here you will find all the essential advice and information you will need during your stay.

AT A GLANCE

EMERGENCY NUMBERS

EMERGENCY	POLICE
112	**117**

AMBULANCE	FIRE SERVICE
144	**118**

TIME ZONE

CET/CEST: Central European Summer Time runs from the last Sunday in March to the last Sunday in October.

TAP WATER

Unless otherwise stated, tap water in Switzerland and water from fountains in towns and villages is safe to drink.

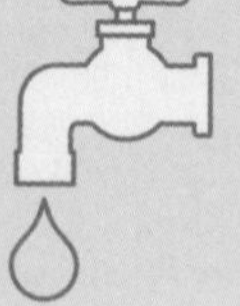

WEBSITES AND APPS

Switzerland Tourism
Produces excellent free apps, including Family Trips, SwitzerlandMobility, Swiss Events and Snow Report *(www.myswitzerland.com).*

Swiss Museums
Discover the latest exhibitions on this app.

Via Michelin
App providing live speed restriction and traffic alerts, navigation and other tools.

Meteo Suisse
The country's official weather app.

Personal Security

Switzerland is a safe country to visit but, like anywhere, petty crime does occur. Pickpockets work known tourist areas, public transport and busy streets. Use your common sense and be alert to your surroundings, and you should enjoy a stress-free trip.

If you do have anything stolen, report the crime within 24 hours to the nearest police station. Obtaining a police report will enable you to make an insurance claim. Contact your embassy if you have your passport stolen, or in the event of a serious crime or accident.

As a rule, the Swiss are accepting of all people, regardless of their race, gender or sexuality. Homosexuality was legalized in 1942 and Zürich has held a huge annual Pride event since 1994. That being said, some forms of homophobic discrimination have only been criminalized since 2020 and same-sex marriage only became legal in 2022. Conservative attitudes prevail, especially outside of urban areas. If you do feel unsafe, head for the nearest police station or contact **Diologai**, an LGBTQ+ association in Geneva.

Diologai
W dialogai.org

Health

Switzerland has a world-class healthcare system, but the country does not have a government health programme, so medical treatment of any kind must be paid for. A reciprocal agreement exists with all EU nations, so if you have an EHIC or GHIC *(p271)*, present this as soon as possible. You may have to pay the fee and claim it back later. Private health insurance is essential, especially if you are planning a skiing, mountaineering or hiking holiday, or any extreme sports.

For minor ailments, seek medical supplies and advice from pharmacies. Search the website of the **SOS-Pharmacy** organization for open emergency pharmacies in your area.

SOS-Pharmacy
W sos-pharmacie.ch

Smoking, Alcohol and Drugs

Smoking is banned on public transport and in enclosed public places, and it is illegal to drive under the influence of alcohol (the blood alcohol content limit is 0.05 per cent). Drug possession is taken very seriously and there are heavy penalties, jail sentences and fines depending on the type of narcotic (possession of very small amounts of cannabis will incur no penalties). Taking drugs across an international border automatically constitutes drug trafficking and incurs a heavy penalty.

ID

By law you must carry valid identification at all times. A photocopy of your passport photo page (and visa if applicable) should suffice.

Local Customs

Be respectful of the religious beliefs and political opinions of the local people and try to adhere to local customs, both at national and cantonal level.

National customs include a commitment to the environment (the Swiss take their recycling seriously and expect tourists to do the same) and punctuality. It'll come as no surprise that a country famed for its timepieces has little tolerance for tardiness, whether you're attending a business meeting or a dinner reservation.

Visiting Churches and Cathedrals

Most churches and cathedrals will not permit visitors during Sunday Mass. Generally, entrance to churches is free, however a fee may apply to enter special areas, like cloisters. When visiting places of worship, ensure that you are dressed respectfully, with your torso, shoulders and knees covered.

Mobile Phones and Wi-Fi

Wi-Fi is widely available throughout Switzerland, and cafés and restaurants will usually give customers their Wi-Fi password. Visitors with EU tariffs are able to use their devices abroad without being affected by roaming charges. Check with your service provider for details.

Post

You can purchase stamps *(Briefmarken/timbres/francobolli)* in post offices and some newsagents. Allow from a couple of days to one or two weeks for delivery of international mail, depending on the service you select.

Taxes and Refunds

Switzerland's standard VAT rate is 8.1 per cent, although there is a reduced rate of 2.6 per cent on certain everyday consumer goods such as food, non-alcoholic beverages, newspapers, magazines, books and medicines. Hotel stays (including breakfast) are taxed at a special rate of 3.7 per cent. Due to the four official languages, VAT may be called Mwst (Mehrwertsteuer), TVA (Taxe sur la valeur ajoutée), IVA (Imposta sul valore aggiunto) or TPV (Taglia sin la Plivalur). Non-EU residents get a tax refund on purchases over SF 300, subject to conditions. Ask for a tax receipt and relevant documentation at the time of purchase, and show these at customs (with ID) when leaving the country for your refund.

Discount Cards

Switzerland Tourism *(p276)* offers a range of passes and tickets exclusively for visitors. Its Swiss Museum Pass allows free entrance into more than 500 museums and galleries and is available from tourist offices, railway stations, post offices and larger museums. It also offers travel passes for three regions – Bernese Oberland, Central Switzerland and Lake Geneva-Alps.

Some cities (Bern, Lucerne, Neuchâtel and Winterthur) offer their own visitors' pass or discount card. Others also cover the cost of public transport, for instance, the **Zürich Card**, the **BaselCard** and the **GenevaPass**. Certain regions (including the Engadin, Davos-Klosters, Arosa-Lenzerheide, Saas Fee, Villars and Adelboden) offer schemes whereby guests staying more than one night in a participating hotel receive free transportation during the summer.

BaselCard
W basel.com/en/BaselCard
GenevaPass
W geneve.com/en/see-do/geneva-pass/
Zürich Card
W zuerich.com/en/zurichcard

INDEX

Index

Page numbers in **bold** refer to main entries.

A

Aarau **197**
Aare, River 76
Aareschlucht 100
Abbeys *see* Monasteries and abbeys
Absinthe **157**
Accommodation
booking 271
see Hotels
Adelboden **104-5**
Aigle **151**
Airolo **232-3**
Air travel 272-3
Alcohol 277
Aletsch Glacier 31, 43, **94-5**
Alphorns 32
Alpines Museum der Schweiz (Bern) **76**
Altdorf **229**
Ammann, Simon 53
Andermatt 237
Antikenmuseum (Basel) **180**
Appenzell **258**
Apps 276
Architecture **40-41**
Schweizerisches Architekturmuseum (Basel) **181**
Arosa **261**
Art
Dada **171**
Switzerland for Art Lovers **38-9**
see Museums and galleries
Art Basel **186**
Ascona **230**, 234
Augusta Raurica 46, **196**
Augustinergasse (Basel) **182**, 189
Augustinerkirche (Zürich) **169**
Avenches 41, 46, **155**

B

Baden **190-93**
map 191
Badenfahrt (Baden) **193**
Bad Ragaz **260**
Bahnhofstrasse (Zürich) 32, **168**
Bains des Pâquis (Geneva) 126
Bärenplatz (Bern) **72**, 78
Barfüsserplatz (Basel) 188
Barrage de la Grande Dixence **109**
Bars 33
Bern 73
Eastern Switzerland and Graubünden 250
Geneva 125
Mittelland, Bernese Oberland and Valais 87
Western Switzerland 139, 145
Zürich 170
Basel 12, 32, **178-89**
architecture 40
for art lovers 38
Fasnacht **181**
map 179
walk 188-9
Basel Münster 32, **184-5**, 189
Bear Park (Bern) **75**
Bears, in Bern **75**
Bearth & Deplazes 41
Beer 33
Bierflaschen Museum (St Gallen) 244
Bellinzona **224-5**
map 225
Bern 10, 16, 32, **62-79**
bars 73
bears **75**
itinerary 22-3
map 64-5
restaurants 74
walk 78-9
Bernatone Alphornbau (Brienz) **89**
Bernese Oberland *see* Mittelland, Bernese Oberland and Valais
Bernina Pass 42-3, **263**
Bernisches Historisches Museum (Bern) 77
Berthod, Madeleine 53
Biel/Bienne **99**
Bike-sledges 52, **102**
Birchermeusli 37
Bischöflicher Hof (Chur) **248**
Bisses (irrigation channels) 110
Boats 42, 274
sailing 49
ZSG (Zürichsee Schifffahrtsgesellschaft) (Zürichsee) 172
Bobsleighs 45, 52
Bodensee **256-7**
Bond, James 51
Bonivard, François 146
Botanical Trail (Zermatt) 43
Botta, Mario 40, 41
Bourbaki Panorama (Lucerne) **208**
Bridges
Chapel Bridge (Lucerne) **204**, 213
Holzbrücke (Baden) **192**
Mittlere Rheinbrücke (Basel) 188
Spreuerbrücke (Lucerne) **206**
Tibetan Bridge (Bellinzona) **225**
Brienz **88-9**
Brienzersee **88-9**
Brig **113**
Brissago 234
Bundeshaus (Bern) **72**
Bundesplatz (Bern) 32, 78
Bündner Kunstmuseum (Chur) **250**
Bündner Naturmuseum (Chur) **251**
Bungee jumps 230
Burghers of Calais (Rodin) 186
Bürglen **229**
Burkart, Erika 197
Buses 274-5
Byron, Lord 146

C

Cabaret Voltaire (Zürich) 39, **171**
Calvin, Jean 57, 127
Canova, Antonio 123
Canyoning 44
Car rental 275
Cars *see* Driving; Tours
Casa Rusca (Locarno) **223**
Castles and fortifications
Castelgrande (Bellinzona) 12, 47, **224**
Castello di Montebello (Bellinzona) 12, 47, **225**
Castello di Sasso Corbaro (Bellinzona) 12, 47, **225**
Castello Visconteo (Locarno) **222**
Château de Chillon 12, 41, 46-7, 51, **146-7**
Château de Grandson 154
Château de Gruyères 152-3
Château de Nyon 144-5
Château de Tourbillon (Sion) 108
Château de Valère (Sion) 108
Château St-Maire (Lausanne) **137**
Château Yverdon-les-Bains 153
Ruine Stein (Baden) **190**
Schloss Oberhofen (Thun) **87**
Schloss Thun (Thun) **86**
Unspunnen Castle (Interlaken) **84-5**
Cathedrals *see* Churches and cathedrals
Cattle descents **152**
Caves, Grottes de Vallorbe 151
Centovalli **230**
Central Switzerland and Ticino 20, **200-237**
driving tours 234-7
hotels 227
itinerary 26-7
map 202-3
restaurants 208, 231
CERN **127**
Chamois 254
Chapel Bridge (Lucerne) **204**, 213
Chaplin, Charlie
Chaplin's World (Vevey) 142, 143
Château d'Oex **150-51**
Châteaux *see* Castles
Cheese
Appenzeller Showcase Dairy (Schaukäserei) 258, 259
fondue 11, 37
Gruyère 152
Schaukäserei (Emmental) 101
Chiesa *see* Churches and cathedrals
Children **34-5**
see Toys

Chillon, Château de 12, 41, 46–7, 51, **146–7**
Chocolate 36
Chur **248–53**
bars 250
map 249
restaurants 251
Chur Cathedral **252–3**
Churches and cathedrals
Augustinerkirche (Zürich) **169**
Baselgia San Jon (Müstair) 263
Basel Münster 32, **184–5**, 189
Cathédrale Notre-Dame (Lausanne) **140–41**
Cathédrale St-Pierre (Geneva) **120–21**, 129
Cattedrale San Lorenzo (Lugano) 220
Château de Valère (Sion) 108
Chiesa Collegiata dei Pietro e Stefano (Bellinzona) **224–5**
Chiesa di San Vittore (Locarno) **223**
Chiesa Nuova (Locarno) **223**
Chiesa San Francesco (Locarno) **222**
Chur Cathedral **252–3**
Église Saint-Laurent (Lausanne) **136**
Franziskanerkirche (Lucerne) **206**
Fraumünster (Zürich) **170–71**
Grossmünster (Zürich) **171**
Jesuit Church (Lucerne) **206**
Kirche St Luzi (Chur) **249**
Kirche St Martin (Zillis) 265
Kirche St Peter (Zürich) **169**
Kirche St Stephen (Chur) **249**
Leonhardskirche (Basel) **180–81**
Martinskirche (Basel) 188
Münster St Vinzenz (Bern) **66–7**, 79
Pfarrkirche Mariä Himmelfahrt (Baden) **190–91**
Pfarrkirche St Mauritius (Zermatt) **91**
Reformierte Kirche (Interlaken) 85
Reformierte Martinskirche (Chur) **249**
San Rocco (Lugano) 221
Santuario della Madonna del Sasso (Locarno) **223**, 234
St Laurenzenkirche (St Gallen) **245**
St Peterskapelle (Lucerne) 213
St Ursen Kathedrale (Solothurn) 98
visiting 277
see Monasteries and abbeys
Cities **32–3**
Climate change 94
Clocks
Zytglogge (Bern) 41, 47, **70–71**, 79
see Watchmaking
Collection de l'Art Brut (Lausanne) **138**
Constance, Lake *see* Bodensee
Cowbell ringing 10
Crans-Montana **111**
Creux du Van 30, **157**
Currency 270, 271
Customs information 270
Cycling 49, 275
bicycle hire 275
mountain biking 45
Simmental Cycle Route 107
Trotti bikes 226

D

Dada 39, **171**
David Presenting Saul with the Head of Goliath (Rembrandt) 186
Davos 53, **261**
Discount cards 277
Dornach **197**
Doyle, Arthur Conan 100
Driving 43, 275
car rental 275
rules of the road 272, 275
speed limits 272
Driving tours
Lake Maggiore 234–5
Three Passes 236–7
Drugs 277

E

Eastern Switzerland and Graubünden 21, 50, **238–67**
bars 250
hotels 265
map 240–41
restaurants 251, 267
Eglisau **199**
Église Saint-Laurent (Lausanne) **136**
Ehrmann, Marianne 259
Eidgenössische Technische Hochschule (Zürich) **172**
Eiger 43, 102
Einsiedeln, Kloster **216–17**
Einstein, Albert, Einsteinhaus (Bern) 73
Electricity supply 270
Emergency numbers 276
Emmental **100–101**
Engadine Valley **262**
Engelberg **227**
Erlacherhof (Bern) **74**
Estavayer-le-Lac **152**
Events *see* Festival and events

F

Falstaff in the Laundry Basket (Füssli) 167
Ferries 274
Festivals and events **54–5**
Art Basel **186**
Badenfahrt (Baden) **193**
Basel Fasnacht **181**
cities 33
food and drink 37
Lötschental **113**
Street Parade (Zürich) **172**
see Sports and outdoor activities
FIFA World Football Museum (Zürich) 49, **173**
Film locations **50–51**
Flon (Lausanne) **137**
Flora, Swiss Alps 93
Fondation de l'Hermitage (Lausanne) **138–9**
Fondation Martin Bodmer (Geneva) **127**
Food and drink
absinthe **157**
beer 33, 244
City Tipples 33
festivals 37
food in St Moritz 264
Switzerland for Foodies **36–7**
whisky 258
see Cheese; Restaurants; Wine
Football **49**
Fotomuseum (Winterthur) **194**
Fountains, Jet d'Eau (Geneva) **124**
Franches-Montagnes **156–7**
Franziskanerkirche (Lucerne) **206**
Frauenfeld **256**
Fraumünster (Zürich) **170–71**
Fribourg **148–9**
map 149
Frogs, Musée des Grenouilles (Estavayer-le-Lac) 152
Furka Pass 237
Furkastrasse 237
Füssli, Johann Heinrich, *Falstaff in the Laundry Basket* 167

G

Galleries *see* Museums and galleries
Gardens *see* Parks and gardens
Gates of Hell, The (Rodin) 166
Geigenbauschule (Brienz) **88**
Geneva 18, 51, **114–29**
bars 125
itinerary 118–19
map 116–17
restaurants 127
walk 128–9

Geneva, Lake **142-7**
map 143
Gerechtigkeitsgasse (Bern) **74-5**, 79
Giessbachfälle **101**
Giger, H R 250
Glacier Express (Zermatt) 42, **91**
Glaciers **93**
Aletsch 31, 43, **94-5**
Glarus **266**
Gletschergarten (Lucerne) **208-9**
Goetheanum (Dornach) 197
Golden eagles 254
Gornergratbahn (Zermatt) **90**
Government advice 270
Grandson **154**
Grand St Bernard Pass **107**
Graubünden *see* Eastern Switzerland and Graubünden
Grimsel Pass 237
Grindelwald **102**
Velogemel (bike-sledge) 52, **102**
Grossmünster (Zürich) **171**
Grottes de Vallorbe 151
Gruyères **152**
Gstaad 41, 53, **106**

H

Hadid, Zaha 40
Haller, Hermann, Atelier Hermann Haller (Zürich) 173
Hauptbahnhof (Zürich) **168**
Haus zum Kirschgarten (Basel) **181**
Healthcare 276
Heimwehfluh (Interlaken) **84**
Helvetic Republic 58
Herzog & de Meuron 41
Hiking 13, 43, 45, 275
Historic buildings
Bischöflicher Hof (Chur) **248**
Bundeshaus (Bern) **72**
Casa Rusca (Locarno) **223**
Haus zum Kirschgarten (Basel) **181**
Ital-Reding-Haus (Schwyz) 228
Käfigturm (Bern) 72
Kornhaus (Bern) 78
Maison Rousseau (Geneva) 128
Maison Tavel (Geneva) **125**, 129
Palais de Rumine (Lausanne) **136-7**
Palazzo Civico (Lugano) 220
Palazzo della Conferenza (Locarno) **223**
Palazzo Riva (Lugano) 220
Rathaus (Basel) **182**, 188
Rathaus (Bern) **75**, 79
Rathaus (Chur) **250**
Rathaus (Lucerne) **207**, 212
Rathaus (Winterthur) **194**
Rathaus (Zürich) **171**
Spalentor (Basel) **178-9**
Stadtturm (Baden) **190**
Villa Ciani (Lugano) 221
see Castles; Churches; Libraries; Monasteries
Historisches Museum Baden **191**
Historisches Museum (Basel) **181**, 189
Historisches Museum (Lucerne) **206**
History **56-9**
Switzerland for History Buffs **46-7**
Hodler, Ferdinand 69
Holmes, Sherlock 100
Holzbrücke (Baden) **192**
Hornussen 10, 49
Hospental 237
Hotels
architecture 40
booking 271
Central Switzerland and Ticino 227
Eastern Switzerland and Graubünden 265
Mittelland, Bernese Oberland and Valais 101, 105

I

Ibex 254
Ice hockey 49
Ice on the River (Monet) 69
ID 277
Île Rousseau (Geneva) **124**
Innertkirchen 237
Insurance 270-71
Interlaken **84-5**
International Red Cross and Red Crescent Museum (Geneva) **126**
Internet access 277
Isole di Brissago 234
Itineraries
2 days in Geneva 118-19
3 days in Zürich 162-3
4 days in Bern and the Bernese Oberland 22-3
5 days in Western Switzerland 24-5
8 days in Central Switzerland 26-7
A week in Valais 28-9

J

Jardin Anglais (Geneva) **124**
Jesuit Church (Lucerne) **206**
Jet d'Eau (Geneva) **124**
Jüdisches Museum der Schweiz (Basel) **178**
Jungfraujoch 11, **102-3**

K

Kaisterstuhl **199**
Kandersteg 34, 96, **105**
Kapellplatz (Lucerne) **207**, 213
Kauffman, Angelica 250
Kirche *see* Churches
KKL (Kultur- und Kongresszentrum) (Lucerne) **204**
Klee, Paul 38, 58, **77**
Kleinbasel (Basel) **183**
Kloster *see* Monasteries and abbeys
Klosters **266**
Koller, Xavier 228
Königsfelden, Kloster **198**
Kornhaus (Bern) 78
Kramgasse (Bern) **73**, 79
Kulturmuseum St Gallen **245**
Kunsthalle (Basel) 38, **181**
Kunsthalle (Bern) **75**
Kunst Halle Sankt Gallen (St Gallen) **245**
Kunsthalle Winterthur **194**
Kunsthaus Interlaken **84**
Kunsthaus Zürich 39, **166-7**
Kunstmuseum Basel 38, 40, **186-7**
Kunstmuseum (Bern) 39, **68-9**
Kunstmuseum (Lucerne) **205**
Kunstmuseum (Thun) **87**
Kunst Museum Winterthur **195**
Küssnacht am Rigi **226**

L

La Chaux-de-Fonds **156**
Lakes 11, 42
Bodensee **256-7**
Brienzersee **88-9**
Lac St Léonard 108
Lake Geneva 42, **142-7**
Lake Lucerne 42, 204
Lake Lugano 31, **218-19**
Lake Maggiore 42, **234-5**
Oeschinensee **96-7**
Thunersee **86-7**
Urnersee **228-9**
Walensee **260**
Zürichsee **172**
Langstrasse (Zürich) 33, **168-9**
Language 271
essential phrases 270
Lausanne **134-41**
map 135
Metro 274
restaurants 138
shopping 137
Lauterbrunnen 50, **103**
Le Bain Turc (Vallotton) 123
Le Locle **155**
Leonhardskirche (Basel) **180-81**
Les Diablerets **150**
Leukerbad **113**
Leysin **150**
LGBTQ+
celebrations 33
safety 277
Libraries
Stadt- und Universitäts-bibliothek (Bern) 74
Stiftsbibliothek (St Gallen) **244-5**
Thomas-Mann-Archiv (Zürich) 172
Limmatquai (Zürich) **171**
Lindenhof (Zürich) **169**
Literature **50-51**

Local customs 277
Locarno **222-3**
map 223
Lötschental, customs **113**
Löwenbräu Complex (Zürich) 39
Löwendenkmal (Lucerne) **207**
Lucerne **204-213**
map 205
restaurants 208
walk 212-13
Lucerne, Lake 42, 204
Lugano, walk 220-21
Lugano, Lake 31, **218-19**

M

Maggiore, Lake **234-5**
Maienfeld **261**
Maison Rousseau (Geneva) 128
Maison Tavel (Geneva) **125**, 129
Mann, Thomas, Thomas-Mann-Archiv (Zürich) 172
Maps
A Short Walk: Old Town (Basel) 188-9
A Short Walk: Old Town (Bern) 78-9
A Short Walk: Old Town (Geneva) 128-9
A Short Walk: Old Town (Lucerne) 212-13
A Short Walk: Old Town (Lugano) 220-21
Baden 191
Basel 179
Bellinzona 225
Bern 64-5
Central Switzerland and Ticino 202-3
Chur 249
Eastern Switzerland and Graubünden 240-41
Fribourg 149
Geneva 116-17
Interlaken 85
Lake Geneva 143
Lake Maggiore driving tour 234-5
Lausanne 135
Locarno 223
Lucerne 205
Mittelland, Bernese Oberland and Valais 82-3
Northern Switzerland 176-7
rail journey planner 273
St Gallen 245
Switzerland 14-15
Three Passes driving tour 236-7
Thun 87
Western Switzerland 132-3
Winterthur 195
Zürich 160-61
Marktgasse (Bern) **73**, 78
Marktplatz (Basel) **180**, 188
Marktplatz (St Gallen) **245**
Marmots 93, 254
Martigny **106**
Martinskirche (Basel) 188
Matterhorn 30, 43, **90-91**
Matterhorn Alpine Crossing **91**
Matterhorn Museum – Zermatlantis (Zermatt) **90**
MEG (Ethnographic Museum of Geneva) **127**
Meienreuss Pass 237
Meiringen **100**
Mère Royaume (Catherine Cheynel) **57**
Mesocco **267**
Metro, Lausanne 274
Migros Museum für Gegenwarts-kunst (Zürich) **168**
Miraculous Draft of Fishes (Witz) 123
Mittelland, Bernese Oberland and Valais 17, **80-113**
bars 87
hotels 101, 105
itinerary 28-9
map 82-3
restaurants 89, 103, 111
Mittlere Rheinbrücke (Basel) 188
Mobile phones 277
Monasteries and abbeys
Kloster Einsiedeln **216-17**
Kloster Königsfelden **198**
Kloster Muri 198
St Gallen Abbey 12, 47, **246-7**
Zisterzienserkloster (Wettingen) 199
Monet, Claude, *Ice on the River* 69
Money 270, 271
Monte Generoso 31
Monte Rosa **111**
Mont Fort 31
Montreux **144**
Monuments
Löwendenkmal (Lucerne) **207**
Mur de la Réformation (Geneva) 127
Morat *see* Murten
Mountain biking 45
Mountains 31
Eiger 43, 102
Jungfraujoch 11, **102-3**
Matterhorn 30, **90-91**
Pilatus 31, **214-15**
Rigi 31, **226-7**
Munch, Edvard, *Wilhelm Wartmann* 167
Münstergasse (Bern) 32, **74**, 79
Münsterplatz (Basel) 189
Münster St Vinzenz (Bern) **66-7**, 79
Muri **198**
Mürren **104**
Murten/Morat **152-3**
Museums and galleries **38-9**
Aargauer Kunsthaus (Aarau) 197
Alpines Museum der Schweiz (Bern) **76**
Altes Zeughaus (Solothurn) 98
Antikenmuseum (Basel) **180**
Appenzeller Brauchtumsmuseum 258
Museums and galleries (cont.)
Appenzell Folklore Museum 258
Atelier Hermann Haller (Zürich) 49, 173
Barryland (Martigny) 106
Basler Papiermühle (Basel) 182
Bernisches Historisches Museum (Bern) 77
Bierflaschen Museum (St Gallen) 244
Bourbaki Panorama (Lucerne) **208**
Bundesbriefmuseum (Schwyz) 228
Bündner Kunstmuseum (Chur) **250**
Bündner Naturmuseum (Chur) **251**
Cabaret Voltaire (Zürich) 39
Caricature and Cartoon Museum (Basel) 39
Centre Pasquart (Biel) 99
Chaplin's World (Vevey) 142, 143
Collection de l'Art Brut (Lausanne) **138**
Dorfmuseum (Riehen) 196
Einsteinhaus (Bern) 73
FIFA World Football Museum (Zürich) **173**
Fondation Beyeler (Riehen) 196
Fondation de l'Hermitage (Lausanne) **138-9**
Fondation Martin Bodmer (Geneva) **127**
Fondation Pierre Gianadda (Martigny) 106
Forum der Schweizer Geschichte (Schwyz) 228
Fotomuseum (Winterthur) **194**
Geigenbauschule (Brienz) **88**
Giovanni-Segantini Museum (St Moritz) 264
Haus zum Kirschgarten (Basel) **181**
Historisches Museum Baden **191**
Historisches Museum (Basel) **181**, 189
Historisches Museum (Lucerne) **206**
International Red Cross and Red Crescent Museum (Geneva) **126**
Jüdisches Museum der Schweiz (Basel) **178**
Kirchner Museum (Davos) 261
Klostermuseum St Georgen (Stein am Rhein) 257
Kulturmuseum St Gallen **245**
Kunsthalle (Basel) 38, **181**
Kunsthalle (Bern) **75**
Kunst Halle Sankt Gallen (St Gallen) **245**
Kunsthalle Winterthur **194**
Kunsthaus Interlaken **84**
Kunsthaus (Zug) 226
Kunsthaus Zürich 39, **166-7**
Kunstmuseum Basel 38, 40, **186-7**

Museums and galleries (cont.)
- Kunstmuseum (Bern) 39, **68-9**
- Kunstmuseum (Lucerne) **205**
- Kunstmuseum (Olten) 98
- Kunstmuseum (Solothurn) 98
- Kunstmuseum (Thun) **87**
- Kunst Museum Winterthur **195**
- Leman Lake Museum (Nyon) 145
- Lindwurm Museum (Stein am Rhein) 257
- Löwenbräu Complex (Zürich) 39
- Maison d'Ailleurs (Yverdon-les-Bains) 153
- Matterhorn Museum – Zermatlantis (Zermatt) **90**
- MEG (Ethnographic Museum of Geneva) **127**
- Migros Museum für Gegenwartskunst (Zürich) **168**
- Musée Barbier-Mueller (Geneva) **124**
- Musée Baud (Sainte-Croix) 154
- Musée d'Art et d'Histoire (Geneva) 39, **122-3**
- Musée de la Vigne et du Vin (Aigle) 151
- Musée des Grenouilles (Estavayer-le-Lac) 152
- Musée du CIMA (Sainte-Croix) 154
- Musée du Fer et du Chemin de Fer (Vallorbe) 151
- Musée Historique (Lausanne) **136**
- Musée Historique (Murten) 153
- Musée International de l'Etiquette (Aigle) 151
- Musée International d'Horlogerie (La Chaux-de-Fonds) 156
- Musée Jenisch (Vevey) 142-3
- Musée Romain (Avenches) 155
- Musée Romain de Lausanne-Vidy (Lausanne) **139**
- Museo Nazionale del San Gottardo 233
- Museo Sasso San Gottardo 46, **233**
- Museum Alpin (Pontresina) 263
- Museum Appenzell 258
- Museum Burg Zug 226
- Museum der Kulturen (Basel) 182, 189
- Museum Engiadinais (St Moritz) 264, 265
- Museum für Gegenwartskunst (Basel) 182
- Museum für Kommunikation (Bern) **76**
- Museum für Urgeschichte(n) (Zug) 226
- Museum Langmatt (Baden) **193**
- Museum Rietberg (Zürich) **173**
- Museum Sammlung Rosengart (Lucerne) **208**
- Museum Tinguely (Basel) 38, **183**

Museums and galleries (cont.)
- Muzeum Kultur & Spiel Riehen 196
- Naturhistorisches Museum (Basel) 182
- Naturhistorisches Museum (Bern) **77**
- Naturmuseum (Lucerne) **207**
- Neues Museum Biel 99
- Nietzsche Haus (Sils) 265
- Nutli-Hüschi (Klosters) 266
- Olympic Museum (Lausanne) 49, **138**
- Palais de Rumine (Lausanne) **136-7**
- Pharmazie-historisches Museum Basel **180**
- Rätisches Museum (Chur) **248**
- Rebbaumuseum (Riehen) 196
- Richard Wagner-Museum (Lucerne) **209**
- Römermuseum 196
- Sammlung Oskar Reinhart am Römerholz (Winterthur) **195**
- Schanfigg Heimatmuseum (Arosa) 261
- Schweizerisches Architekturmuseum (Basel) **181**
- Schweizerisches Nationalmuseum (Zürich) 35, 46, **164-5**
- Schweizer Kindermuseum (Baden) 35, **193**
- Sherlock Holmes Museum (Meiringen) 100
- Spielzeug Welten Museum Basel **179**
- Swiss Open-Air Museum Ballenberg **89**
- Technorama (Winterthur) **194**
- Tell Museum (Bürglen) 229
- Textilmuseum (St Gallen) **244**
- Top 4 best art museums 39
- Tourismuseum (Interlaken) 85
- Verkehrshaus der Schweiz (Lucerne) **210-211**
- Wine Museum Sierre 108-9
- Zentrum Paul Klee (Bern) 38, **77**
- Zunfthaus zur Meisen (Zürich) **169**
- *see* Castles and fortifications; Historic buildings

Müstair **262-3**

N

National Parks, Swiss National Park **254-5**
Natural wonders **30-31**
Naturhistorisches Museum (Bern) **77**
Naturmuseum (Lucerne) **207**
Neuchâtel **154**
Neutrality 58-9
Niederdorf (Zürich) **171**
Nietzsche, Friedrich, Nietzsche Haus (Sils) 265
Nightlife, Zürich 13
Night sledging 151
Northern Switzerland 19, **174-99**
- map 176-7
- restaurants 199

Nyon **144-5**

O

Obere Gasse (Chur) **251**
Oeschinensee 31, **96-7**
Old Town (Bellinzona) **224**
Olten **98**
Olympic Museum (Lausanne) 49, **138**
Opening hours 271
Opernhaus (Zürich) **172-3**
Ouchy (Lausanne) **139**
Outdoor activities *see* Sports and outdoor activities

P

Palais de Rumine (Lausanne) **136-7**
Palais des Nations (Geneva) **126-7**
Palazzo della Conferenza (Locarno) **223**
Paragliding 44
Parks and gardens
- Bear Park (Bern) **75**
- Chinagarten (Zürich) 173
- Gletschergarten (Lucerne) **208-9**
- Jardin Anglais (Geneva) **124**
- Parc des Bastions (Geneva) **127**
- Parc Mon-Repos (Lausanne) **139**
- Schadau Park (Thun) 86
- Städtische Sukkulentensammlung (Zürich) **173**
- Zürichhorn Park (Zürich) **173**
- *see* National parks; Theme parks

Parliament, Bundeshaus (Bern) **72**
Passes
- Bernina Pass 42-3, **263**
- Furka Pass 237
- Grand St Bernard Pass **107**
- Grimsel Pass 237
- Meienreuss Pass 237
- San Bernardino Pass **265**
- Simplon Pass **112**
- St Gotthard Pass 43, **233**
- Three Passes driving tour **236-7**
- Umbrail Pass 43

Passports 270, 277
Personal security 276
Pfarrkirche Mariä Himmelfahrt (Baden) **190-91**
Pfarrkirche St Mauritius (Zermatt) **91**
Pharmacies 276
Pharmazie-historisches Museum Basel **180**

Photography, Fotomuseum (Winterthur) **194**
Piano, Renzo 40
Piazza Grande (Locarno) **222**
Picasso, Pablo 58
Pilatus 31, **214-15**
Piz Gloria 51
Place de la Palud (Lausanne) **134**
Place du Bourg-de-Four (Geneva) **124-5**, 129
Place St-François (Lausanne) **136**
Police 276
Pontresina **263**
Poschiavo **267**
Postal services 277
Promenade Lungolago Giuseppe Motta (Locarno) **223**
Public holidays 271
Public transport 272, 274

Q

Quartier Des Bains (Geneva) **126**

R

Rafting 45
Railways *see* Train travel
Rapperswil **259**
Rathaus *see* Historic buildings
Rätisches Museum (Chur) **248**
Reasons to Love Switzerland **10-13**
Reformation 56, 127
Regensberg **199**
Regierungsplatz (Chur) **250-51**
Reinhart, Oskar, Sammlung Oskar Reinhart am Römerholz (Winterthur) **195**
Rembrandt, *David Presenting Saul with the Head of Goliath* 186
Restaurants
  Bern 74
  Central Switzerland and Ticino 208, 231
  Eastern Switzerland and Graubünden 251, 267
  Geneva 127
  Lausanne 138
  Lucerne 208
  Mittelland, Bernese Oberland and Valais 89, 103, 111
  Northern Switzerland 199
  Western Switzerland 138, 139, 143, 155
  Zürich 169
  see Food and drink
Rhaetian Railway **257**
Rheinfall 242, **256**
Rhine, River 32, 42
Richard Wagner-Museum (Lucerne) **209**
Riehen **196**
Rigi 31, **226-7**
Rochers-de-Naye 31
Rodin, Auguste
  Burghers of Calais 186
  Gates of Hell, The 166
Romans 56
  Augusta Raurica **196**
  Avenches 41, 46, **155**
  Musée Romain de Lausanne-Vidy (Lausanne) **139**
Ronco 234
Rothorn Bahn (Brienz) **88**
Rousseau, Jean-Jacques, Maison Rousseau (Geneva) 128
Ruine Stein (Baden) **190**
Rules of the road 272, 275
Rütli meadow (Lucerne) 46, 57

S

Saas-Fee **112**
Safety 270
  personal security 276
Sailing 49
Sainte-Croix **154**
Salle Métropole (Lausanne) **135**
Sammlung Oskar Reinhart am Römerholz (Winterthur) **195**
San Bernardino Pass **265**
Santuario della Madonna del Sasso (Locarno) **223**, 234
Sasso San Gottardo, Museo 46, **233**
Schadau Park (Thun) **86**
Schaffhausen 42, **242-3**
Schloss Oberhofen (Thun) **87**
Schloss Thun (Thun) **86**
Schneider, Vreni 53
Schweizerisches Architekturmuseum (Basel) **181**
Schweizerisches Nationalmuseum (Zürich) 35, 46, **164-5**
Schweizer Kindermuseum (Baden) 35, **193**
Schwingen (Swiss wrestling) 10, 49
Schwyz **228**
Segantini, Giovanni 264
Shelley, Mary 51
Shopping 32
  Lausanne 137
  Lucerne's markets **207**
  taxes and refunds 277
Sierre **108-9**
Sils **265**
Simmental **107**
Simplon Pass **112**
Sion **108**
Skiing 12, 52-3
  cross-country skiing in the Engadine 262
Sledging 11
  night sledging 151
  Velogemel (bike-sledge) 52, **102**
Smoking 277
Snow Tubing 53
Solothurn **98**
Spalentor (Basel) **178-9**
Spa resorts
  Bad Ragaz **260**
  Centre Thermal (Yverdon-les-Bains) 153
Spa resorts (cont.)
  Leukerbad **113**
  Quartier Des Bains (Geneva) **126**
  Spa Quarter (Baden) **192**
  St Moritz **264-5**
  Thermalbad and Spa Zürich 173
  Yverdon-les-Bains **153**
Specific requirements, travellers with 271
Speed limits 272
Spielzeug Welten Museum Basel **179**
Sports and outdoor activities
  children 34
  Olympic Museum (Lausanne) 49, **138**
  Schwingen (Swiss wrestling) 32, 49
  Switzerland for Outdoor adventures **44-5**
  Switzerland for Sports Fans **48-9**
  traditional sports 49
  winter sports **52-3**
Spreuerbrücke (Lucerne) **206**
Spyri, Johanna 50
Stadthaus (Baden) **191**
Städtische Sukkulentensammlung (Zürich) **173**
Stadtturm (Baden) **190**
St Alban (Basel) **182**
Stans **227**
St Beatus Höhlen (Thun) **87**
Stein am Rhein 42, **257**
Steiner, Rudolf 197
Steintossen 49
St Gallen 41, **244-7**
  map 245
St Gallen Abbey 12, 47, **246-7**
St Gotthard Pass 43, **233**
  Museo Nazionale del San Gottardo **233**
  Museo Sasso San Gottardo 46, **233**
Stiftsbibliothek (St Gallen) **244-5**
St Laurenzenkirche (St Gallen) **245**
St Moritz 53, **264-5**
St-Pierre-de-Clages **108**
Street Parade (Zürich) **172**
St-Saphorin **144**
St-Ursanne **157**
Susten Pass 237
Swiss Alps, The **92-3**
Swissminiatur 35
Swiss National Park **254-5**
Swiss Open-Air Museum Ballenberg (Brienz) **89**

T

Tap water 276
Taxes 277
Taxis 275
Technorama (Winterthur) **194**
Telephone services 277
Tell, William **229**

Tenero 234
Tennis 48
Textilmuseum (St Gallen) **244**
Theme parks
Heididorf 35, 51
Swissminiatur 35
Three Passes driving tour **236-7**
Thun **86-7**
Thun Altstadt **86**
Thunersee **86-7**
Tibetan Bridge (Bellinzona) **225**
Ticino *see* Central Switzerland and Ticino
Time zone 276
Tinguely, Jean 38, **183**
Tipping 271
Titlis Cliff Walk (Engelberg) 45
Toggenburg **259**
Tolkien, J R R 50
Tour Bel-Air (Lausanne) **135**
Tours
Lake Maggiore driving tour **234-5**
Three Passes driving tour **236-7**
Town halls *see* Rathaus; Stadthaus
Toys
Muzeum Kultur & Spiel Riehen 196
Schweizer Kindermuseum (Baden) 35, **193**
Spielzeug Welten Museum Basel **179**
Trauffer World of Experiences (Brienz) **88**
Traditional sports 49
Traditions 10
Train travel 10, 272
Bernina Express 42
Centovalli Railway 230
children 35
cogwheel railway (Pilatus) 214
Funicular (Giessbachfälle) 101
Glacier Express 42, **91**
Gornergratbahn (Zermatt) **90**
Hauptbahnhof (Zürich) **168**
journey planner map 273
mountain railways 42
Musée du Fer et du Chemin de Fer (Vallorbe) 151
Rhaetian Railway **257**
Rothorn Bahn (Brienz) 88
Trams 274
Trauffer World of Experiences (Brienz) **88**
Travel **272-5**
government advice 270
Scenic Journeys **42-3**
Verkehrshaus de Schweiz (Lucerne) **210-211**
Trient Valley **109**
Trotti bikes 226

U

Umbrail Pass 43
UNESCO 47
United Nations **126-7**
Universität (Basel) **178**
Unspunnen Castle (Interlaken) **84-5**
Unterseen (Interlaken) **85**
Urnersee **228-9**

V

Vaccinations 271
Valais *see* Mittelland, Bernese Oberland and Valais
Val Bavona **232**
Val Bregaglia **264**
Val d'Anniviers **110-111**
Val d'Hérens **110**
Valle di Blenio **232**
Vallée de Joux **155**
Valle Maggia **231**
Valle Verzasca **230-31**
Vallorbe **151**
Vallotton, Félix, *Le Bain Turc* 123
Velogemel (bike-sledge) 52, **102**
Verbier 53, **106-7**
Verkehrshaus der Schweiz (Lucerne) **210-211**
VerticAlp Emosson 109
Vevey **142**
Via ferrata 45, **96**
Villars-sur-Ollon **150**
Vineyards, St-Saphorin **144**
Vipers, northern 254
Vira 234
Visas 270
Vitznau **226-7**

W

Wagner, Richard, Richard Wagner-Museum (Lucerne) **209**
Walensee **260**
Walking 275
Walks
A Short Walk: Old Town (Basel) **188-9**
A Short Walk: Old Town (Bern) **78-9**
A Short Walk: Old Town (Geneva) **128-9**
A Short Walk: Old Town (Lucerne) **212-13**
A Short Walk: Old Town (Lugano) **220-21**
Watchmaking industry 155
Musée International d'Horlogerie (La Chaux-de-Fonds) 156
Water, drinking 276
Waterfalls
Reichenbachfälle 100
Rheinfall 242, **256**
Websites 276
Weinmarkt (Lucerne) **209**, 212
Weissenstein **98-9**
Wengen 34, **104**
Western Switzerland 18, **130-57**
bars 139, 145
itinerary 24-5
map 132-3
restaurants 138, 139, 143, 155
Wettingen **199**
Whisky 258
Whitewater rafting 45
Wi-Fi 277
Wildlife
bears in Bern **75**
marmots 93
Top Five Alpine Animals **254**
Wilhelm Wartmann (Munch) 167
Wine 13
Musée de la Vigne et du Vin (Aigle) 151
Musée International de l'Etiquette (Aigle) 151
Rebbaumuseum (Riehen) 196
Wine Museum Sierre 108-9
Winter sports 52-3
Winterthur **194-5**
map 195
Witz, Konrad, *Miraculous Draft of Fishes* 123
Wocher Panorama (Thun) 86, 87
Womens' suffrage **58**
World War I 58
World War II 58-9

Y

Yverdon-les-Bains **153**

Z

Zentrum Paul Klee (Bern) 38, **77**
Zermatt 30, 53, **90-91**
Zillis **265**
Ziplines 44, 102
Zofingen **196-7**
Zug **226**
Zunfthaus zur Meisen (Zürich) **169**
Zürich 18, 32, **158-73**
bars 170
itinerary 162-3
map 160-61
nightlife 13
restaurants 169
Zürichhorn Park (Zürich) **173**
Zürichsee **172**
Zytglogge (Bern) 41, 47, **70-71**, 79

PHRASEBOOK

German is the most widely spoken language in Switzerland, followed by French and Italian. Swiss German, which is used in everyday speech, differs from standard German, so some of the most commonly used expressions in Swiss German are marked here by an asterisk.

IN EMERGENCY	German	French	Italian
Help!	*Hilfe!*	*Au secours!*	*Aiuto!*
Stop!	*Halt!*	*Arrêtez!*	*Alt!*
Call a doctor!	*Holen Sie einen Artz!*	*Appelez un médecin!*	*Chiami un medico!*
... an ambulance!	*... einen Krankenwagen!*	*... une ambulance!*	*... una ambulanza!*
... the police!	*... die Polizei!*	*... la police!*	*... la polizia!*
Where is the hospital?	*Wo finde ich das Krankenhaus?*	*Où est l'hôpital?*	*Dov'è l'ospedale?*

COMMUNICATION ESSENTIALS

Yes	*Ja*	*Oui*	*Si*
No	*Nein*	*Non*	*No*
Please	*Bitte*	*S'il vous plaît*	*Per favore*
Thank you	*Danke vielmals*	*Merci*	*Grazie*
Excuse me	*Entschuldigen Sie* **Äxgüsi*	*Excusez-moi*	*Mi scusi*
Hello	*Guten Tag* **Grüezi*	*Salut*	*Salve/Ciao*
Goodbye	*Auf Widersehen* **Ufwiederluege*	*Au revoir*	*Arrivederci*
Bye!	*Tschüss!*	*Salut!*	*Ciao!*
here	*hier*	*ici*	*qui*
there	*dort*	*là*	*la*
What?	*Was?*	*Quel/Quelle?*	*Quale?*
When?	*Wann?*	*Quand?*	*Quando?*
Where?	*Wo/Wohin?*	*Oé?*	*Dove?*

USEFUL PHRASES AND WORDS

Where is ...?	*Wo befindet sich...?*	*Où est ...?*	*Dov'è...?*
Where are ...?	*Wo befinden sich...?*	*Où sont...?*	*Dove sono...?*
Do you speak English?	*Sprechen Sie Englisch?*	*Parlez-vous anglais?*	*Parla inglese?*
I understand	*Ich verstehe*	*Je comprends*	*Capisco*
I don't understand	*Ich verstehe nicht*	*Je ne comprends pas*	*Non capisco*
I'm sorry	*Es tut mir leid*	*Je suis désolé*	*Mi dispiace*
big	*gross*	*grand*	*grande*
small	*klein*	*petit*	*piccolo*
open	*auf/offen*	*ouvert*	*aperto*
closed	*zu/geschlossen*	*fermé*	*chiuso*
left	*links*	*à gauche*	*a sinistra*
right	*rechts*	*à droite*	*a destra*
near	*in der Nähe*	*près*	*vicino*
far	*weit*	*loin*	*lontano*
early	*früh*	*de bonne heure*	*presto*
late	*spät*	*en retard*	*tardi*
entrance	*Eingang/Einfahrt*	*l'entrée*	*l'entrata*
exit	*Ausgang/Ausfahrt*	*la sortie*	*l'uscita*
toilet	*WC/Toilette*	*les toilettes/les WCs*	*il gabinetto*
this	*diese*	*ce*	*questo*
that	*das*	*cette*	*quello*

MAKING A TELEPHONE CALL

I'd like to make a long-distance call.	*Ich möchte ein Ferngespräch machen.*	*Je voudrais faire un interurbain.*	*Vorrei fare una interurbana.*
I'll try again later.	*Ich versuche es später noch einmal.*	*Je rapellerai plus tard.*	*Ritelefono pié tardi.*
Can I leave a message?	*Kann ich etwas ausrichten?*	*Est ce que je peux laisser un message?*	*Posso lasciare un messaggio?*

STAYING IN A HOTEL

Do you have a vacant room?	*Haben Sie ein Zimmer frei?*	*Est-ce que vous avez une chambre libre?*	*Avete camere libere?*
double room	*ein Doppelzimmer*	*une chambre à deux*	*una camera doppia*
twin room	*ein Doppelzimmer mit zwei Betten*	*une chambre à deux lits*	*una camera con due letti*
single room	*ein Einzelzimmer*	*une chambre à une personne*	*una camera singola*
with a bath/shower	*mit Bad/Dusche*	*avec salle de bains/douche*	*con bagno/doccia*
How much is the room?	*Wievel kostet das Zimmer?*	*Combien coûte la chambre?*	*Quanto costa la camera?*
Where is the bathroom?	*Wo ist das Bad?*	*Où est la salle de bain?*	*Dov'è il bagno?*
with breakfast	*mit Frühstück*	*avec petit-déjeuner*	*con prima colazione*
with half-board	*mit Halbpension*	*en demi-pension*	*mezza pensione*
dormitory	*Schlafsaal*	*le dortoir*	*il dormitorio*
key	*Schlüssel*	*la clef*	*la chiave*
I have a reservation	*Ich habe ein Zimmer reserviert*	*J'ai fait une réservation*	*Ho fatto una prenotazione*

SIGHTSEEING

bus	*der Bus*	*l'autobus*	*el autobus*
tram	*die Strassenbahn*	*le tramway*	*el tram*
train	*der Zug*	*le train*	*il treno*
bus station	*der Busbahnhof*	*la gare routière*	*l'autostazione*
train station	*der Bahnhof*	*la gare*	*la stazione*
boat	*das Boot*	*le bateau*	*la barca*
parking	*der Parkplatz*	*la place de stationnement*	*il parcheggio*
car park	*das Parkhaus*	*le parking*	*l'autosilo*
(hire) bicycle	*das Fahrrad/das Mietvelo*	*le vélo (de location)*	*la bicicletta (a noleggio)*
airport	*der Flughafen*	*l'aéroport*	*l'aeroporto*
church	*die Kirche*	*l'église*	*la chiesa*
cathedral	*der Dom*	*la cathédrale*	*il duomo/la cattedrale*
main square	*der Hauptplatz*	*la place centrale*	*la piazza principale*
post office	*das Postamt*	*le bureau de poste*	*la posta*
tourist office	*das Verkehrsamt*	*l'office du tourisme*	*l'ente turistico*

TIME

morning	*der Morgan*	*le matin*	*la mattina*
afternoon	*der Nachmittag*	*l'après-midi*	*il pomeriggio*
evening	*das Abend*	*le soir*	*la sera*
yesterday	*gestern*	*hier*	*ieri*
today	*heute*	*aujourd'hui*	*oggi*
tomorrow	*morgen*	*demain*	*domani*
Monday	*Montag*	*lundi*	*lunedì*
Tuesday	*Dienstag*	*mardi*	*martedì*
Wednesday	*Mittwoch*	*mercredi*	*mercoledì*
Thursday	*Donnerstag*	*jeudi*	*giovedì*
Friday	*Freitag*	*vendredi*	*venerdì*
Saturday	*Samstag/*Sonnabend*	*samedi*	*sabato*
Sunday	*Sonntag*	*dimanche*	*domenica*

SHOPPING

How much does this cost?	*Wieviel kostet das?*	*C'est combien, s'il vous plaît?*	*Quant'è, per favore?*
I would like...	*Ich hätte gern...*	*Je voudrais...*	*Vorrei...*
Do you have...?	*Haben Sie...?*	*Est-ce que vous avez...?*	*Avere...?*
bank	*Bank*	*la banque*	*la banca*
chemist/pharmacy	*Apotheke*	*la pharmacie*	*la farmacia*
market	*Markt*	*le marché*	*il mercato*
travel agent	*Reisebüro*	*l'agence de voyages*	*l'agenzia di viaggi*

EATING OUT

Have you got a table for...?	*Haben sie einen Tisch für ...?*	*Avez-vous une table pour...?*	*Avete una tavola per ...?*
The bill/check, please	*Zahlen, bitte*	*L'addition, s'il vous plaît*	*Il conto, per favore*
I am a vegetarian	*Ich bin Vegetarier(in)*	*Je suis végétarien(ne)*	*Sono vegetariano(a)*
waitress/waiter	*Fräulein/Herr Ober*	*Mademoiselle/Monsieur*	*Cameriera/Camariere*
menu	*die Spiesekarte*	*le menu/la carte*	*il mené*
wine list	*die Weinkarte*	*la carte des vins*	*la lista dei vini*
breakfast	*das Frühstück*	*le petit-déjeuner*	*la prima colazione*
lunch	*das Mittagessen*	*le déjeuner*	*il pranzo*
dinner	*das Abendessen*	*le dîner*	*la cena*

MENU DECODER

baked	*gebacken*	*cuit au four*	*al forno*
beans	*Bohnen*	*des haricots*	*fagioli*
beef	*Rindfleisch*	*boeuf*	*manzo*
boiled	*gekocht*	*bouilli*	*bollito*
cheese	*Käse*	*fromage*	*formaggio*
chicken	*Hendle/Hahn/Huhn*	*poulet*	*pollo*
chocolate	*Schokolade*	*chocolat*	*cioccolato*
cream	*Schlag*	*crème*	*crema*
egg	*Ei*	*oeuf*	*uovo*
fish	*Fisch*	*poisson*	*pesce*
garlic	*Knoblauch*	*ail*	*aglio*
grilled	*vom Grill*	*grillé*	*alla griglia*
ham	*Schinken/Speck*	*jambon*	*prosciutto*
ice cream	*Eis*	*glace*	*gelato*
lamb	*Lamm*	*agneau*	*agnello*
meat	*Fleisch*	*viande*	*carne*
milk	*Milch*	*lait*	*latte*
pepper	*Pfeffer*	*poivre*	*pepe*
poached	*pochiert*	*poché*	*in camicia*
pork	*Schwein*	*porc*	*carne di miale*
potato	*Kartoffel/Erdäpfel*	*pomme de terre*	*patate*
red/white wine	*Rot-/Weisswein*	*vin rouge/blanc*	*vino rosso/blanco*
roasted	*gebraten*	*rôti*	*arrosto*
salad	*Salat*	*salade*	*insalata*
salt	*Salz*	*sel*	*sale*
sausage	*Wurst*	*saucisse*	*salsiccia*
seafood	*Meeresfrüchte*	*fruits de mer*	*frutti di mare*
vegetables	*Gemüse*	*légumes*	*contorni*
water	*Wasser*	*l'eau*	*acqua*

ACKNOWLEDGMENTS

DK would like to thank the following for their contribution to the previous edition: Caroline Bishop, Anthony Lambert, Craig Turp.

The publisher would like to thank the following for their kind permission to reproduce their photographs:

Key: a-above; b-below/bottom; c-centre; f-far; l-left; r-right; t-top

123RF.com: Roman Babakin 29tr, 122-23b; Stefan Ember 218cl; Janos Gaspar 22crb; jakobradlgruber 118cr; Chon Kit Leong 242bl; Narongsak Nagadhana 68cra; photogearch 242clb; rudi1976 248-9t; ruslankphoto 46tr; Fedor Selivanov 246bl; theyok 162bl; Eleonora Travostino 222t.

4Corners: Andreas Gerth 30bl; Gianni Krattli 19, 174; Luca Da Ros 76-7b.

akg-images: 166cl; Cameraphoto 69tl; André Held 191br.

Alamy Stock Photo: age fotostock 67br, 126cra, 157tr; Agencja Fotograficzna Caro / Bastian 255ca; AGF Srl 153tr; Stephen Allen 56bc; Leonid Andronov 67t; Anvalo 251tl; AR Photo 150tr; Architecture2000 186clb; Arco / J. Pfeiffer 255t; ART Collection 57cra; Arterra Picture Library 228tr; Udo Bernhart 36-7t; Eva Bocek 214-15b, 266t; Tibor Bognar 18bl, 158; byvalet 75b; Josse Christophel 58tl; Aiden Clarke 263b; Sorin Colac 72b; Chris Craggs 112tl; Peter Crighton 251br; Ian Dagnall 22bl; dpa picture alliance 112-13b; Ros Drinkwater 194-95t; Pavel Dudek 145tl; eFesenko 32-33t; Reiner Elsen 168bl; Stefan Ember 232b; EThamPhoto 49br; Archie Fisher 230bl; Francesco Gavazzeni 264-5b; GFC Collection 24t, 55tl; Godong 121bc; Tim Graham 262tl; Granger Historical Picture Archive 58bc; hemis.fr 118bl, 154bl, 173tr / Giuglio Gil 24crb / Ludovic Maisant 123ca / Bertrand Rieger 187; The History Collection 181bc; imageBROKER 17t, 31b, 197b, 198clb, 198b, 232tl / Werner Dieterich 220bl / Marina Horvat 94bl / Iris Kürschner 254-5b / Meinrad Riedo 210t / Harald Wenzel – Orf 250bl; imageBROKER.com GmbH & Co. KG / Daniel Schoenen 40b; Johner Images 44-45t; Image Professionals GmbH / Bernard van Dierendonck 44bl / Ingrid Firmhofer 53cla / LOOK-foto 40-41t, 45cl; INTERFOTO / Fine Arts 167cra; JBTravel 118crb, 147bl; Michael Jenner 267b; Christian Kober 96cr, 259br; Bogdan Lazar 41clb; Jitraporn Leeniva 227b; MARKA / giulio andreini/ *exhibition of work by Sigmar Ploke at art museum, Kunsthaus, Zürich* © The Estate of Sigmar Polke, Cologne / DACS 2018 167tr / giovanni mereghetti 214ca; Hilke Maunder 28cla; mauritius images GmbH 13cr, 53br, 107br, 127br, 199tl, 221cr, 258-9t, 265t / Walter Bibikow 35b / enricocacciafotografie 221t; McPhoto / Protze 49c; mediacolor's 162crb; Melba Photo Agency 24cr; Hercules Milas 16, 62; MLouisphotography 39cla; Roberto Moiola 42-43b; Peter Moulton 112cb; National Geographic Image Collection / Robbie Shone 94cra; Sérgio Nogueira 147br; Alexander Novikov 256-7b; George Oze 162t; Panther Media GmbH 99t, 150b, 228tr, / Elena Klippert 150b / xbrchx 32b; vichai phububphapan 104b, 162cr; PjrTravel 182b, 184clb; Prisma Archivo 56crb; Prisma by Dukas Presseagentur GmbH 10clb, 11cr, 98bl, 103br, 108b, 110t, 110bl, 154-55t, 156tl, 156-57b, 207tl, 228-29b, Olaf Protze 46tl / Sonderegger Christof 52bl; Simon Reddy 74tr; Paolo Romiti 117bl; RossHelen editorial 226tl, 33cla; Alistair Scott 54clb, 55bl, 152-53b, 152-53b; Kumar Sriskandan 261tr; Dominic Steinmann 97clb; Geoffrey Taunton 100bl; Erik Tham / *template / variant / friend / stranger* by Tony Oursler at the modern art show "Art Basel 2016" 54cr; The Protected Art Archive 56t; Glyn Thomas 170cra; Rosengart Museum, Lucerne / TravelCollection / Inga Wandinger *works by Picasso* © Succession Picasso/ DACS, London 2018 208tr; travelstock44 8clb, 169t, 171br, 178cr; travelstock44.de / Juergen Held 161cl; Jorge Tutor 117ca; Universal Images Group North America LLC 123cra, 186bl; Sebastian Wasek 100-01t; Westend61 GmbH 8cl, 121t / Werner Dieterich 130bl; Peter Wey 95; Scott Wilson 41ca; World History Archive 57br; Juriaan Wossink 120bl; Patrizia Wyss 188bl, 258bl; YesPhotographers 260-1b; Mikalai Zastsenski 172b.

AWL Images: Jon Arnold 129tl; Jean-Francois Hagenmuller 60-1; Christian Kober 210cr, 211; Doug Pearson 218cb.

Bern Welcome: 70cra.

Cabaret Voltaire: *Thus I Spoke- «Dying on Stage»,* Performance by Christodoulos Panayiotou & Jean Capeille 39br.

Chur Tourismus: Andrea Bradrutt 249tr.

Crans-Montana Tourisme & Congrès: 111bl.

Depositphotos Inc: pandionhiatus3 170t.

Dorling Kindersley: Katarzyna Medrzakowie / Wojciech Medrzakowie 121fbl, 252bl, 253tr.

Dreamstime.com: Akulamatiau 54cla; Alexirina27000 138tr; Andreykr 124tl; Leonid Andronov 43tr, 80-81, 148, 184bl; Astra490 217tr; Baselxg 181tr; Eva Bocek 97bc, 206-07b; Roberto Cerruti 93br; Elena Duvernay 17bl, 114; Stefano Ember 48-49t, 215ca, 79br; Janos Gaspar 255cla; Gayane 138-39b; Diego Grandi 70c; Jojjik 90-91t; Thomas Jurkowski 121cra; Rachapol Kitjanukit 20, 200; Makasanaphoto 93cla; Mihai-bogdan Lazar 136-37t; Minnystock 42tl; Emanuele Leoni 109ca; Lianem 218b; Milosk50 192-93b; Moniphoto 142bc; Monner 54cra; Morseicinque 224-25t; Dmytro Nikitin 231t; Nuvisage 46-7b; Vichai Phububphapan 94clb; Ivano Piacenza 93tr; Ppy2010ha 36bl; Prasit Rodphan 59tr; Rosshelen 70bl, 128b, 192tr; Sculpies 96-97t; Sforzza1 166-67b; Sophyphotos 37tc; Michal Stipek 109t; Susazoom 253tl; Swisshippo 47cl, 55cr, 242br, 243; Tnuangthong 59crb; Verryfe 97br; Victorflowerfly 213tr; Vogelsp 30-1t; Bram De Vrind 43cb; Xantana 26cla, 86b, 178t, 204-05t.

The Fondation Beyeler: Mark Niedermann 149tl.

Getty Images: AFP / Fabrice Coffrini 24cl, 51cb, 68-9b; AGF / Hermes Images 247t; Ascent Xmedia / Milo Zanecchia 2-3; Bettmann 58cla, 59clb; cdbrphotography 50-1b; Corbis / VCG / Francis G. Mayer 68clb; Harold Cunningham 69tr, 69cla; EyeEm / Marcus Fischer 26t; Fine Art Images / Heritage Images 123t; Sean Gallup 31cl; Gamma-Rapho / Marc Deville 28tl; Historical 58clb; Hulton Deutsch 58-9t; Lightcapturing by Björn Abt 190-91t; Frank Lukasseck 8-9; March Of Time 57tl; Francesco Meroni 21, 238; Martin Moos 189tr; Neumann 228-9; Matteo Placucci / NurPhoto 33cb; Mathieu Polak 59bc; robertharding / Julian Elliott 4; Michele Tantussi / *Accumulation: Searching for Destination* (2014-2016) by Chiharu Shiota, Art Basel 2016 © DACS 2018 12-3b; Jean Bernard Vernier 57bl; VCG Wilson 38b; Suphanat Wongsanuphat 8cla; xenotar 18tl, 130; Lingxiao Xie 36br.

Heididorf: Gaudenz Danuser 50tl.

Getty Images / iStock: AleksandarGeorgiev 213br; alxpin 216bl; Leonid Andronov 178br; anouchka 78tr, 144-45b; antares71 141tr; AsianDream 217cra; assalve 55tr; bhidethescene 22t, 121br; cdbrphotography 12clb, 28-9t; Dmitry Chulov 215cr; dblight 121tr; E+ / Bim 142-43t / mbbirdy 52-53t; elettro24 134-35t, 151br; fotoember 214clb, 233tr; fotoVoyager 22cr; Gatsi 180b; Aleksandar Georgiev 6-7; Andreas Haas 257tr; Yuliia Hrozian 26-7t; Janoka82 10-11b; Alexander Jung 102t; JurgaR 11t; LianeM 27tr; lucentius 105tl, 210cl; MatteoCozzi 141cr; merc67 11br; Mor65 236, 253ca; OGphoto 51tr, 141crb; olli0815 186crb; PixHound 208-09b; RomanBabakin 24bl, 73t; Rostislavv 66bl; Juergen Sack 55br; Saro17 45br; Oleh Slobodeniuk 268-9; Somatuscani 88-89t; Michal Stipek 215ca; swisshippo 13br; syolacan 219; TheShihan 28-9ca; taranchic 84-85t; TomasSereda 254cra; Flavio Vallenari 57tr; Rafael_Wiedenmeier 93c; Xantana 26cra; yanisapae 210br; zorazhuang 106t.

Kunsthaus Zürich: 167cla.

Kunstmuseum Basel: Julian Salinas / *La femme et l'enfant* (1922, r) and *Les deux figures (Nus sur fonds rouge)* (1923) by Fernand Léger © ADAGP, Paris and DACS, London 2018, *L'automne* (1948) by Henri Laurens, © ADAGP, Paris and DACS, London 2018 38-9t.

La Gruyère Tourisme: 54cl.

MICR: Alain Germond 126t.

Musée du Fer et du Chemin de Fer: 148tl.

Museum der Kulturen Basel: Omar Lemke 182tl.

Museum fur Kommunikation: Thijs Wolzak 76t.

Museum Tinguely: Daniel Spehr / Donation Micheline and Claude Renard / *Incitation á la Création* (1981) by Jean Tinguely right and Donation Niki de Saint Phalle / *Bosch No. 2* (1974) by Jean Tinguely back © ADAGP, Paris and DACS, London 2018 183t.

Robert Harding Picture Library: Menno Boermans 13t; Sonderegger Christof 26-7ca; Stuart Dee 244t; Christian Kober 149tr; Roberto Moiola 34bl; Travelstock44 161br.

Schweizer Kindermuseum: Steve Jaeckle 193tr.

Shutterstock.com: Eva Bocek 101br; Benoit Bruchez 118t; EPA / Martial Trezzini 48bl / Peter Schneider 55cl; EPA-EFE / Patrick Huerlimann 172tr; M.Antonello Photography 54b; WestEnd61 235.

Swiss Children's Museum, Baden: 34-35t, 35ca.

Swiss National Museum, Zürich / Schweizerisches Nationalmuseum: 164cra, 164bl, 165tc, 165tr AURA / Emanuel Ammon 165cra / Gabriel Ammon 164-65b.

Front flap:
Alamy Stock Photo: Archie Fisher bl; Jitraporn Leeniva t; George Oze cla; **Depositphotos Inc:** pandionhiatus3 c; **Dreamstime.com:** Victorflowerfly br; **Getty Images / iStock:** merc67 cra.

Cover images:
Front and spine: **Getty Images / iStock:** Andrew_Mayovskyy.
Back: **Alamy Stock Photo:** Hercules Milas cla; **123RF.com:** Xantana c; **Getty Images:** Frank Lukasseck tr; **Getty Images / iStock:** Andrew_Mayovskyy b.

For further information see: www.dkimages.com

Illustrators: Michal Burkiewicz, Paweł Marczak

MIX
Paper | Supporting responsible forestry
FSC™ C018179

This book was made with Forest Stewardship Council™ certified paper – one small step in DK's commitment to a sustainable future.
For more information go to www.dk.com/our-green-pledge

A NOTE FROM DK EYEWITNESS

The rate at which the world is changing is constantly keeping the DK Eyewitness team on our toes. While we've worked hard to ensure that this edition of Switzerland is accurate and up-to-date, we know that opening hours alter, standards shift, prices fluctuate, places close and new ones pop up in their stead. So, if you notice we've got something wrong or left something out, we want to hear about it. Please get in touch at travelguides@dk.com

This edition updated by
Contributor Mike MacEacheran
Senior Editors Dipika Dasgupta, Alison McGill
Senior Art Editor Vinita Venugopal
Project Editor Anuroop Sanwalia
Editor Alex Pathe
Art Editor Bandana Paul
Proofreader Samantha Cook
Indexer Helen Peters
Picture Research Administrator Vagisha Pushp
Picture Research Manager Taiyaba Khatoon
Publishing Assistant Simona Velikova
Jacket Designer Jordan Lambley
Cartographer Ashif
Cartography Manager Suresh Kumar
Senior DTP Designer Tanveer Zaidi
Senior Production Editor Jason Little
Production Controller Kariss Ainsworth
Managing Editors Shikha Kulkarni, Beverly Smart, Hollie Teague
Senior Managing Art Editor Priyanka Thakur
Art Director Maxine Pedliham
Publishing Director Georgina Dee

First edition 2005

Published in Great Britain by Dorling Kindersley Limited, DK, One Embassy Gardens, 8 Viaduct Gardens, London SW11 7BW, UK

The authorized representative in the EEA is Dorling Kindersley Verlag GmbH. Arnulfstr. 124, 80636 Munich, Germany

Published in the United States by DK Publishing, 1745 Broadway, 20th Floor, New York, NY 10019, USA

23 24 25 26 10 9 8 7 6 5 4 3 2 1

A CIP catalogue record for this book is available from the British Library.

A catalogue record for this book is available from the Library of Congress.

ISSN: 1542 1554
ISBN: 978 0 2416 6452 0

Printed and bound in China.

www.dk.com